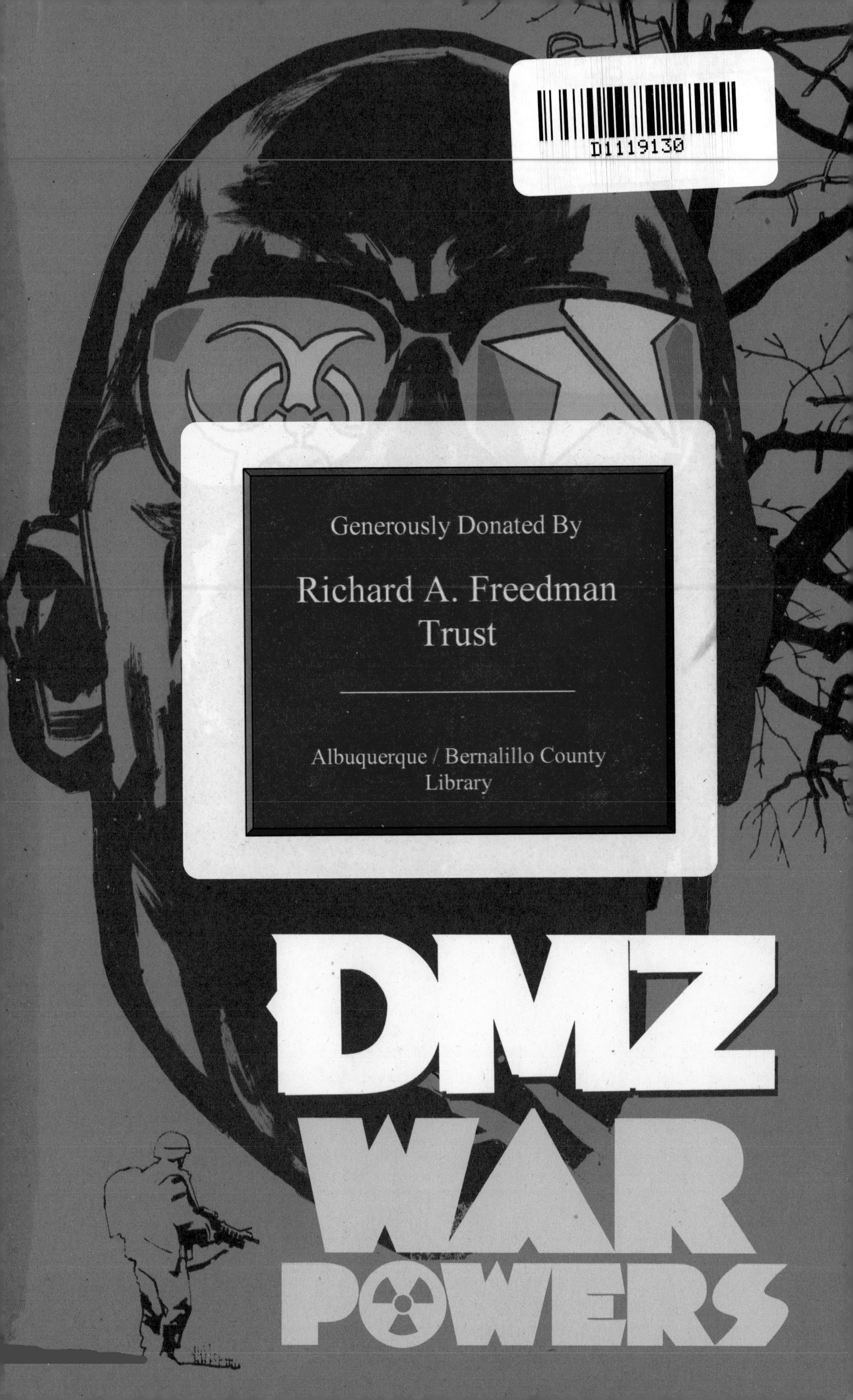
DMZ
WAR
POWERS

BRIAN WOOD WRITER

THE ISLAND CHAPTERS 1–2
KRISTIAN DONALDSON
ARTIST

WAR POWERS CHAPTERS 1–4
RICCARDO BURCHIELLI
ARTIST

ZEE, DMZ
NIKKI COOK
ARTIST

JEROMY COX
COLORIST

JARED K. FLETCHER
LETTERER

ORIGINAL SERIES COVERS BY
JOHN PAUL LEON

DMZ CREATED BY **BRIAN WOOD**
AND **RICCARDO BURCHIELLI**

DMZ
WAR POWERS

3907504767 2164

Will Dennis Editor – Original Series **Robbin Brosterman** Design Director – Books
Amelia Grohman Publication Design **Karen Berger** Senior VP – Executive Editor, Vertigo
Bob Harras VP – Editor-in-Chief **Diane Nelson** President **Dan DiDio** and **Jim Lee** Co-Publishers
Geoff Johns Chief Creative Officer **John Rood** Executive VP – Sales, Marketing and Business Development
Amy Genkins Senior VP – Business and Legal Affairs **Nairi Gardiner** Senior VP – Finance
Jeff Boison VP – Publishing Operations **Mark Chiarello** VP – Art Direction and Design
John Cunningham VP – Marketing **Terri Cunningham** VP – Talent Relations and Services
Alison Gill Senior VP – Manufacturing and Operations **Hank Kanalz** Senior VP – Digital
Jay Kogan VP – Business and Legal Affairs, Publishing **Jack Mahan** VP – Business Affairs, Talent
Nick Napolitano VP – Manufacturing Administration **Sue Pohja** VP – Book Sales
Courtney Simmons Senior VP – Publicity **Bob Wayne** Senior VP – Sales

Cover illustration by Brian Wood Logo designed by Brian Wood

DMZ: WAR POWERS
Published by DC Comics. Cover and compilation Copyright © 2009 DC Comics. All Rights Reserved.
Originally published in single magazine form as DMZ 35–41. Copyright © 2008, 2009 Brian Wood and
Riccardo Burchielli. All Rights Reserved. VERTIGO and all characters, their distinctive likenesses and
related elements featured in this publication are trademarks of DC Comics. The stories, characters
and incidents featured in this publication are entirely fictional. DC Comics does not
read or accept unsolicited submissions of ideas, stories or artwork.

DC Comics, 1700 Broadway, New York, NY 10019
A Warner Bros. Entertainment Company.
Printed in the USA. Third Printing.
ISBN: 978-1-4012-2430-1

SUSTAINABLE
FORESTRY
INITIATIVE

Certified Chain of Custody
Promoting Sustainable Forestry
www.sfiprogram.org
SFI-01042
APPLIES TO TEXT STOCK ONLY

THE ISLAND

CHAPTER ONE

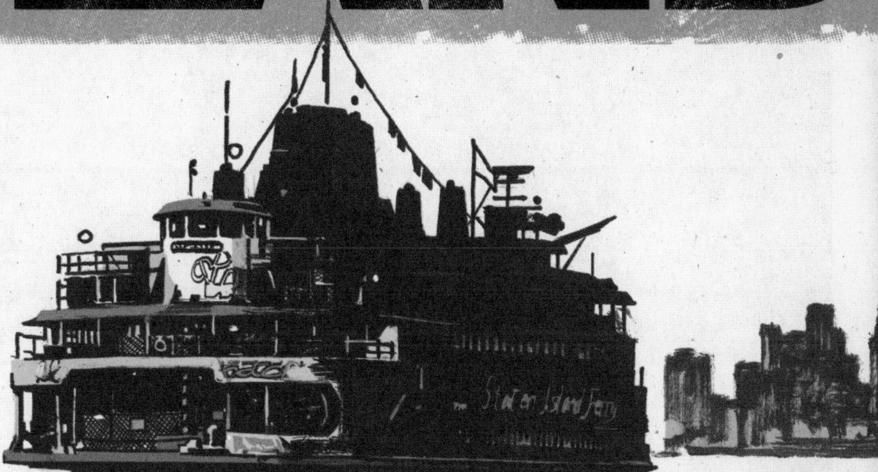
Staten Island Ferry

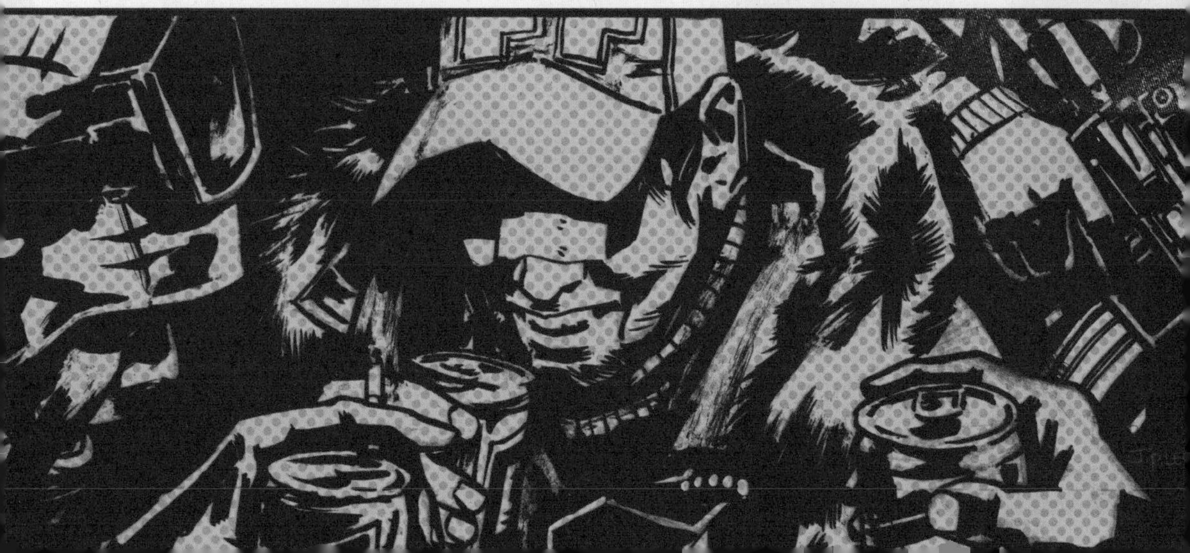

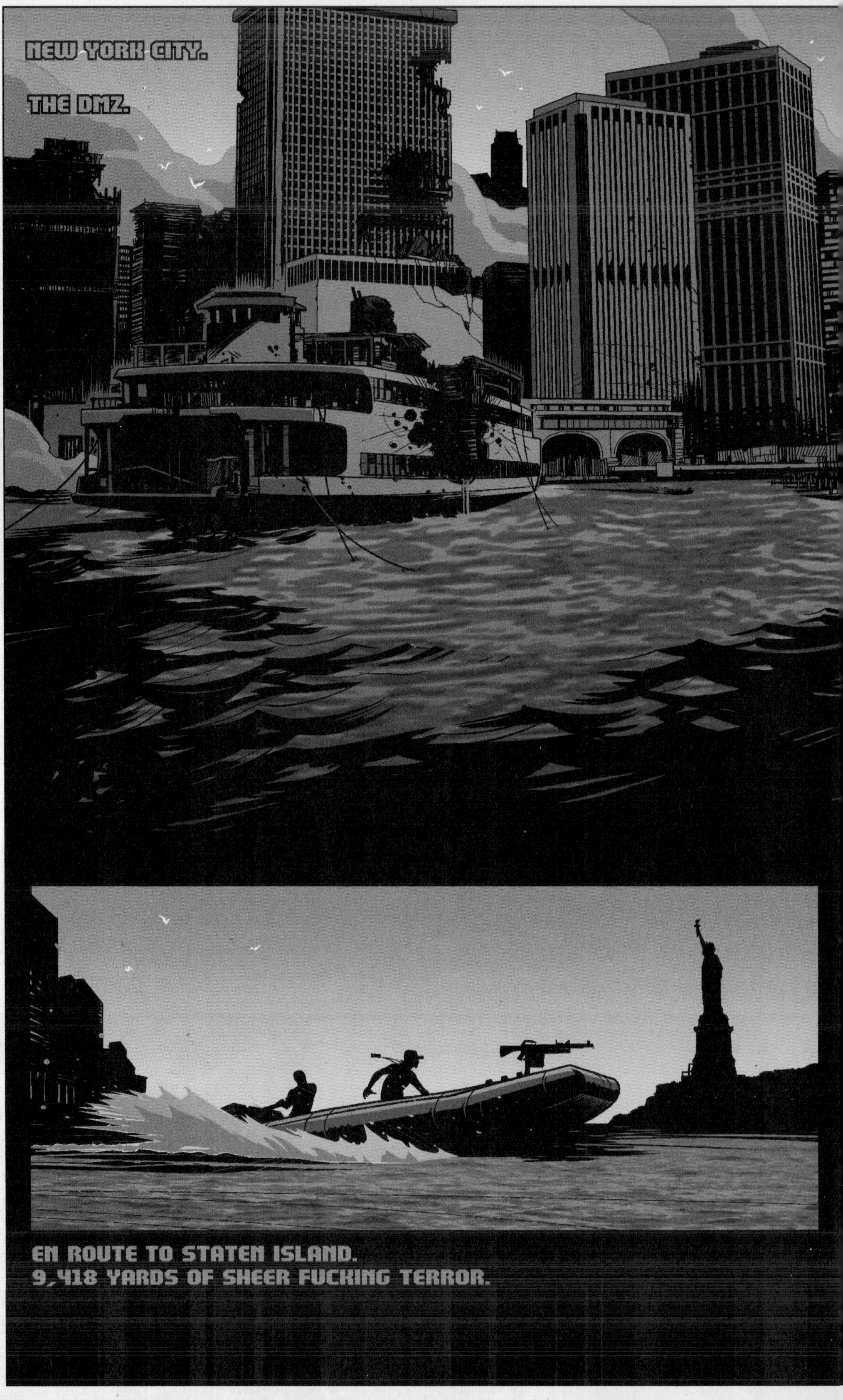
NEW YORK CITY.
THE DMZ.
EN ROUTE TO STATEN ISLAND.
9,418 YARDS OF SHEER FUCKING TERROR.

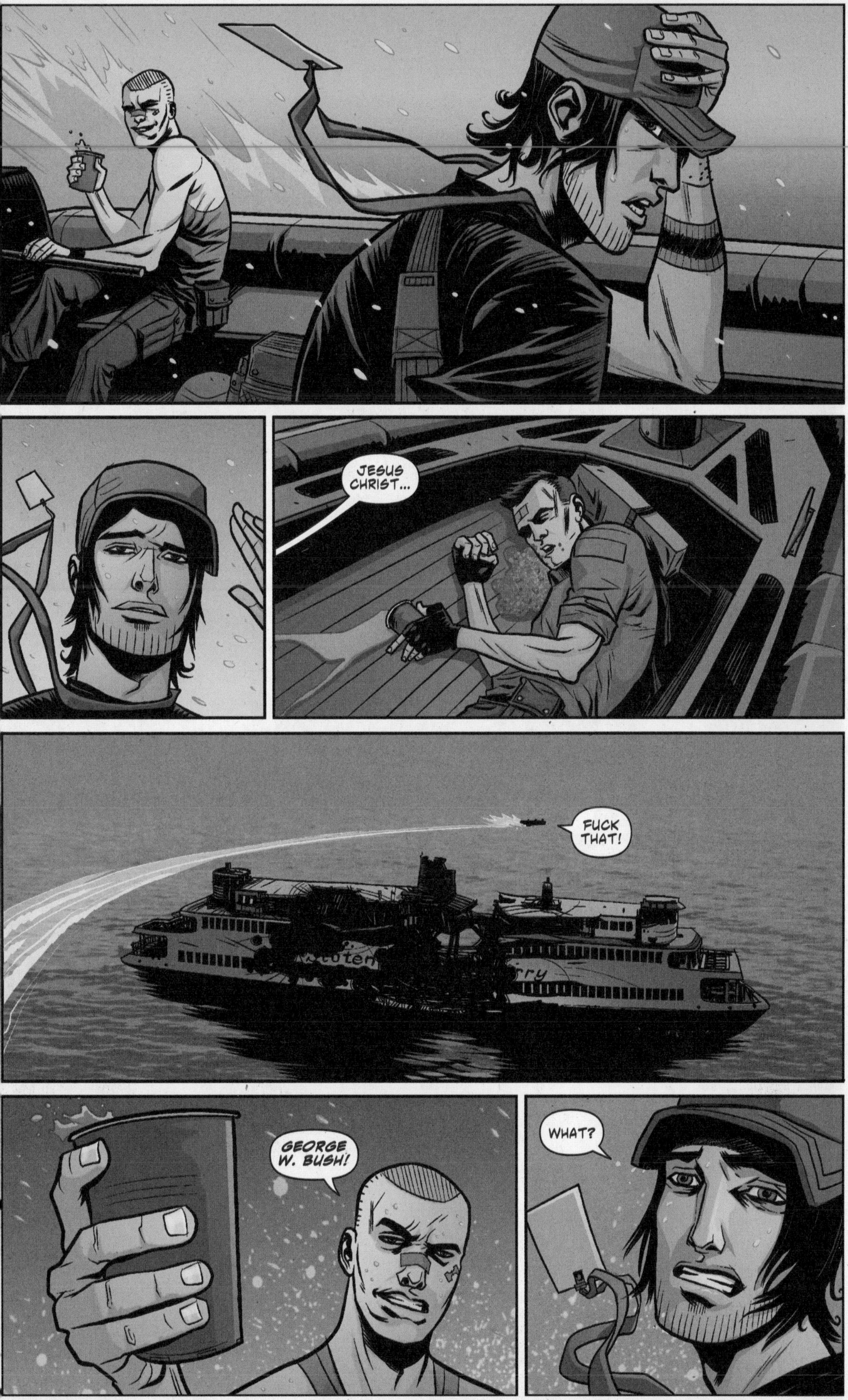
JESUS CHRIST...
FUCK THAT!
GEORGE W. BUSH!
WHAT?

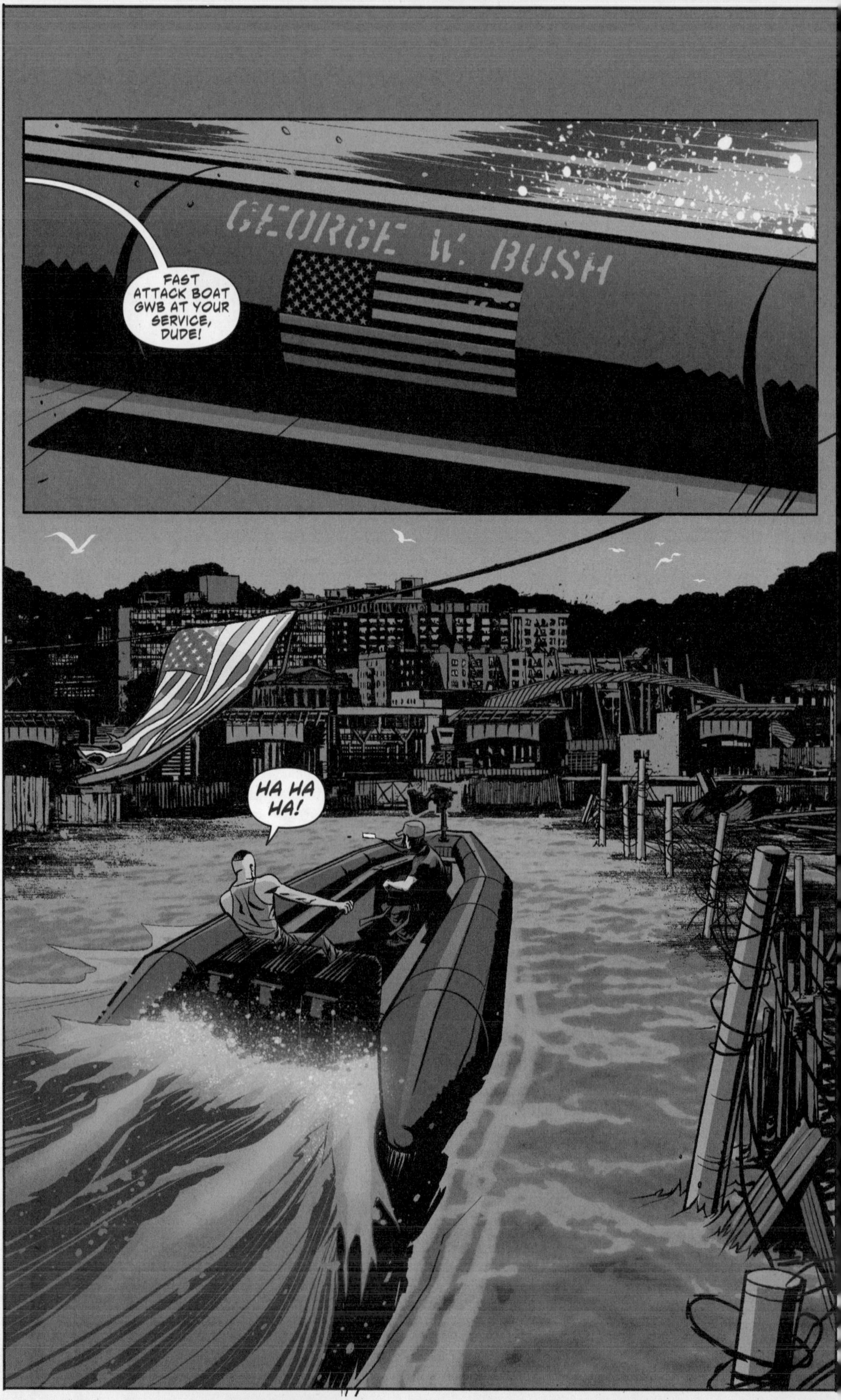
GEORGE W. BUSH
FAST ATTACK BOAT GWB AT YOUR SERVICE, DUDE!
HA HA HA!

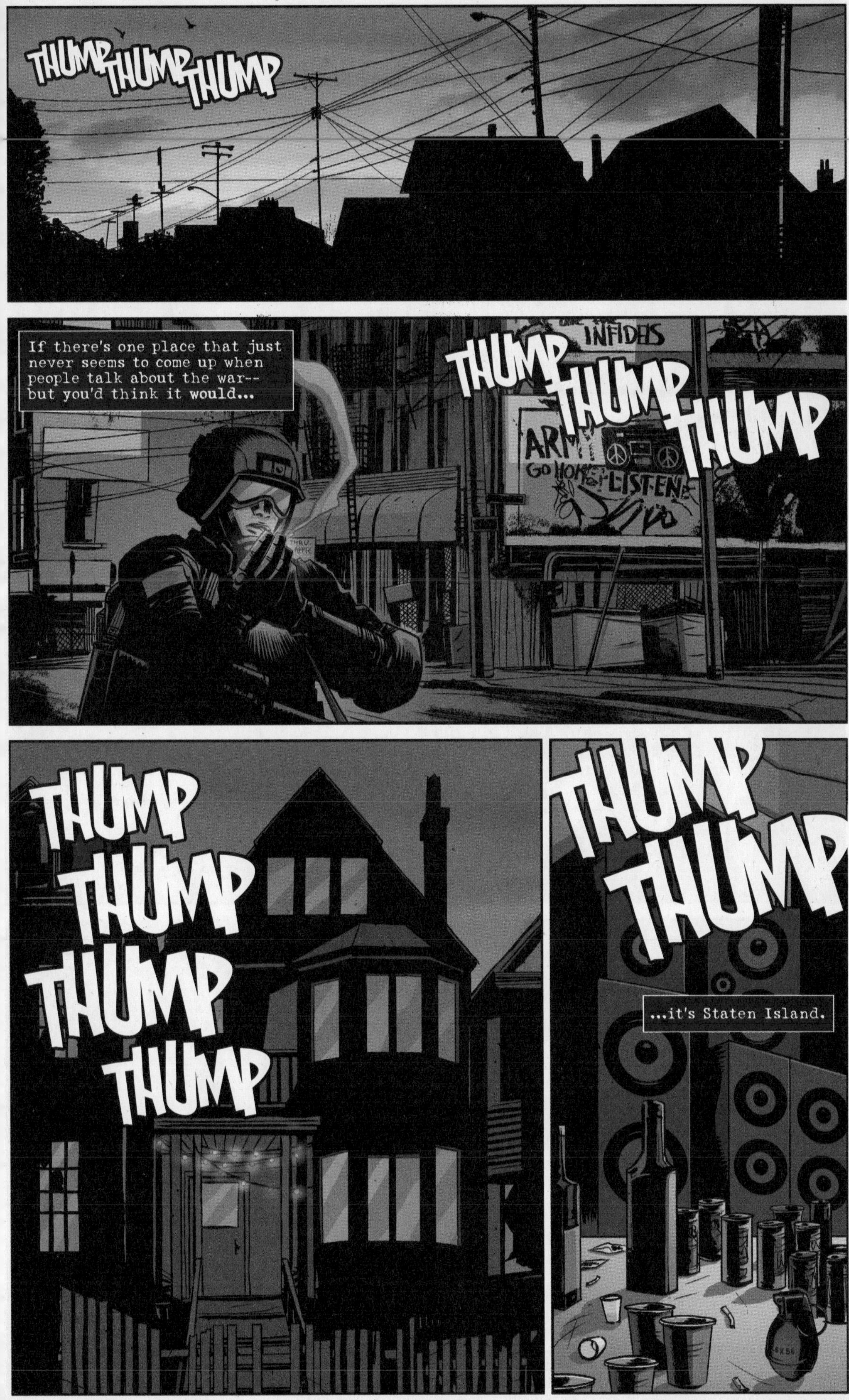
THUMP THUMP THUMP
If there's one place that just never seems to come up when people talk about the war--but you'd think it would...
THUMP THUMP THUMP
THUMP THUMP THUMP THUMP
THUMP THUMP
...it's Staten Island.

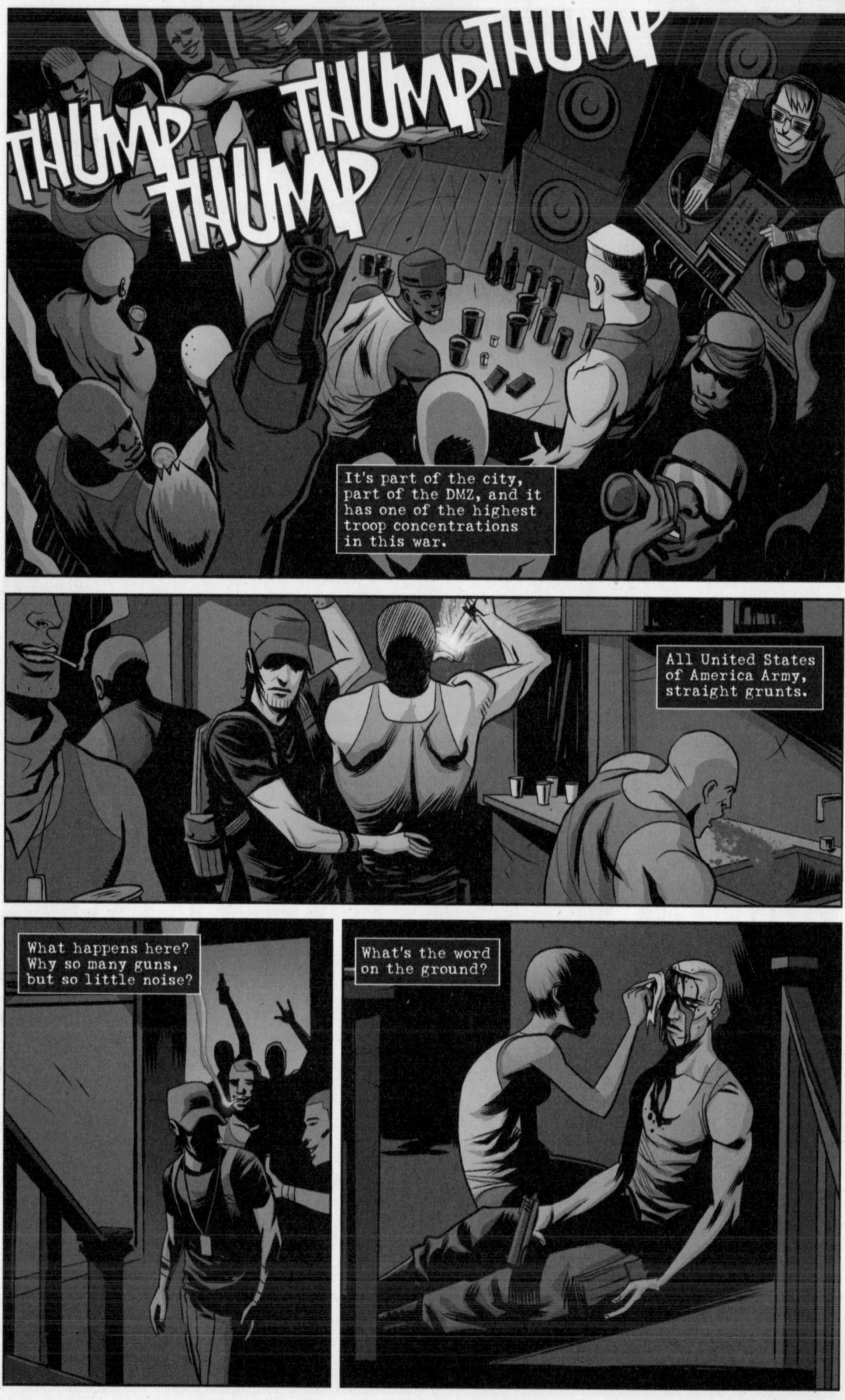
THUMP THUMP THUMP THUMP
It's part of the city, part of the DMZ, and it has one of the highest troop concentrations in this war.
All United States of America Army, straight grunts.
What happens here? Why so many guns, but so little noise?
What's the word on the ground?

Apparently in certain foreign markets, people are obsessed with this shit. Culture of war, psychology of frontline troops, stress under fire, stuff like that.

MATTY! *BRO!* GET OVER HERE!

CLIP!

RAT-A-TAT-A-TAT-A-TAT

Life in the DMZ.

MARCUSO HERE IS THE UNDISPUTED *KING* OF THIS SHIT! SEE, THE *FUCKING ARC*, MAN! THE TRACER! YOU CAN SEE IT LAND!

WE GOT A TARGET, A FUCKING *TARGET* DOWN THERE, BRO! HE *NAILS* IT, *EVERY FUCKING TIME!*

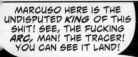

If all of this reads like a pitch, it basically is.

YOSHUTTHEFUCKUP!

FOURTH CLIP!

Cut off from Liberty, and all other friendly outlets taking a wait-and-see approach with the incoming administration...

UNREAL!

...and also, apparently, with my *loyalties...*

It's time to get my hustle on.

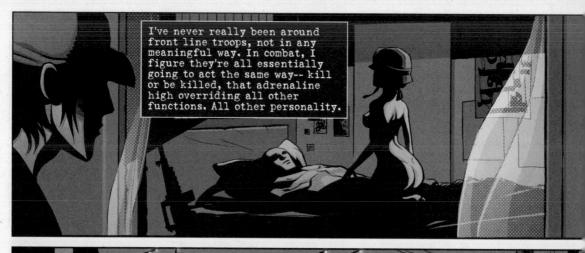

I've never really been around front line troops, not in any meaningful way. In combat, I figure they're all essentially going to act the same way-- kill or be killed, that adrenaline high overriding all other functions. All other personality.

But troops stationed somewhere, on base, standing by, keeping watch... what's that all about? What's their P.O.V.? What's it like to get this close to Manhattan and all you can do is stare at it from across the harbor?

Beyond the rah-rah shit, beyond the shit talk, beyond the sound bites...

These invisible troops in the forgotten borough.

What's their deal?

CLIP!

THERE'S GOTTA BE SOMETHING HERE...

ARE YOU MATTY ROTH?

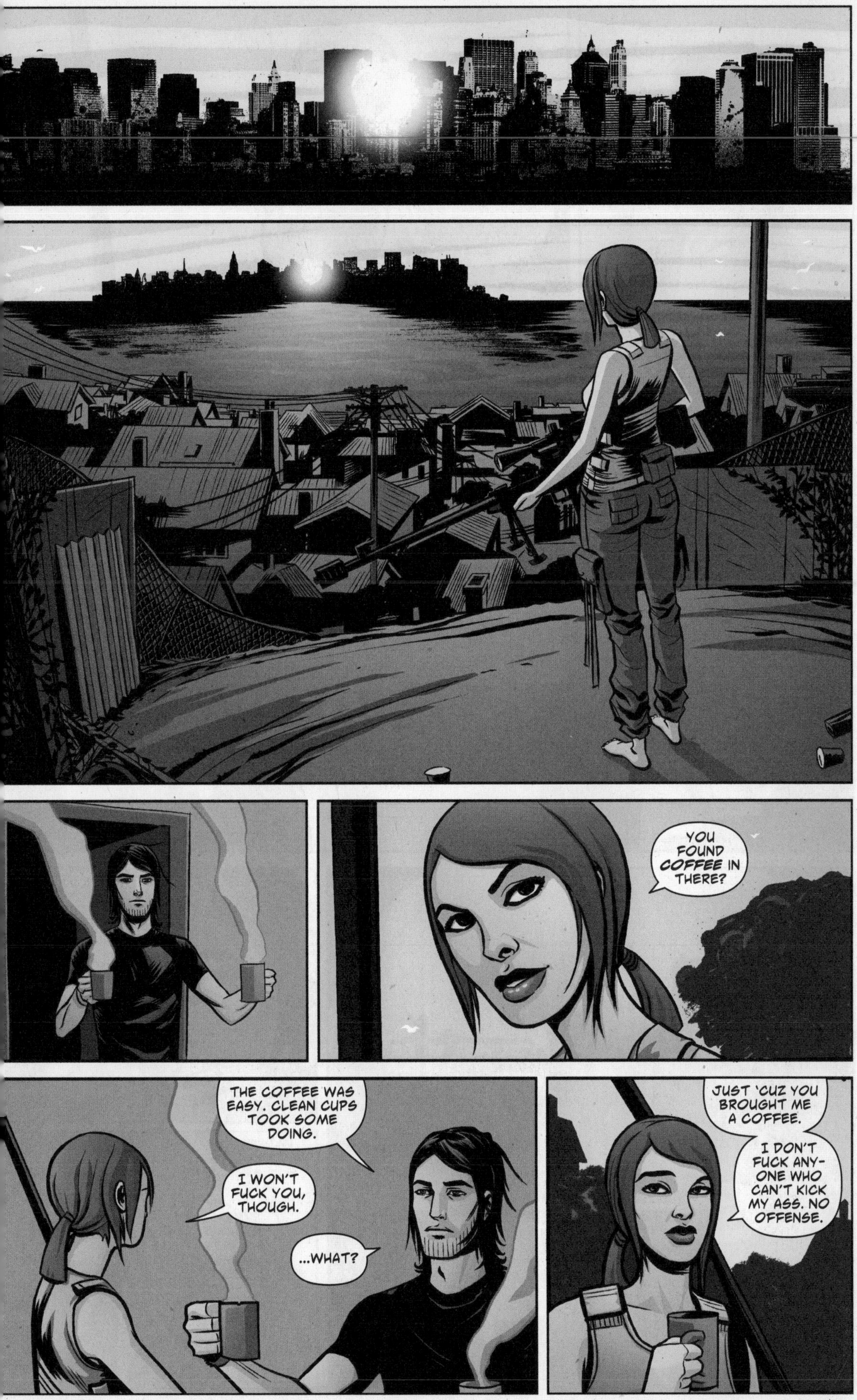
YOU FOUND COFFEE IN THERE?
THE COFFEE WAS EASY. CLEAN CUPS TOOK SOME DOING.
I WON'T FUCK YOU, THOUGH.
...WHAT?
JUST 'CUZ YOU BROUGHT ME A COFFEE.
I DON'T FUCK ANY-ONE WHO CAN'T KICK MY ASS. NO OFFENSE.

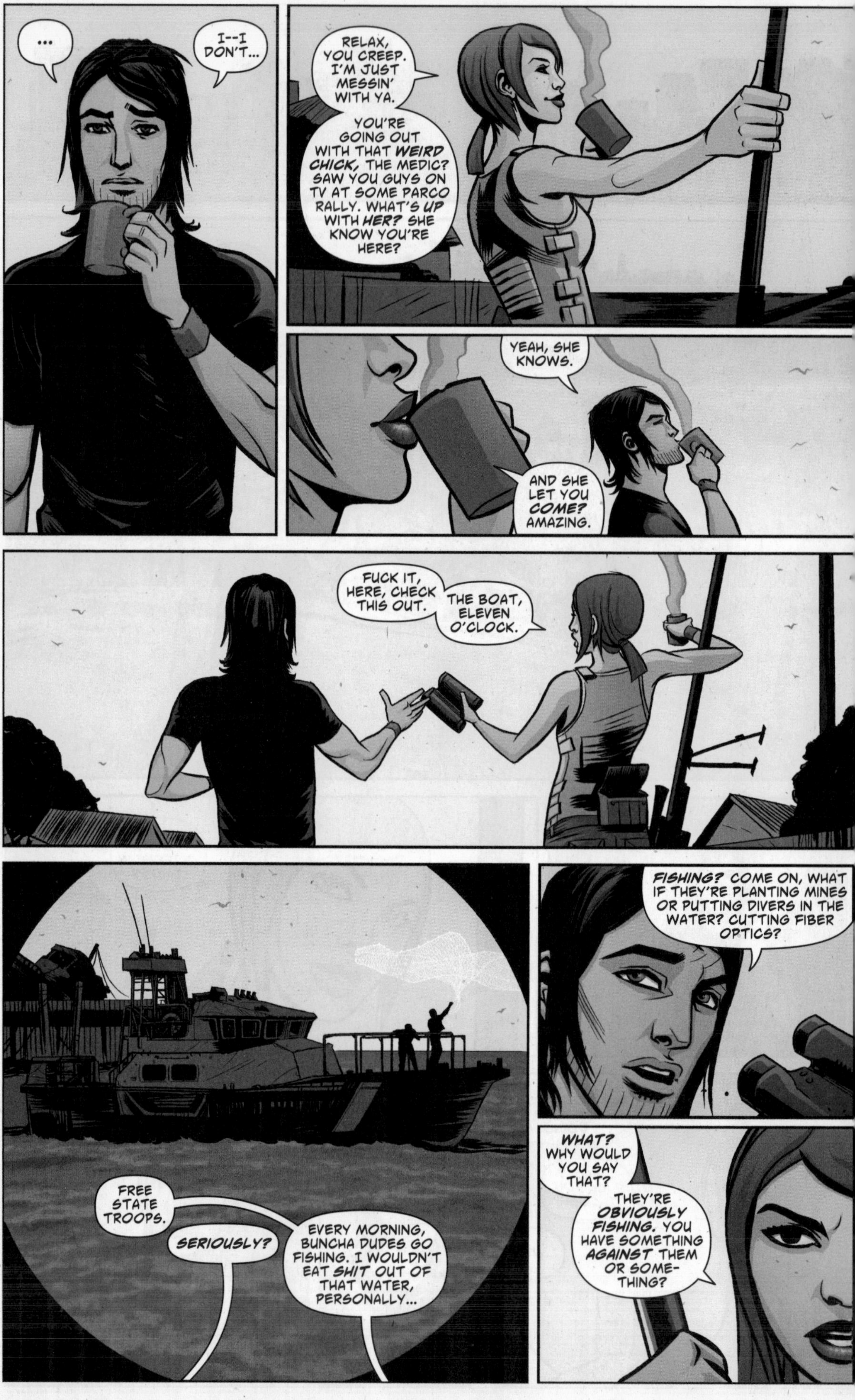
...
I--I DON'T...
RELAX, YOU CREEP. I'M JUST MESSIN' WITH YA.
YOU'RE GOING OUT WITH THAT WEIRD CHICK, THE MEDIC? SAW YOU GUYS ON TV AT SOME PARCO RALLY. WHAT'S UP WITH HER? SHE KNOW YOU'RE HERE?
YEAH, SHE KNOWS.
AND SHE LET YOU COME? AMAZING.
FUCK IT, HERE, CHECK THIS OUT.
THE BOAT, ELEVEN O'CLOCK.
FREE STATE TROOPS.
SERIOUSLY?
EVERY MORNING, BUNCHA DUDES GO FISHING. I WOULDN'T EAT SHIT OUT OF THAT WATER, PERSONALLY...
FISHING? COME ON, WHAT IF THEY'RE PLANTING MINES OR PUTTING DIVERS IN THE WATER? CUTTING FIBER OPTICS?
WHAT? WHY WOULD YOU SAY THAT?
THEY'RE OBVIOUSLY FISHING. YOU HAVE SOMETHING AGAINST THEM OR SOME-THING?

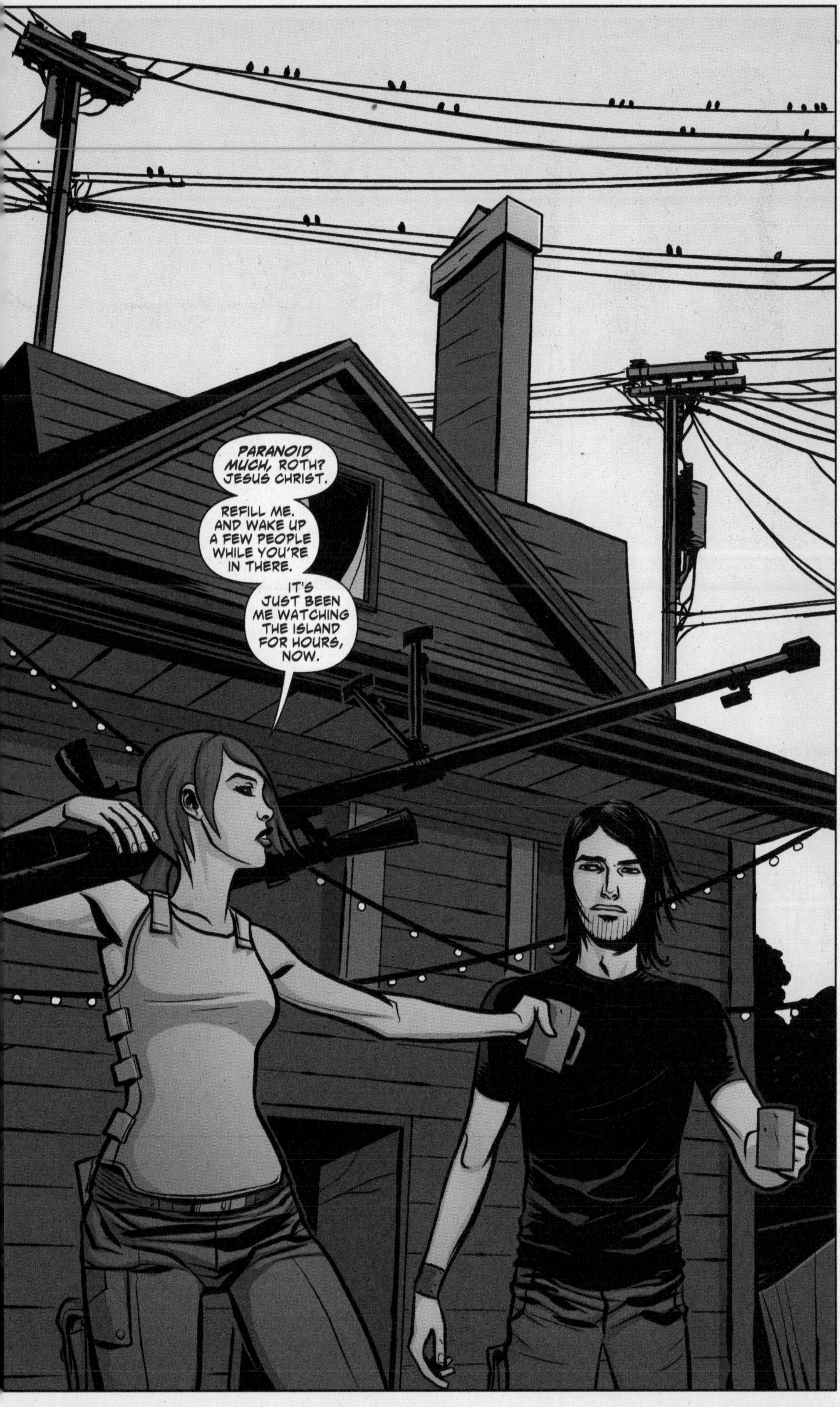
PARANOID MUCH, ROTH? JESUS CHRIST.
REFILL ME. AND WAKE UP A FEW PEOPLE WHILE YOU'RE IN THERE.
IT'S JUST BEEN ME WATCHING THE ISLAND FOR HOURS, NOW.

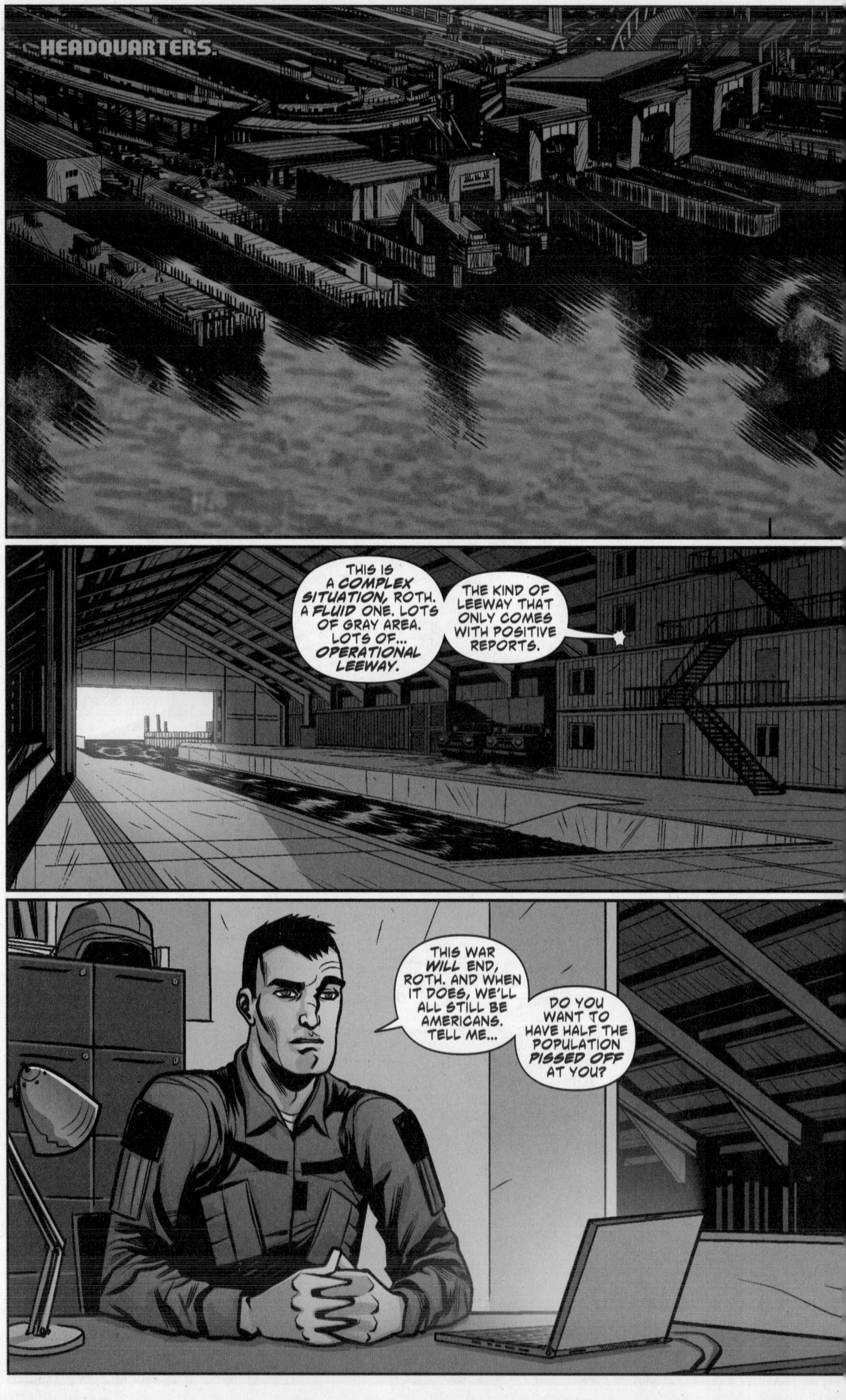

HEADQUARTERS.
THIS IS A COMPLEX SITUATION, ROTH. A FLUID ONE. LOTS OF GRAY AREA. LOTS OF... OPERATIONAL LEEWAY.
THE KIND OF LEEWAY THAT ONLY COMES WITH POSITIVE REPORTS.
THIS WAR WILL END, ROTH. AND WHEN IT DOES, WE'LL ALL STILL BE AMERICANS. TELL ME...
DO YOU WANT TO HAVE HALF THE POPULATION PISSED OFF AT YOU?

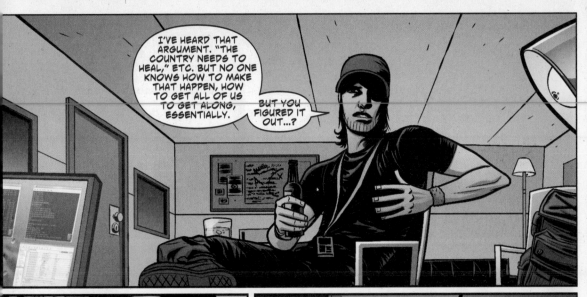

I'VE HEARD THAT ARGUMENT. "THE COUNTRY NEEDS TO HEAL," ETC. BUT NO ONE KNOWS HOW TO MAKE THAT HAPPEN, HOW TO GET ALL OF US TO GET ALONG, ESSENTIALLY.

BUT YOU FIGURED IT OUT...?

FUCK YEAH I DID.

WE CHOSE NOT TO FIGHT IN THE FIRST PLACE.

THIS IS STILL OFF THE RECORD, BY THE WAY.

YEAH, AND *FUCK* YOU FOR THAT, BY THE WAY.

I STILL DON'T GET HOW YOU GET AWAY WITH IT.

SHIT, MAN, HOW DO I *NOT* GET AWAY WITH IT?

THEY PUT US HERE, EYES AND GUNS TRAINED ON THE *ENEMY*. THE ENEMY, THEY PUT THEIR *OWN* GUYS IN PLACE TO WATCH *US*.

SO ONE DAY I JUST SENT SOME BOOZE AND SOME GUYS OVER IN A ZODIAC TO SAY "WHAT'S UP?".

EASY, RIGHT?

He made it that easy.

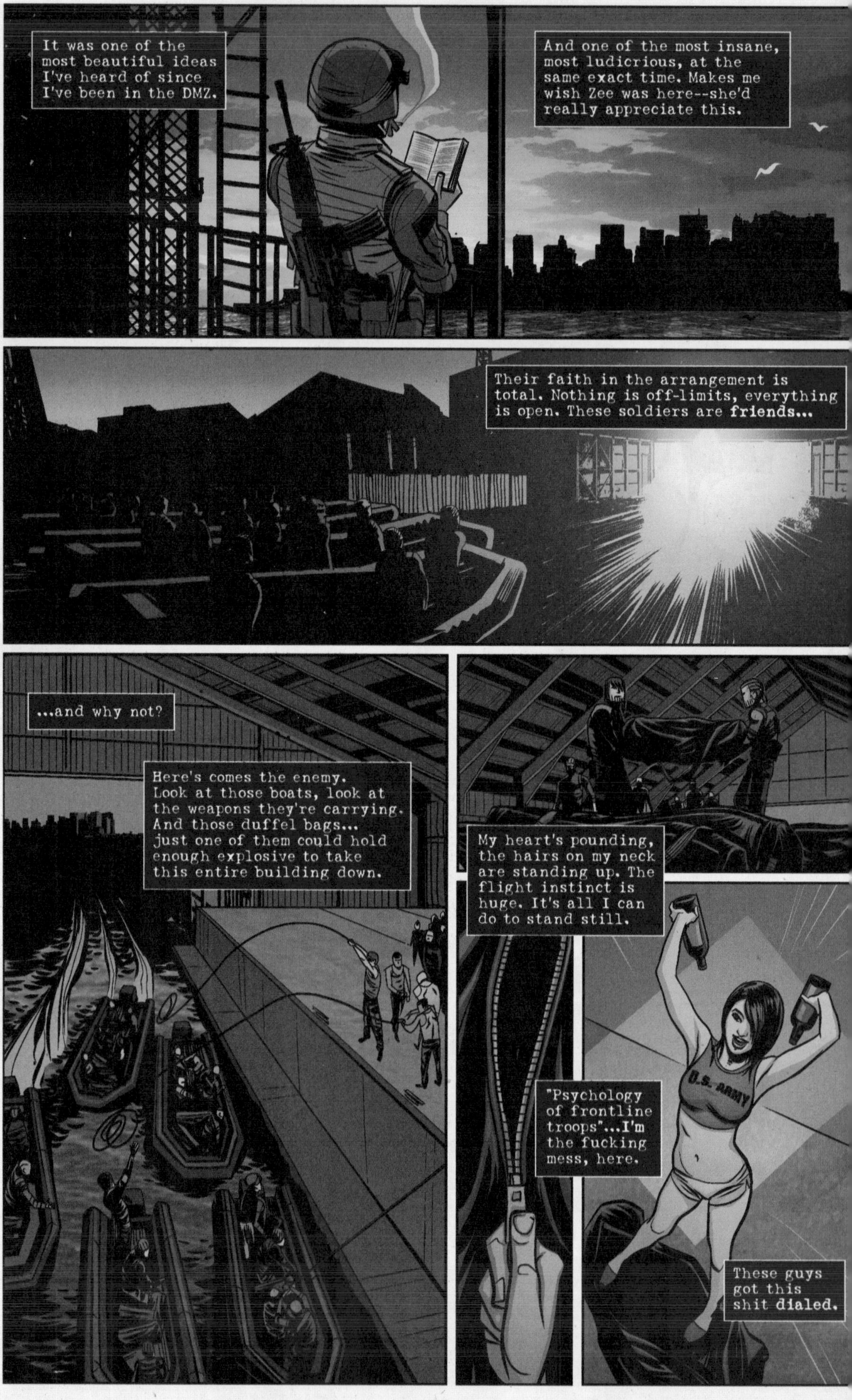
It was one of the most beautiful ideas I've heard of since I've been in the DMZ.
And one of the most insane, most ludicrious, at the same exact time. Makes me wish Zee was here--she'd really appreciate this.
Their faith in the arrangement is total. Nothing is off-limits, everything is open. These soldiers are **friends...**
...and why not?
Here's comes the enemy. Look at those boats, look at the weapons they're carrying. And those duffel bags... just one of them could hold enough explosive to take this entire building down.
My heart's pounding, the hairs on my neck are standing up. The flight instinct is huge. It's all I can do to stand still.
U.S. ARMY
"Psychology of frontline troops"...**I'm** the fucking mess, here.
These guys got this shit **dialed.**

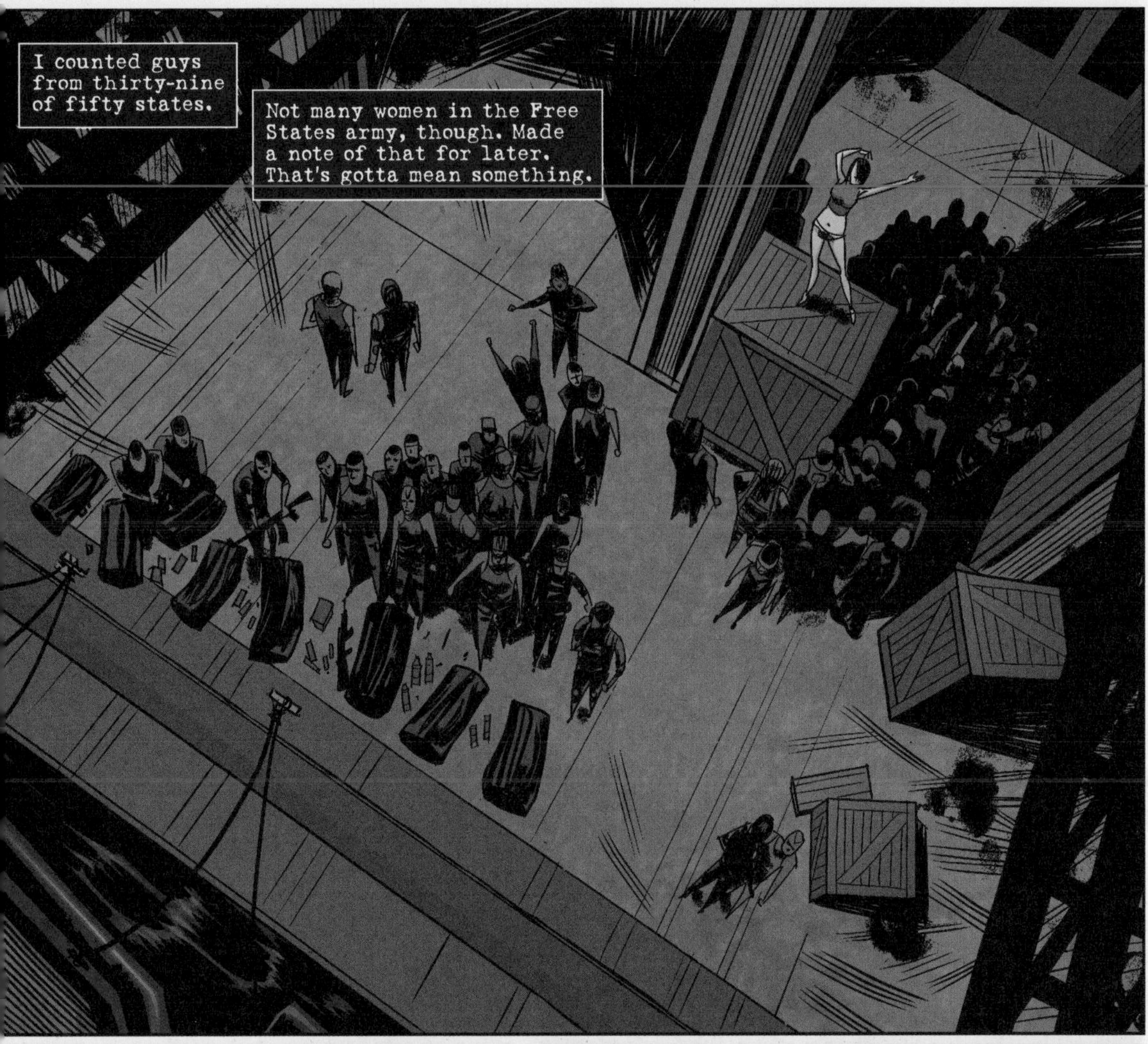
I counted guys from thirty-nine of fifty states.
Not many women in the Free States army, though. Made a note of that for later. That's gotta mean something.

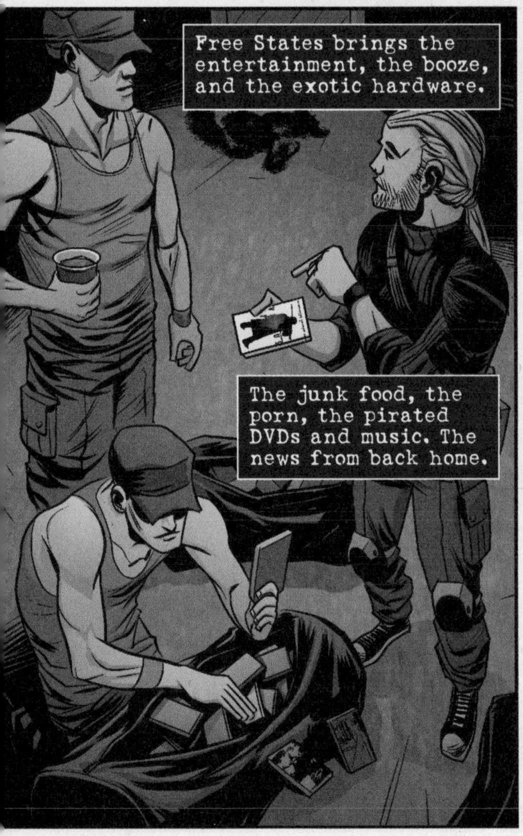
Free States brings the entertainment, the booze, and the exotic hardware.
The junk food, the porn, the pirated DVDs and music. The news from back home.

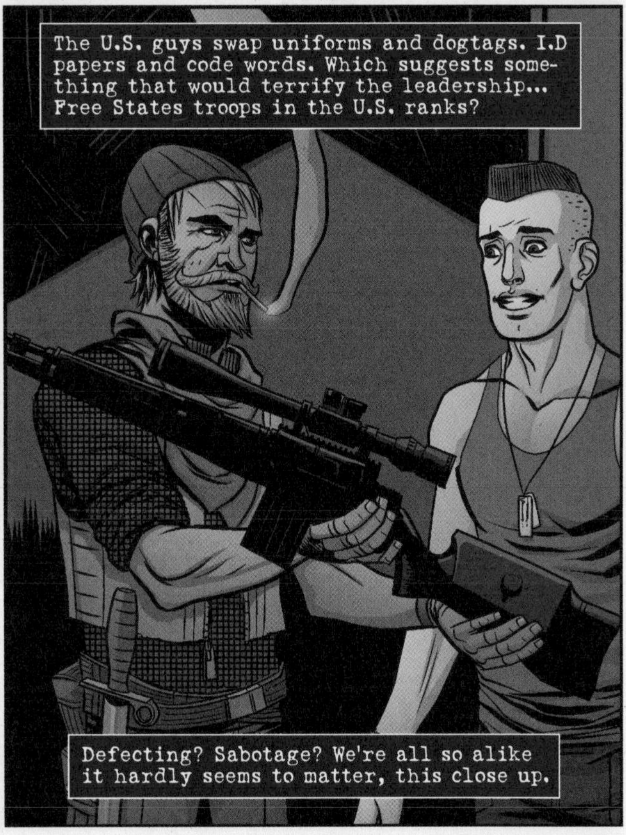
The U.S. guys swap uniforms and dogtags. I.D papers and code words. Which suggests something that would terrify the leadership... Free States troops in the U.S. ranks?
Defecting? Sabotage? We're all so alike it hardly seems to matter, this close up.

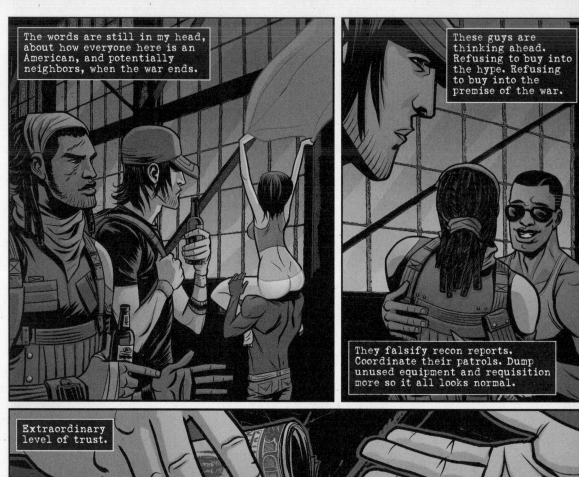

The words are still in my head, about how everyone here is an American, and potentially neighbors, when the war ends.

These guys are thinking ahead. Refusing to buy into the hype. Refusing to buy into the premise of the war.

They falsify recon reports. Coordinate their patrols. Dump unused equipment and requisition more so it all looks normal.

Extraordinary level of trust.

But I suppose they all got a good thing going, and to fuck over one side means both sides are fucked.

Nice deterrent.

CHECK THIS OUT.

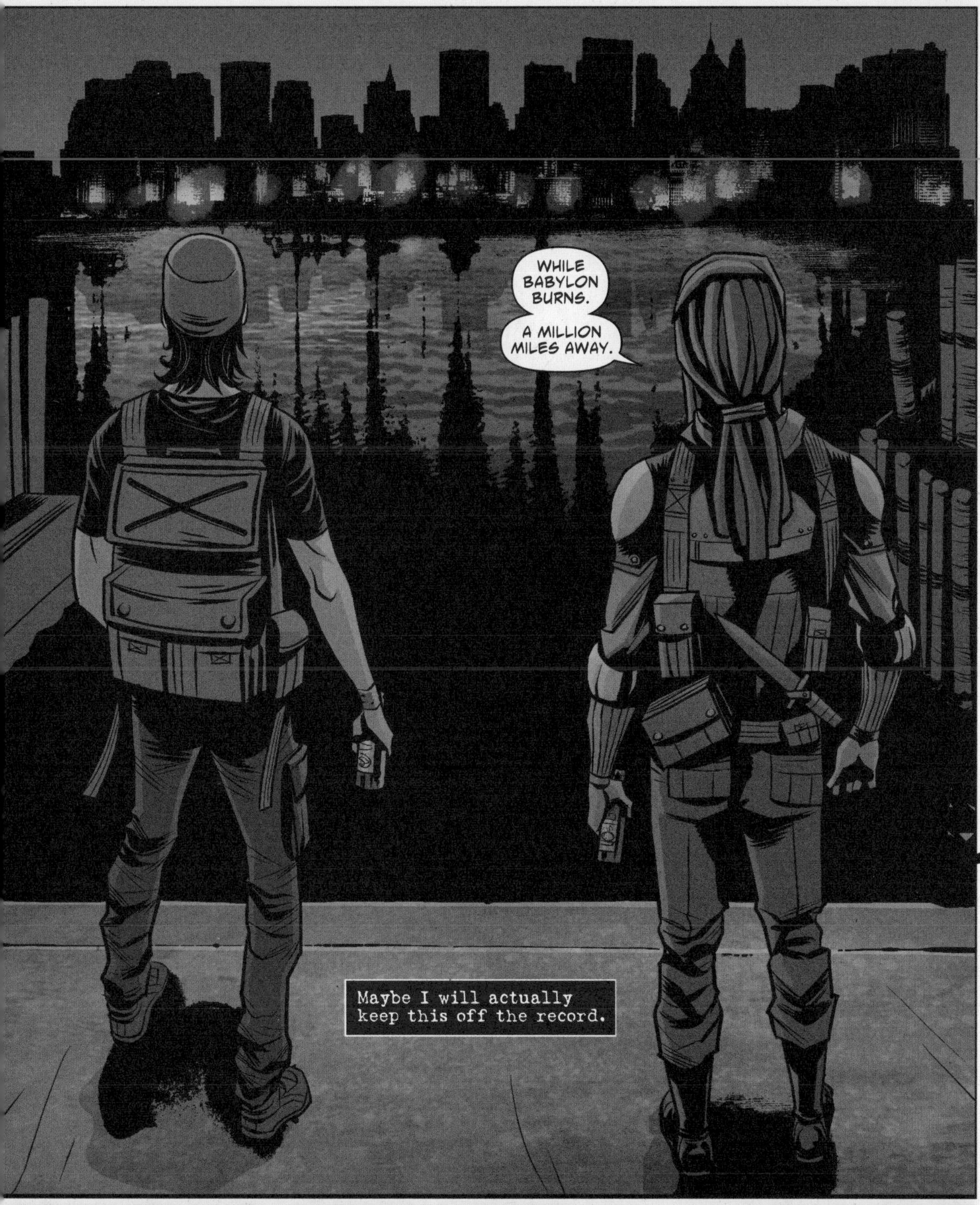
WHILE BABYLON BURNS.
A MILLION MILES AWAY.
Maybe I will actually keep this off the record.

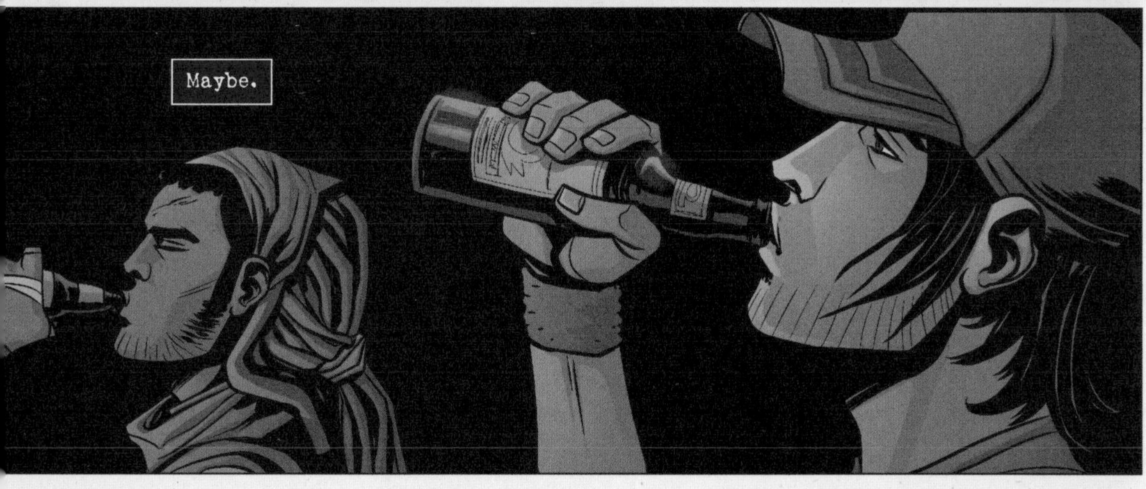
Maybe.

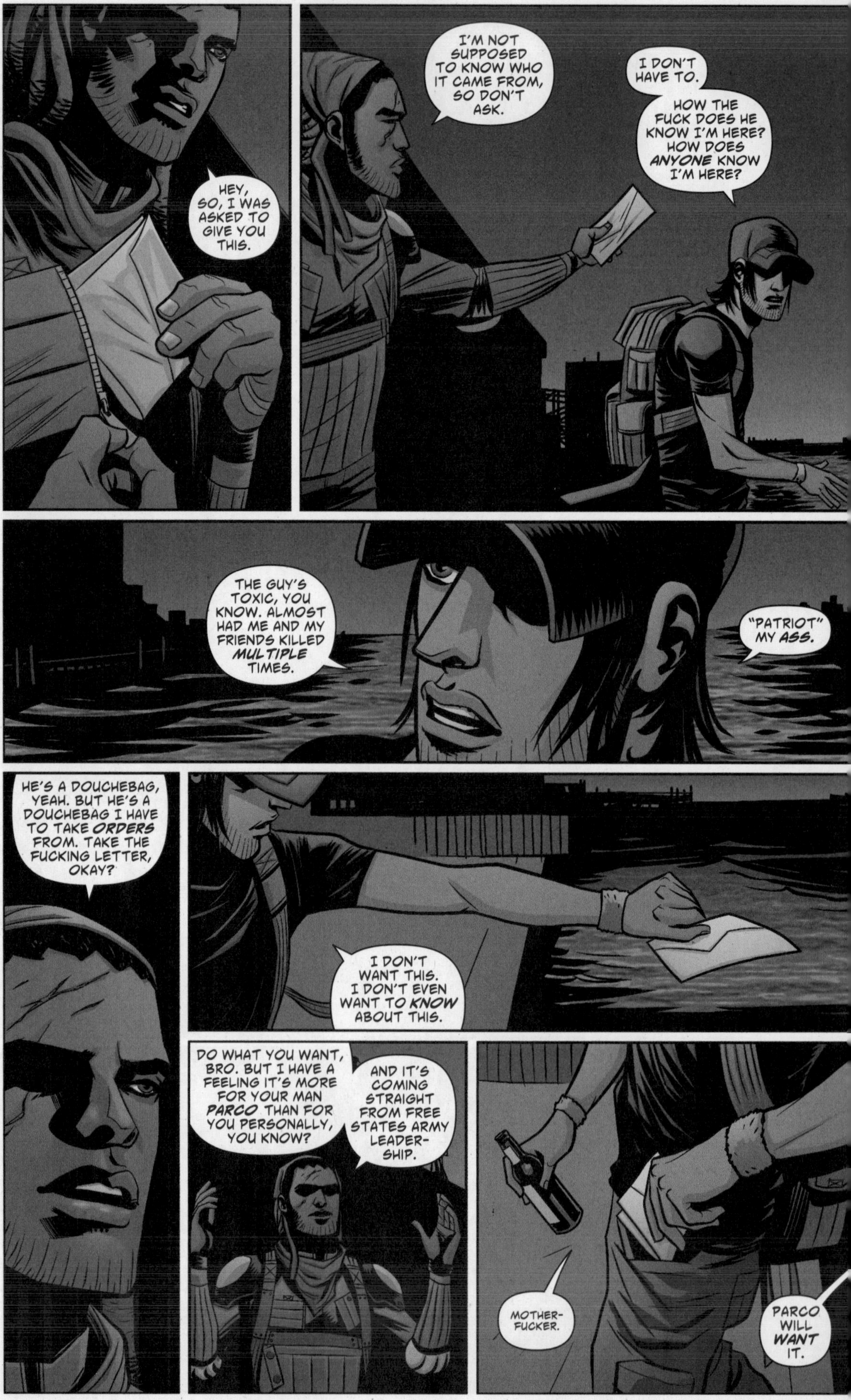
HEY, SO, I WAS ASKED TO GIVE YOU THIS.
I'M NOT SUPPOSED TO KNOW WHO IT CAME FROM, SO DON'T ASK.
I DON'T HAVE TO.
HOW THE FUCK DOES HE KNOW I'M HERE? HOW DOES ANYONE KNOW I'M HERE?
THE GUY'S TOXIC, YOU KNOW. ALMOST HAD ME AND MY FRIENDS KILLED MULTIPLE TIMES.
"PATRIOT" MY ASS.
HE'S A DOUCHEBAG, YEAH. BUT HE'S A DOUCHEBAG I HAVE TO TAKE ORDERS FROM. TAKE THE FUCKING LETTER, OKAY?
I DON'T WANT THIS. I DON'T EVEN WANT TO KNOW ABOUT THIS.
DO WHAT YOU WANT, BRO. BUT I HAVE A FEELING IT'S MORE FOR YOUR MAN PARCO THAN FOR YOU PERSONALLY, YOU KNOW?
AND IT'S COMING STRAIGHT FROM FREE STATES ARMY LEADER-SHIP.
MOTHER-FUCKER.
PARCO WILL WANT IT.

MUCH LATER...

ZZZ...

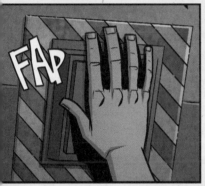

FAP

AwOOOOGA!
AwOOOOGA!
AwOOOOGA!
AwOOOOGA!

?

HEY!

FUCKING MOVE, ASSHOLE!

SHIT.

PUT THAT FUCKING THING AWAY OR I'LL KICK THE LIVING SHIT OUT OF YOU MYSELF!

OFF. THE. RECORD.

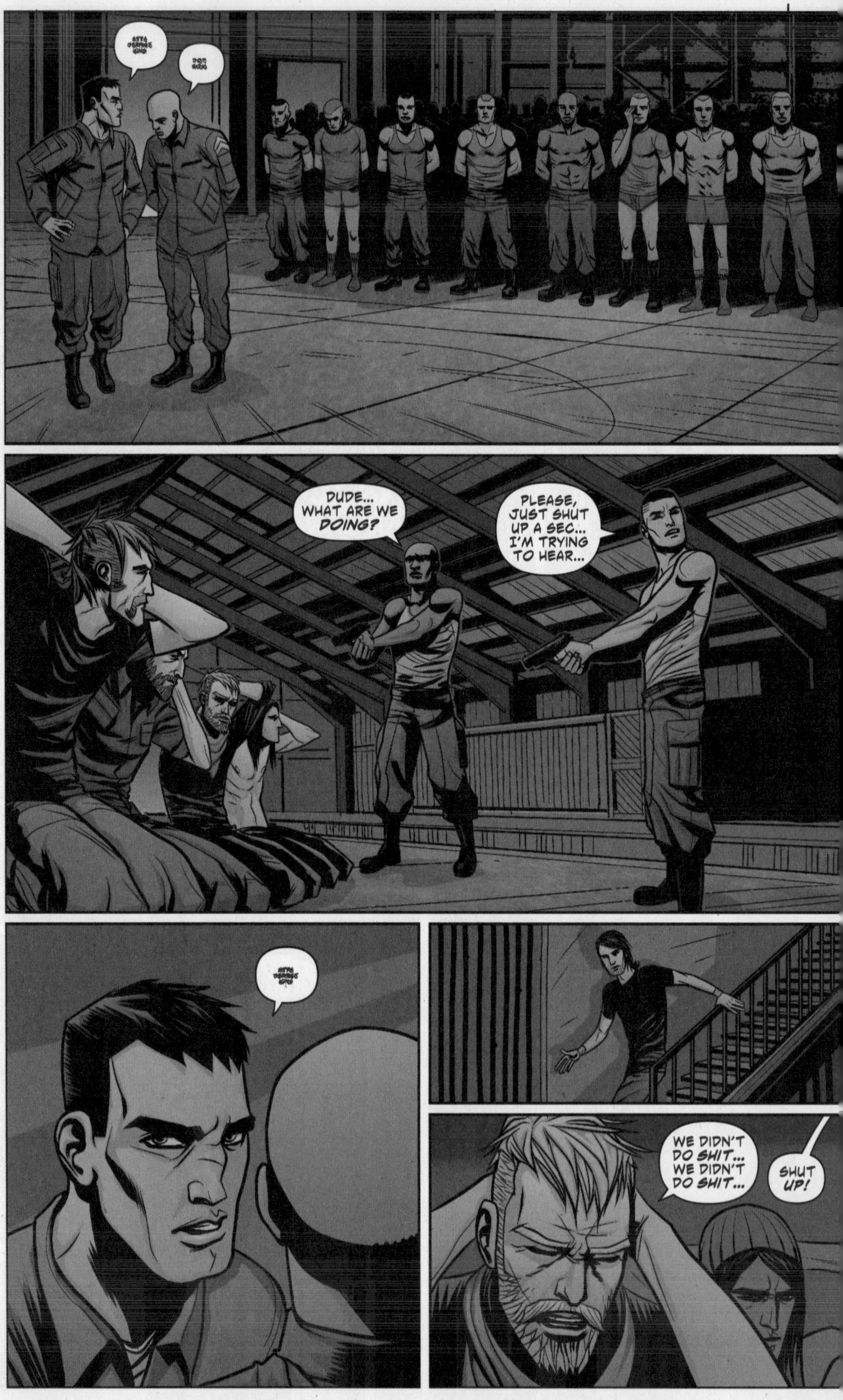
DUDE... WHAT ARE WE DOING?
PLEASE, JUST SHUT UP A SEC... I'M TRYING TO HEAR...
WE DIDN'T DO SHIT... WE DIDN'T DO SHIT...
SHUT UP!

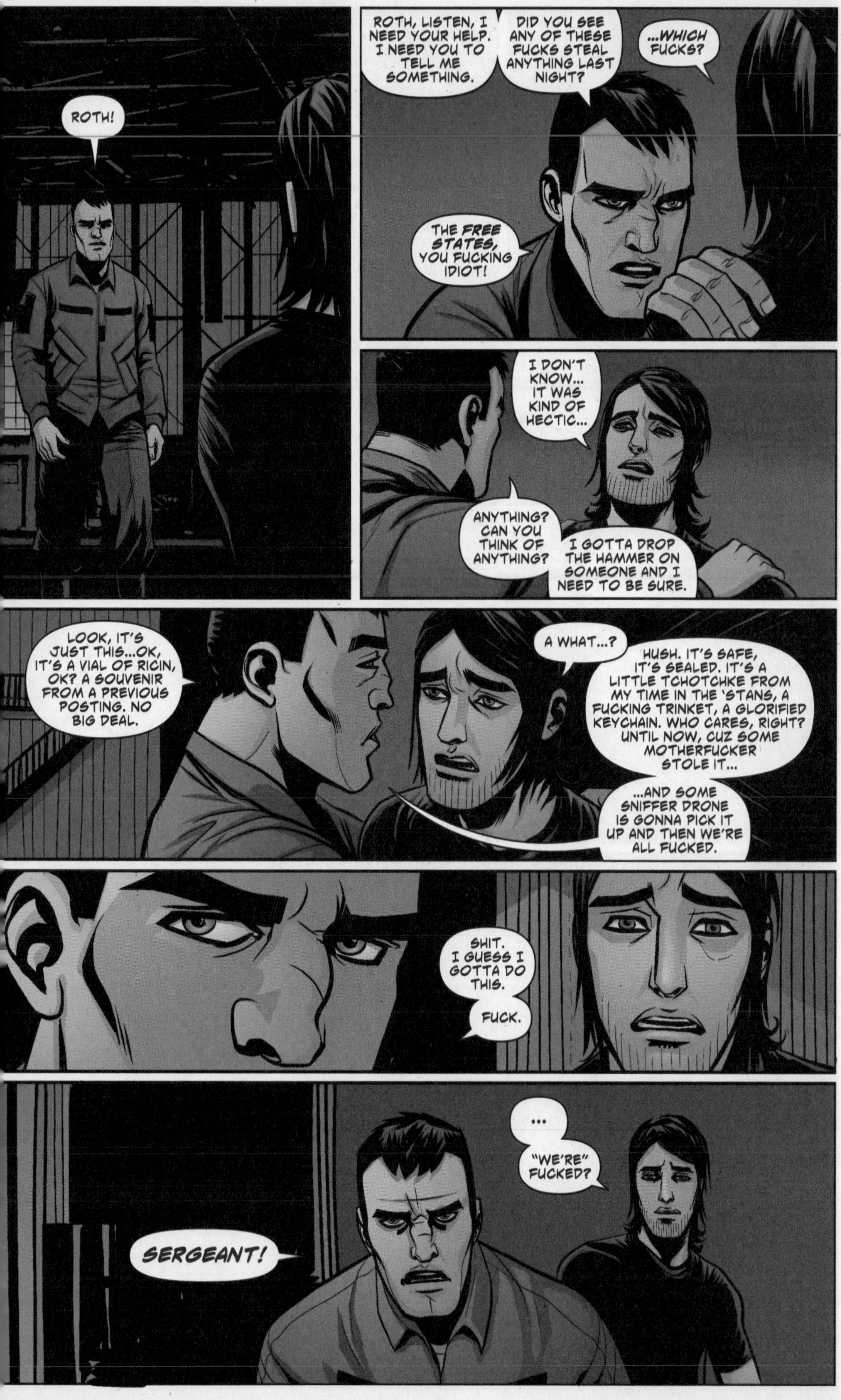
ROTH!
ROTH, LISTEN, I NEED YOUR HELP. I NEED YOU TO TELL ME SOMETHING.
DID YOU SEE ANY OF THESE FUCKS STEAL ANYTHING LAST NIGHT?
...WHICH FUCKS?
THE FREE STATES, YOU FUCKING IDIOT!
I DON'T KNOW... IT WAS KIND OF HECTIC...
ANYTHING? CAN YOU THINK OF ANYTHING?
I GOTTA DROP THE HAMMER ON SOMEONE AND I NEED TO BE SURE.
LOOK, IT'S JUST THIS...OK, IT'S A VIAL OF RICIN, OK? A SOUVENIR FROM A PREVIOUS POSTING. NO BIG DEAL.
A WHAT...?
HUSH. IT'S SAFE, IT'S SEALED. IT'S A LITTLE TCHOTCHKE FROM MY TIME IN THE 'STANS, A FUCKING TRINKET, A GLORIFIED KEYCHAIN. WHO CARES, RIGHT? UNTIL NOW, CUZ SOME MOTHERFUCKER STOLE IT...
...AND SOME SNIFFER DRONE IS GONNA PICK IT UP AND THEN WE'RE ALL FUCKED.
SHIT. I GUESS I GOTTA DO THIS.
FUCK.
...
"WE'RE" FUCKED?
SERGEANT!

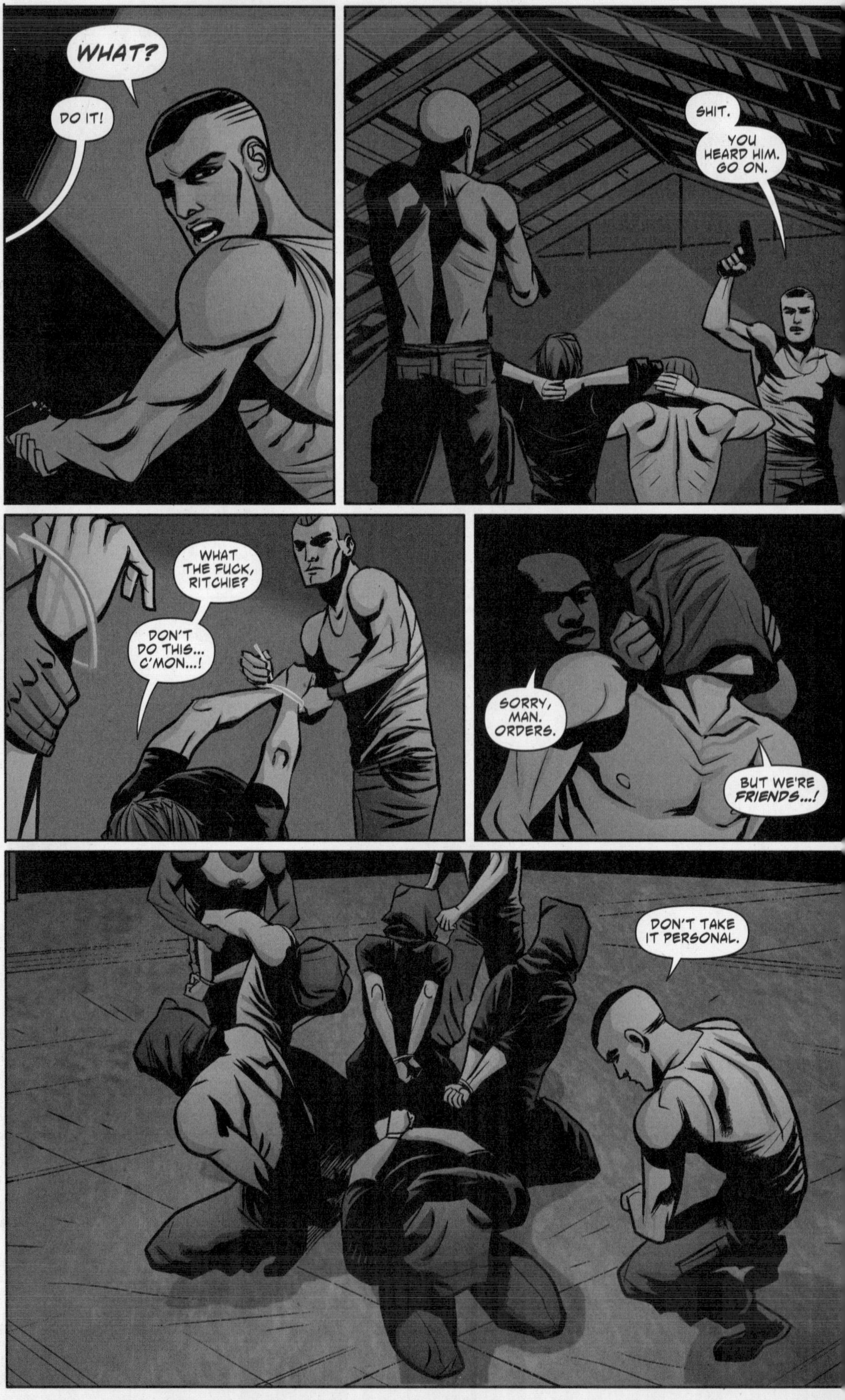
WHAT?
DO IT!
SHIT.
YOU HEARD HIM. GO ON.
WHAT THE FUCK, RITCHIE?
DON'T DO THIS... C'MON...!
SORRY, MAN. ORDERS.
BUT WE'RE FRIENDS...!
DON'T TAKE IT PERSONAL.

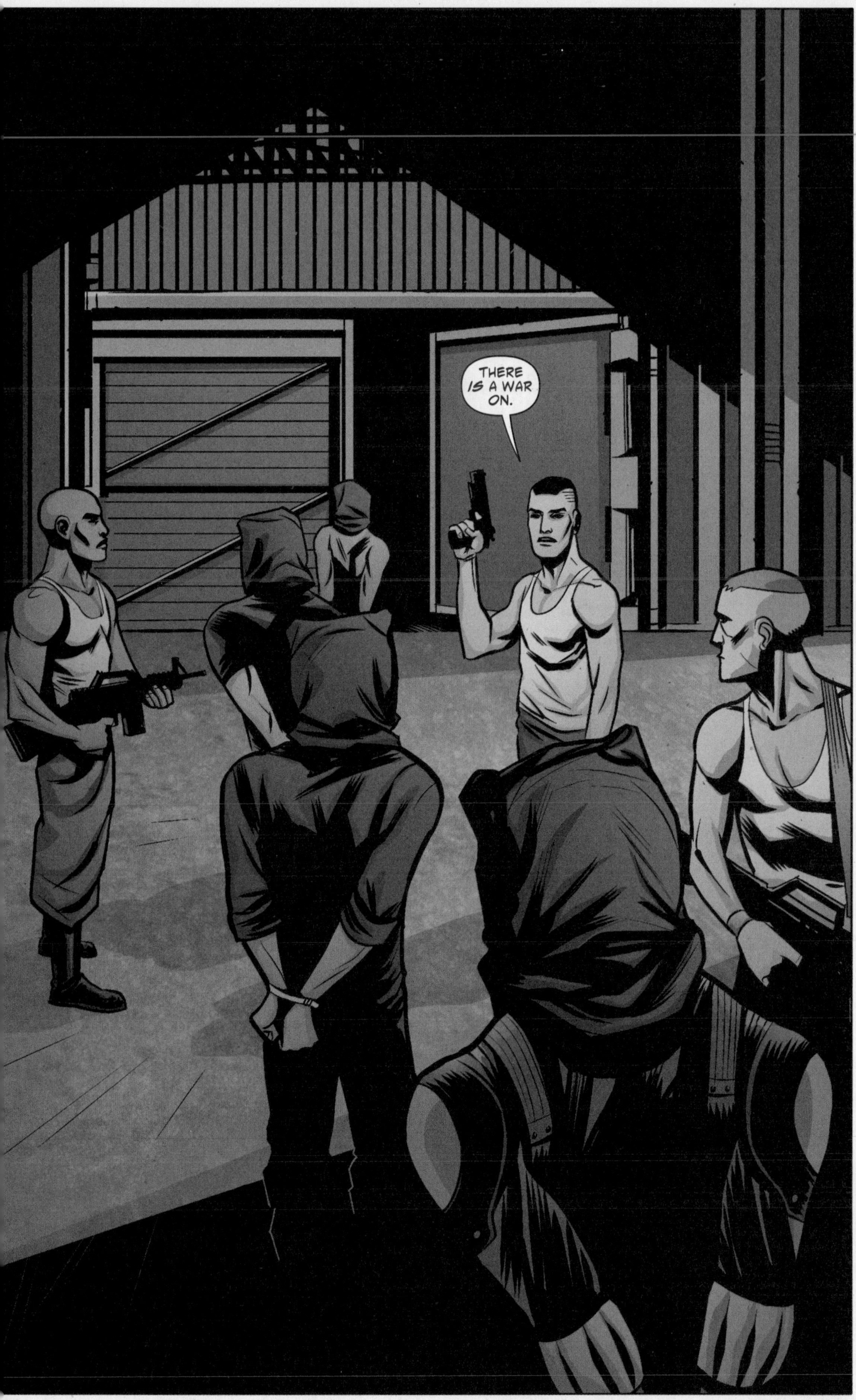
THERE IS A WAR ON.

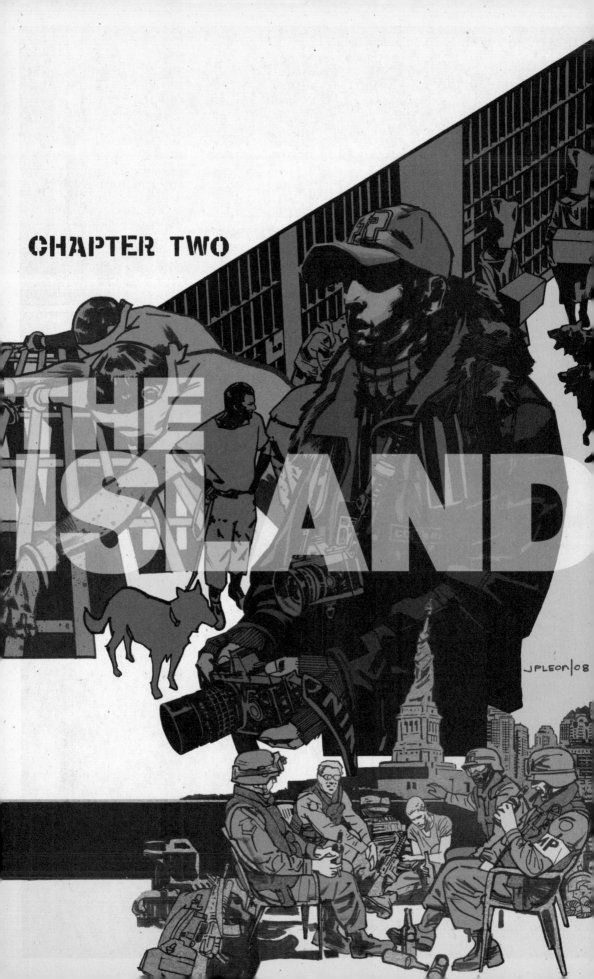

CHAPTER TWO

THE ISLAND

JPLEON/08

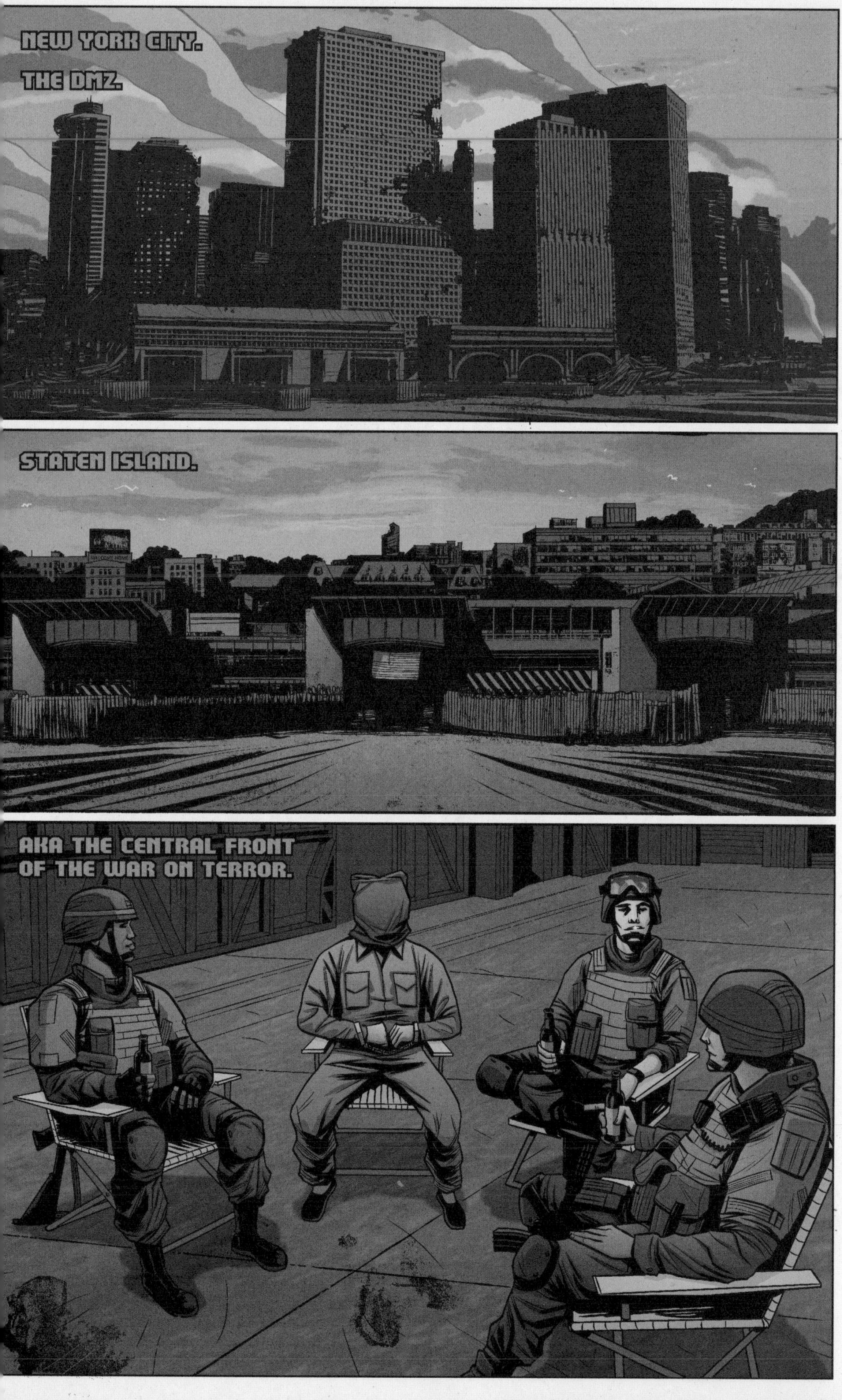
NEW YORK CITY.
THE DMZ.
STATEN ISLAND.
AKA THE CENTRAL FRONT OF THE WAR ON TERROR.

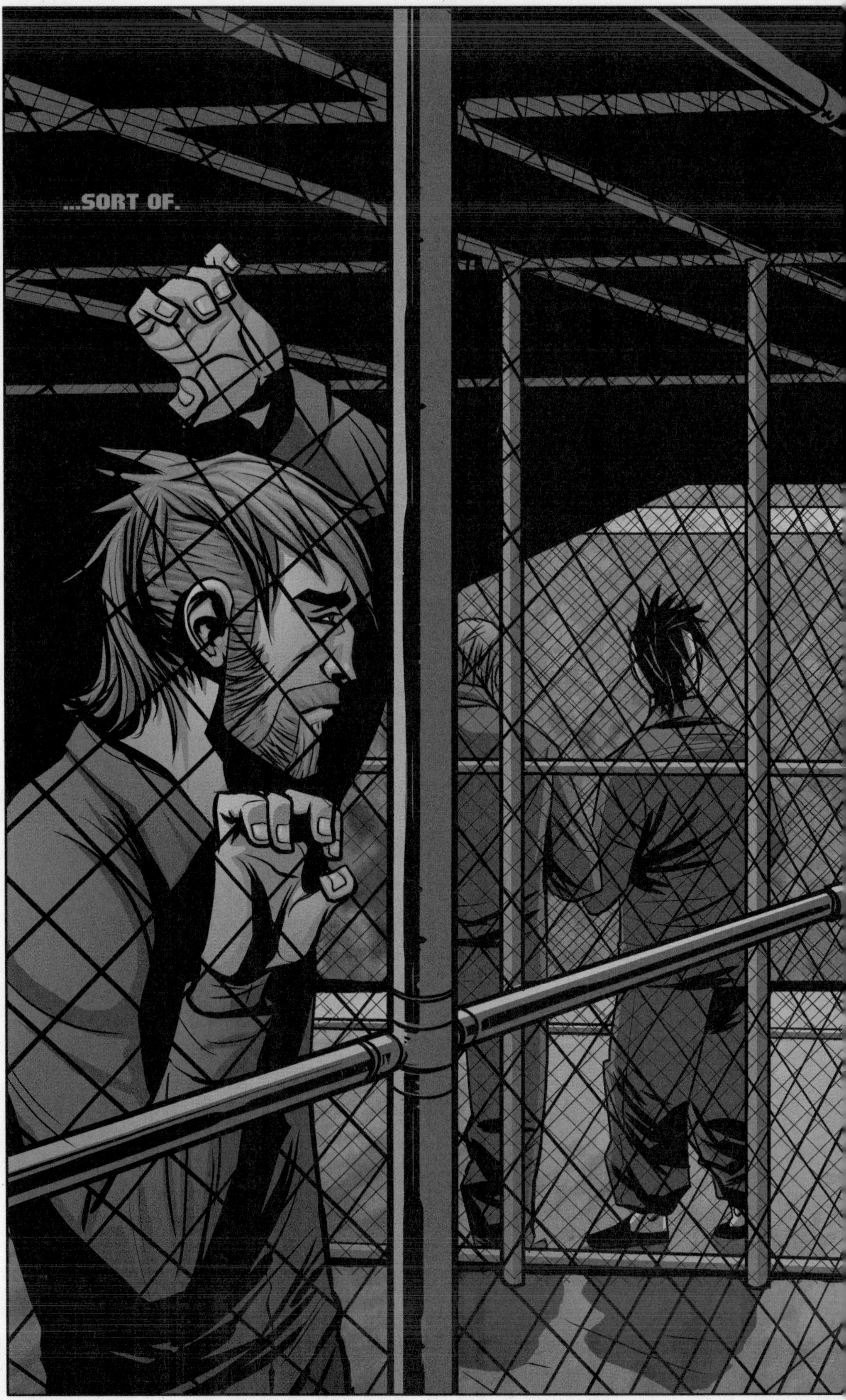
...SORT OF.

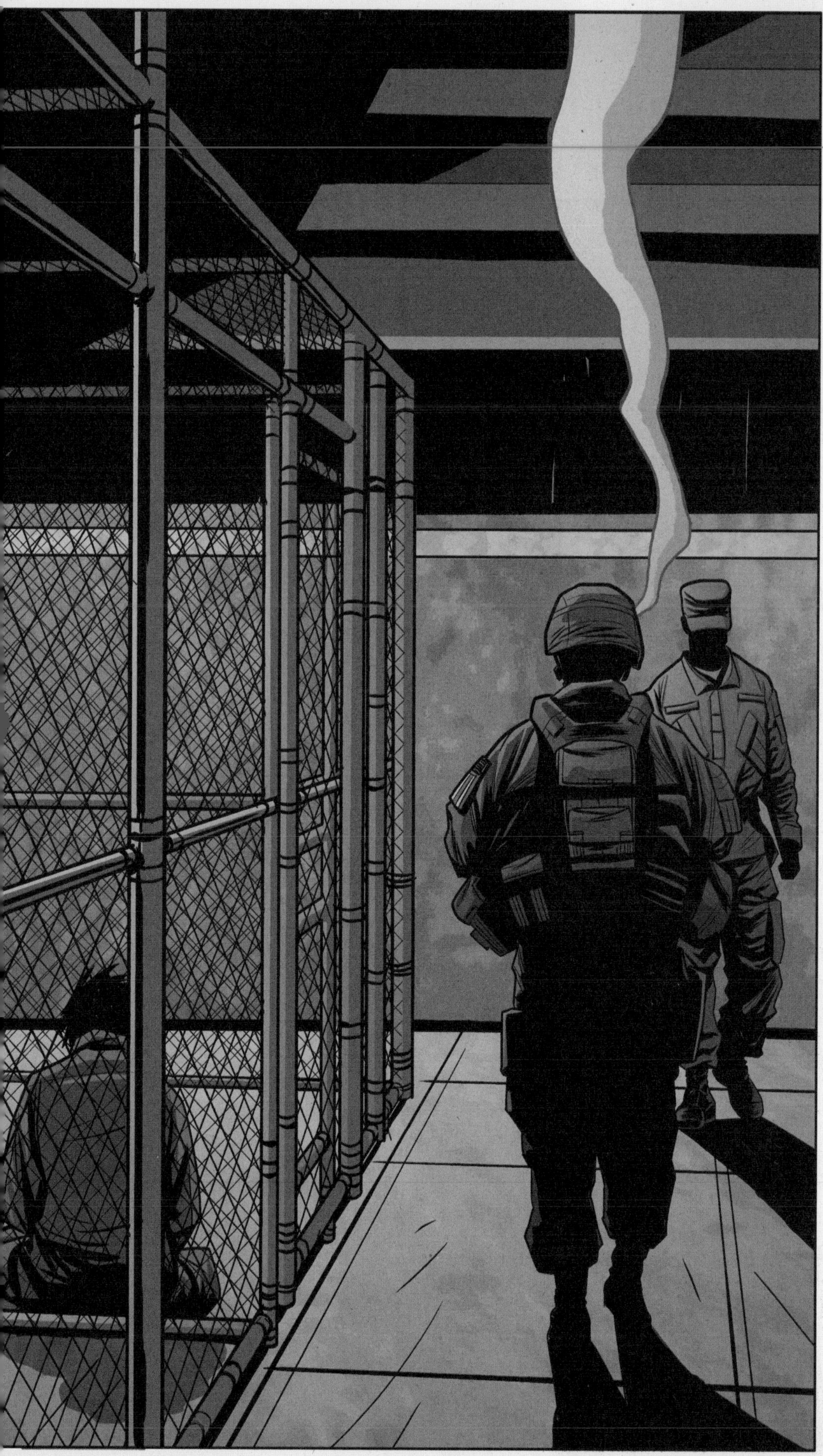

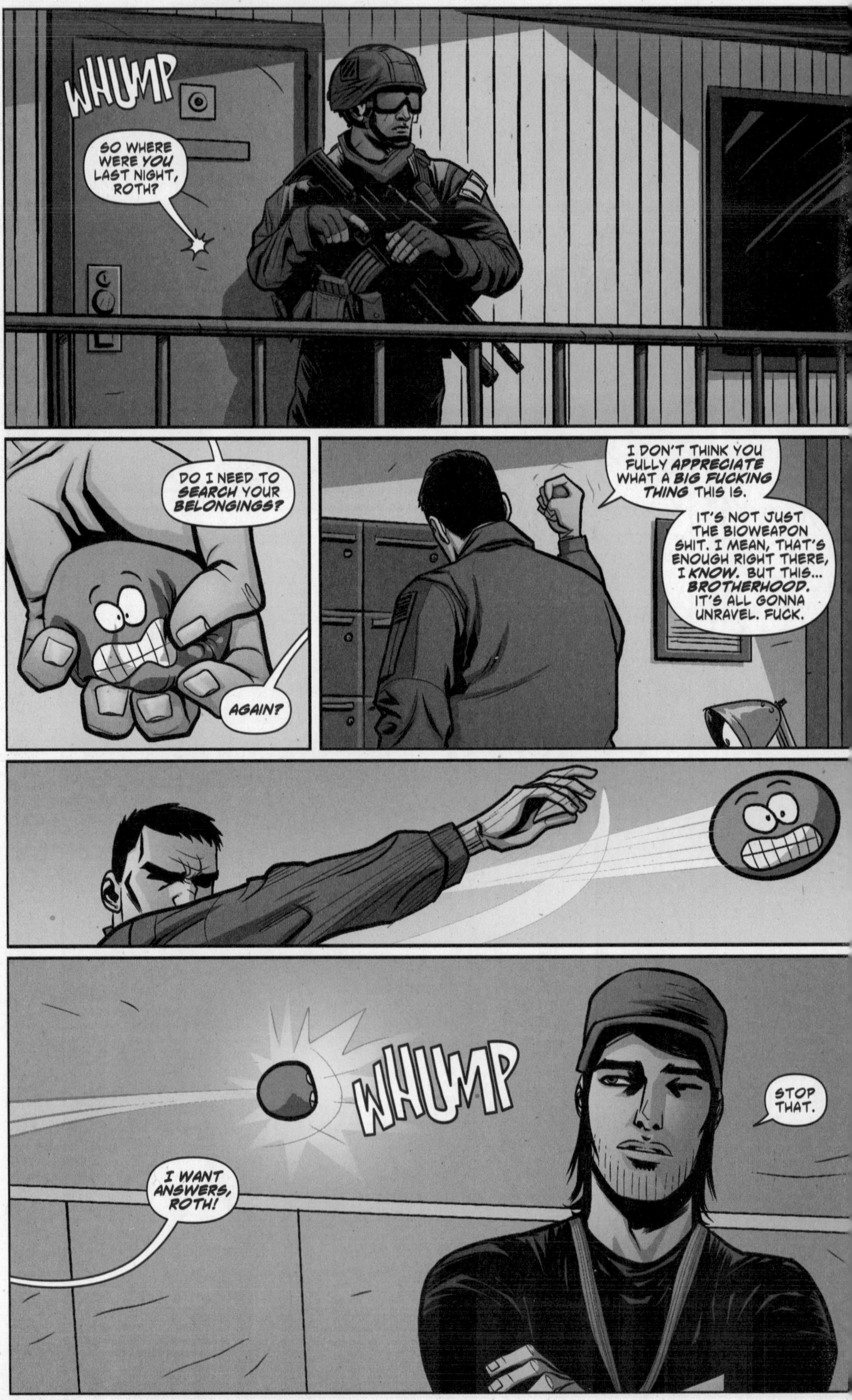
WHUMP
SO WHERE WERE YOU LAST NIGHT, ROTH?
DO I NEED TO SEARCH YOUR BELONGINGS?
AGAIN?
I DON'T THINK YOU FULLY APPRECIATE WHAT A BIG FUCKING THING THIS IS.
IT'S NOT JUST THE BIOWEAPON SHIT. I MEAN, THAT'S ENOUGH RIGHT THERE, I KNOW. BUT THIS... BROTHERHOOD. IT'S ALL GONNA UNRAVEL. FUCK.
WHUMP
STOP THAT.
I WANT ANSWERS, ROTH!

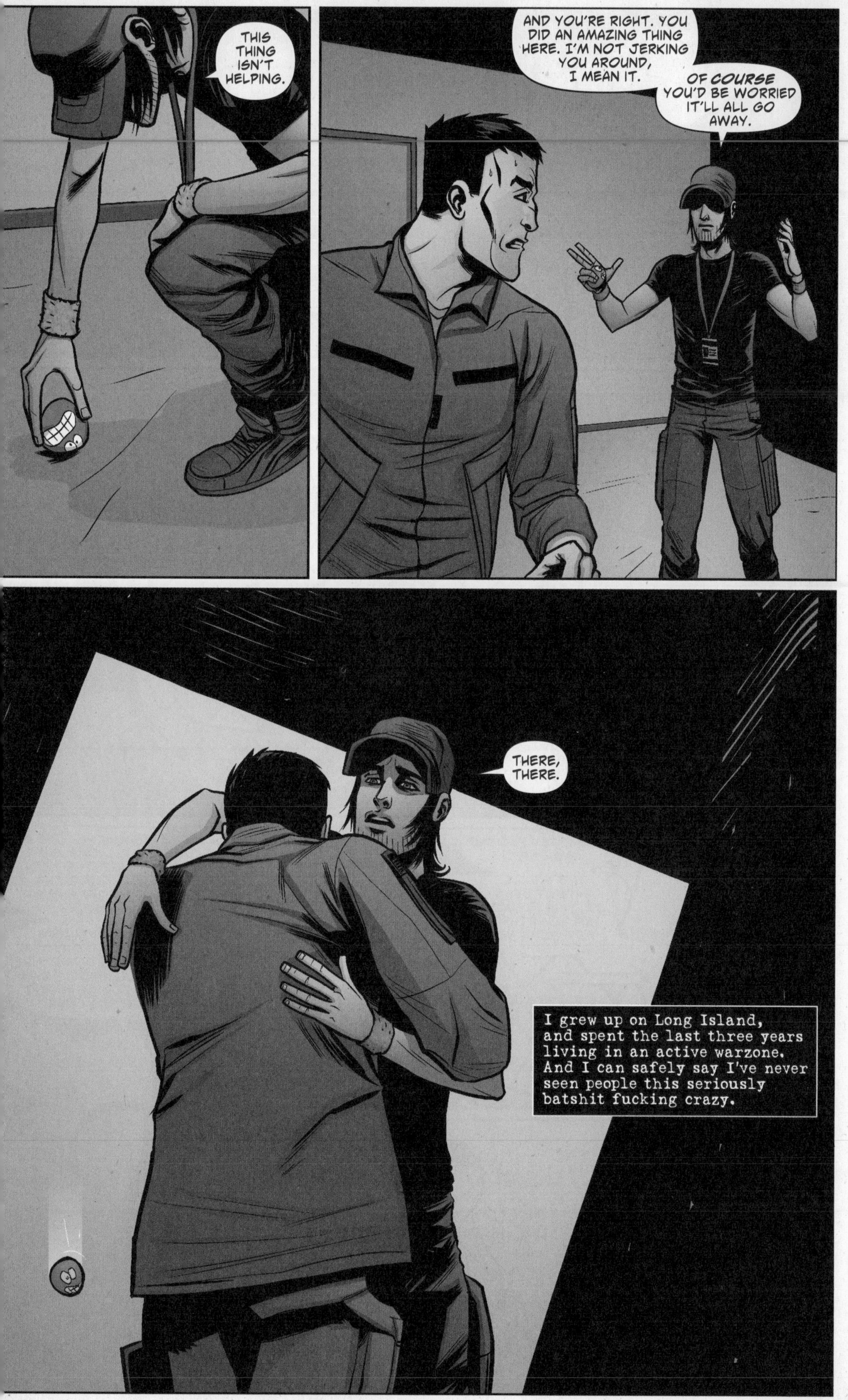
THIS THING ISN'T HELPING.
AND YOU'RE RIGHT. YOU DID AN AMAZING THING HERE. I'M NOT JERKING YOU AROUND, I MEAN IT.
OF COURSE YOU'D BE WORRIED IT'LL ALL GO AWAY.
THERE, THERE.
I grew up on Long Island, and spent the last three years living in an active warzone. And I can safely say I've never seen people this seriously batshit fucking crazy.

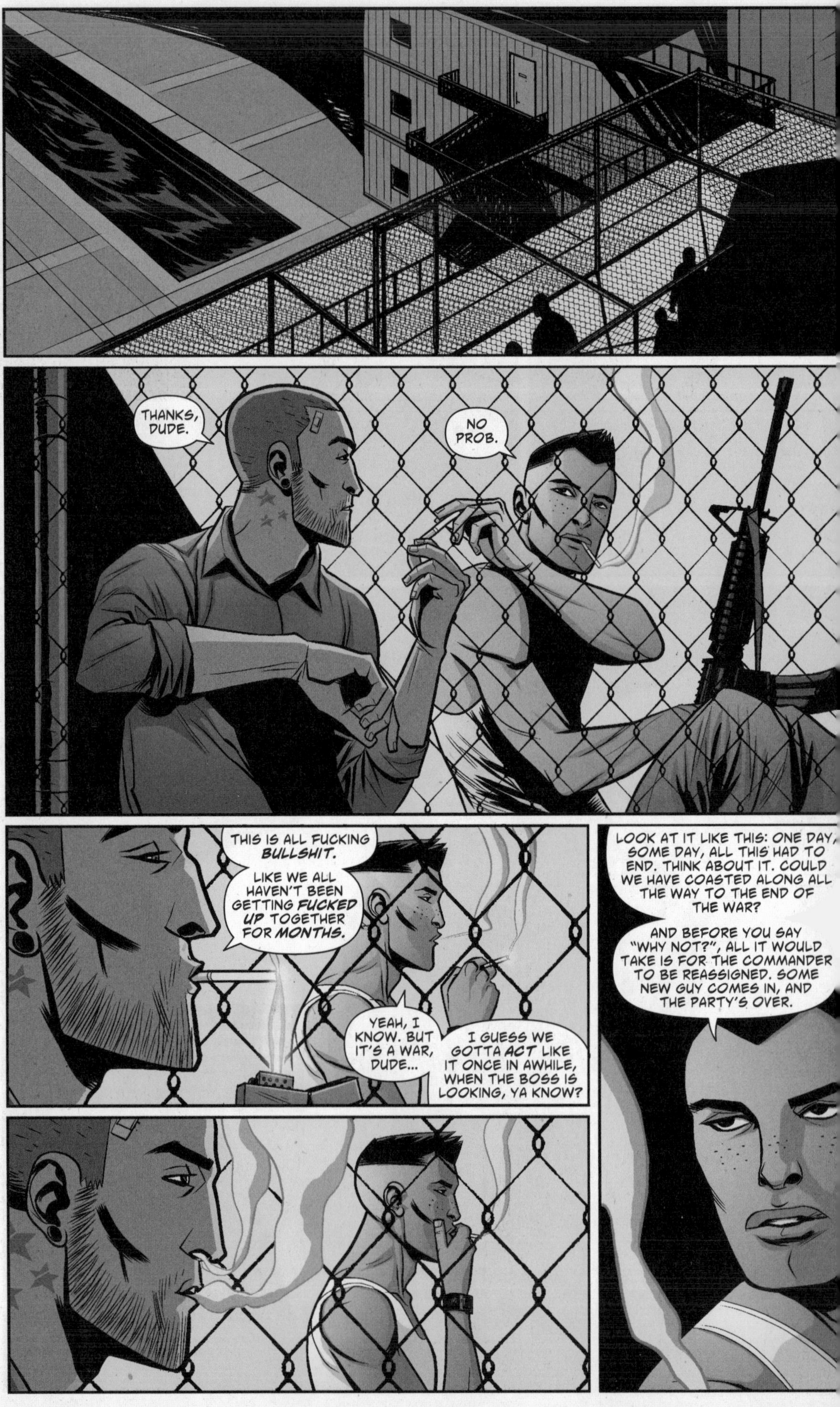
THANKS, DUDE.
NO PROB.
THIS IS ALL FUCKING **BULLSHIT.**
LIKE WE ALL HAVEN'T BEEN GETTING **FUCKED UP** TOGETHER FOR **MONTHS.**
YEAH, I KNOW. BUT IT'S A WAR, DUDE...
I GUESS WE GOTTA **ACT** LIKE IT ONCE IN AWHILE, WHEN THE BOSS IS LOOKING, YA KNOW?
LOOK AT IT LIKE THIS: ONE DAY, SOME DAY, ALL THIS HAD TO END. THINK ABOUT IT. COULD WE HAVE COASTED ALONG ALL THE WAY TO THE END OF THE WAR?
AND BEFORE YOU SAY "WHY NOT?", ALL IT WOULD TAKE IS FOR THE COMMANDER TO BE REASSIGNED. SOME NEW GUY COMES IN, AND THE PARTY'S OVER.

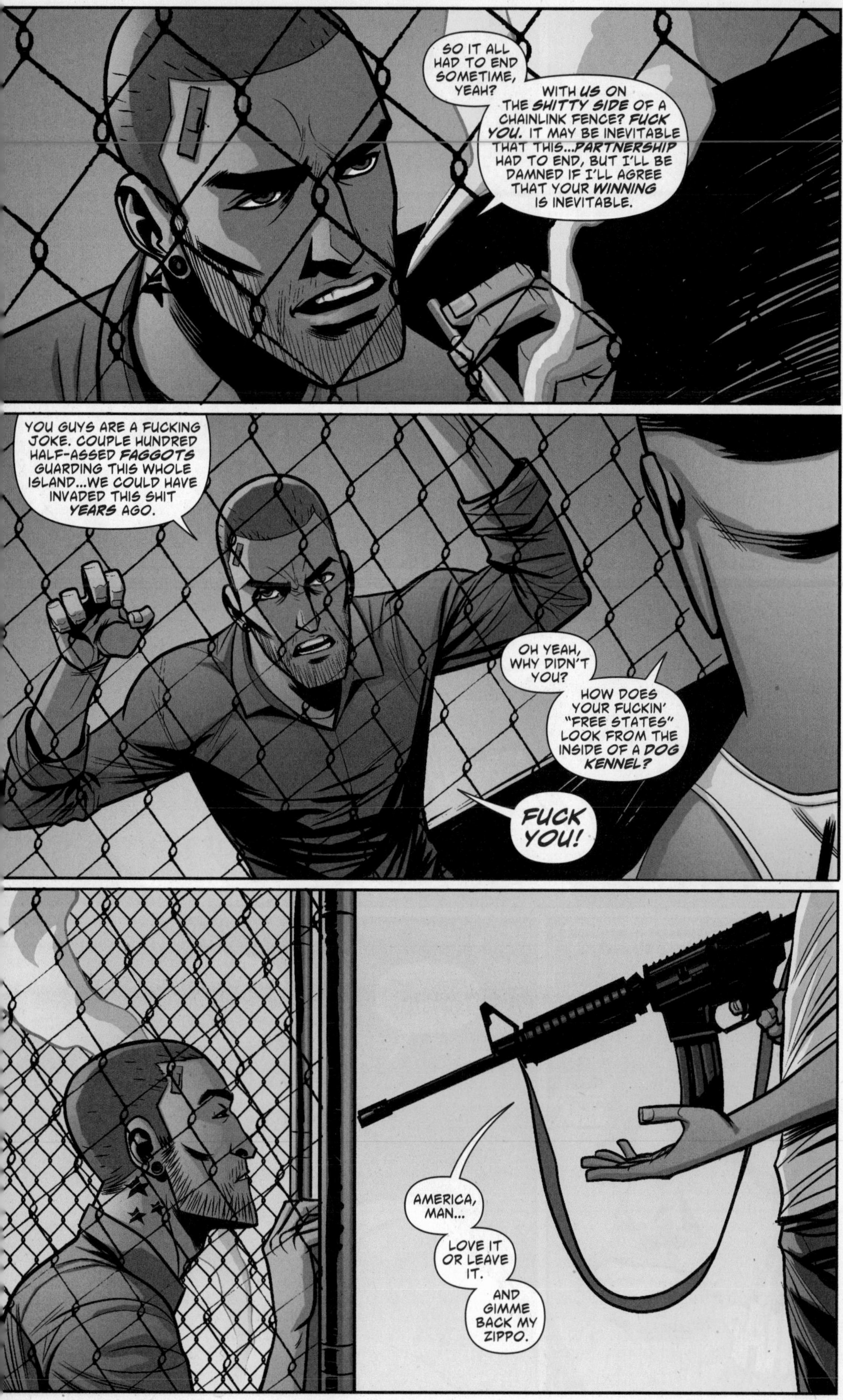
SO IT ALL HAD TO END SOMETIME, YEAH?
WITH US ON THE SHITTY SIDE OF A CHAINLINK FENCE? FUCK YOU. IT MAY BE INEVITABLE THAT THIS...PARTNERSHIP HAD TO END, BUT I'LL BE DAMNED IF I'LL AGREE THAT YOUR WINNING IS INEVITABLE.
YOU GUYS ARE A FUCKING JOKE. COUPLE HUNDRED HALF-ASSED FAGGOTS GUARDING THIS WHOLE ISLAND...WE COULD HAVE INVADED THIS SHIT YEARS AGO.
OH YEAH, WHY DIDN'T YOU?
HOW DOES YOUR FUCKIN' "FREE STATES" LOOK FROM THE INSIDE OF A DOG KENNEL?
FUCK YOU!
AMERICA, MAN...
LOVE IT OR LEAVE IT.
AND GIMME BACK MY ZIPPO.

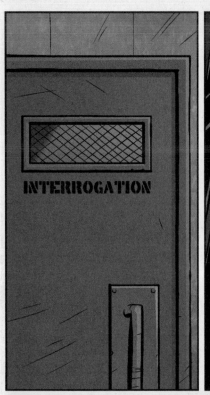

INTERROGATION

TELL ME WHERE IT IS.

...TELL YOU WHERE **WHAT** IS?

WHAP

GAHHHH!

Why am I here?

This is a **disaster**. These guys are panicking...they have no idea what they're doing.

WHAP

FUCK! THAT FUCKING **HURT,** MAN!

TELL ME WHERE THE **VIAL** IS, ASSHOLE!

And that makes this whole thing so dangerous.

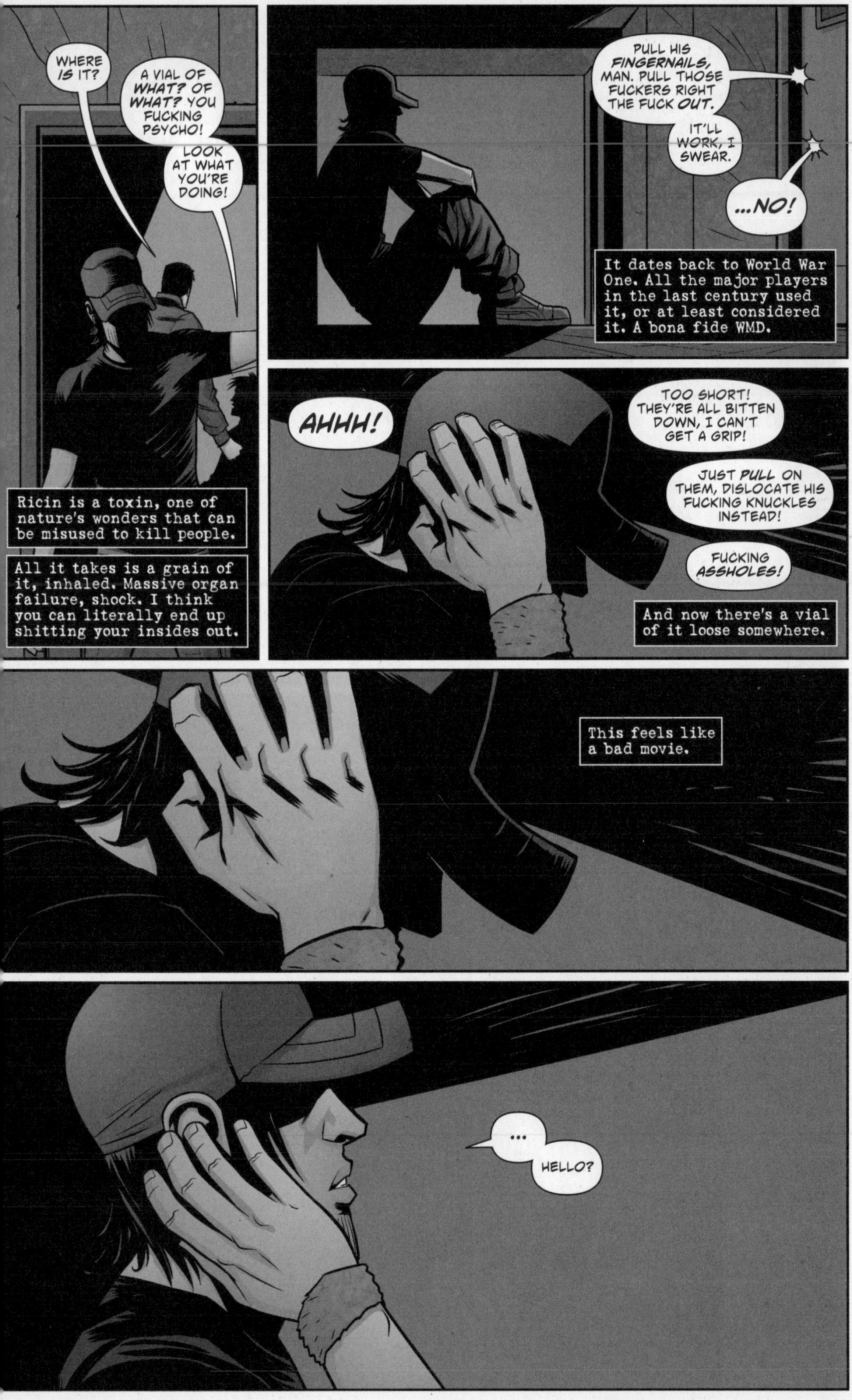
WHERE IS IT?
A VIAL OF WHAT? OF WHAT? YOU FUCKING PSYCHO!
LOOK AT WHAT YOU'RE DOING!
Ricin is a toxin, one of nature's wonders that can be misused to kill people.
All it takes is a grain of it, inhaled. Massive organ failure, shock. I think you can literally end up shitting your insides out.
PULL HIS FINGERNAILS, MAN. PULL THOSE FUCKERS RIGHT THE FUCK OUT.
IT'LL WORK, I SWEAR.
...NO!
It dates back to World War One. All the major players in the last century used it, or at least considered it. A bona fide WMD.
AHHH!
TOO SHORT! THEY'RE ALL BITTEN DOWN, I CAN'T GET A GRIP!
JUST PULL ON THEM, DISLOCATE HIS FUCKING KNUCKLES INSTEAD!
FUCKING ASSHOLES!
And now there's a vial of it loose somewhere.
This feels like a bad movie.
...
HELLO?

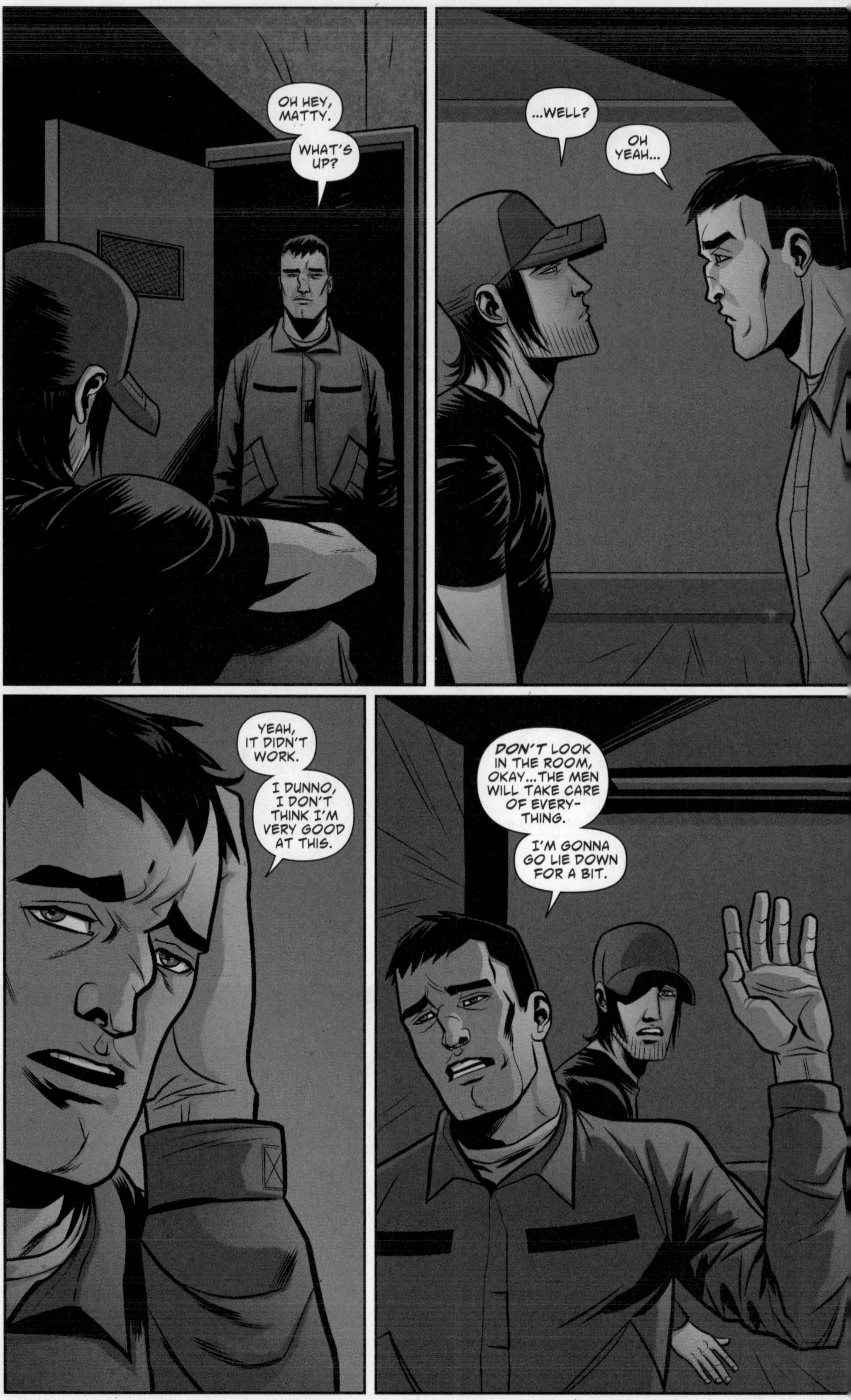
OH HEY, MATTY.
WHAT'S UP?
...WELL?
OH YEAH...
YEAH, IT DIDN'T WORK.
I DUNNO, I DON'T THINK I'M VERY GOOD AT THIS.
DON'T LOOK IN THE ROOM, OKAY...THE MEN WILL TAKE CARE OF EVERY-THING.
I'M GONNA GO LIE DOWN FOR A BIT.

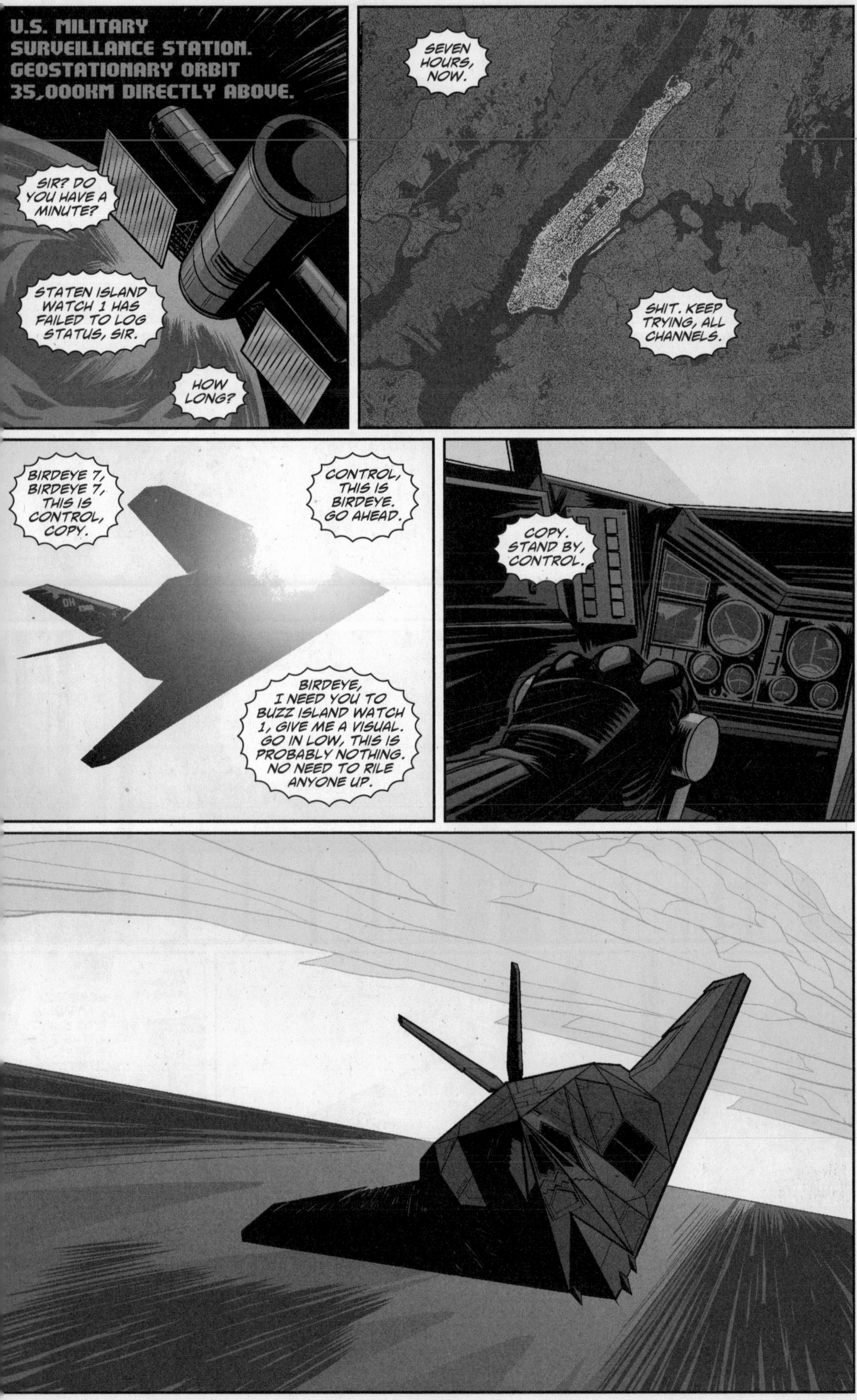
U.S. MILITARY SURVEILLANCE STATION. GEOSTATIONARY ORBIT 35,000KM DIRECTLY ABOVE.
SIR? DO YOU HAVE A MINUTE?
STATEN ISLAND WATCH 1 HAS FAILED TO LOG STATUS, SIR.
HOW LONG?
SEVEN HOURS, NOW.
SHIT. KEEP TRYING, ALL CHANNELS.
BIRDEYE 7, BIRDEYE 7, THIS IS CONTROL, COPY.
CONTROL, THIS IS BIRDEYE. GO AHEAD.
BIRDEYE, I NEED YOU TO BUZZ ISLAND WATCH 1, GIVE ME A VISUAL. GO IN LOW, THIS IS PROBABLY NOTHING. NO NEED TO RILE ANYONE UP.
COPY. STAND BY, CONTROL.

WHOOOOSH

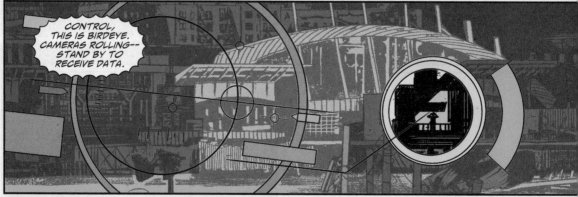

CONTROL, THIS IS BIRDEYE. CAMERAS ROLLING-- STAND BY TO RECEIVE DATA.

MAN ON STATION, ALL LOOKS WELL.

BIRDEYE FLIGHT TO ISLAND WATCH 1. YOU OKAY DOWN THERE? RESPOND WITH DAY CODE, OVER.

BIRDEYE, WE'RE TOTALLY COOL. RADIO CONTROL, TELL THEM IT'S JUST TECH TROUBLE, NO WORRIES. DAY CODE DELTA DELTA BRAVO FOXTROT.

CONFIRMED, OVER. TAKE IT EASY, SOLDIER.

YEAH, YEAH. FUCKIN' FAGGOT. HEY BRO, CONTROL'S GETTING CURIOUS. TELL THE BOSS WE NEED TO FILE STATUS, PRONTO.

HE NEEDS TO GET HIS HEAD IN THE GAME!

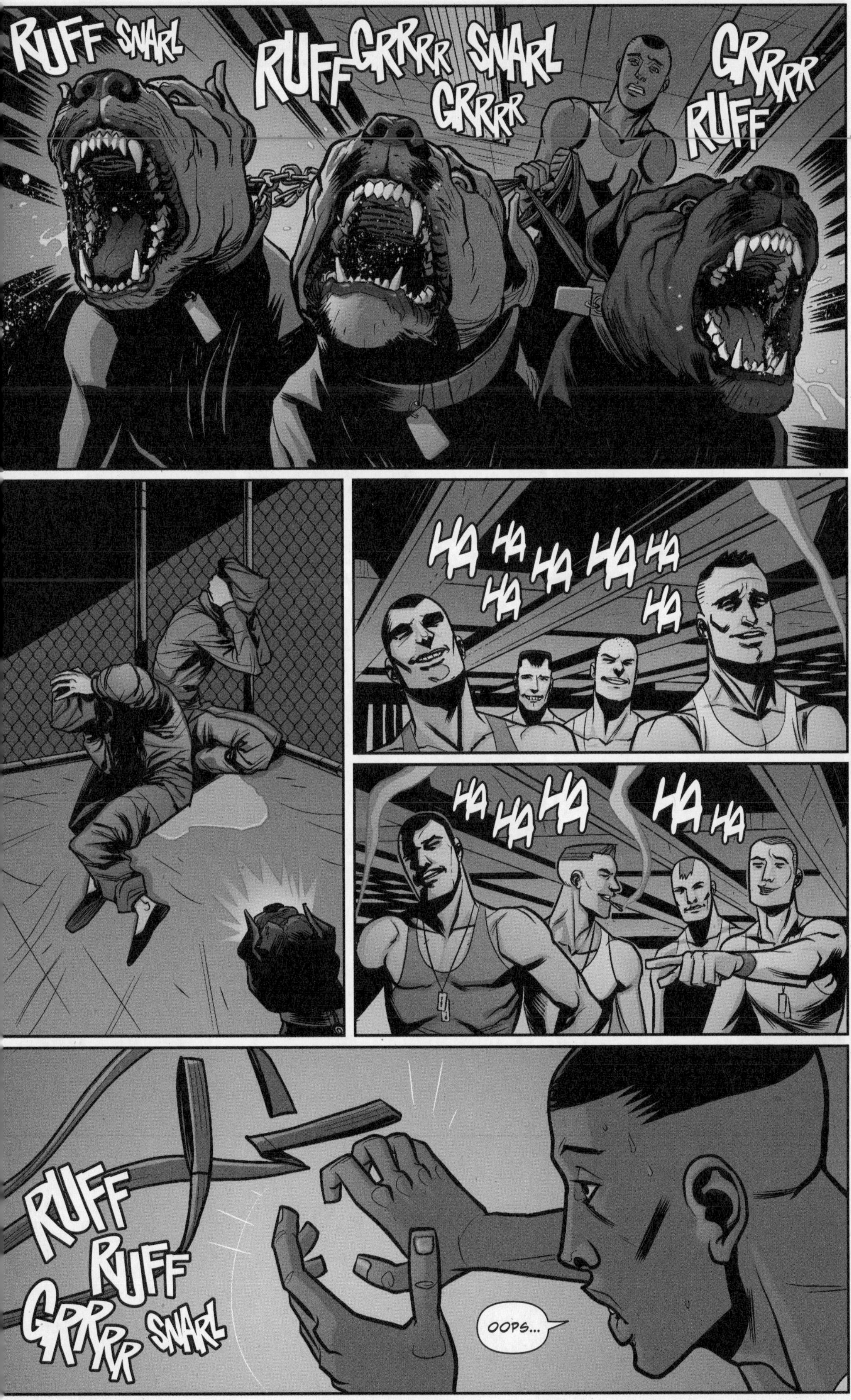
RUFF SNARL
RUFF GRRRRR SNARL GRRRRR
GRRRRR RUFF
HA HA HA HA HA HA HA HA
HA HA HA HA HA
RUFF RUFF GRRRRR SNARL
OOPS...

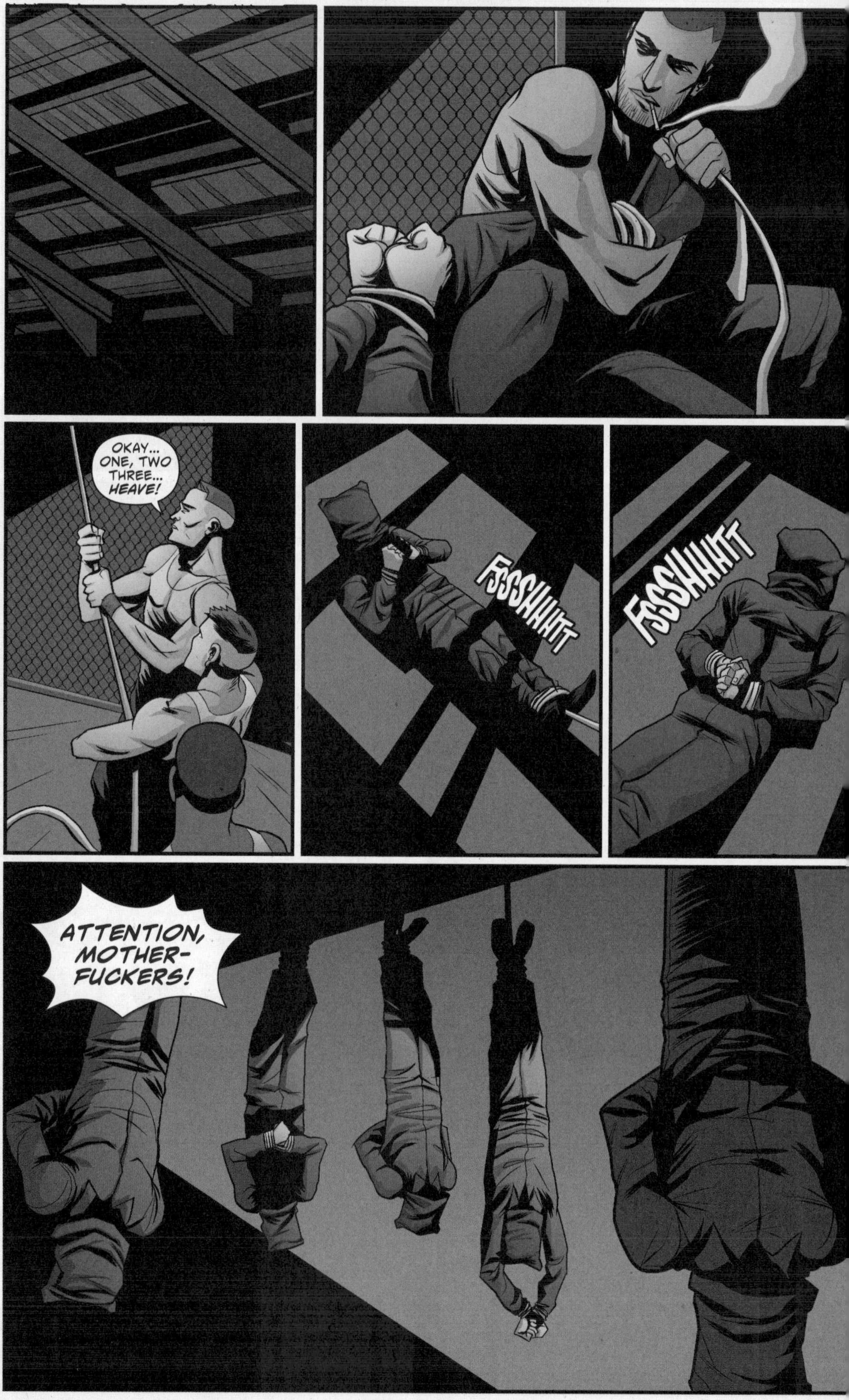
OKAY... ONE, TWO THREE... HEAVE!
FSSSHHHTT
FSSSHHHTT
ATTENTION, MOTHER-FUCKERS!

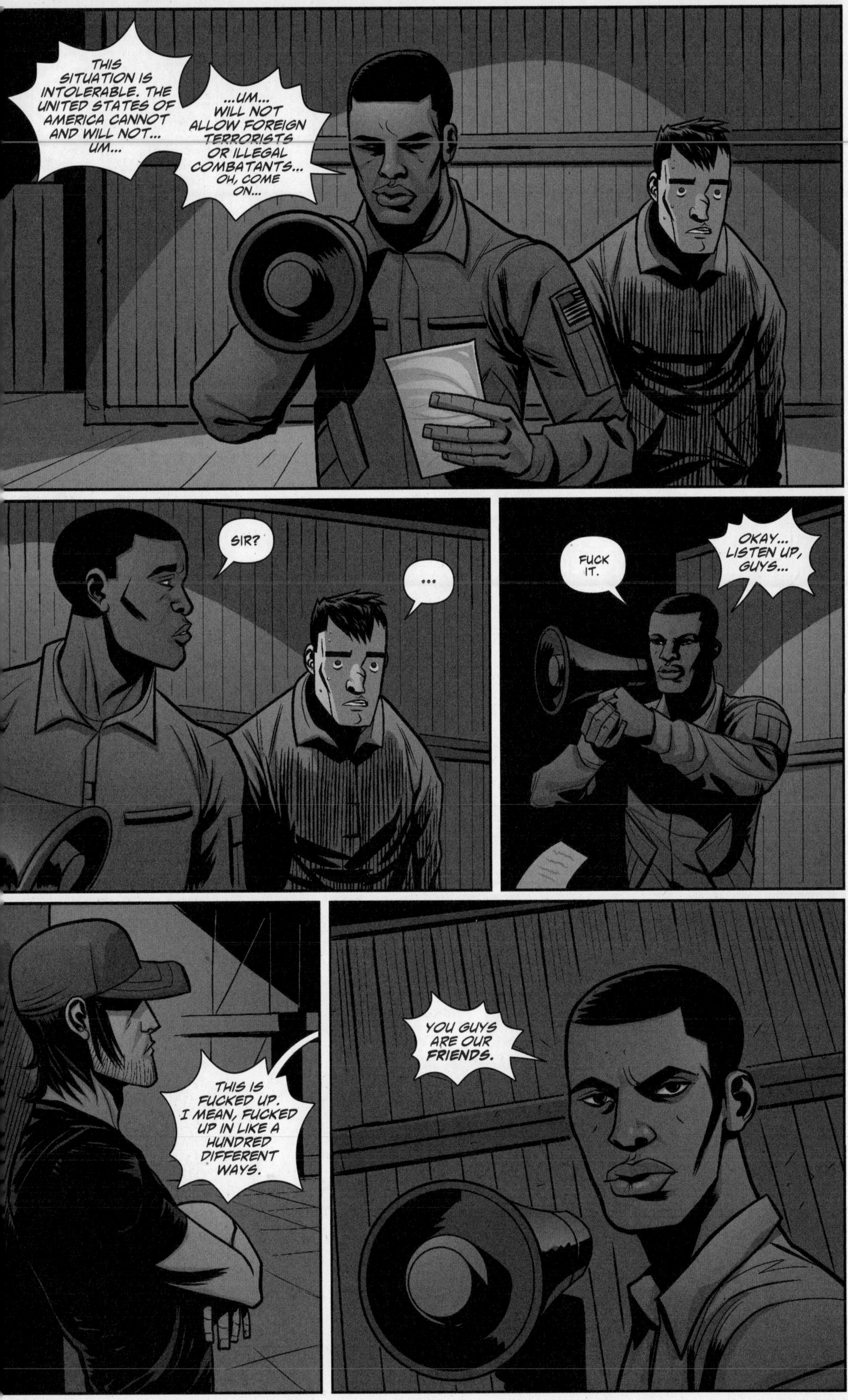
THIS SITUATION IS INTOLERABLE. THE UNITED STATES OF AMERICA CANNOT AND WILL NOT... UM...
...UM... WILL NOT ALLOW FOREIGN TERRORISTS OR ILLEGAL COMBATANTS... OH, COME ON...
SIR?
...
FUCK IT.
OKAY... LISTEN UP, GUYS...
THIS IS FUCKED UP. I MEAN, FUCKED UP IN LIKE A HUNDRED DIFFERENT WAYS.
YOU GUYS ARE OUR FRIENDS.

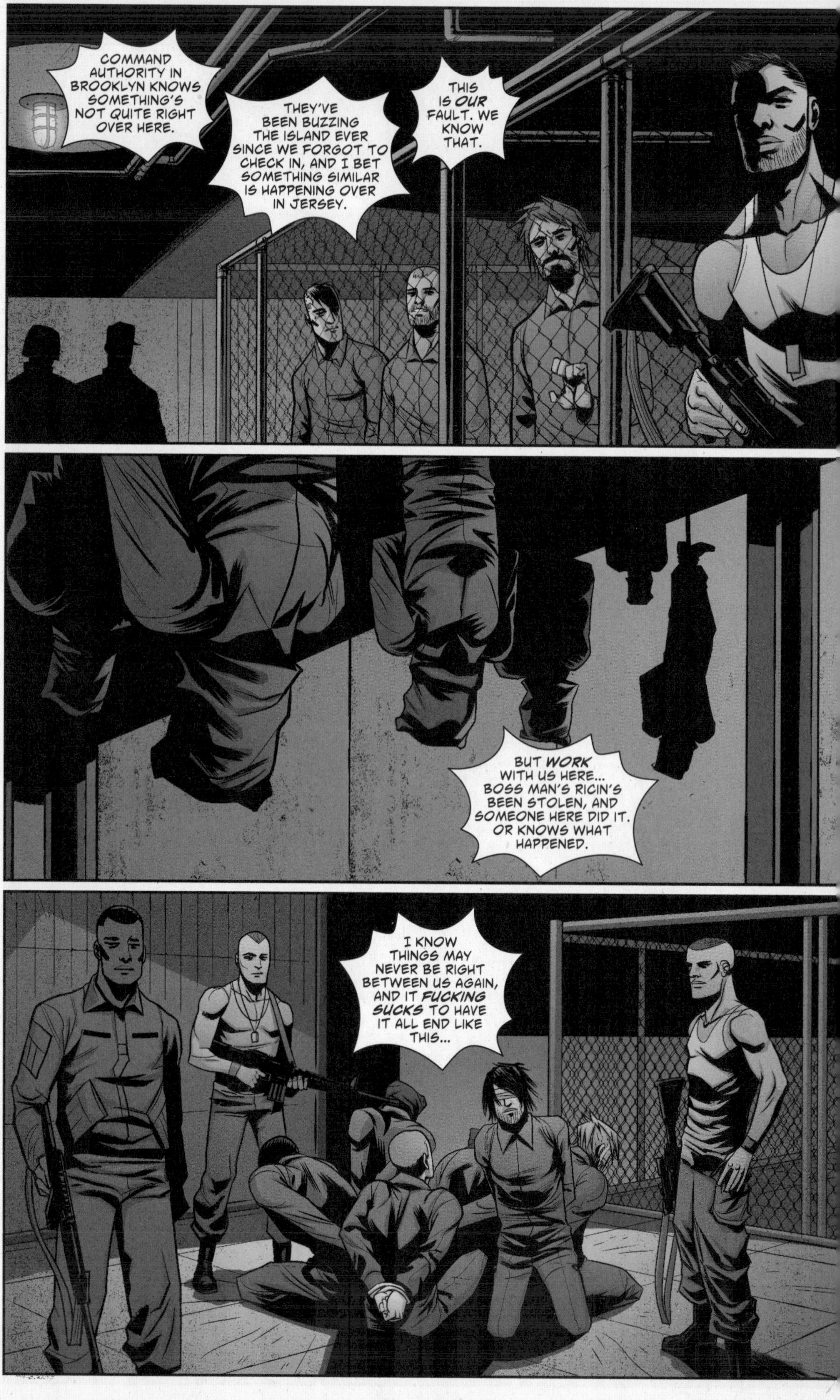
COMMAND AUTHORITY IN BROOKLYN KNOWS SOMETHING'S NOT QUITE RIGHT OVER HERE.
THEY'VE BEEN BUZZING THE ISLAND EVER SINCE WE FORGOT TO CHECK IN, AND I BET SOMETHING SIMILAR IS HAPPENING OVER IN JERSEY.
THIS IS *OUR* FAULT. WE KNOW THAT.
BUT *WORK* WITH US HERE... BOSS MAN'S RICIN'S BEEN STOLEN, AND SOMEONE HERE DID IT. OR KNOWS WHAT HAPPENED.
I KNOW THINGS MAY NEVER BE RIGHT BETWEEN US AGAIN, AND IT *FUCKING SUCKS* TO HAVE IT ALL END LIKE THIS...

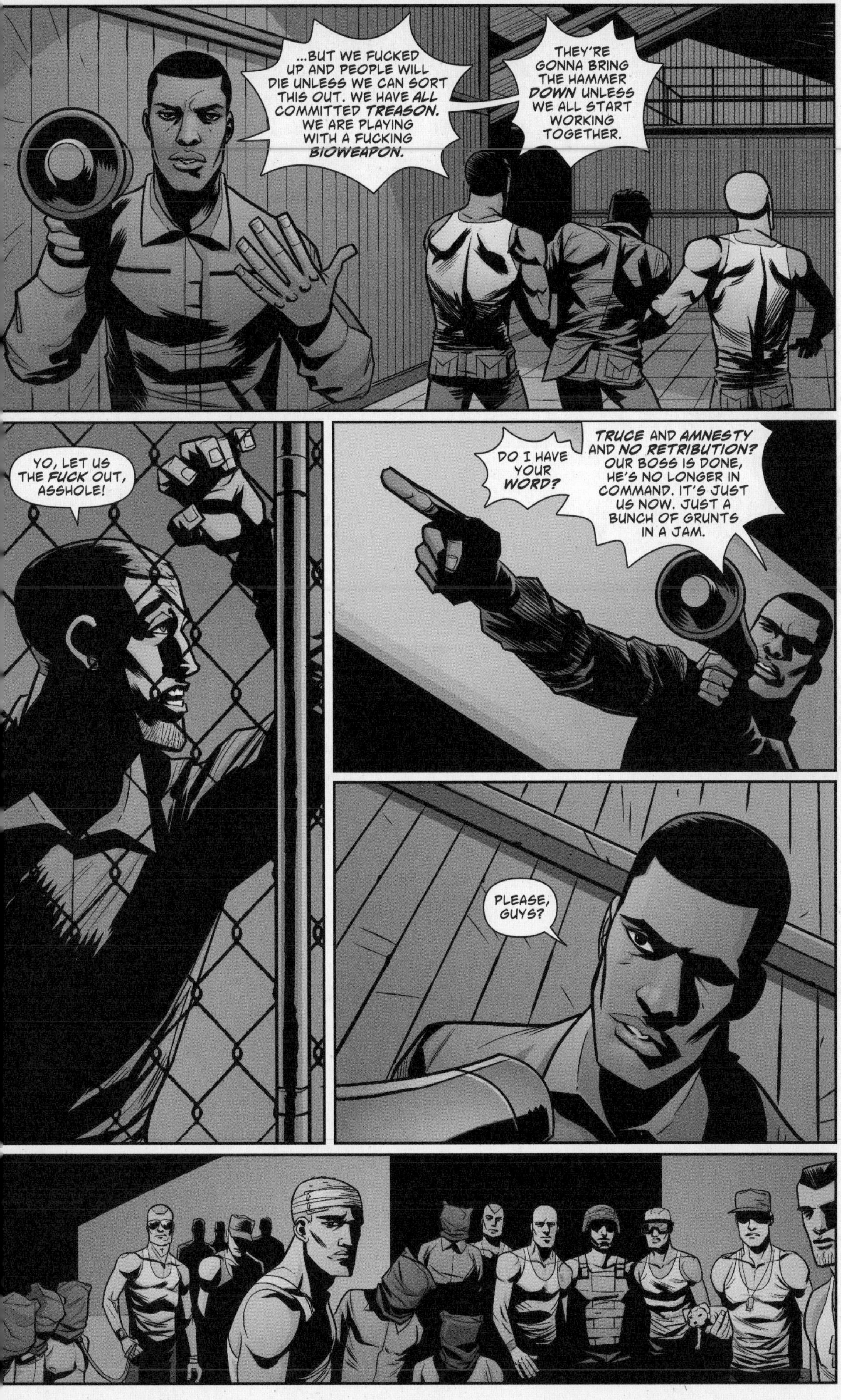
...BUT WE FUCKED UP AND PEOPLE WILL DIE UNLESS WE CAN SORT THIS OUT. WE HAVE ALL COMMITTED TREASON. WE ARE PLAYING WITH A FUCKING BIOWEAPON.
THEY'RE GONNA BRING THE HAMMER DOWN UNLESS WE ALL START WORKING TOGETHER.
YO, LET US THE FUCK OUT, ASSHOLE!
DO I HAVE YOUR WORD?
TRUCE AND AMNESTY AND NO RETRIBUTION? OUR BOSS IS DONE, HE'S NO LONGER IN COMMAND. IT'S JUST US NOW. JUST A BUNCH OF GRUNTS IN A JAM.
PLEASE, GUYS?

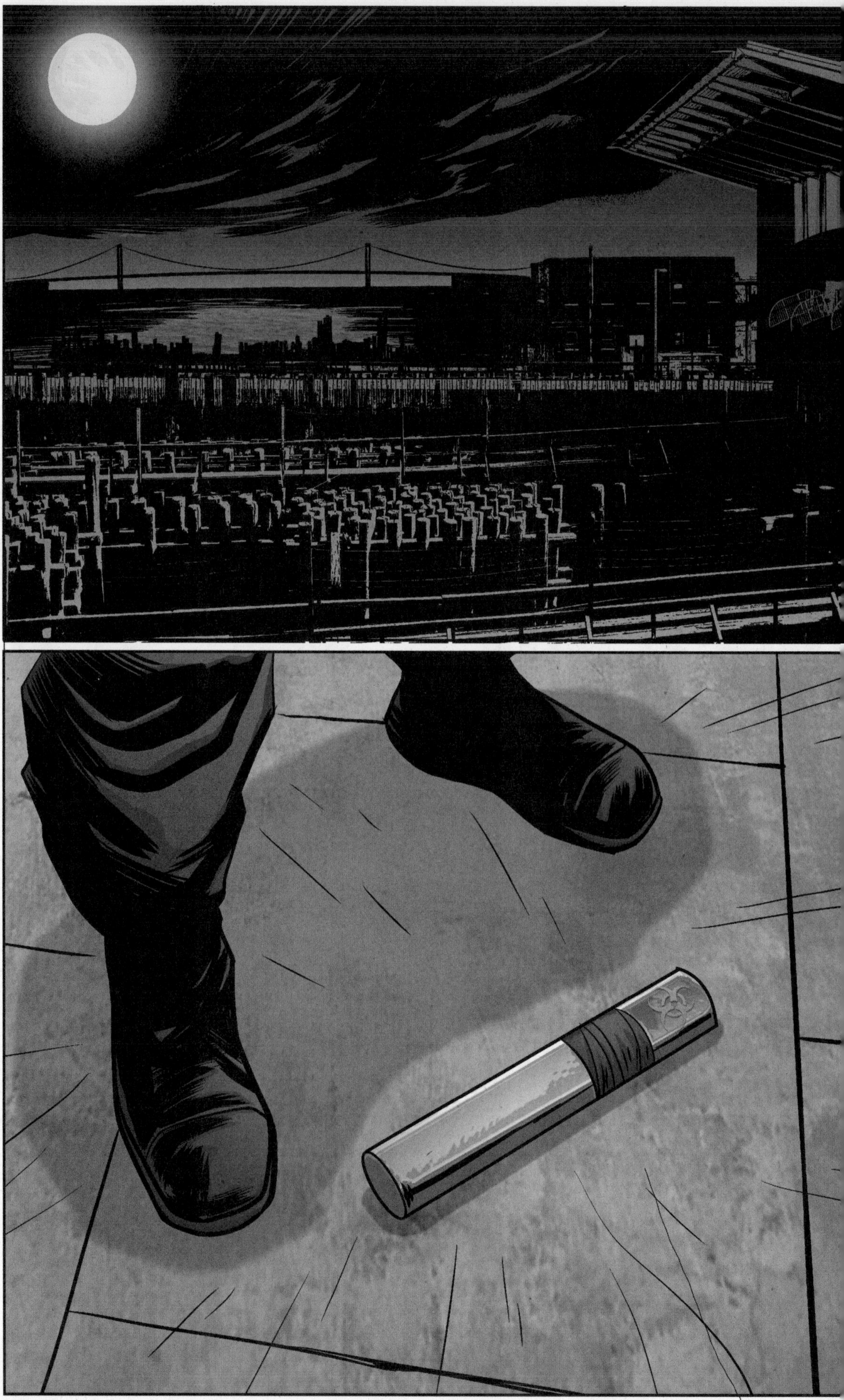

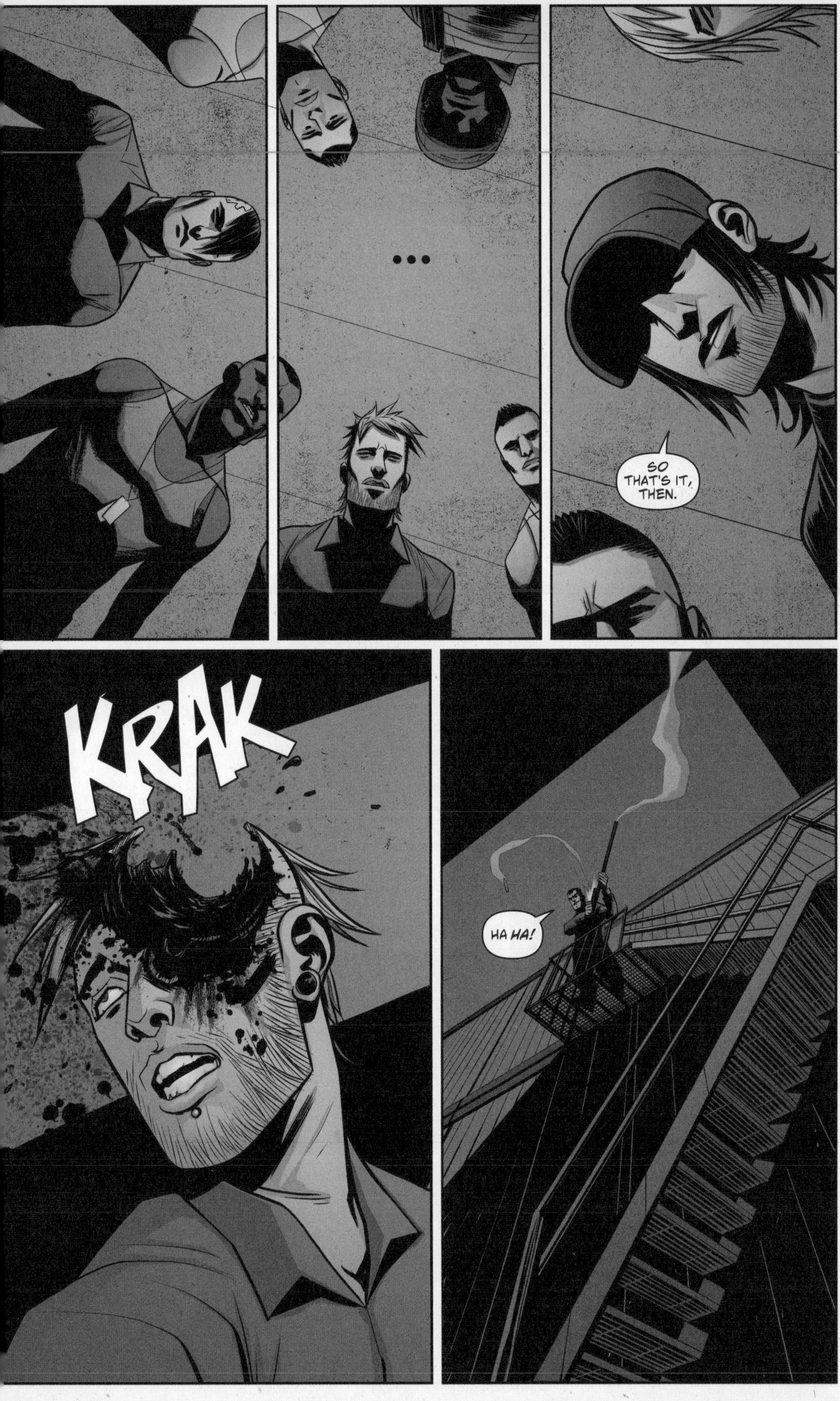
...
SO THAT'S IT, THEN.
KRAK
HA HA!

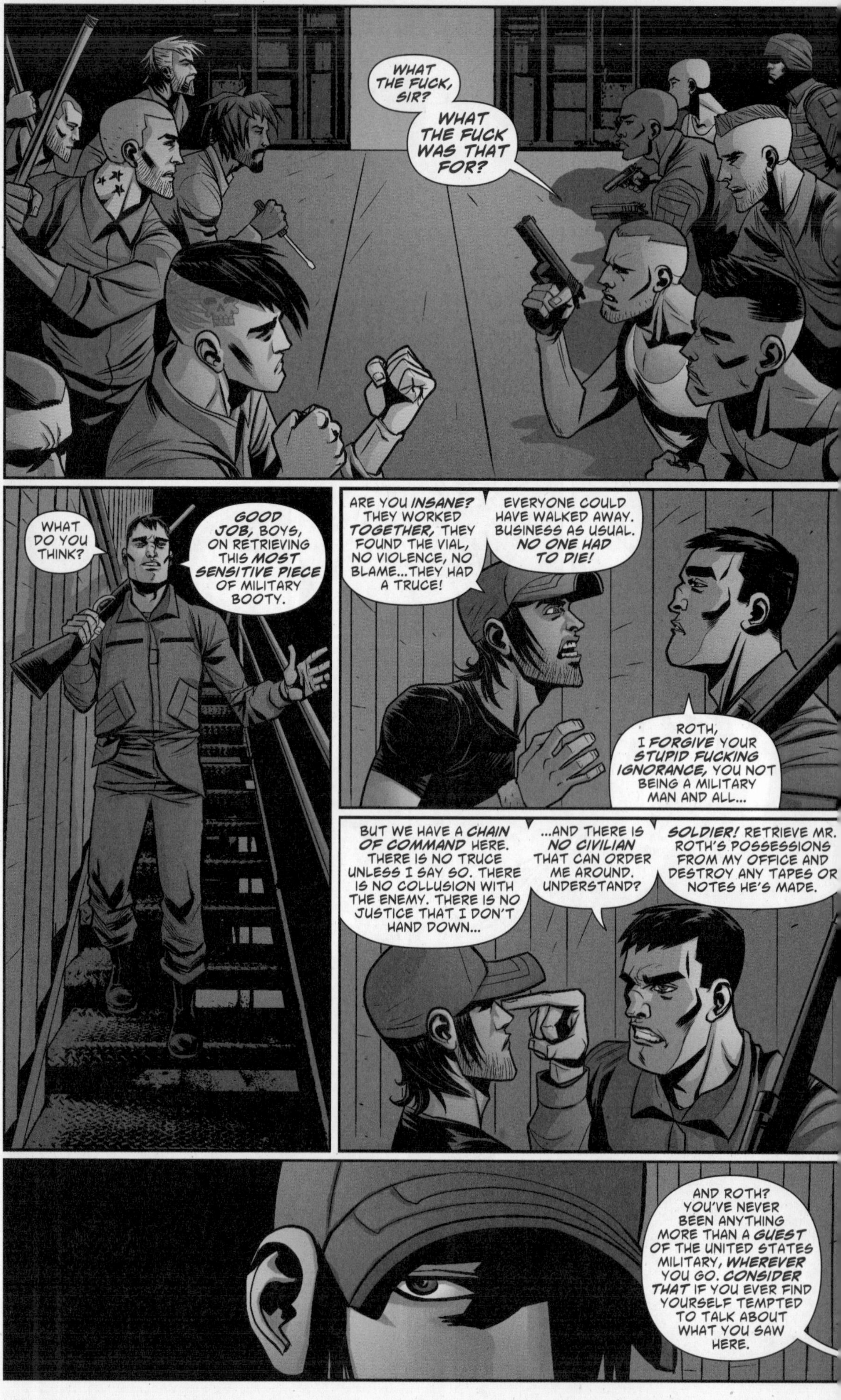
WHAT THE FUCK, SIR?
WHAT THE FUCK WAS THAT FOR?
WHAT DO YOU THINK?
GOOD JOB, BOYS, ON RETRIEVING THIS MOST SENSITIVE PIECE OF MILITARY BOOTY.
ARE YOU INSANE? THEY WORKED TOGETHER, THEY FOUND THE VIAL, NO VIOLENCE, NO BLAME...THEY HAD A TRUCE!
EVERYONE COULD HAVE WALKED AWAY. BUSINESS AS USUAL. NO ONE HAD TO DIE!
ROTH, I FORGIVE YOUR STUPID FUCKING IGNORANCE, YOU NOT BEING A MILITARY MAN AND ALL...
BUT WE HAVE A CHAIN OF COMMAND HERE. THERE IS NO TRUCE UNLESS I SAY SO. THERE IS NO COLLUSION WITH THE ENEMY. THERE IS NO JUSTICE THAT I DON'T HAND DOWN...
...AND THERE IS NO CIVILIAN THAT CAN ORDER ME AROUND. UNDERSTAND?
SOLDIER! RETRIEVE MR. ROTH'S POSSESSIONS FROM MY OFFICE AND DESTROY ANY TAPES OR NOTES HE'S MADE.
AND ROTH? YOU'VE NEVER BEEN ANYTHING MORE THAN A GUEST OF THE UNITED STATES MILITARY, WHEREVER YOU GO. CONSIDER THAT IF YOU EVER FIND YOURSELF TEMPTED TO TALK ABOUT WHAT YOU SAW HERE.

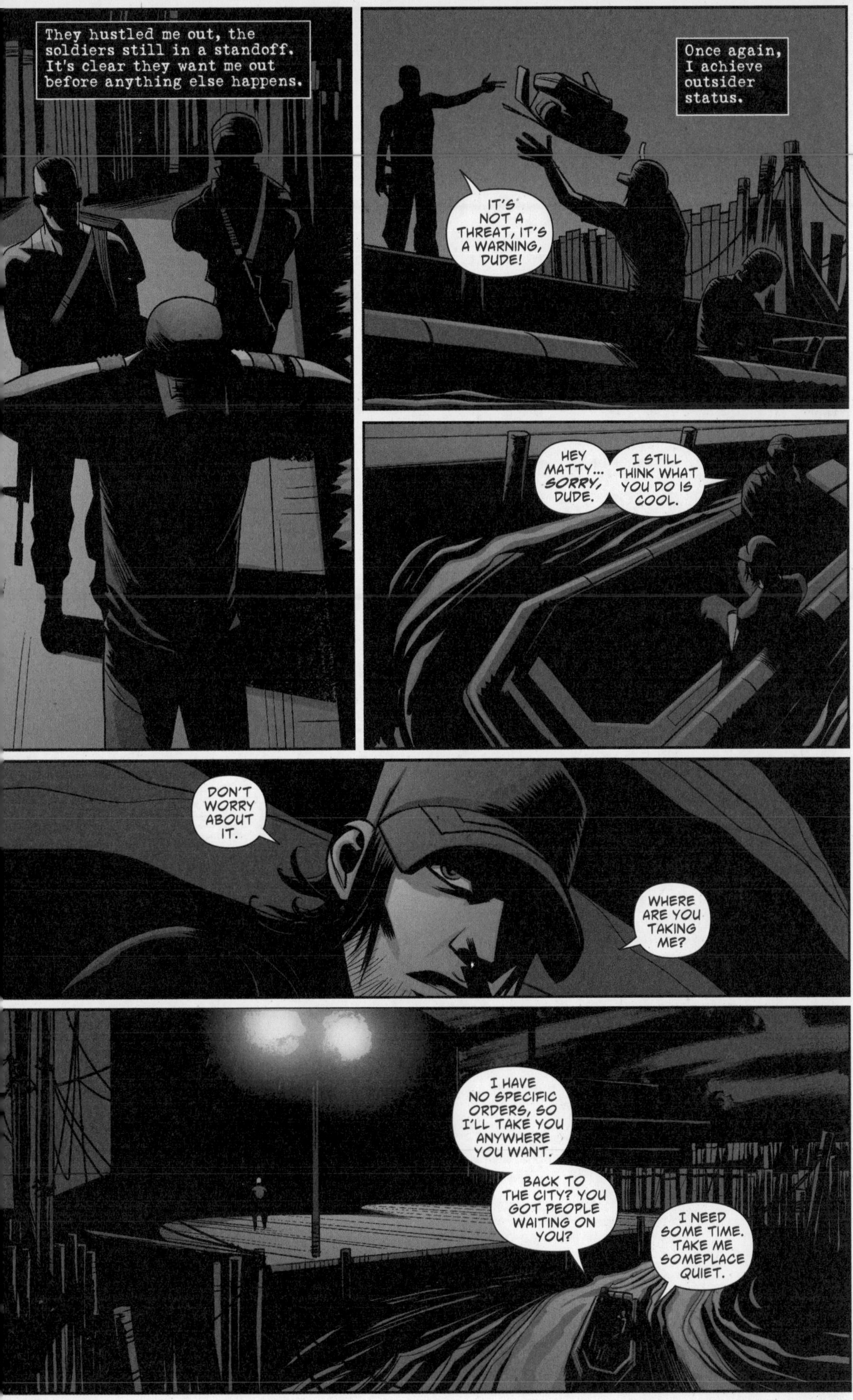
They hustled me out, the soldiers still in a standoff. It's clear they want me out before anything else happens.
Once again, I achieve outsider status.
IT'S NOT A THREAT, IT'S A WARNING, DUDE!
HEY MATTY... SORRY, DUDE.
I STILL THINK WHAT YOU DO IS COOL.
DON'T WORRY ABOUT IT.
WHERE ARE YOU TAKING ME?
I HAVE NO SPECIFIC ORDERS, SO I'LL TAKE YOU ANYWHERE YOU WANT.
BACK TO THE CITY? YOU GOT PEOPLE WAITING ON YOU?
I NEED SOME TIME. TAKE ME SOMEPLACE QUIET.

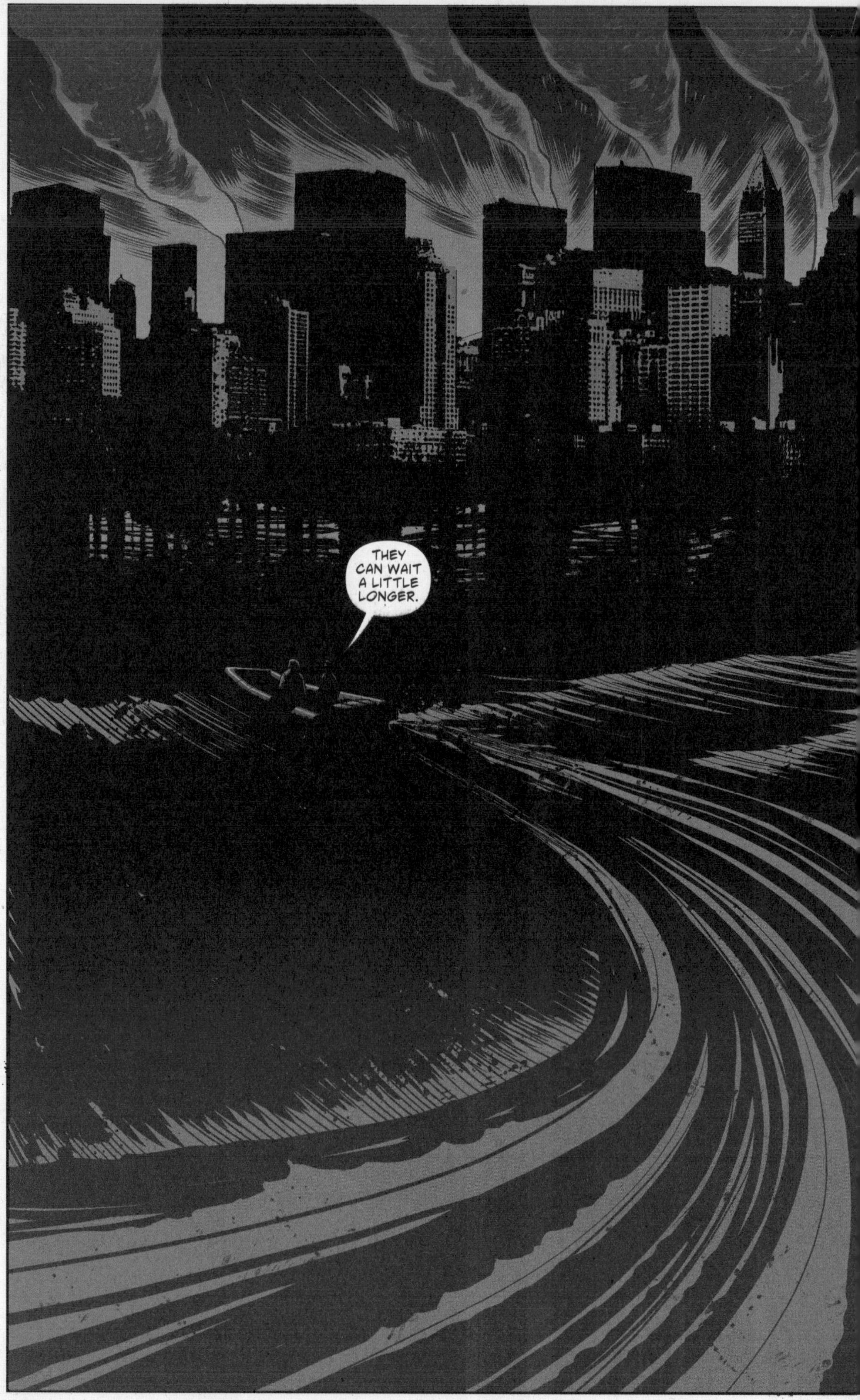
THEY CAN WAIT A LITTLE LONGER.

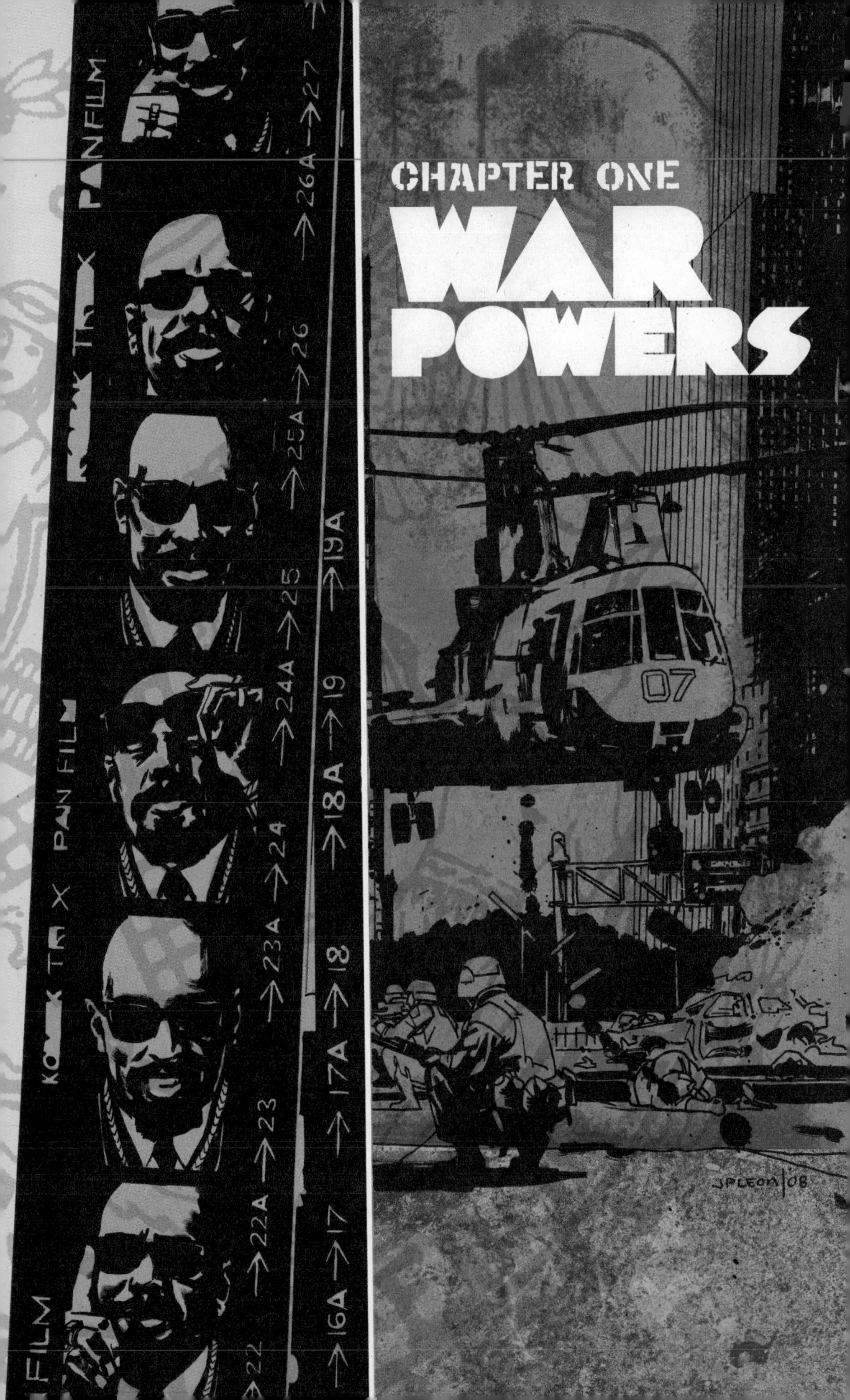
CHAPTER ONE
WAR POWERS
07
JPLEON|08

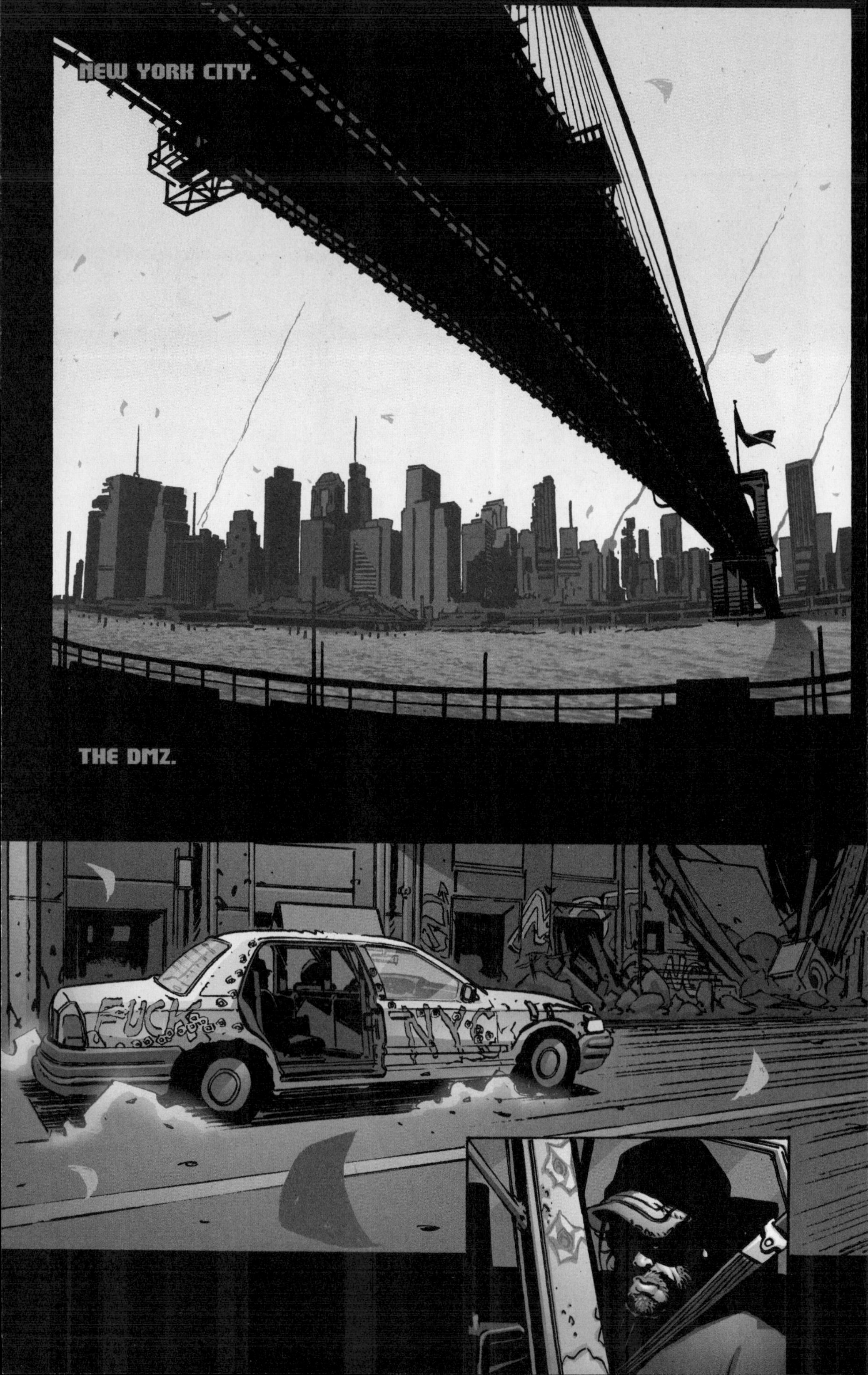
NEW YORK CITY.
THE DMZ.
FUCK
NYC

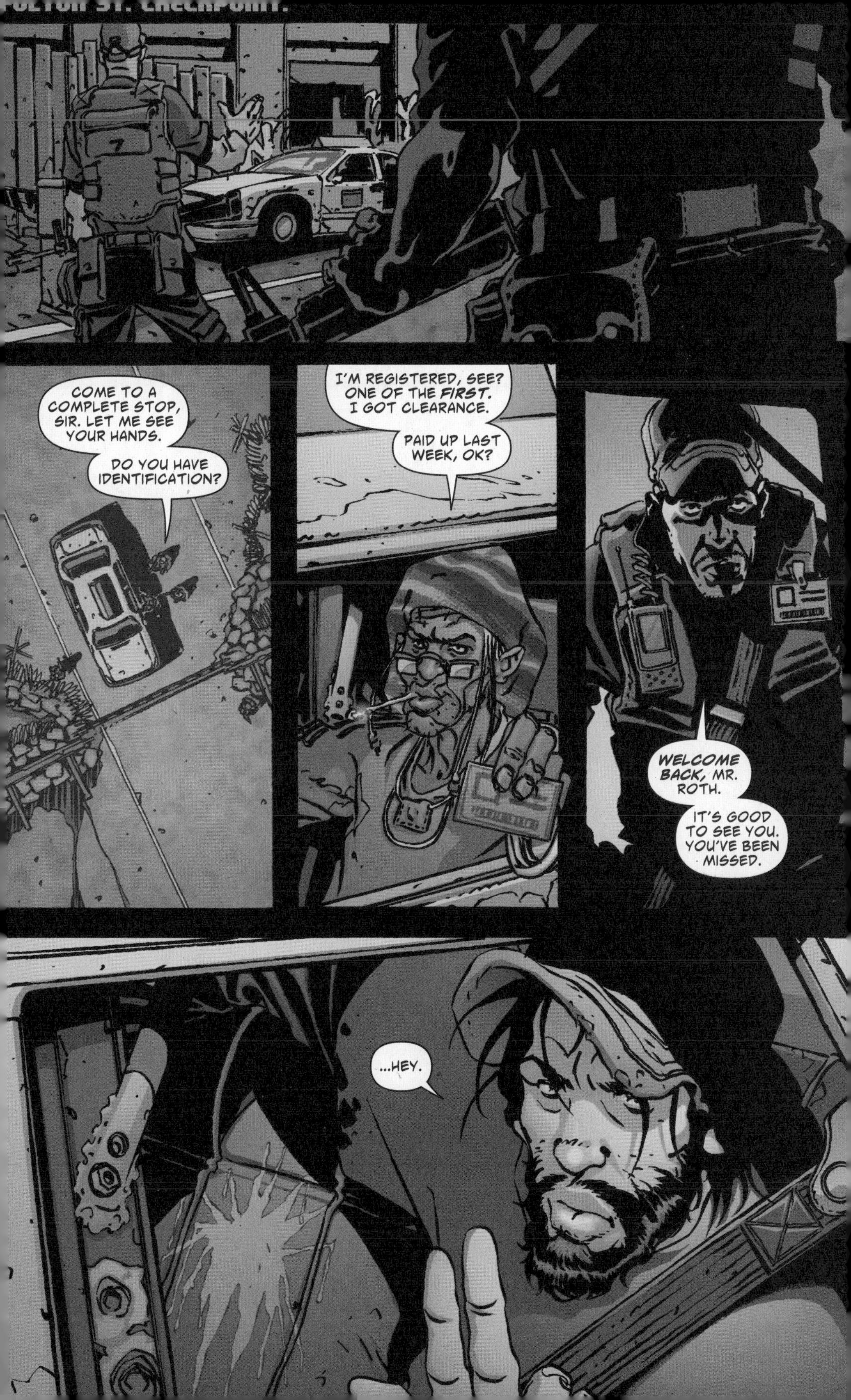
COME TO A COMPLETE STOP, SIR. LET ME SEE YOUR HANDS.
DO YOU HAVE IDENTIFICATION?
I'M REGISTERED, SEE? ONE OF THE FIRST. I GOT CLEARANCE.
PAID UP LAST WEEK, OK?
WELCOME BACK, MR. ROTH.
IT'S GOOD TO SEE YOU. YOU'VE BEEN MISSED.
...HEY.

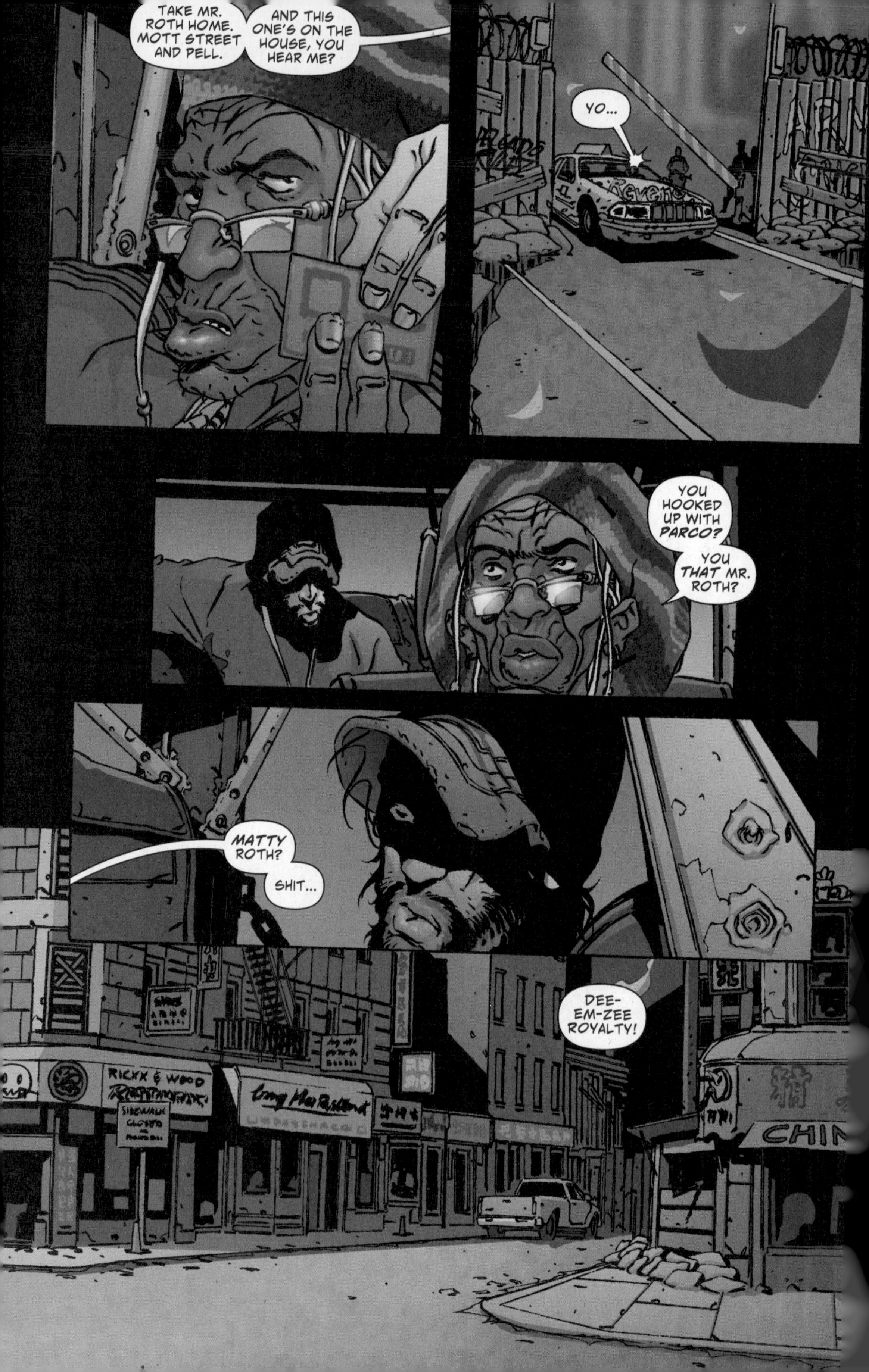
TAKE MR. ROTH HOME. MOTT STREET AND PELL.
AND THIS ONE'S ON THE HOUSE, YOU HEAR ME?
YO...
YOU HOOKED UP WITH PARCO?
YOU THAT MR. ROTH?
MATTY ROTH?
SHIT...
DEE-EM-ZEE ROYALTY!
CHIN

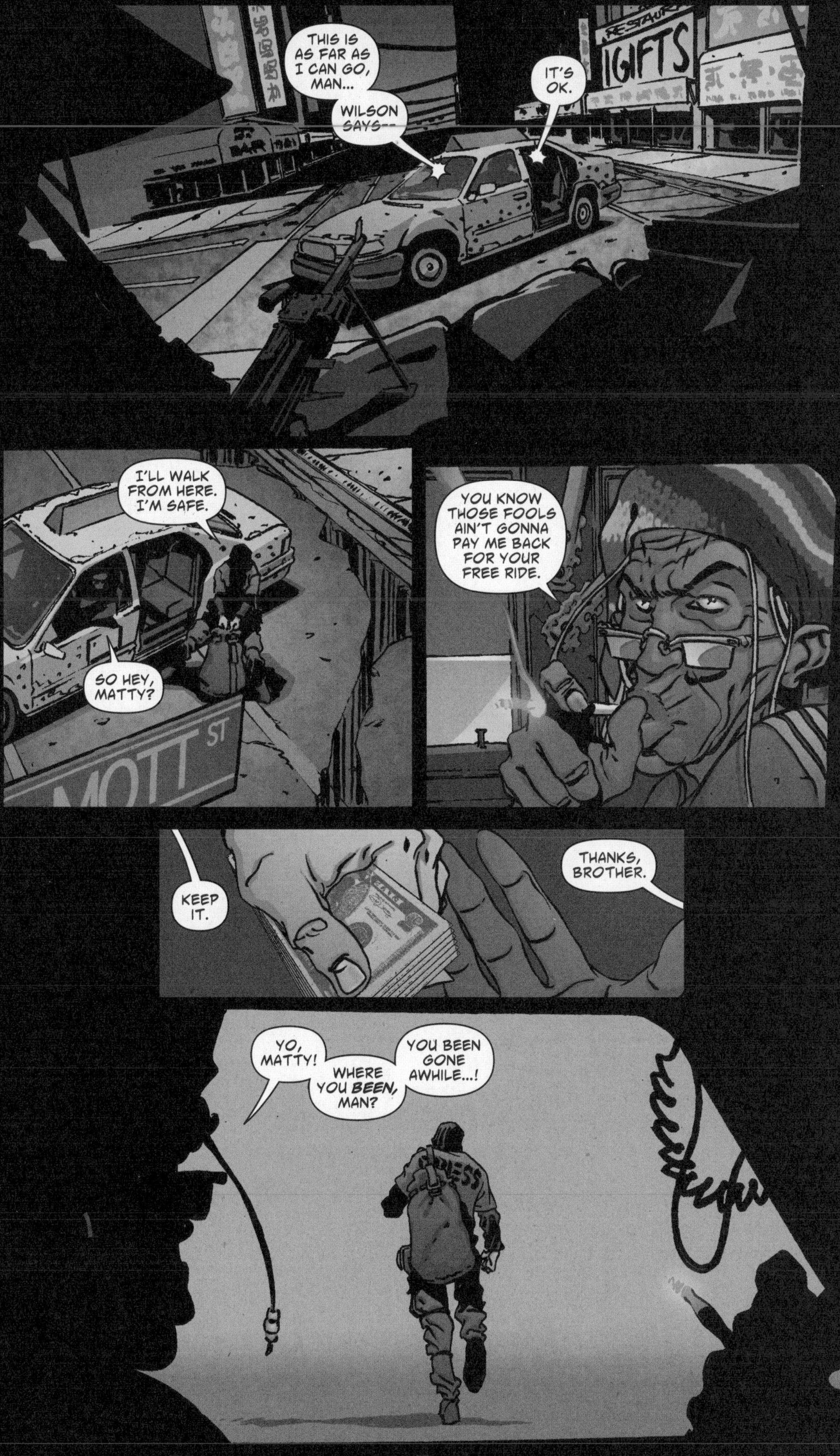
THIS IS AS FAR AS I CAN GO, MAN...
WILSON SAYS--
IT'S OK.
GIFTS
RESTAURANT
I'LL WALK FROM HERE. I'M SAFE.
SO HEY, MATTY?
MOTT ST
YOU KNOW THOSE FOOLS AIN'T GONNA PAY ME BACK FOR YOUR FREE RIDE.
KEEP IT.
THANKS, BROTHER.
YO, MATTY!
WHERE YOU BEEN, MAN?
YOU BEEN GONE AWHILE...!

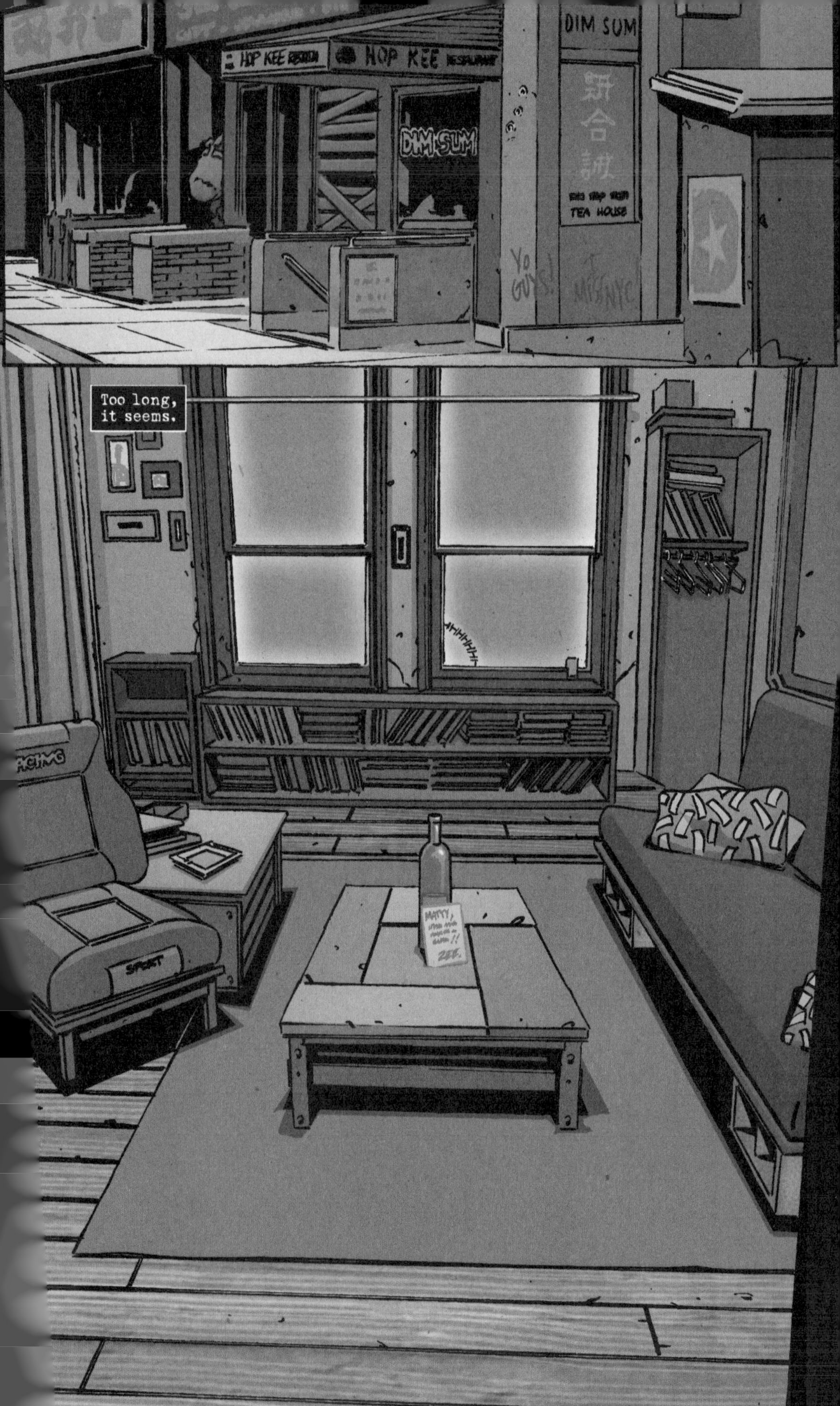
HOP KEE
HOP KEE RESTAURANT
DIM SUM
DIM SUM
TEA HOUSE
Yo GUYS!
Too long, it seems.

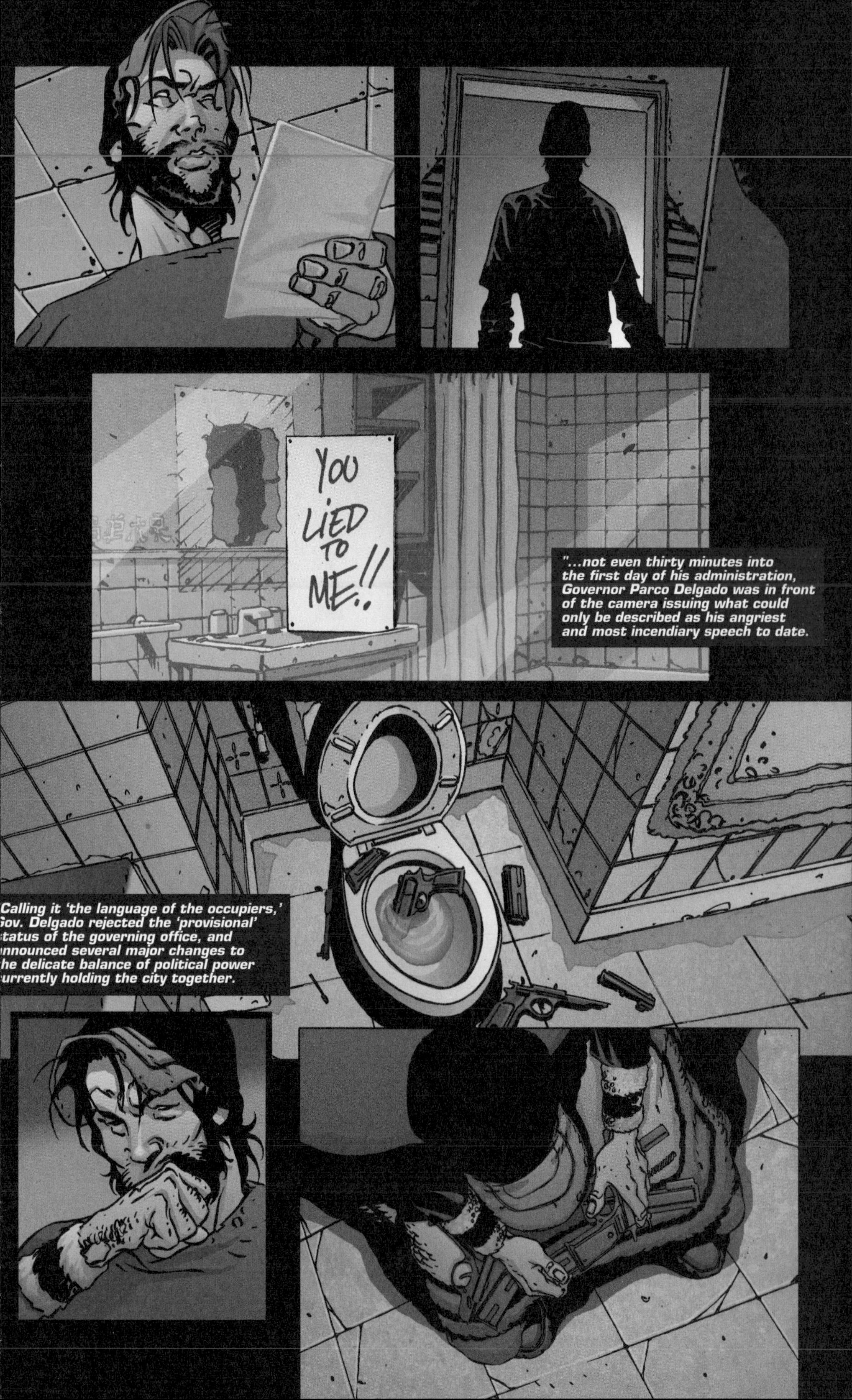

YOU LIED TO ME!!
"...not even thirty minutes into the first day of his administration, Governor Parco Delgado was in front of the camera issuing what could only be described as his angriest and most incendiary speech to date.
Calling it 'the language of the occupiers,' ov. Delgado rejected the 'provisional' tatus of the governing office, and nnounced several major changes to he delicate balance of political power urrently holding the city together.

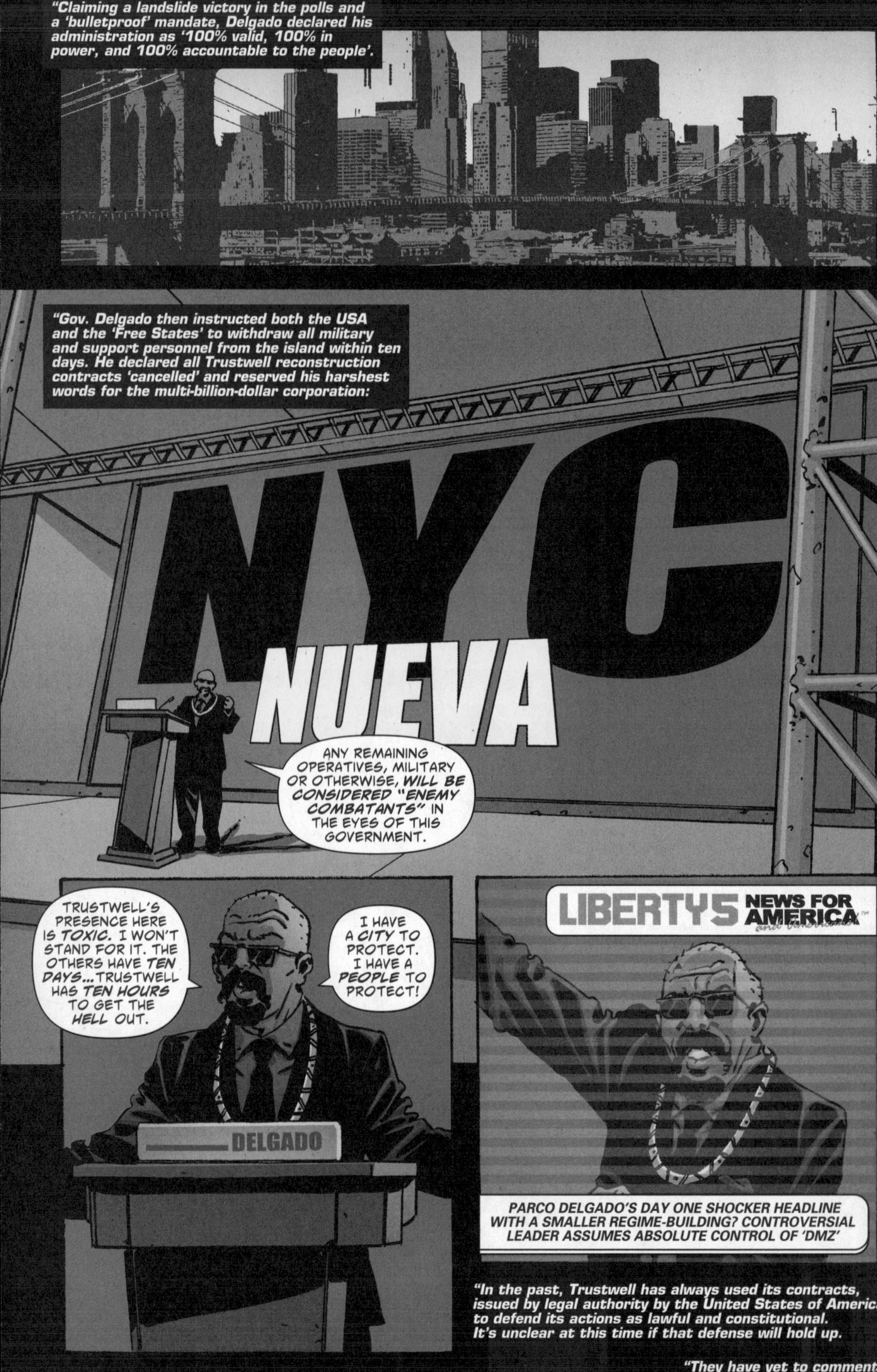
"Claiming a landslide victory in the polls and a 'bulletproof' mandate, Delgado declared his administration as '100% valid, 100% in power, and 100% accountable to the people'.
"Gov. Delgado then instructed both the USA and the 'Free States' to withdraw all military and support personnel from the island within ten days. He declared all Trustwell reconstruction contracts 'cancelled' and reserved his harshest words for the multi-billion-dollar corporation:
NYC
NUEVA
ANY REMAINING OPERATIVES, MILITARY OR OTHERWISE, WILL BE CONSIDERED "ENEMY COMBATANTS" IN THE EYES OF THIS GOVERNMENT.
TRUSTWELL'S PRESENCE HERE IS TOXIC. I WON'T STAND FOR IT. THE OTHERS HAVE TEN DAYS... TRUSTWELL HAS TEN HOURS TO GET THE HELL OUT.
I HAVE A CITY TO PROTECT. I HAVE A PEOPLE TO PROTECT!
DELGADO
LIBERTY5 NEWS FOR AMERICA
PARCO DELGADO'S DAY ONE SHOCKER HEADLINE WITH A SMALLER REGIME-BUILDING? CONTROVERSIAL LEADER ASSUMES ABSOLUTE CONTROL OF 'DMZ'
"In the past, Trustwell has always used its contracts, issued by legal authority by the United States of America to defend its actions as lawful and constitutional. It's unclear at this time if that defense will hold up.
"They have yet to comment.

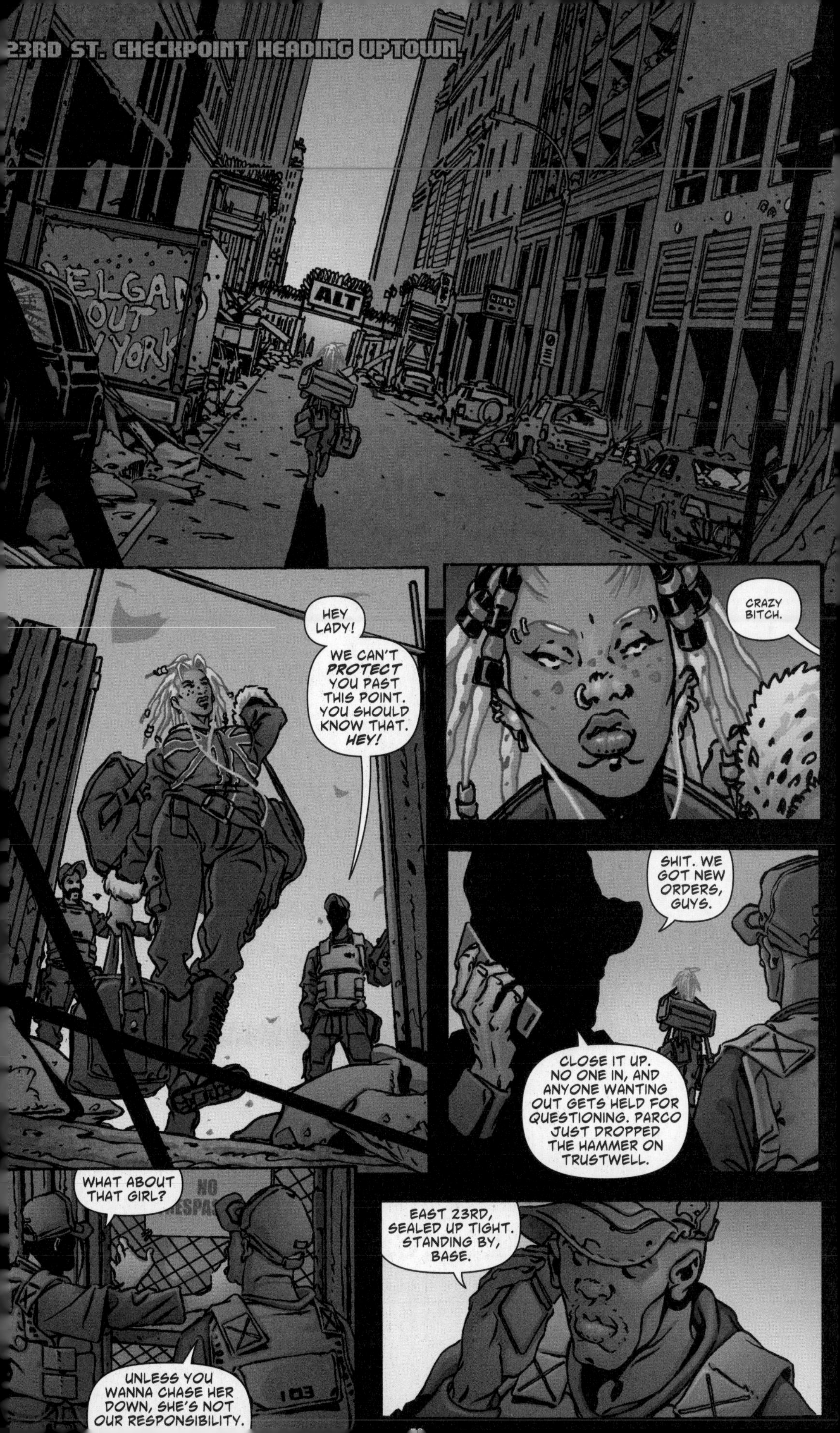

23RD ST. CHECKPOINT HEADING UPTOWN.
ALT
DELGADO OUT NEW YORK
HEY LADY!
WE CAN'T PROTECT YOU PAST THIS POINT. YOU SHOULD KNOW THAT. HEY!
CRAZY BITCH.
SHIT. WE GOT NEW ORDERS, GUYS.
CLOSE IT UP. NO ONE IN, AND ANYONE WANTING OUT GETS HELD FOR QUESTIONING. PARCO JUST DROPPED THE HAMMER ON TRUSTWELL.
WHAT ABOUT THAT GIRL?
UNLESS YOU WANNA CHASE HER DOWN, SHE'S NOT OUR RESPONSIBILITY.
EAST 23RD, SEALED UP TIGHT. STANDING BY, BASE.

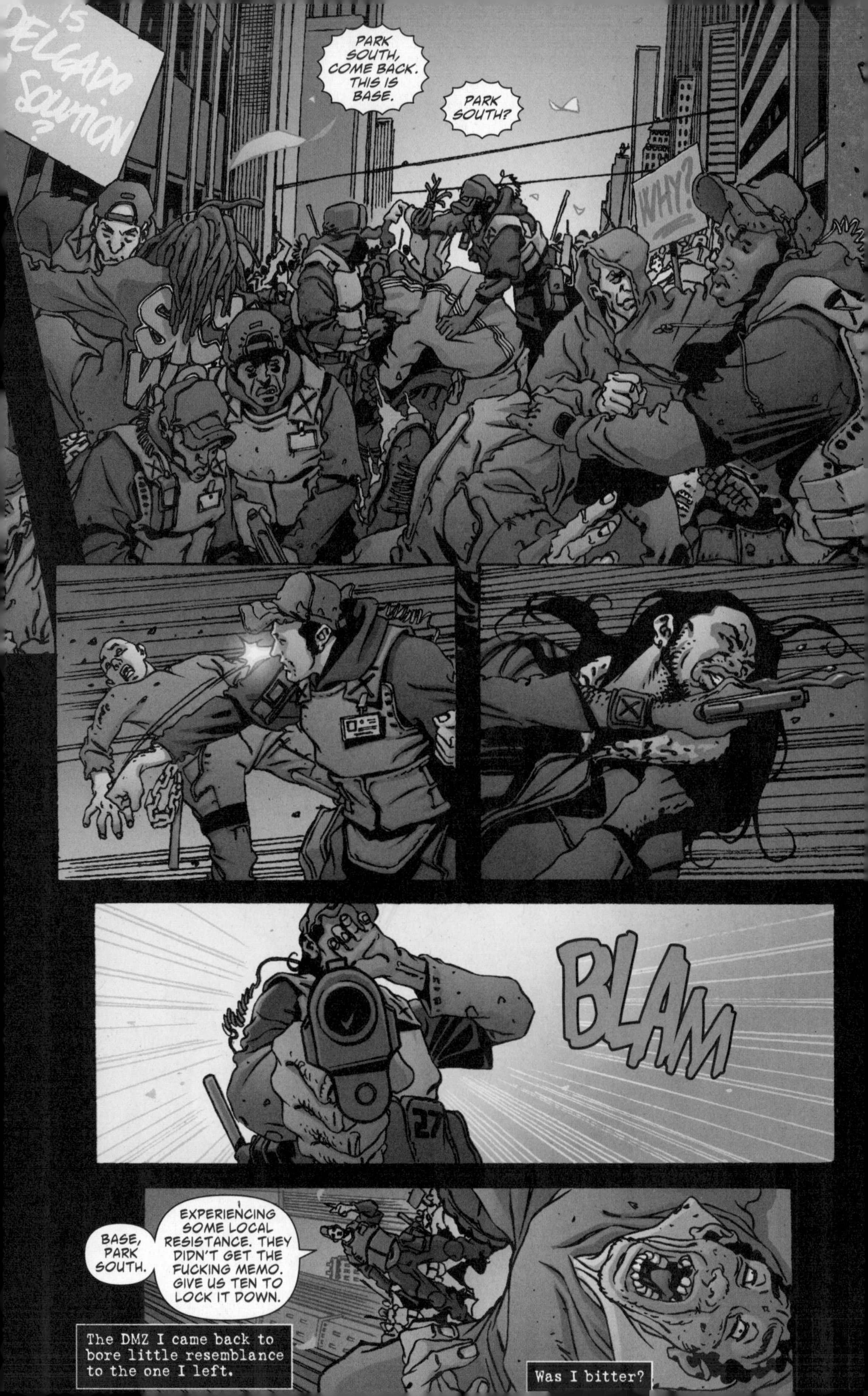
IS DELGADO SOLUTION?
PARK SOUTH, COME BACK. THIS IS BASE.
PARK SOUTH?
WHY?
BLAM
BASE, PARK SOUTH.
EXPERIENCING SOME LOCAL RESISTANCE. THEY DIDN'T GET THE FUCKING MEMO. GIVE US TEN TO LOCK IT DOWN.
The DMZ I came back to bore little resemblance to the one I left.
Was I bitter?

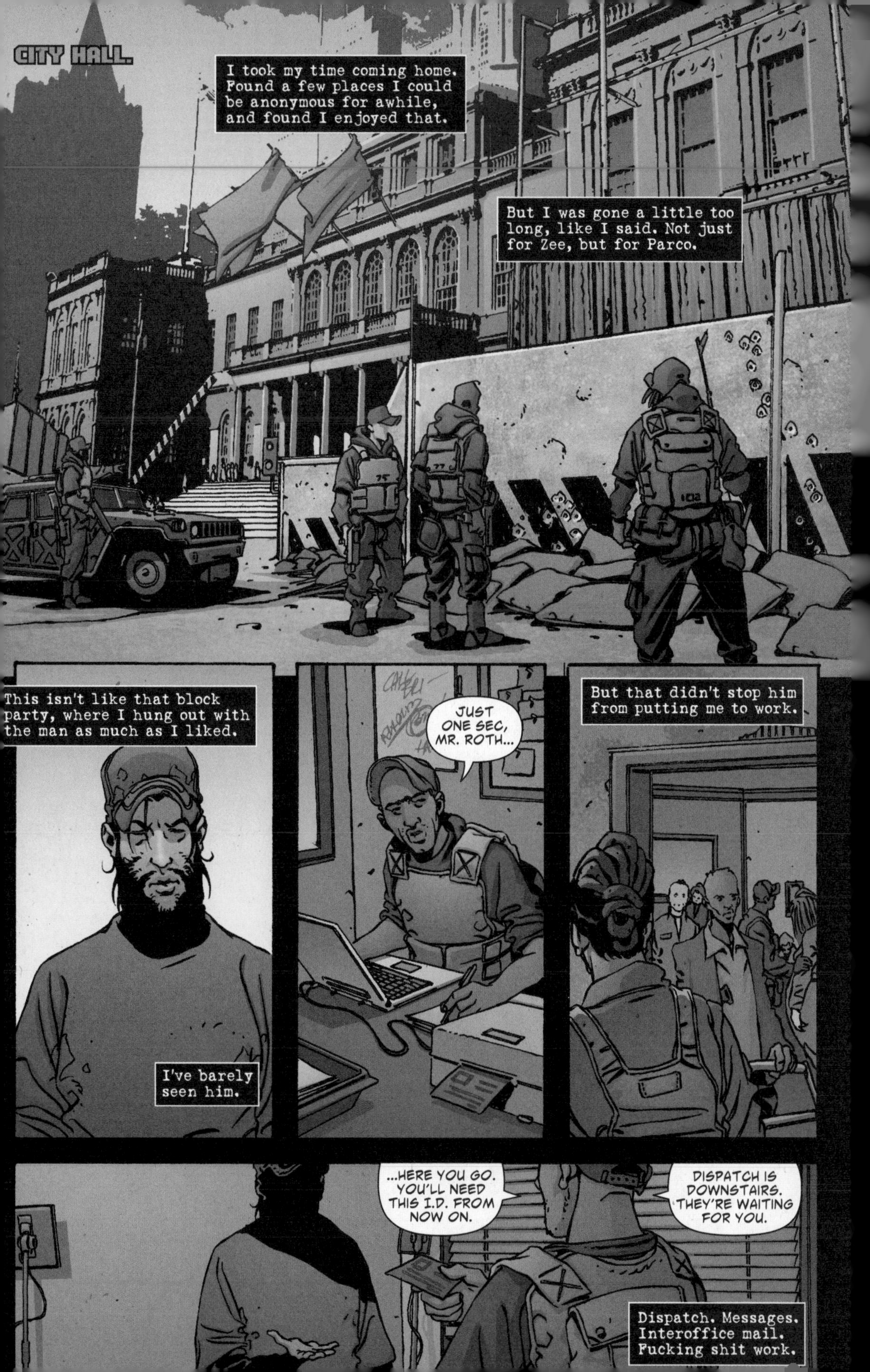
CITY HALL.
I took my time coming home. Found a few places I could be anonymous for awhile, and found I enjoyed that.
But I was gone a little too long, like I said. Not just for Zee, but for Parco.
This isn't like that block party, where I hung out with the man as much as I liked.
I've barely seen him.
JUST ONE SEC, MR. ROTH...
But that didn't stop him from putting me to work.
...HERE YOU GO. YOU'LL NEED THIS I.D. FROM NOW ON.
DISPATCH IS DOWNSTAIRS. THEY'RE WAITING FOR YOU.
Dispatch. Messages. Interoffice mail. Fucking shit work.

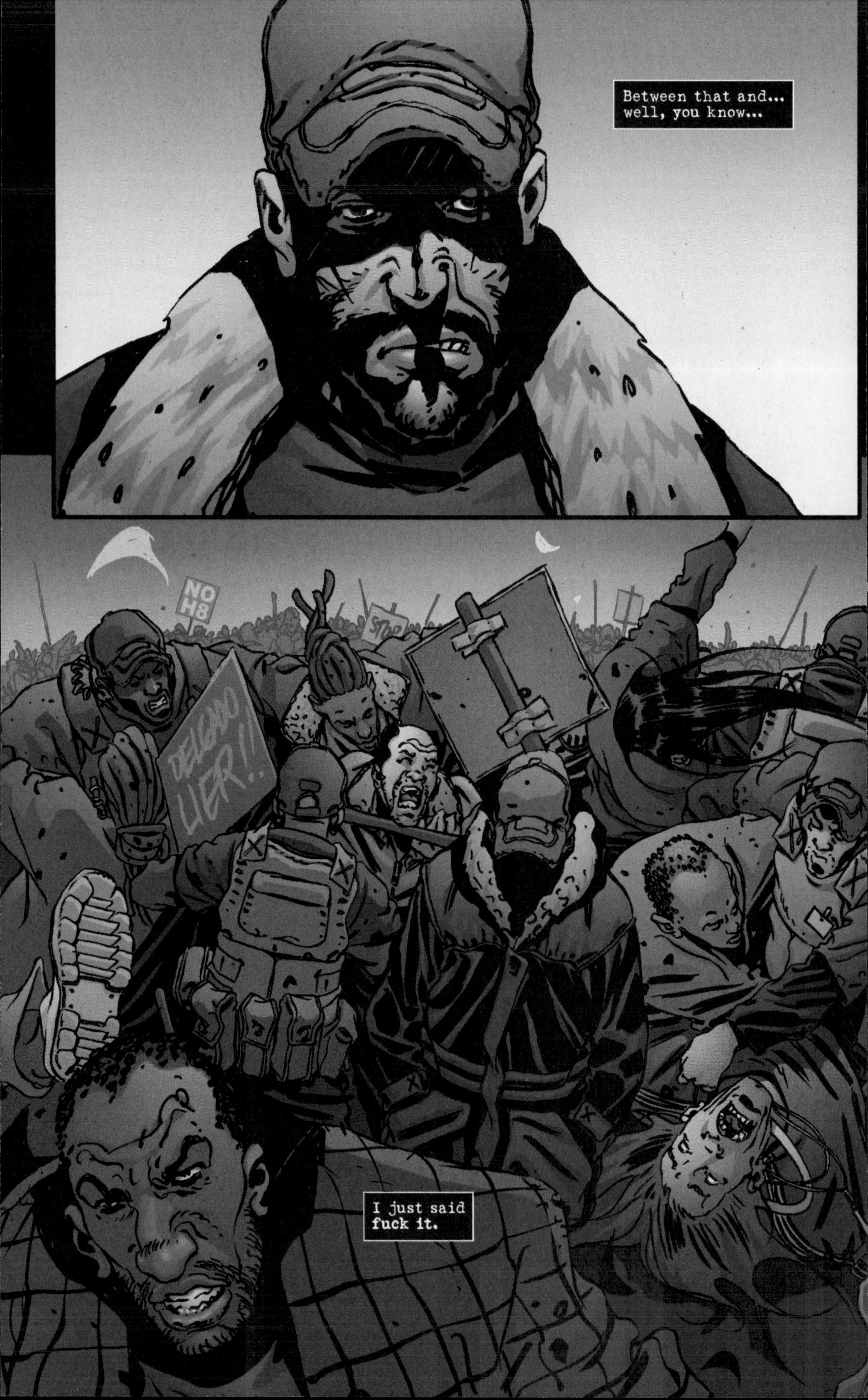
Between that and... well, you know...
NO H8
STOP
DELGADO LIER!!
I just said fuck it.

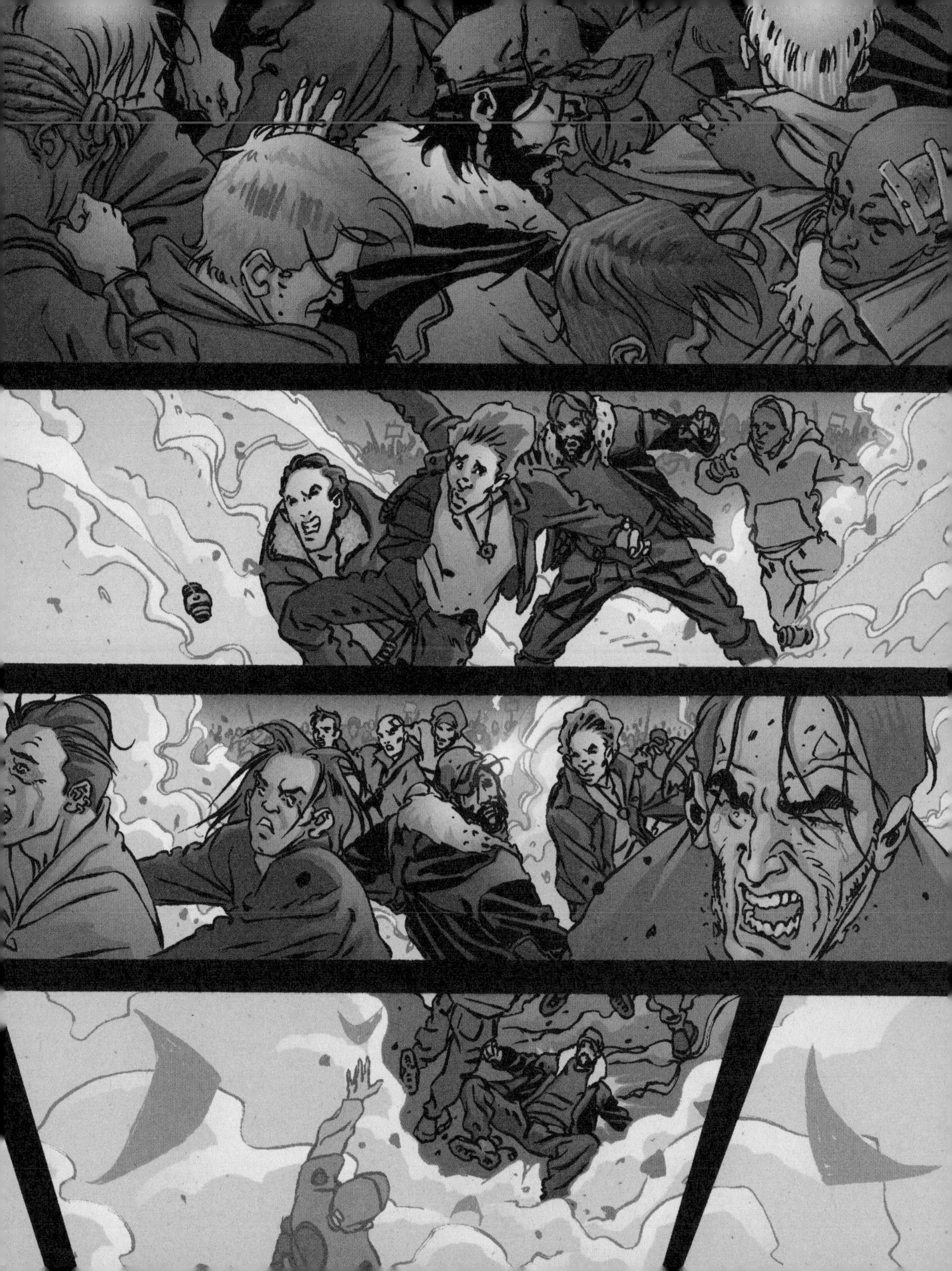

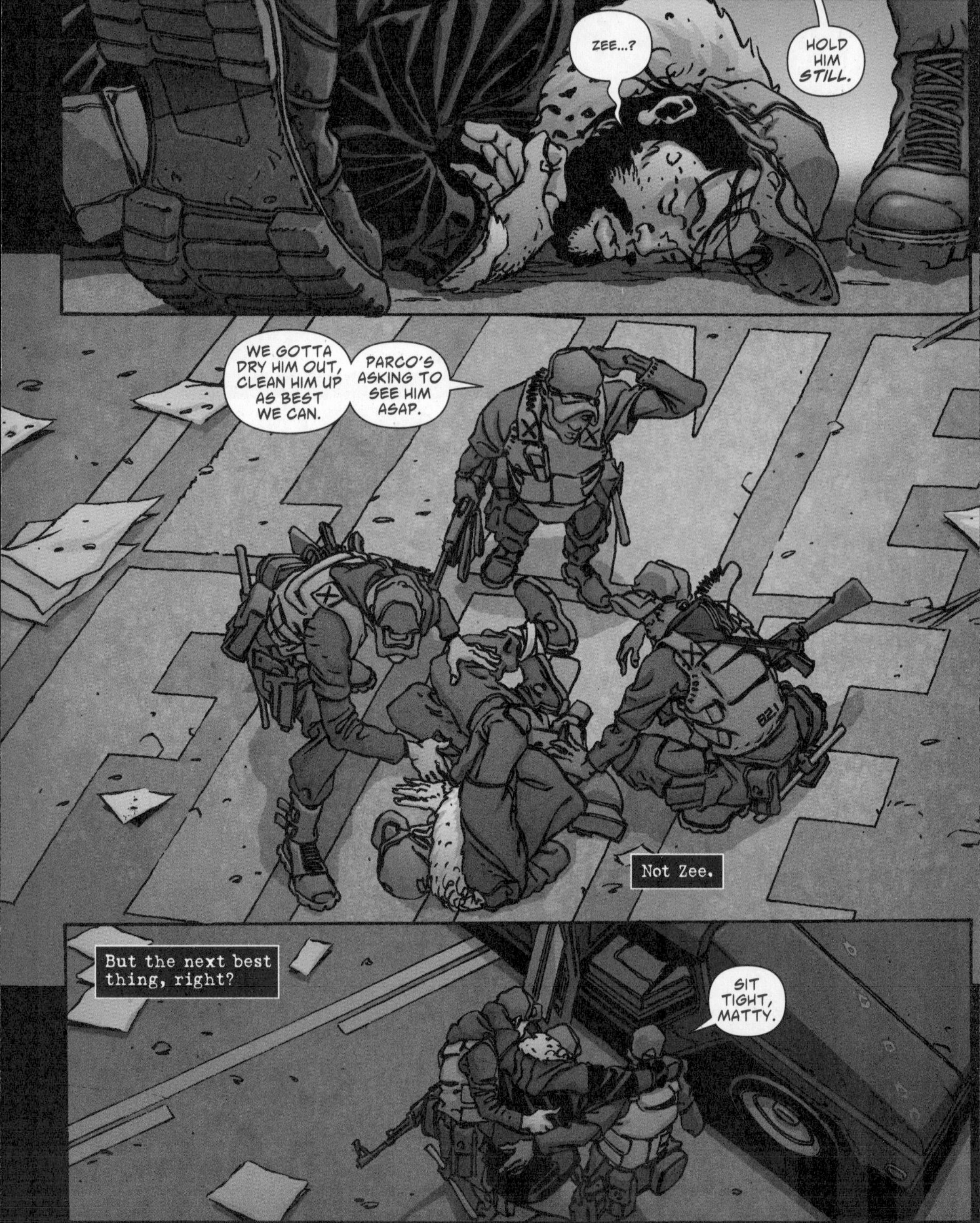
ZEE...?
HOLD HIM STILL.
WE GOTTA DRY HIM OUT, CLEAN HIM UP AS BEST WE CAN.
PARCO'S ASKING TO SEE HIM ASAP.
Not Zee.
But the next best thing, right?
SIT TIGHT, MATTY.

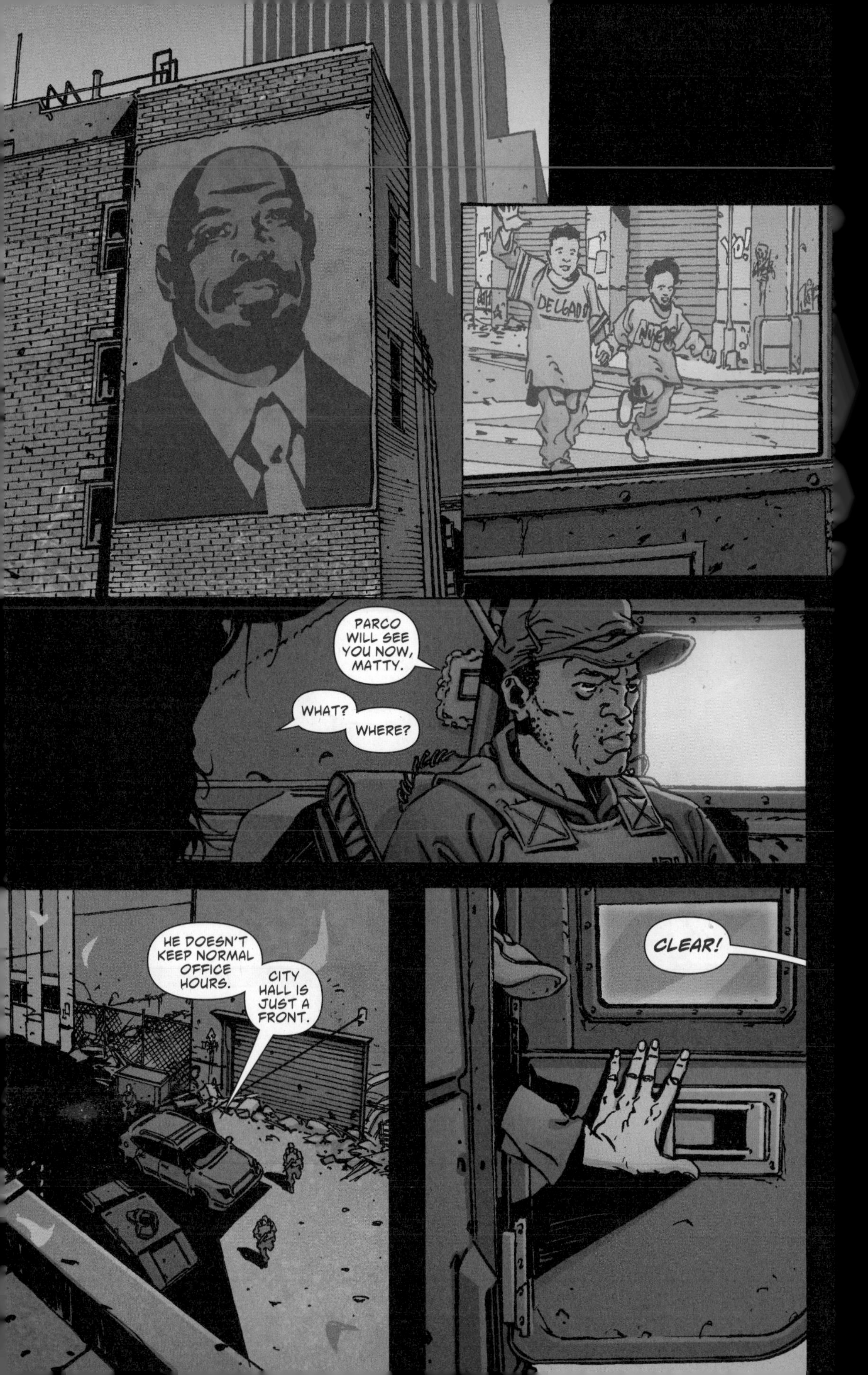
DELGADO
YO!
PARCO WILL SEE YOU NOW, MATTY.
WHAT?
WHERE?
HE DOESN'T KEEP NORMAL OFFICE HOURS.
CITY HALL IS JUST A FRONT.
CLEAR!

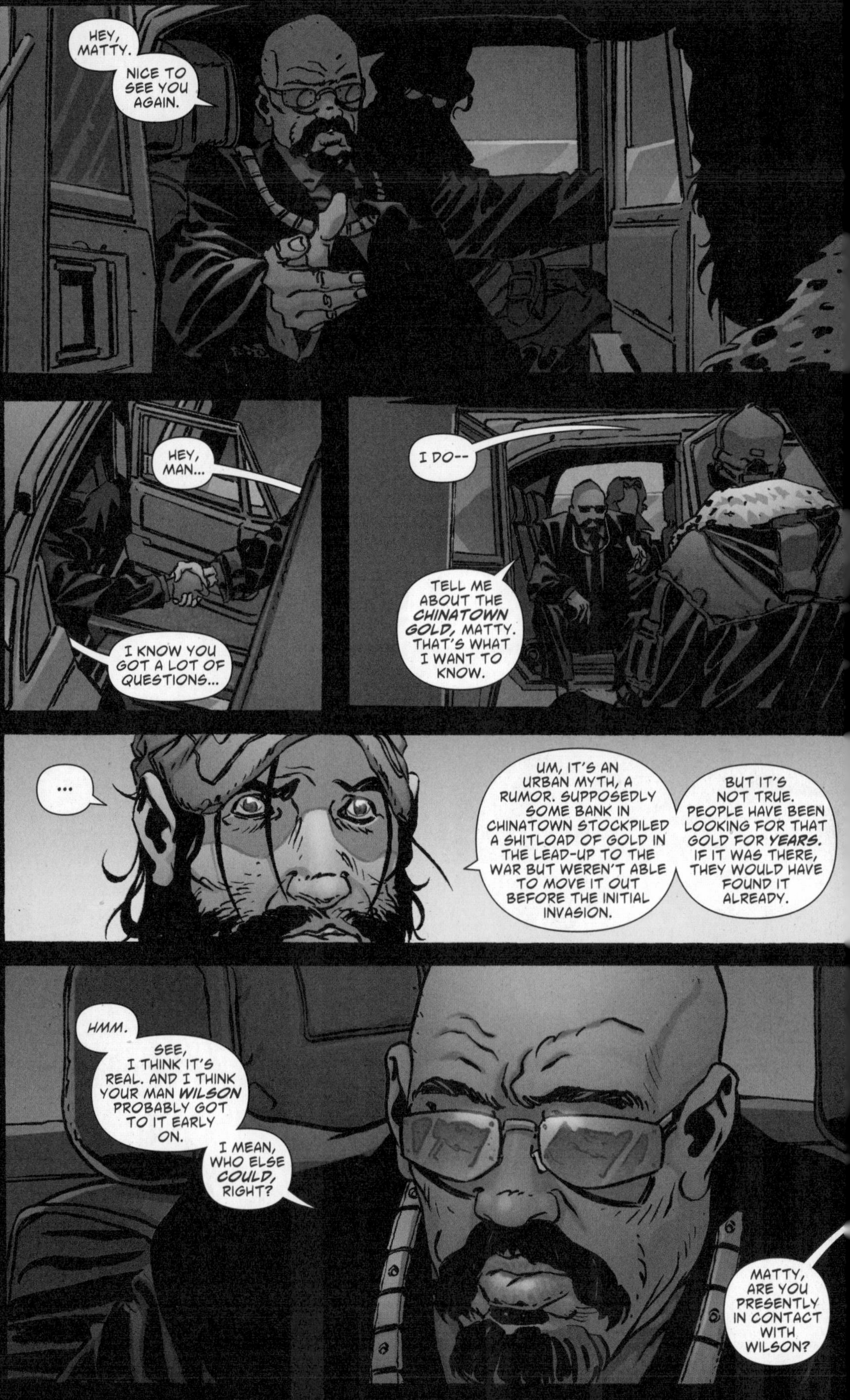

HEY, MATTY.
NICE TO SEE YOU AGAIN.
HEY, MAN...
I KNOW YOU GOT A LOT OF QUESTIONS...
I DO--
TELL ME ABOUT THE CHINATOWN GOLD, MATTY. THAT'S WHAT I WANT TO KNOW.
...
UM, IT'S AN URBAN MYTH, A RUMOR. SUPPOSEDLY SOME BANK IN CHINATOWN STOCKPILED A SHITLOAD OF GOLD IN THE LEAD-UP TO THE WAR BUT WEREN'T ABLE TO MOVE IT OUT BEFORE THE INITIAL INVASION.
BUT IT'S NOT TRUE. PEOPLE HAVE BEEN LOOKING FOR THAT GOLD FOR YEARS. IF IT WAS THERE, THEY WOULD HAVE FOUND IT ALREADY.
HMM.
SEE, I THINK IT'S REAL. AND I THINK YOUR MAN WILSON PROBABLY GOT TO IT EARLY ON.
I MEAN, WHO ELSE COULD, RIGHT?
MATTY, ARE YOU PRESENTLY IN CONTACT WITH WILSON?

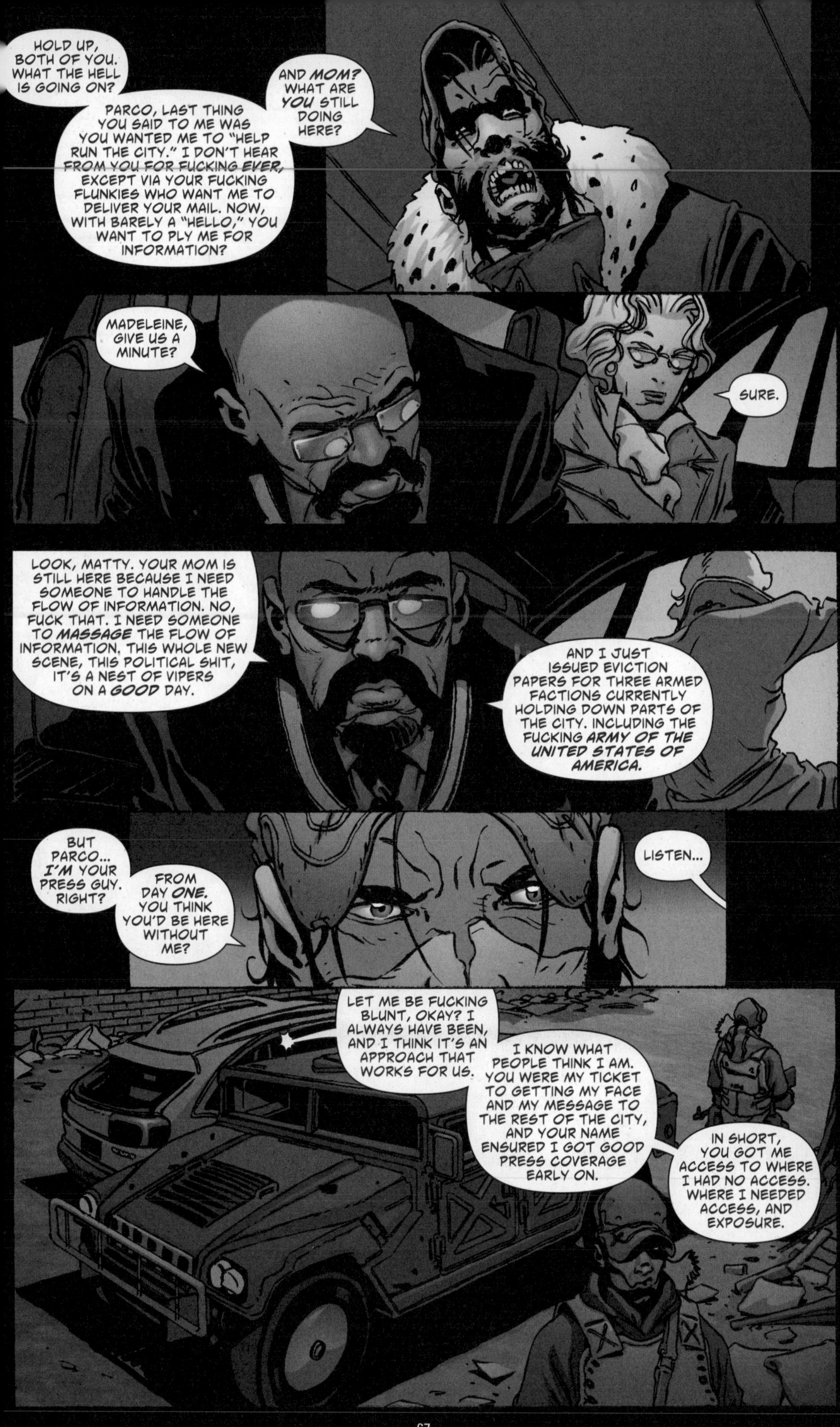
HOLD UP, BOTH OF YOU. WHAT THE HELL IS GOING ON?
AND MOM? WHAT ARE YOU STILL DOING HERE?
PARCO, LAST THING YOU SAID TO ME WAS YOU WANTED ME TO "HELP RUN THE CITY." I DON'T HEAR FROM YOU FOR FUCKING EVER, EXCEPT VIA YOUR FUCKING FLUNKIES WHO WANT ME TO DELIVER YOUR MAIL. NOW, WITH BARELY A "HELLO," YOU WANT TO PLY ME FOR INFORMATION?
MADELEINE, GIVE US A MINUTE?
SURE.
LOOK, MATTY. YOUR MOM IS STILL HERE BECAUSE I NEED SOMEONE TO HANDLE THE FLOW OF INFORMATION. NO, FUCK THAT. I NEED SOMEONE TO MASSAGE THE FLOW OF INFORMATION. THIS WHOLE NEW SCENE, THIS POLITICAL SHIT, IT'S A NEST OF VIPERS ON A GOOD DAY.
AND I JUST ISSUED EVICTION PAPERS FOR THREE ARMED FACTIONS CURRENTLY HOLDING DOWN PARTS OF THE CITY. INCLUDING THE FUCKING ARMY OF THE UNITED STATES OF AMERICA.
BUT PARCO... I'M YOUR PRESS GUY. RIGHT?
FROM DAY ONE. YOU THINK YOU'D BE HERE WITHOUT ME?
LISTEN...
LET ME BE FUCKING BLUNT, OKAY? I ALWAYS HAVE BEEN, AND I THINK IT'S AN APPROACH THAT WORKS FOR US.
I KNOW WHAT PEOPLE THINK I AM. YOU WERE MY TICKET TO GETTING MY FACE AND MY MESSAGE TO THE REST OF THE CITY, AND YOUR NAME ENSURED I GOT GOOD PRESS COVERAGE EARLY ON.
IN SHORT, YOU GOT ME ACCESS TO WHERE I HAD NO ACCESS. WHERE I NEEDED ACCESS, AND EXPOSURE.

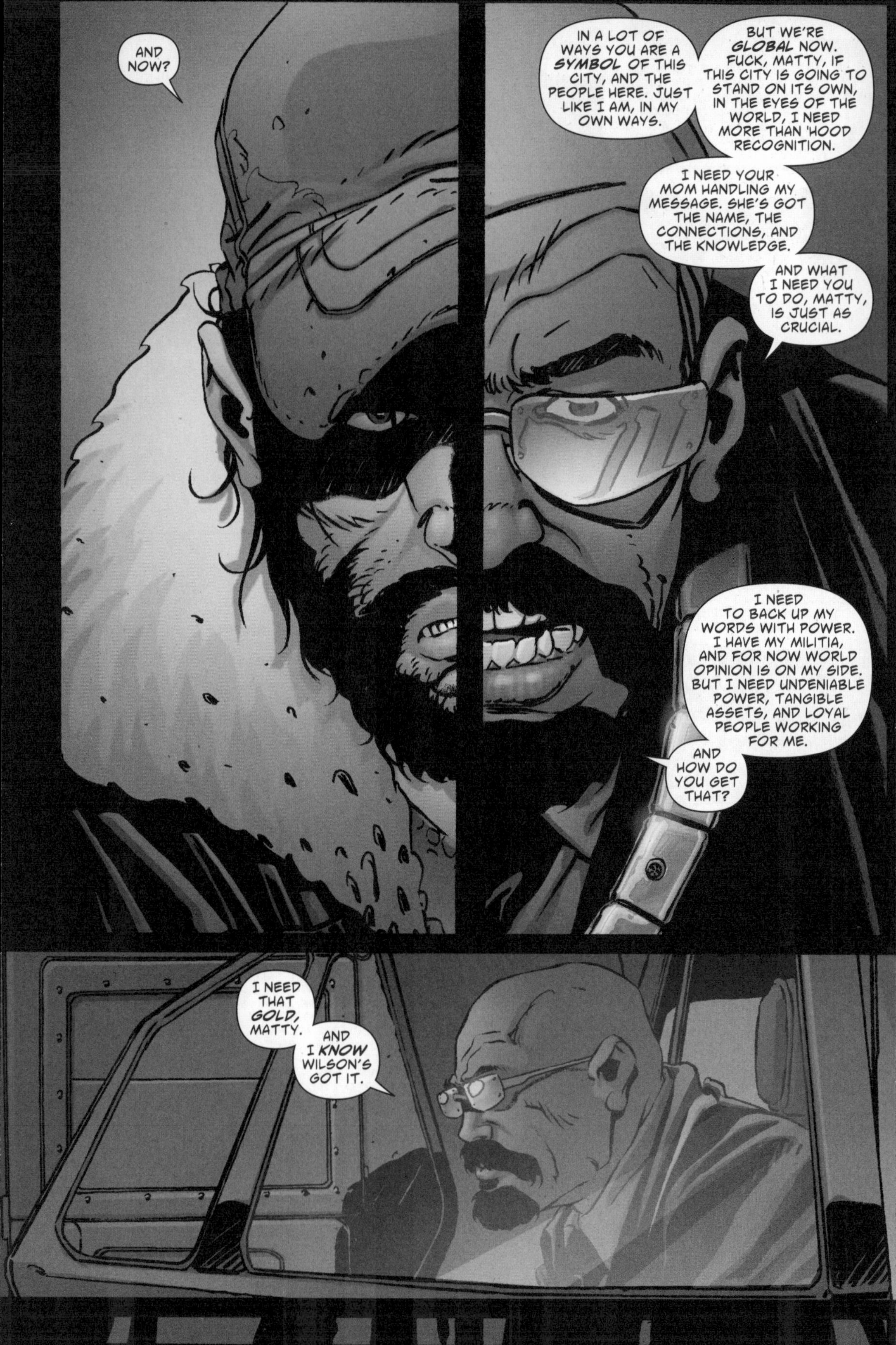
AND NOW?
IN A LOT OF WAYS YOU ARE A SYMBOL OF THIS CITY, AND THE PEOPLE HERE. JUST LIKE I AM, IN MY OWN WAYS.
BUT WE'RE GLOBAL NOW. FUCK, MATTY, IF THIS CITY IS GOING TO STAND ON ITS OWN, IN THE EYES OF THE WORLD, I NEED MORE THAN 'HOOD RECOGNITION.
I NEED YOUR MOM HANDLING MY MESSAGE. SHE'S GOT THE NAME, THE CONNECTIONS, AND THE KNOWLEDGE.
AND WHAT I NEED YOU TO DO, MATTY, IS JUST AS CRUCIAL.
I NEED TO BACK UP MY WORDS WITH POWER. I HAVE MY MILITIA, AND FOR NOW WORLD OPINION IS ON MY SIDE. BUT I NEED UNDENIABLE POWER, TANGIBLE ASSETS, AND LOYAL PEOPLE WORKING FOR ME.
AND HOW DO YOU GET THAT?
I NEED THAT GOLD, MATTY.
AND I KNOW WILSON'S GOT IT.

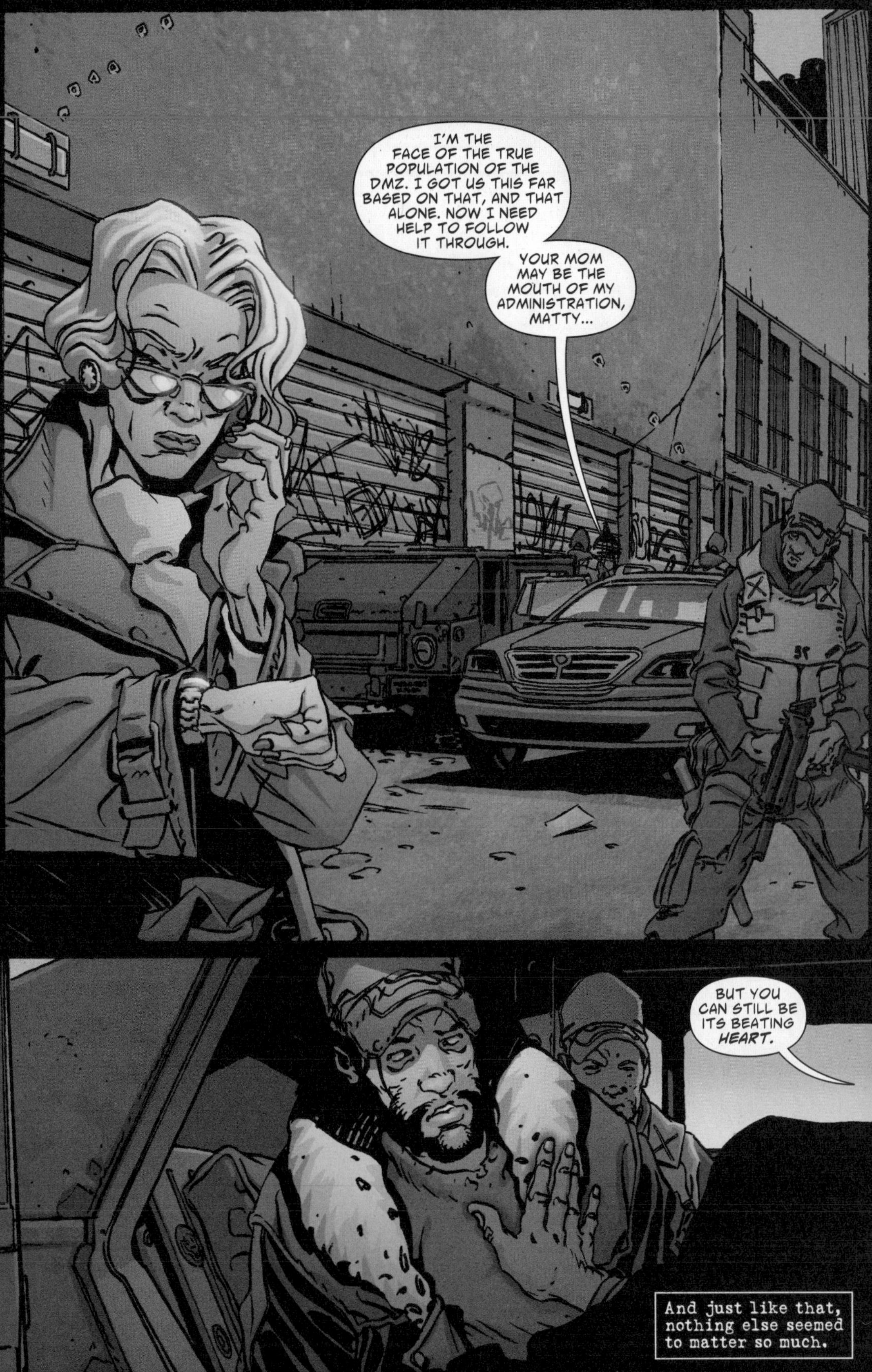
I'M THE FACE OF THE TRUE POPULATION OF THE DMZ. I GOT US THIS FAR BASED ON THAT, AND THAT ALONE. NOW I NEED HELP TO FOLLOW IT THROUGH.
YOUR MOM MAY BE THE MOUTH OF MY ADMINISTRATION, MATTY...
BUT YOU CAN STILL BE ITS BEATING *HEART*.
And just like that, nothing else seemed to matter so much.

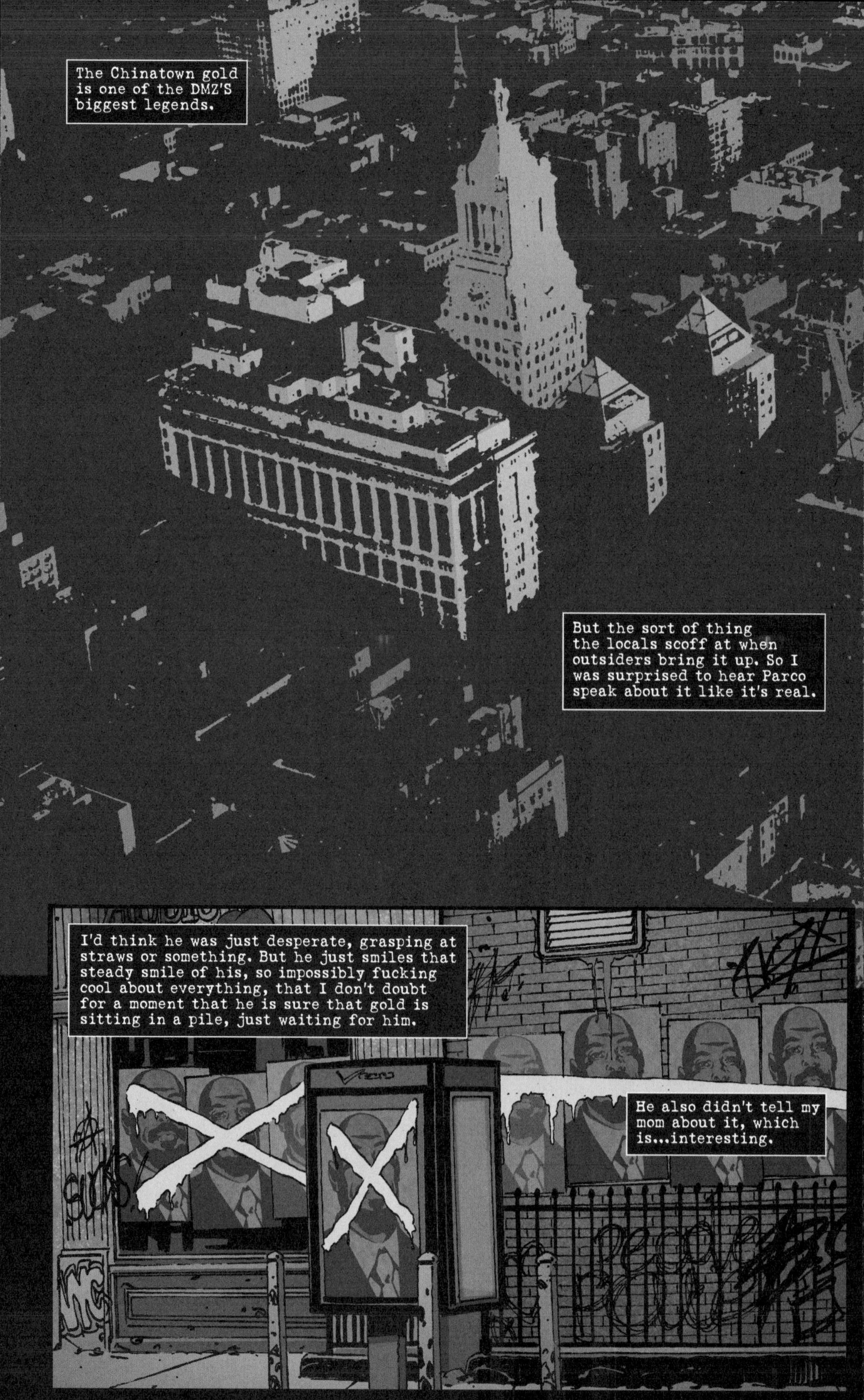
The Chinatown gold is one of the DMZ'S biggest legends.
But the sort of thing the locals scoff at when outsiders bring it up. So I was surprised to hear Parco speak about it like it's real.
I'd think he was just desperate, grasping at straws or something. But he just smiles that steady smile of his, so impossibly fucking cool about everything, that I don't doubt for a moment that he is sure that gold is sitting in a pile, just waiting for him.
He also didn't tell my mom about it, which is...interesting.

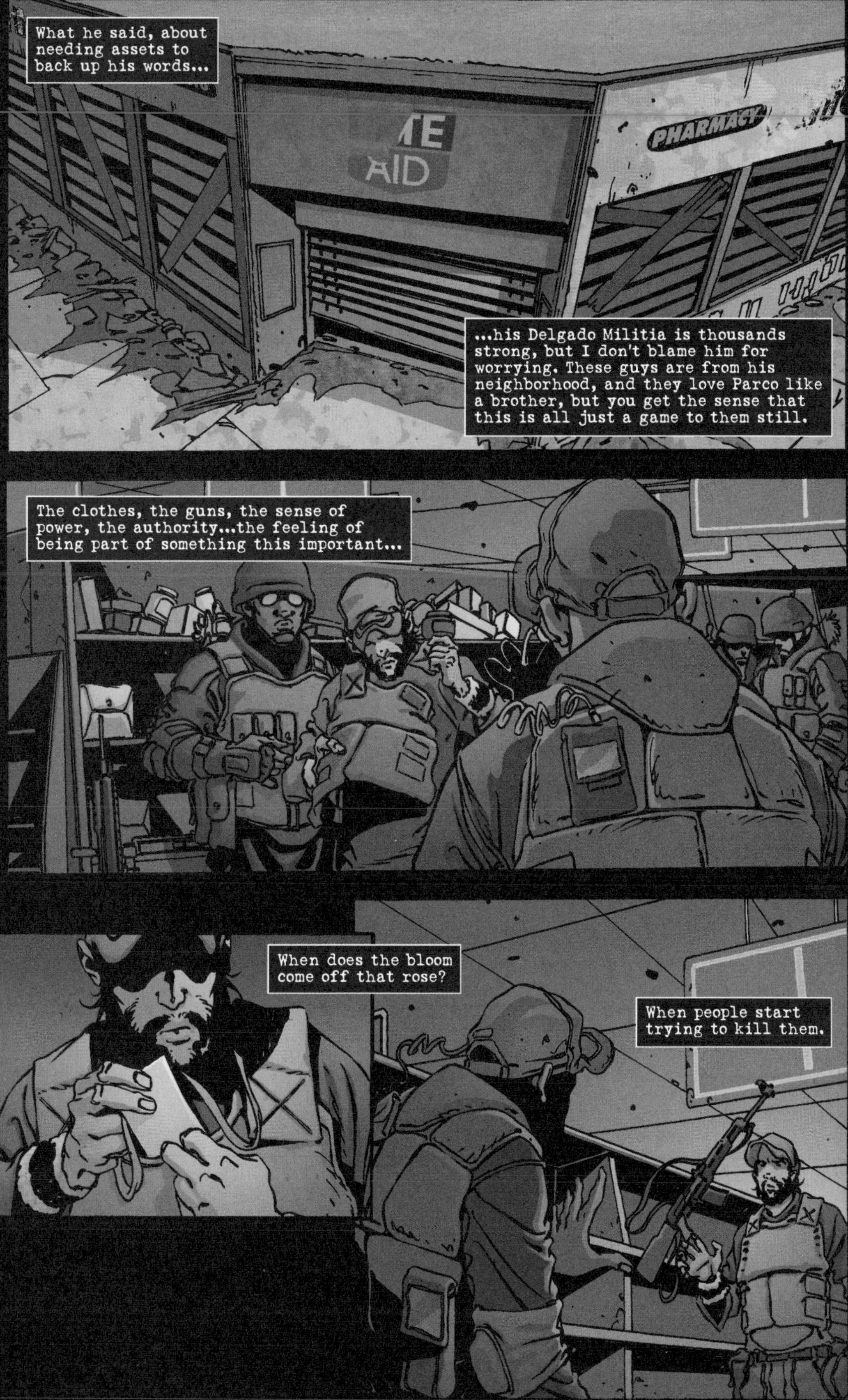
What he said, about needing assets to back up his words...
TE
AID
PHARMACY
...his Delgado Militia is thousands strong, but I don't blame him for worrying. These guys are from his neighborhood, and they love Parco like a brother, but you get the sense that this is all just a game to them still.
The clothes, the guns, the sense of power, the authority...the feeling of being part of something this important...
When does the bloom come off that rose?
When people start trying to kill them.

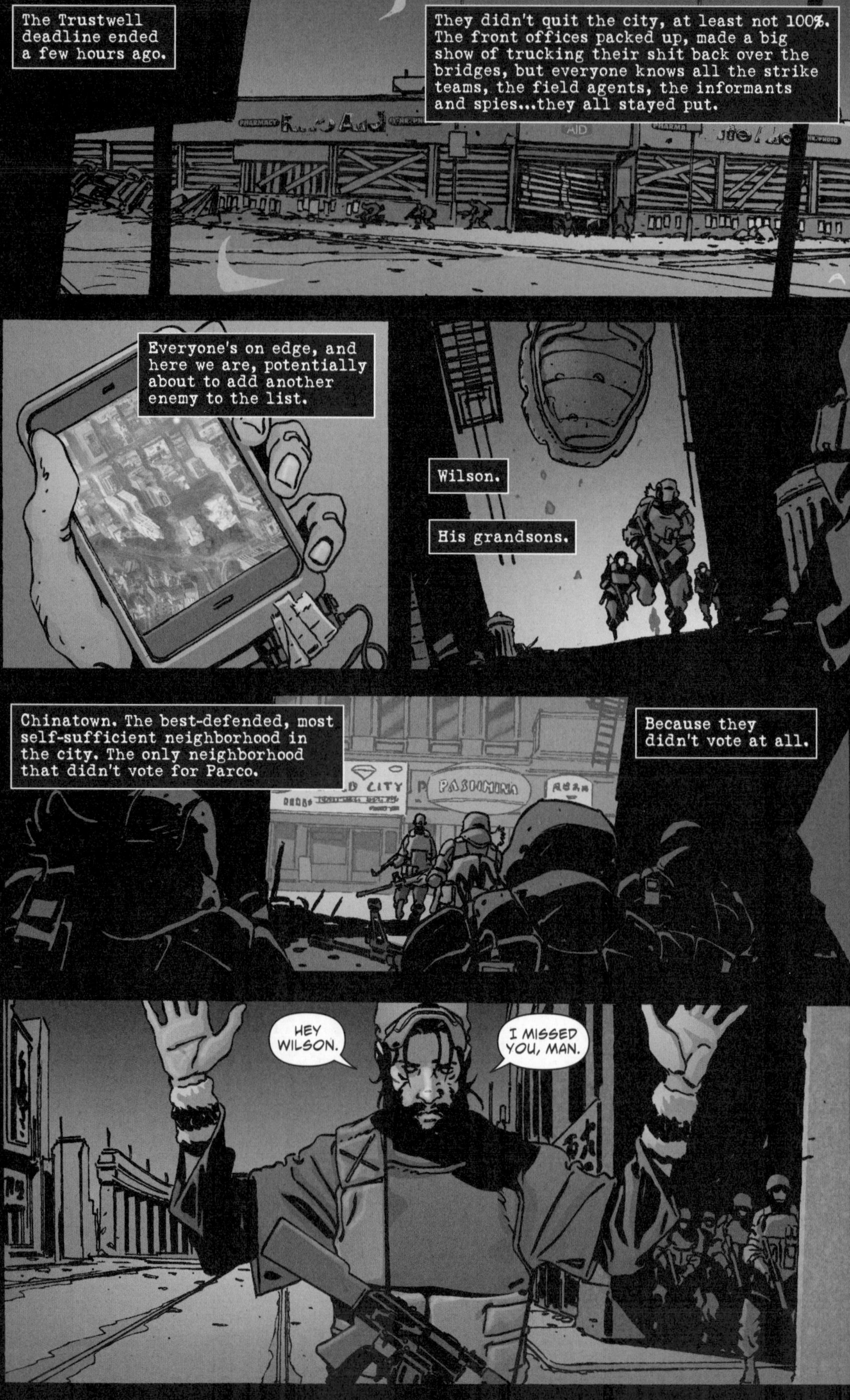

The Trustwell deadline ended a few hours ago.
They didn't quit the city, at least not 100%. The front offices packed up, made a big show of trucking their shit back over the bridges, but everyone knows all the strike teams, the field agents, the informants and spies...they all stayed put.
Everyone's on edge, and here we are, potentially about to add another enemy to the list.
Wilson.
His grandsons.
Chinatown. The best-defended, most self-sufficient neighborhood in the city. The only neighborhood that didn't vote for Parco.
Because they didn't vote at all.
PASHMINA
HEY WILSON.
I MISSED YOU, MAN.

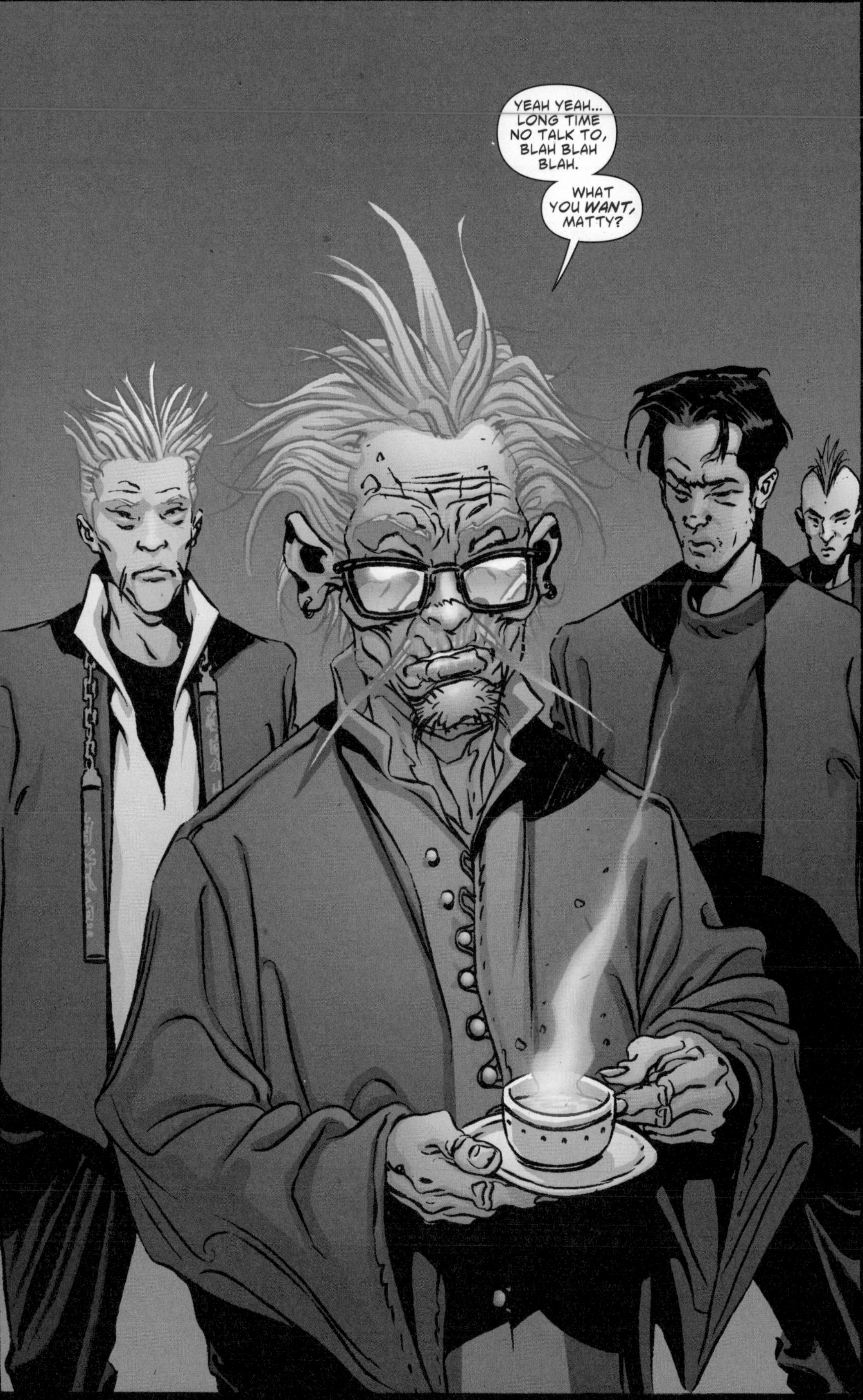
YEAH YEAH... LONG TIME NO TALK TO, BLAH BLAH BLAH.
WHAT YOU *WANT*, MATTY?

WAR POWERS

CHAPTER TWO

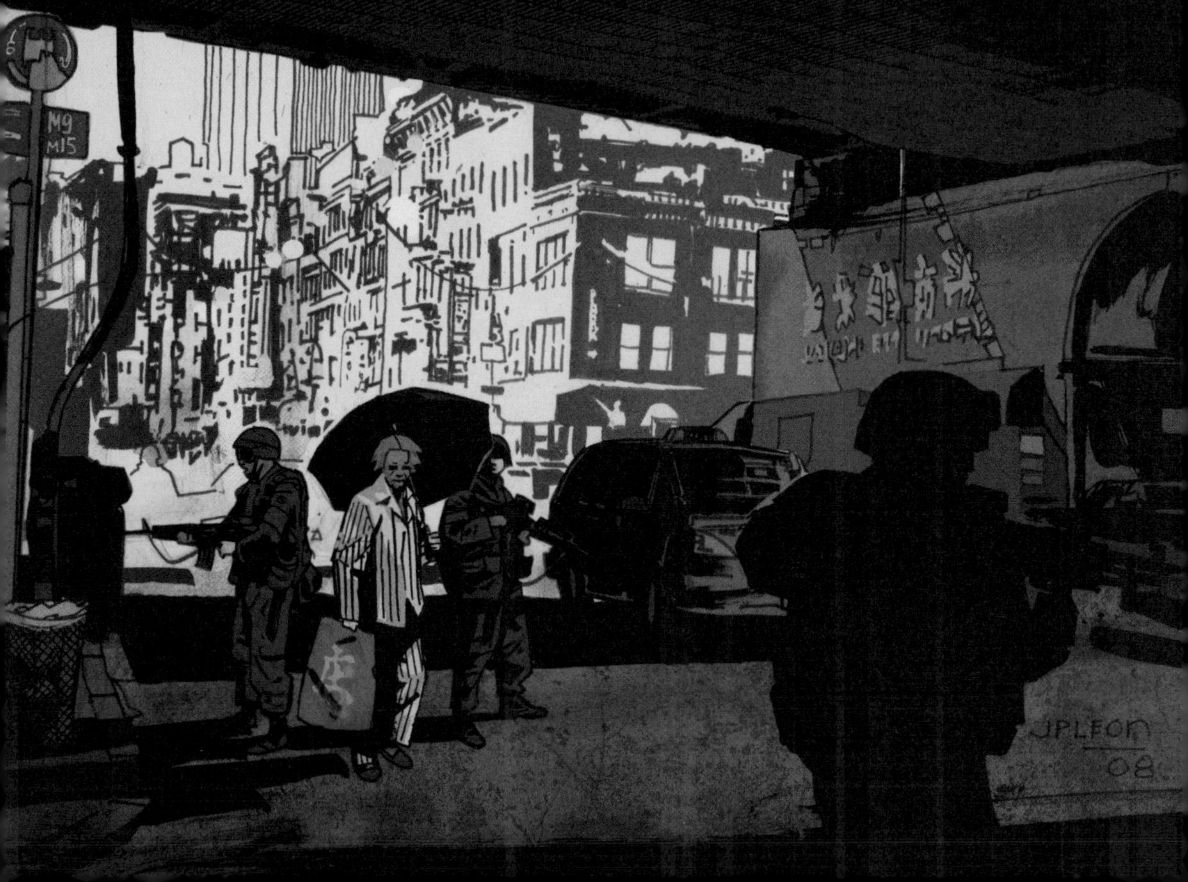
M9
M15
JPLEON
08

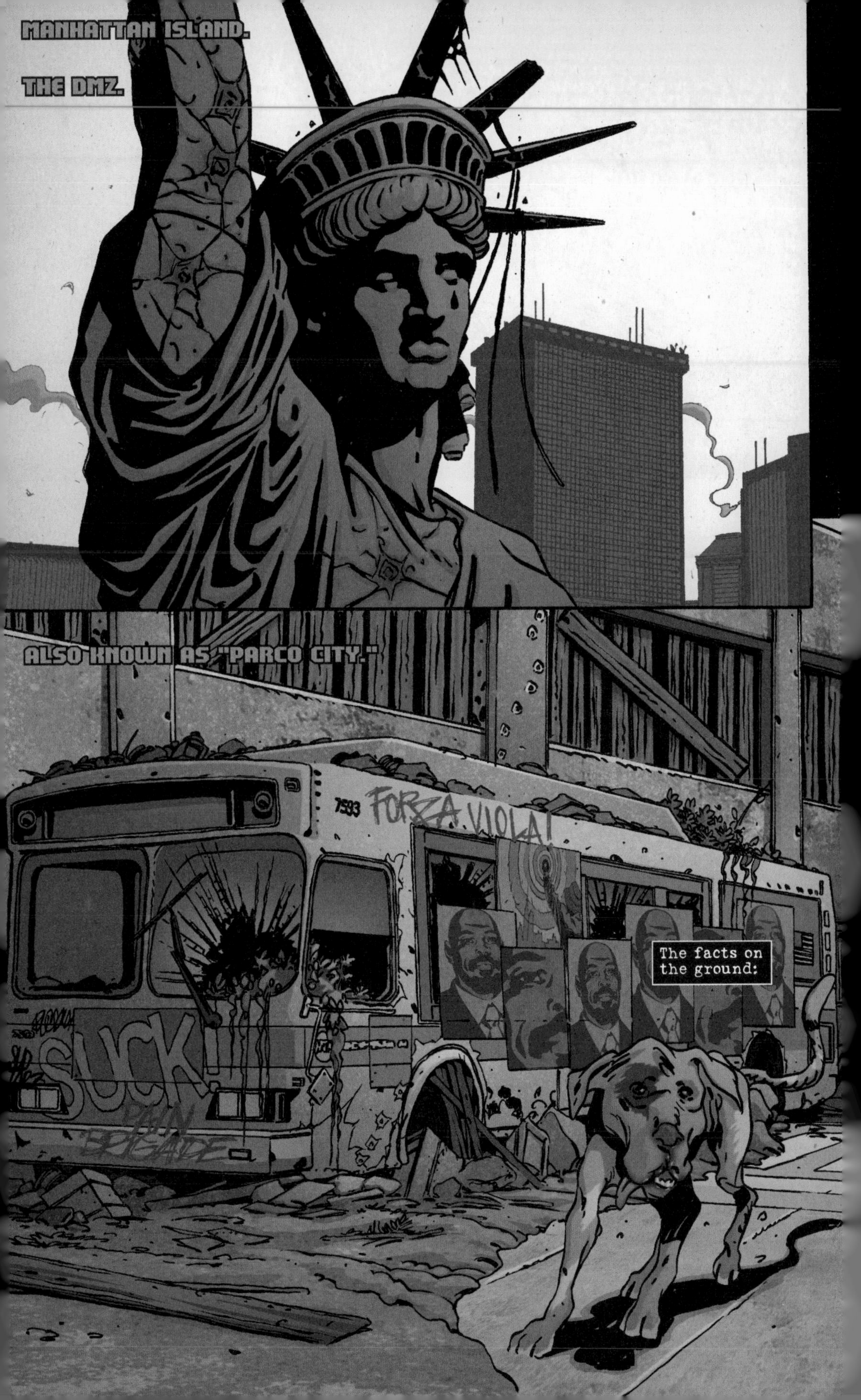
MANHATTAN ISLAND.
THE DMZ.
ALSO KNOWN AS "PARCO CITY."
7593
FORZA VIOLA!
The facts on the ground:
SUCK!!

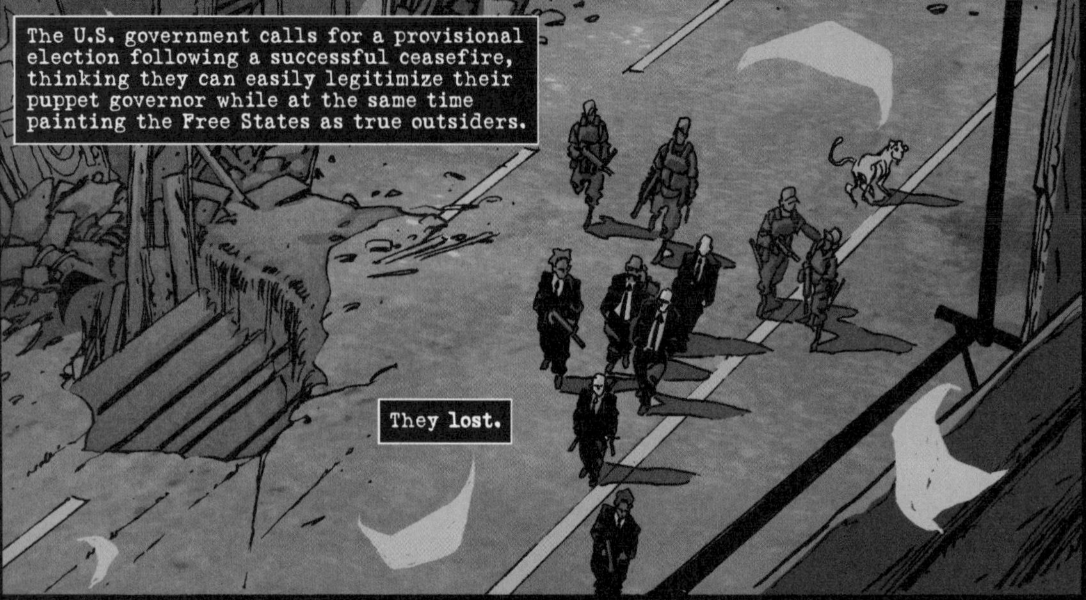
The U.S. government calls for a provisional election following a successful ceasefire, thinking they can easily legitimize their puppet governor while at the same time painting the Free States as true outsiders.
They **lost.**

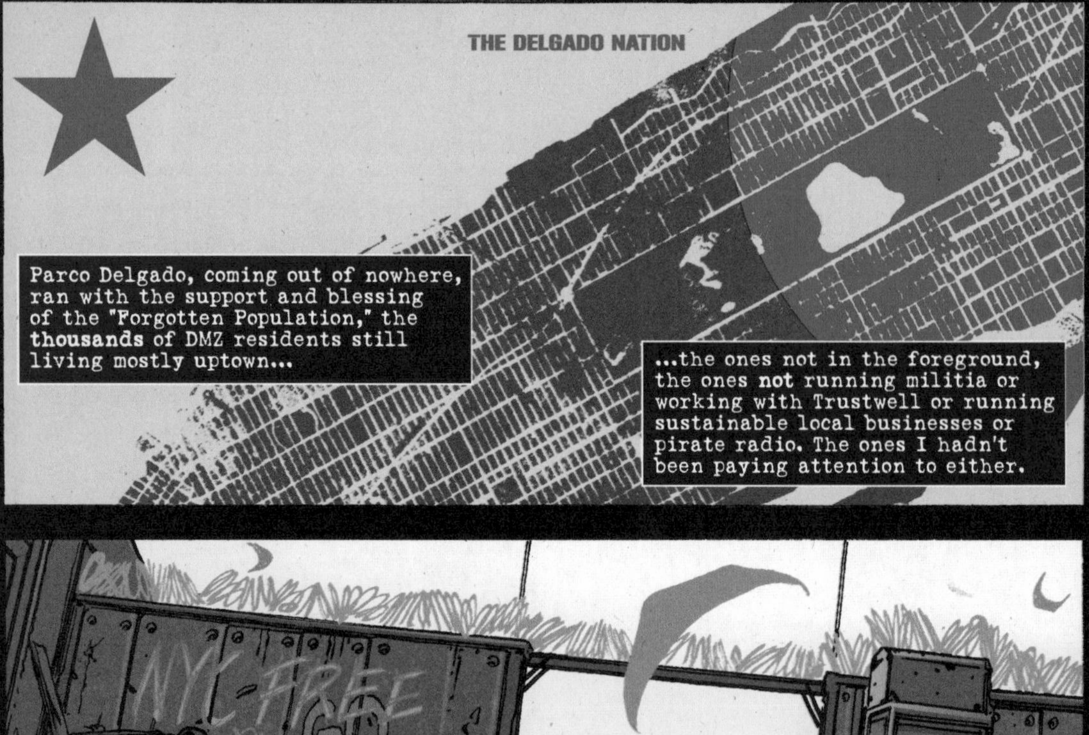
THE DELGADO NATION
Parco Delgado, coming out of nowhere, ran with the support and blessing of the "Forgotten Population," the **thousands** of DMZ residents still living mostly uptown...
...the ones not in the foreground, the ones **not** running militia or working with Trustwell or running sustainable local businesses or pirate radio. The ones I hadn't been paying attention to either.

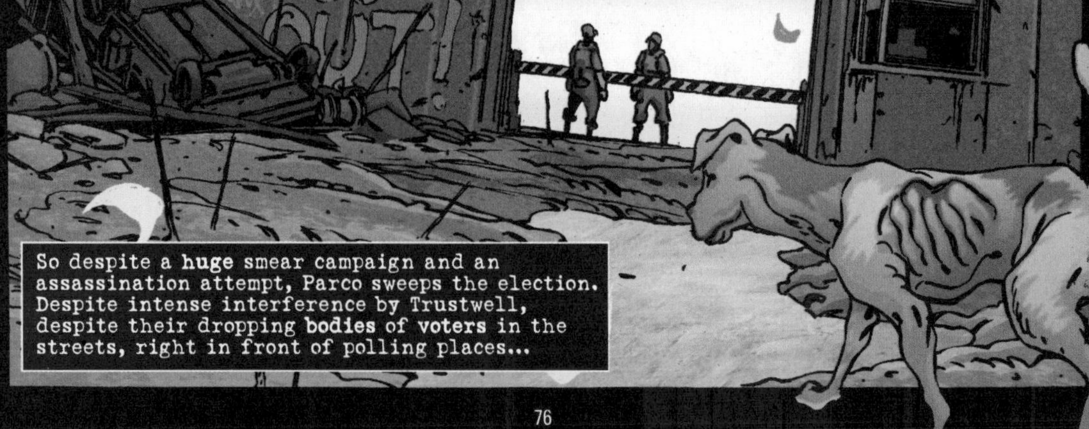
NYC FREE
GO OUT!
So despite a **huge** smear campaign and an assassination attempt, Parco sweeps the election. Despite intense interference by Trustwell, despite their dropping **bodies** of **voters** in the streets, right in front of polling places...

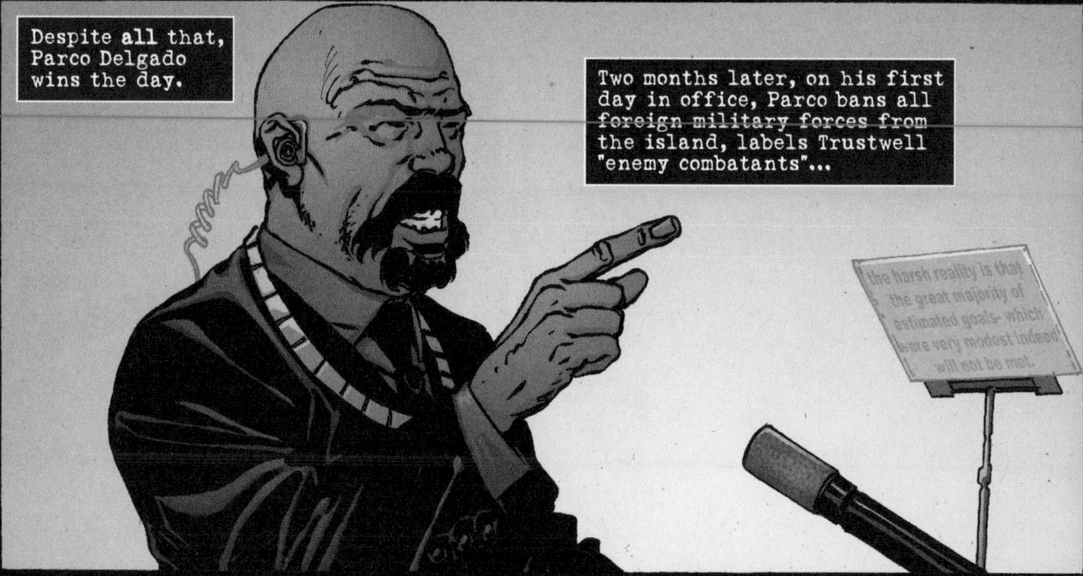
Despite **all** that, Parco Delgado wins the day.
Two months later, on his first day in office, Parco bans all foreign military forces from the island, labels Trustwell "enemy combatants"...
the harsh reality is that the great majority of estimated goals- which were very modest indeed will not be met.

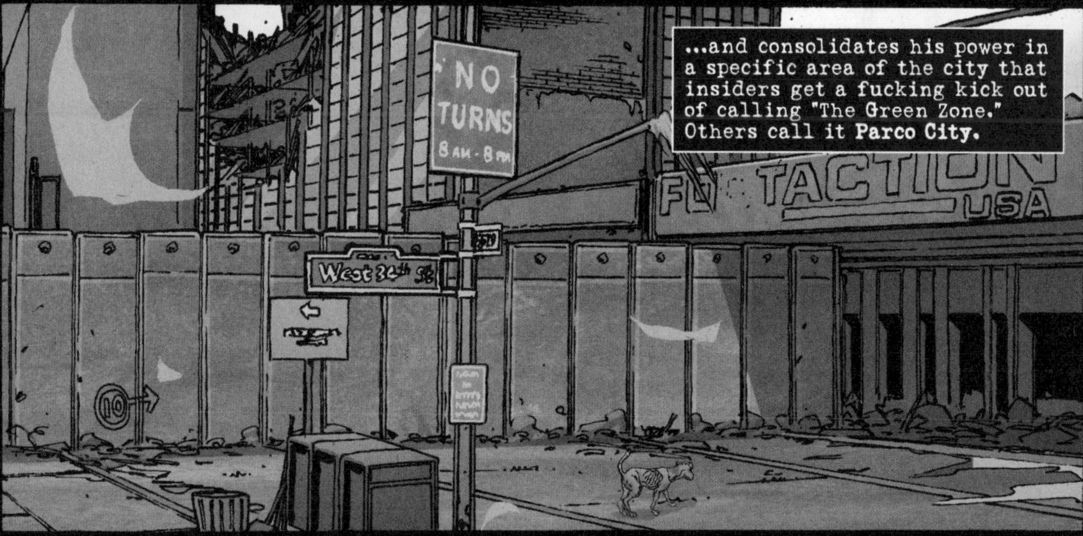
...and consolidates his power in a specific area of the city that insiders get a fucking kick out of calling "The Green Zone." Others call it **Parco City.**
NO TURNS 8 AM - 8 PM
West 34th St
TACTION
USA

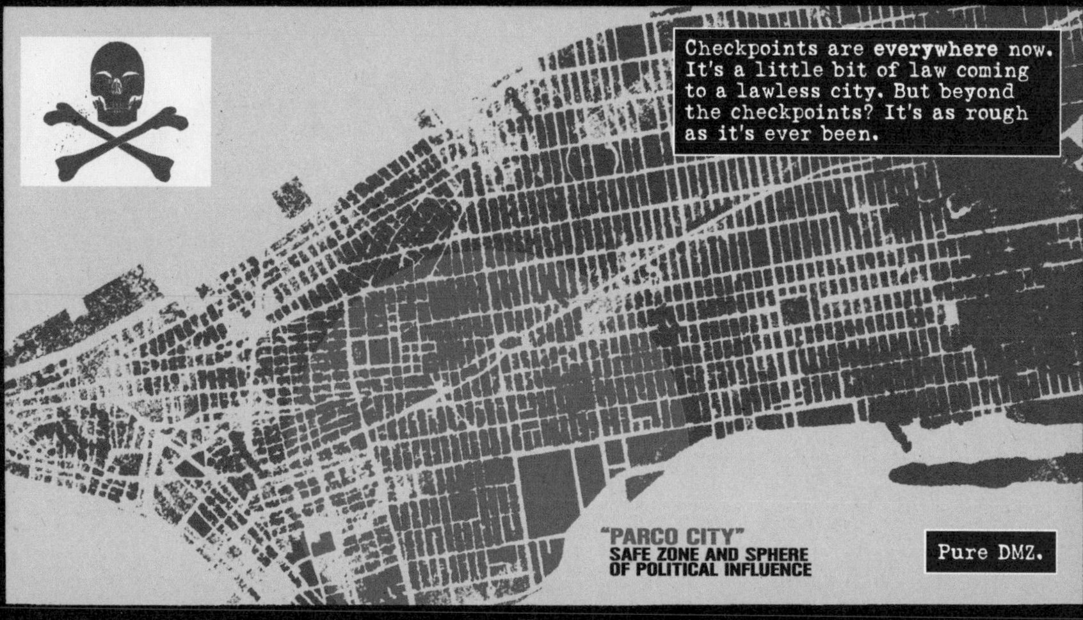
Checkpoints are **everywhere** now. It's a little bit of law coming to a lawless city. But beyond the checkpoints? It's as rough as it's ever been.
"PARCO CITY"
SAFE ZONE AND SPHERE OF POLITICAL INFLUENCE
Pure DMZ.

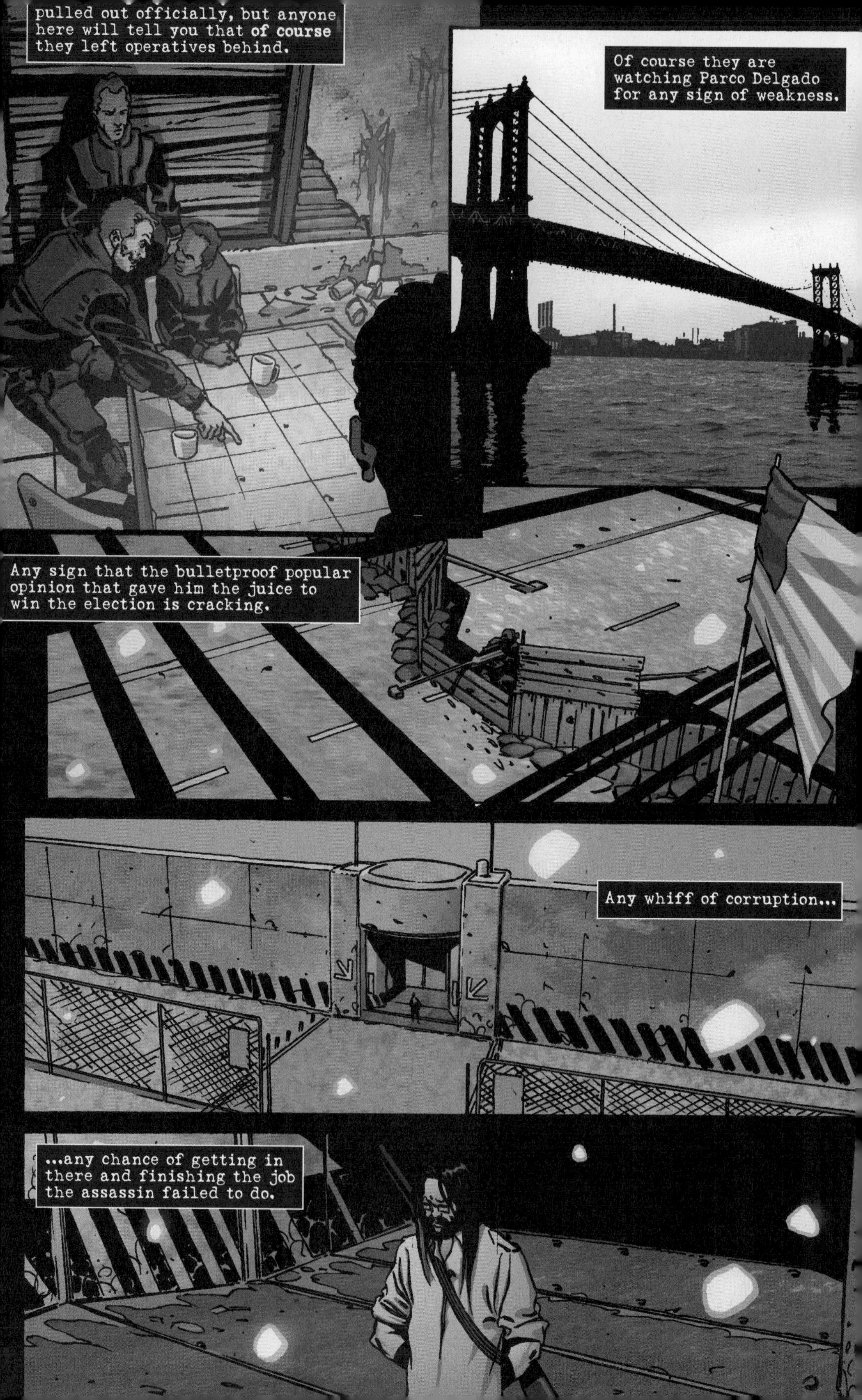
pulled out officially, but anyone here will tell you that **of course** they left operatives behind.
Of course they are watching Parco Delgado for any sign of weakness.
Any sign that the bulletproof popular opinion that gave him the juice to win the election is cracking.
Any whiff of corruption...
...any chance of getting in there and finishing the job the assassin failed to do.

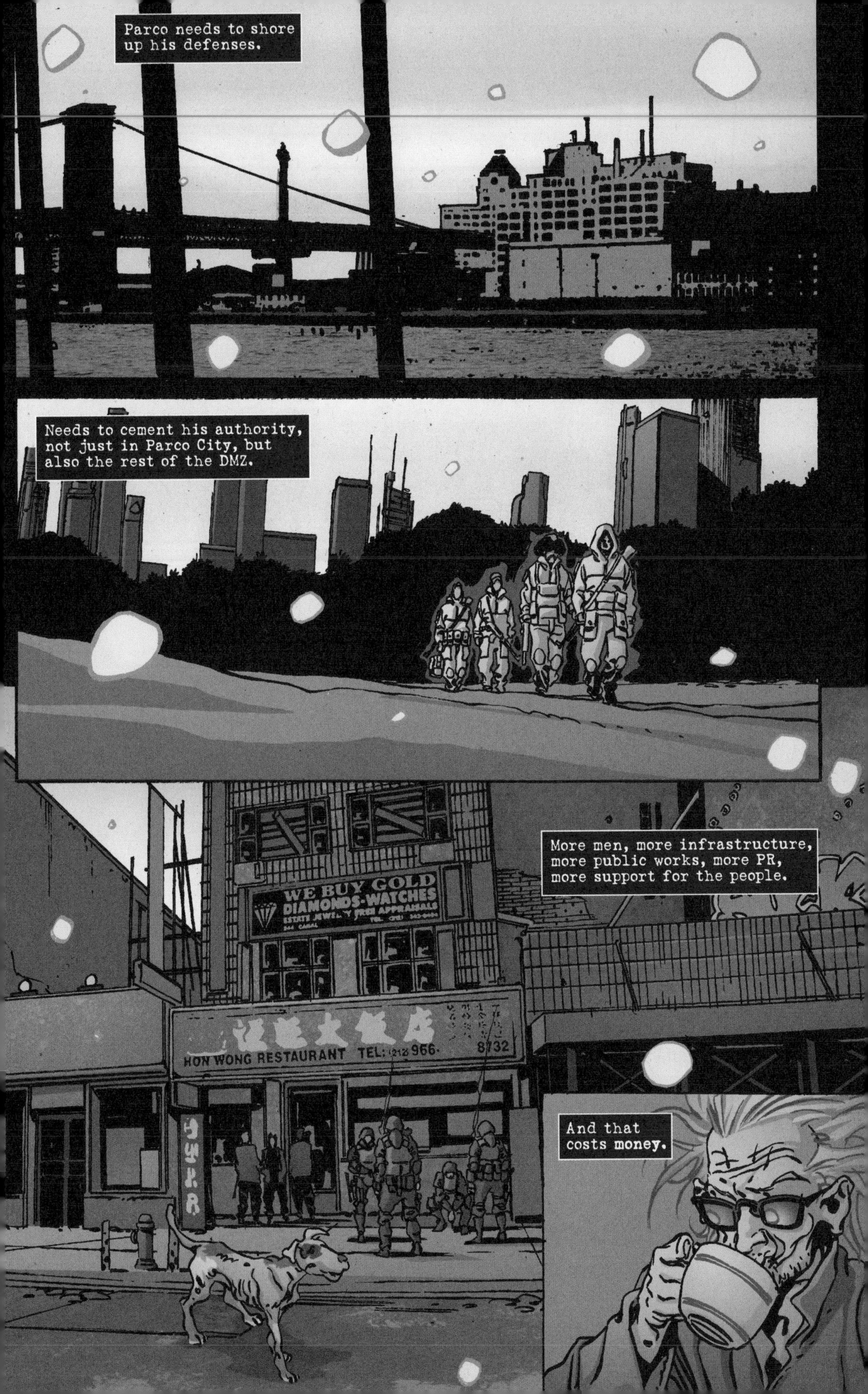

Parco needs to shore up his defenses.
Needs to cement his authority, not just in Parco City, but also the rest of the DMZ.
WE BUY GOLD
DIAMONDS-WATCHES
HON WONG RESTAURANT
More men, more infrastructure, more public works, more PR, more support for the people.
And that costs **money.**

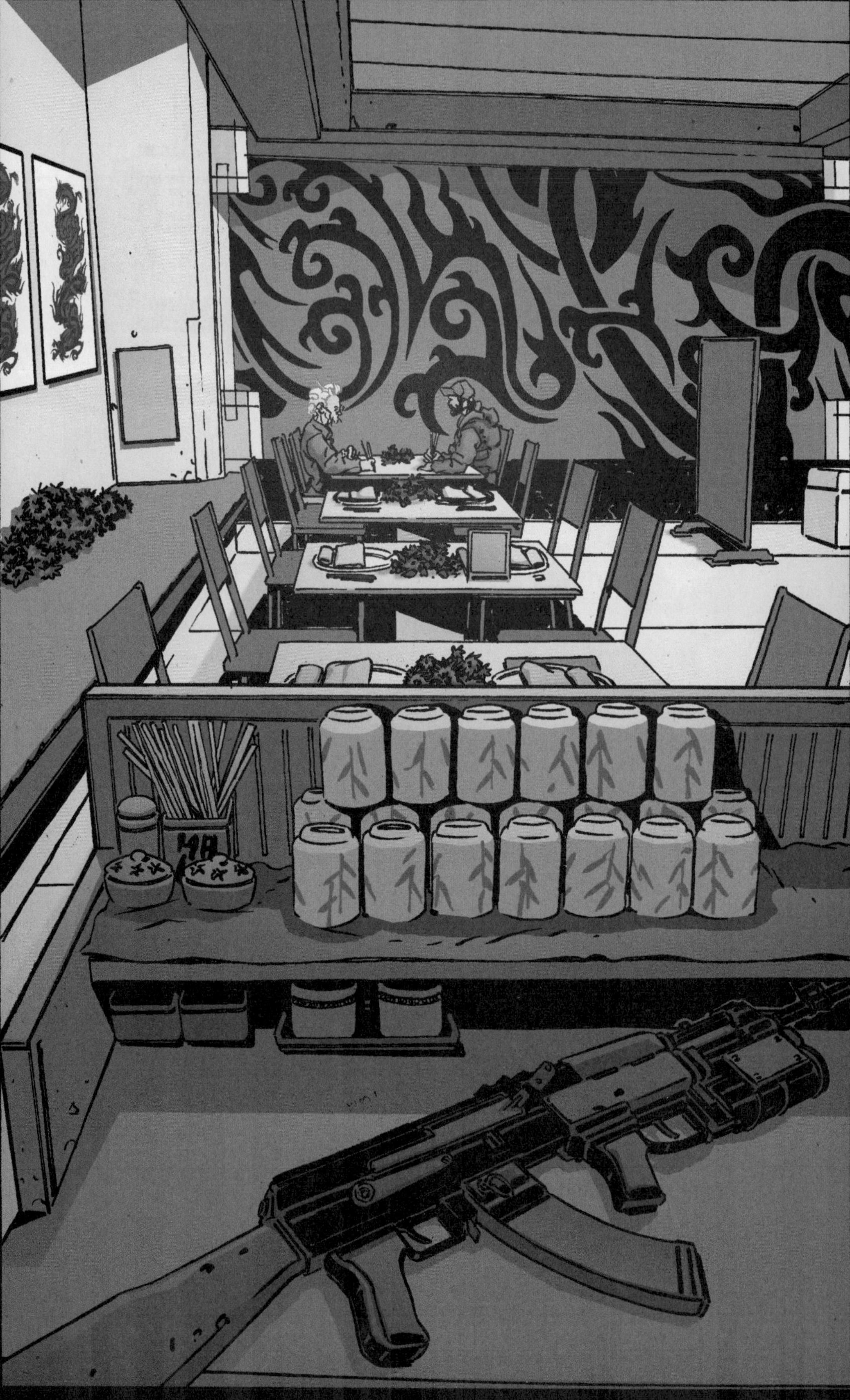
MA

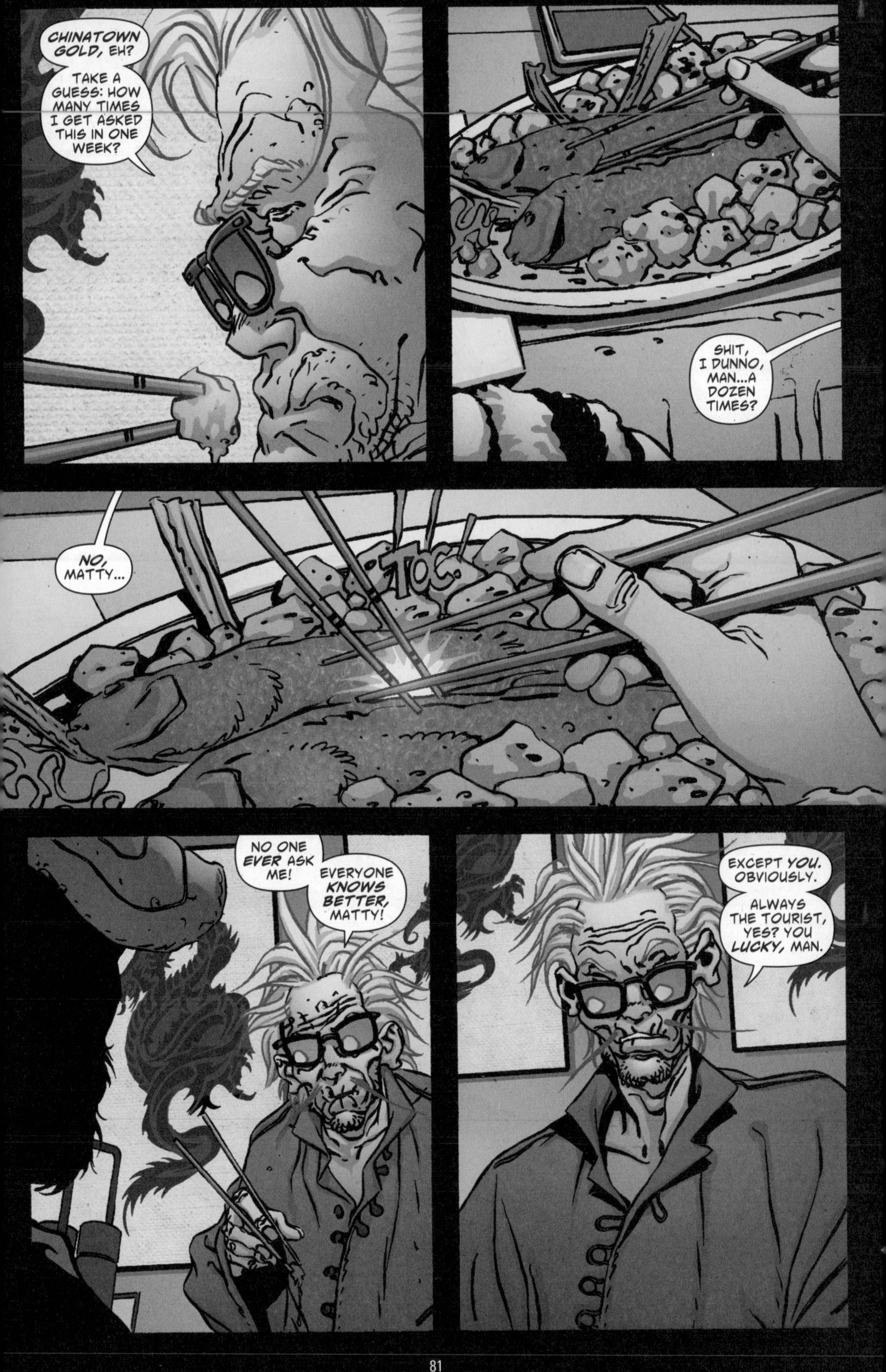
CHINATOWN GOLD, EH?
TAKE A GUESS: HOW MANY TIMES I GET ASKED THIS IN ONE WEEK?
SHIT, I DUNNO, MAN...A DOZEN TIMES?
NO, MATTY...
TOC!
NO ONE EVER ASK ME!
EVERYONE KNOWS BETTER, MATTY!
EXCEPT YOU. OBVIOUSLY.
ALWAYS THE TOURIST, YES? YOU LUCKY, MAN.

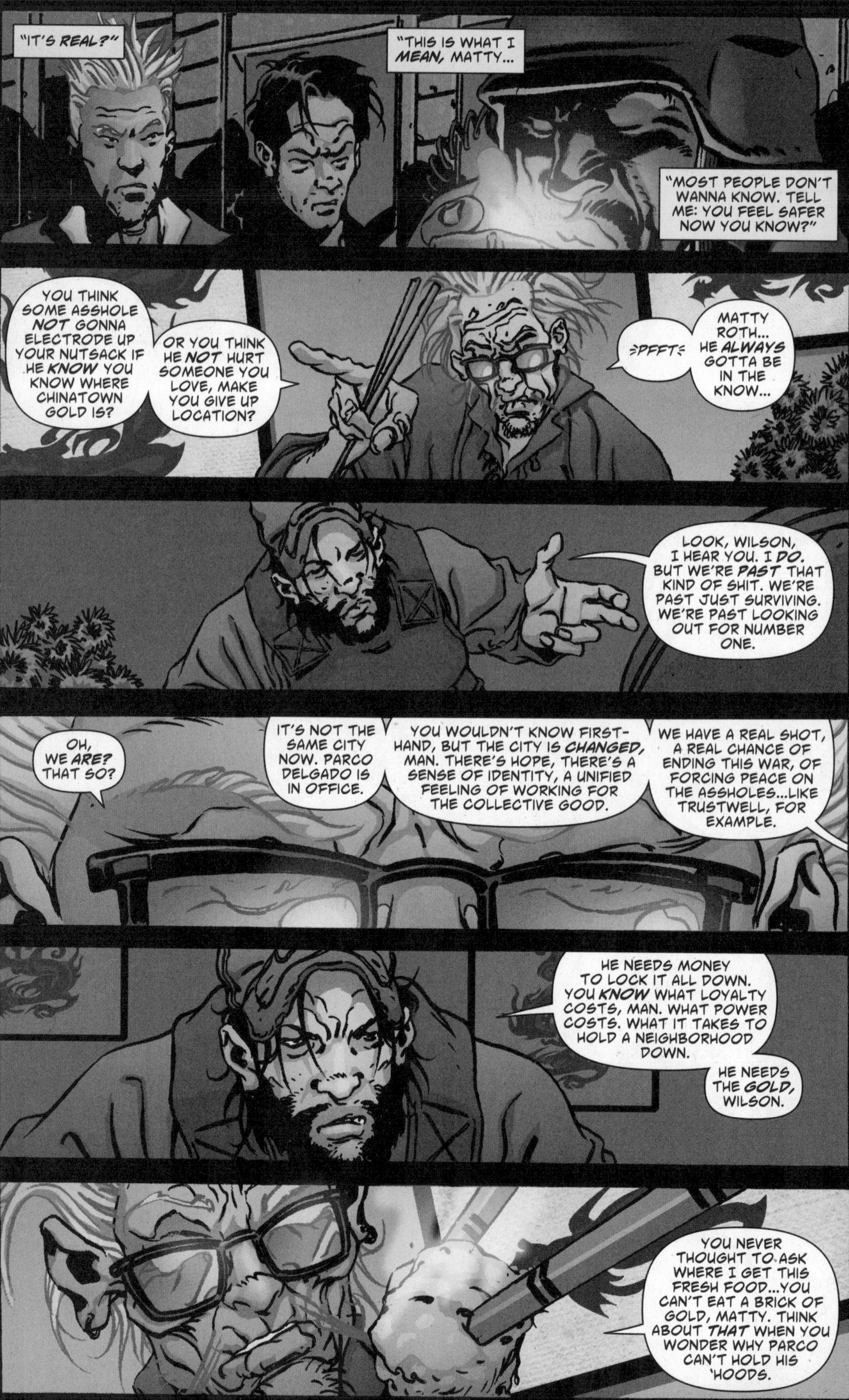
"IT'S REAL?"
"THIS IS WHAT I MEAN, MATTY...
"MOST PEOPLE DON'T WANNA KNOW. TELL ME: YOU FEEL SAFER NOW YOU KNOW?"
YOU THINK SOME ASSHOLE NOT GONNA ELECTRODE UP YOUR NUTSACK IF HE KNOW YOU KNOW WHERE CHINATOWN GOLD IS?
OR YOU THINK HE NOT HURT SOMEONE YOU LOVE, MAKE YOU GIVE UP LOCATION?
PFFT
MATTY ROTH... HE ALWAYS GOTTA BE IN THE KNOW...
LOOK, WILSON, I HEAR YOU. I DO. BUT WE'RE PAST THAT KIND OF SHIT. WE'RE PAST JUST SURVIVING. WE'RE PAST LOOKING OUT FOR NUMBER ONE.
OH, WE ARE? THAT SO?
IT'S NOT THE SAME CITY NOW. PARCO DELGADO IS IN OFFICE.
YOU WOULDN'T KNOW FIRST-HAND, BUT THE CITY IS CHANGED, MAN. THERE'S HOPE, THERE'S A SENSE OF IDENTITY, A UNIFIED FEELING OF WORKING FOR THE COLLECTIVE GOOD.
WE HAVE A REAL SHOT, A REAL CHANCE OF ENDING THIS WAR, OF FORCING PEACE ON THE ASSHOLES...LIKE TRUSTWELL, FOR EXAMPLE.
HE NEEDS MONEY TO LOCK IT ALL DOWN. YOU KNOW WHAT LOYALTY COSTS, MAN. WHAT POWER COSTS. WHAT IT TAKES TO HOLD A NEIGHBORHOOD DOWN.
HE NEEDS THE GOLD, WILSON.
YOU NEVER THOUGHT TO ASK WHERE I GET THIS FRESH FOOD...YOU CAN'T EAT A BRICK OF GOLD, MATTY. THINK ABOUT THAT WHEN YOU WONDER WHY PARCO CAN'T HOLD HIS 'HOODS.

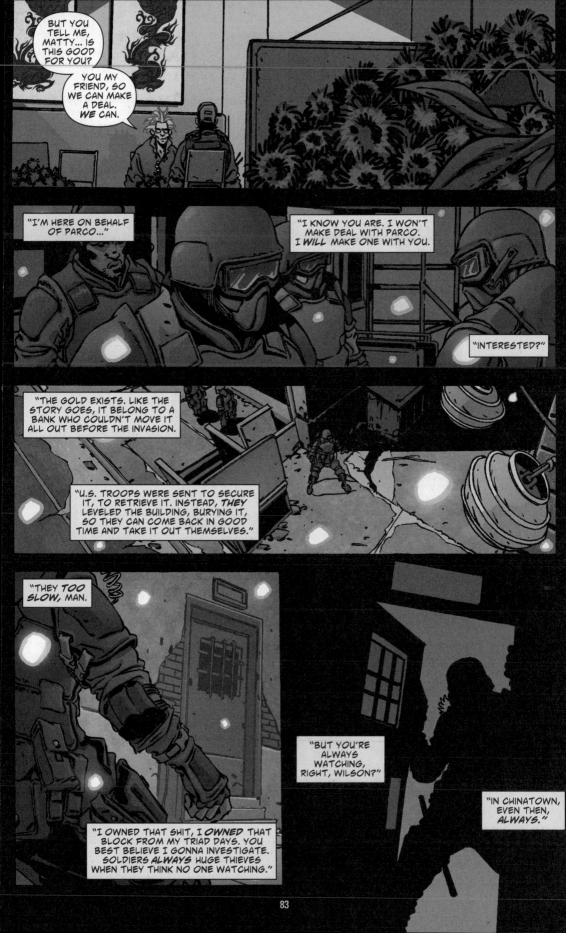

BUT YOU TELL ME, MATTY... IS THIS GOOD FOR YOU?

YOU MY FRIEND, SO WE CAN MAKE A DEAL. WE CAN.

"I'M HERE ON BEHALF OF PARCO..."

"I KNOW YOU ARE. I WON'T MAKE DEAL WITH PARCO. I WILL MAKE ONE WITH YOU.

"INTERESTED?"

"THE GOLD EXISTS. LIKE THE STORY GOES, IT BELONG TO A BANK WHO COULDN'T MOVE IT ALL OUT BEFORE THE INVASION.

"U.S. TROOPS WERE SENT TO SECURE IT, TO RETRIEVE IT. INSTEAD, THEY LEVELED THE BUILDING, BURYING IT, SO THEY CAN COME BACK IN GOOD TIME AND TAKE IT OUT THEMSELVES."

"THEY TOO SLOW, MAN.

"BUT YOU'RE ALWAYS WATCHING, RIGHT, WILSON?"

"IN CHINATOWN, EVEN THEN, ALWAYS."

"I OWNED THAT SHIT, I OWNED THAT BLOCK FROM MY TRIAD DAYS. YOU BEST BELIEVE I GONNA INVESTIGATE. SOLDIERS ALWAYS HUGE THIEVES WHEN THEY THINK NO ONE WATCHING."

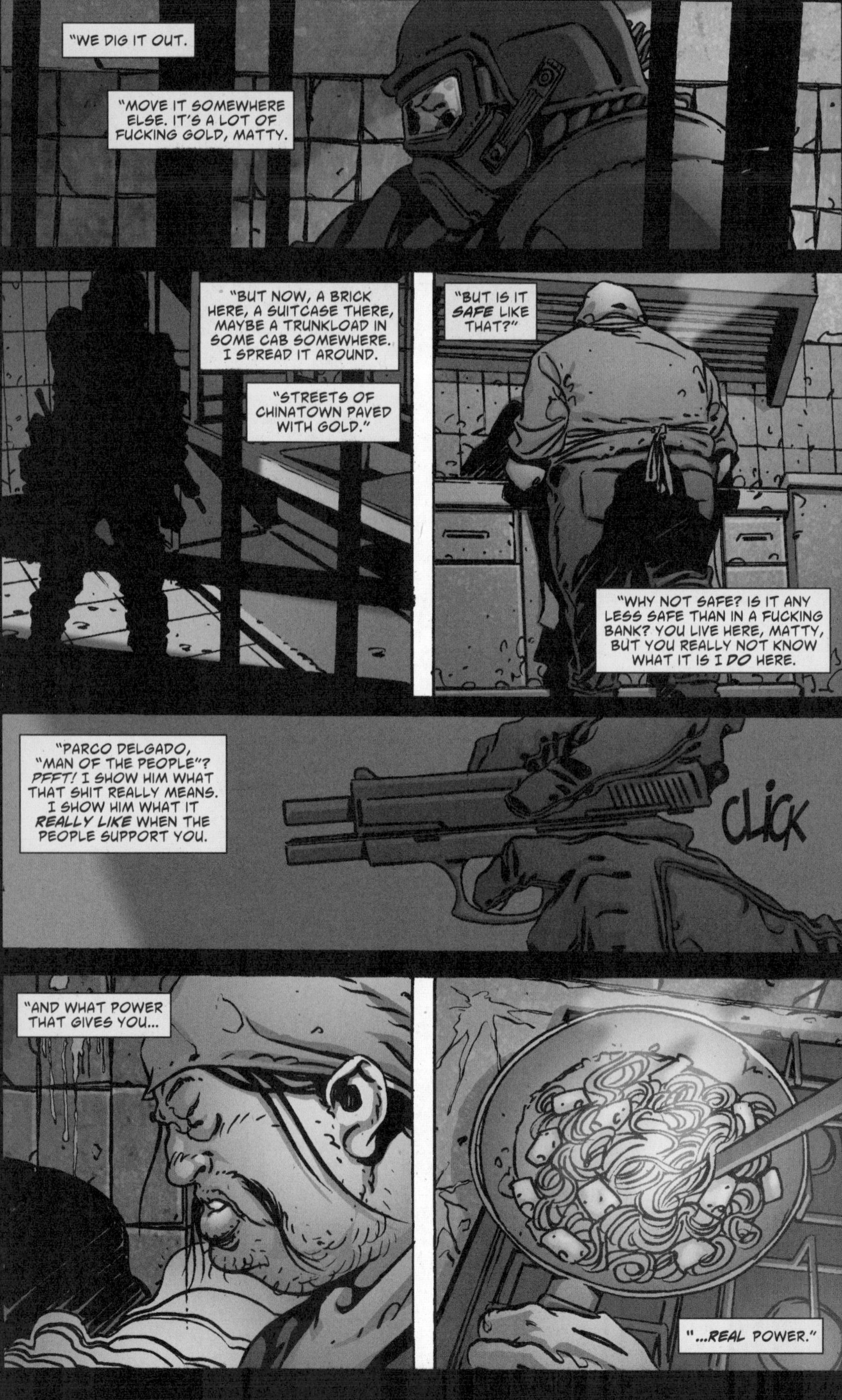
"WE DIG IT OUT.
"MOVE IT SOMEWHERE ELSE. IT'S A LOT OF FUCKING GOLD, MATTY.
"BUT NOW, A BRICK HERE, A SUITCASE THERE, MAYBE A TRUNKLOAD IN SOME CAB SOMEWHERE. I SPREAD IT AROUND.
"STREETS OF CHINATOWN PAVED WITH GOLD."
"BUT IS IT SAFE LIKE THAT?"
"WHY NOT SAFE? IS IT ANY LESS SAFE THAN IN A FUCKING BANK? YOU LIVE HERE, MATTY, BUT YOU REALLY NOT KNOW WHAT IT IS I DO HERE.
"PARCO DELGADO, "MAN OF THE PEOPLE"? PFFT! I SHOW HIM WHAT THAT SHIT REALLY MEANS. I SHOW HIM WHAT IT REALLY LIKE WHEN THE PEOPLE SUPPORT YOU.
CLICK
"AND WHAT POWER THAT GIVES YOU...
"...REAL POWER."

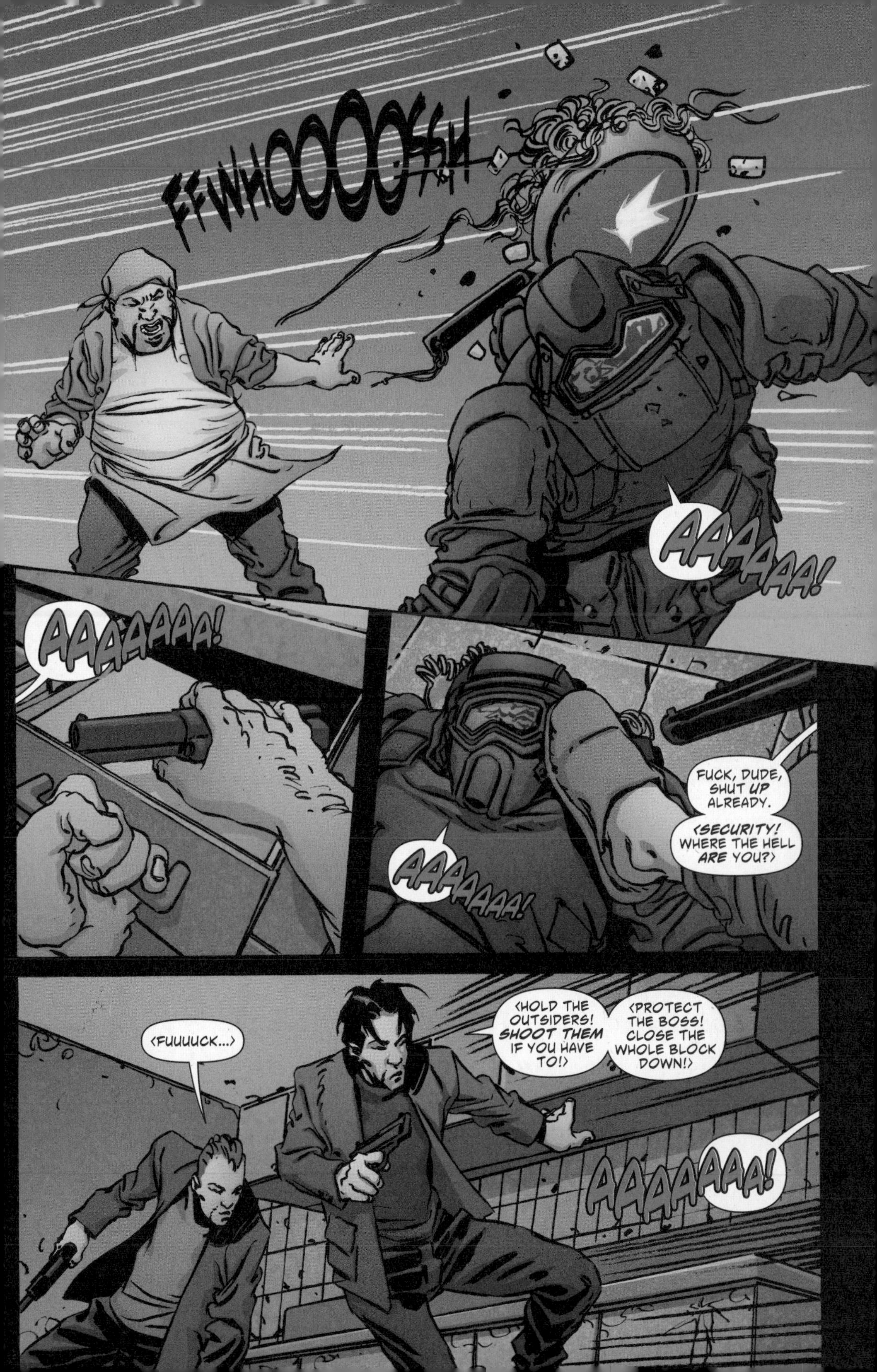
FFWHOOOOOSSH
AAAAAAA!
AAAAAAA!
AAAAAAA!
FUCK, DUDE, SHUT UP ALREADY.
‹SECURITY! WHERE THE HELL ARE YOU?›
‹FUUUUCK...›
‹HOLD THE OUTSIDERS! SHOOT THEM IF YOU HAVE TO!›
‹PROTECT THE BOSS! CLOSE THE WHOLE BLOCK DOWN!›
AAAAAAA!

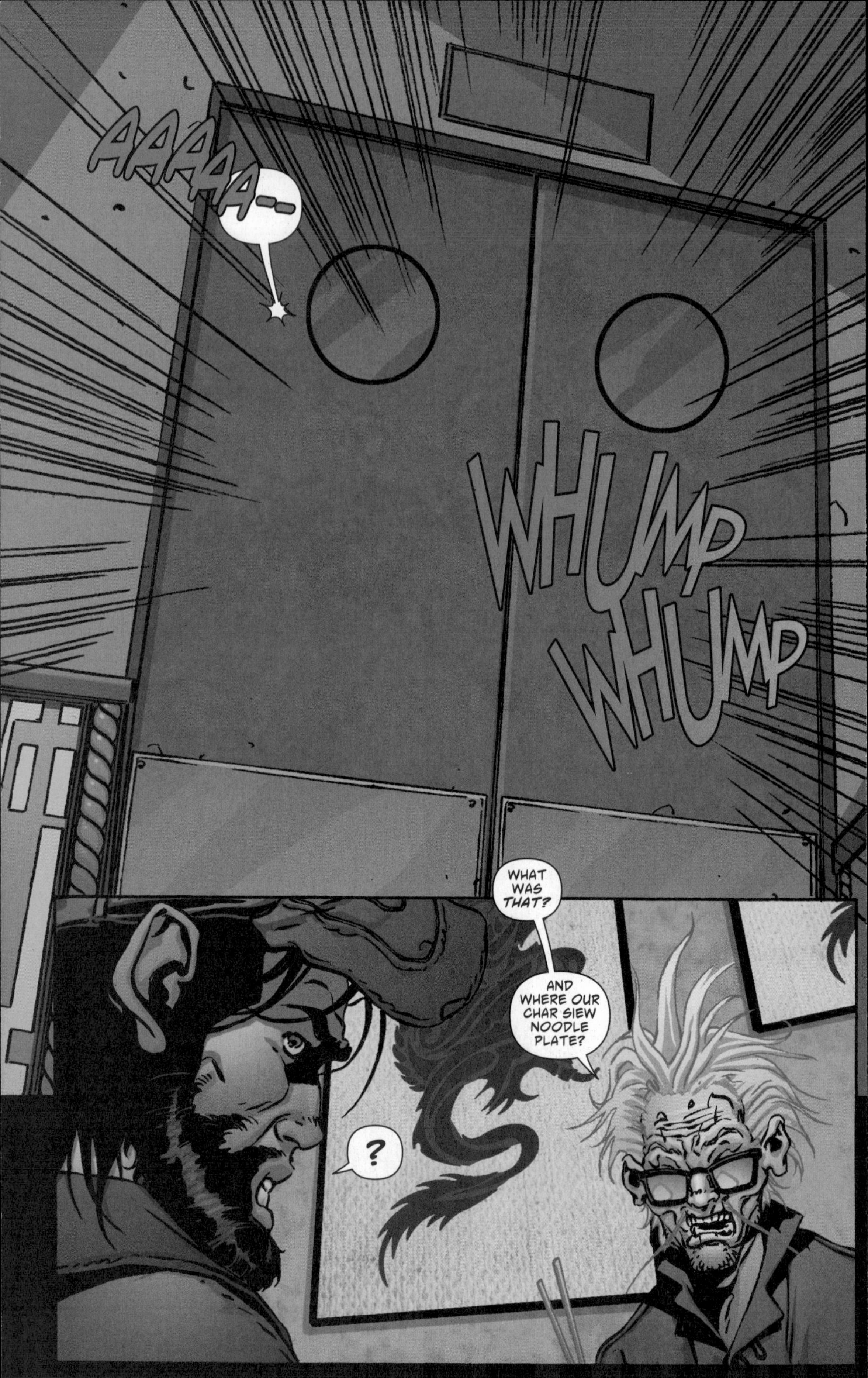
AAAAA--
WHUMP
WHUMP
WHAT WAS THAT?
AND WHERE OUR CHAR SIEW NOODLE PLATE?
?

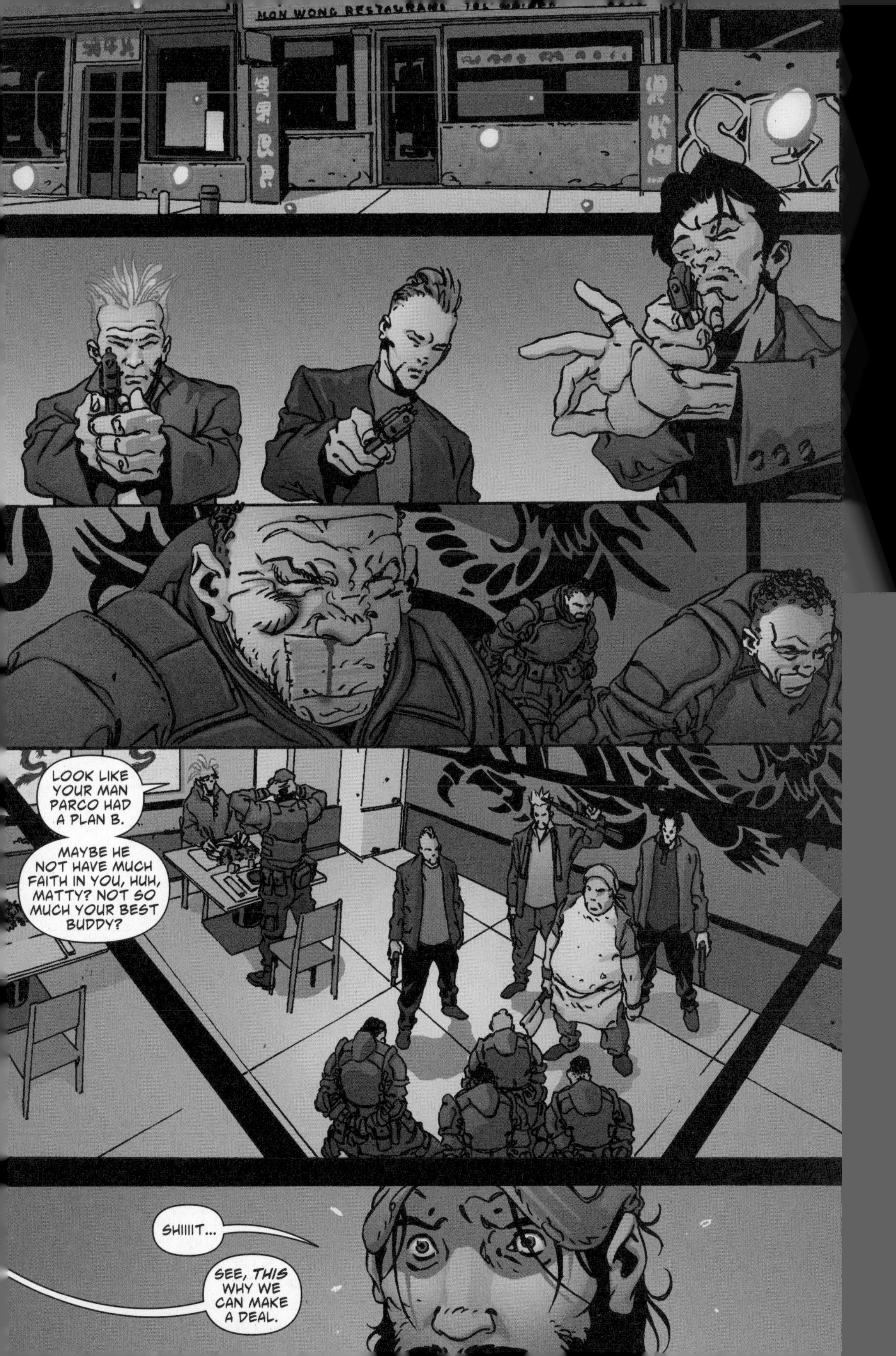
MON WONG RESTAURANT
LOOK LIKE YOUR MAN PARCO HAD A PLAN B.
MAYBE HE NOT HAVE MUCH FAITH IN YOU, HUH, MATTY? NOT SO MUCH YOUR BEST BUDDY?
SHIIIIT...
SEE, *THIS* WHY WE CAN MAKE A DEAL.

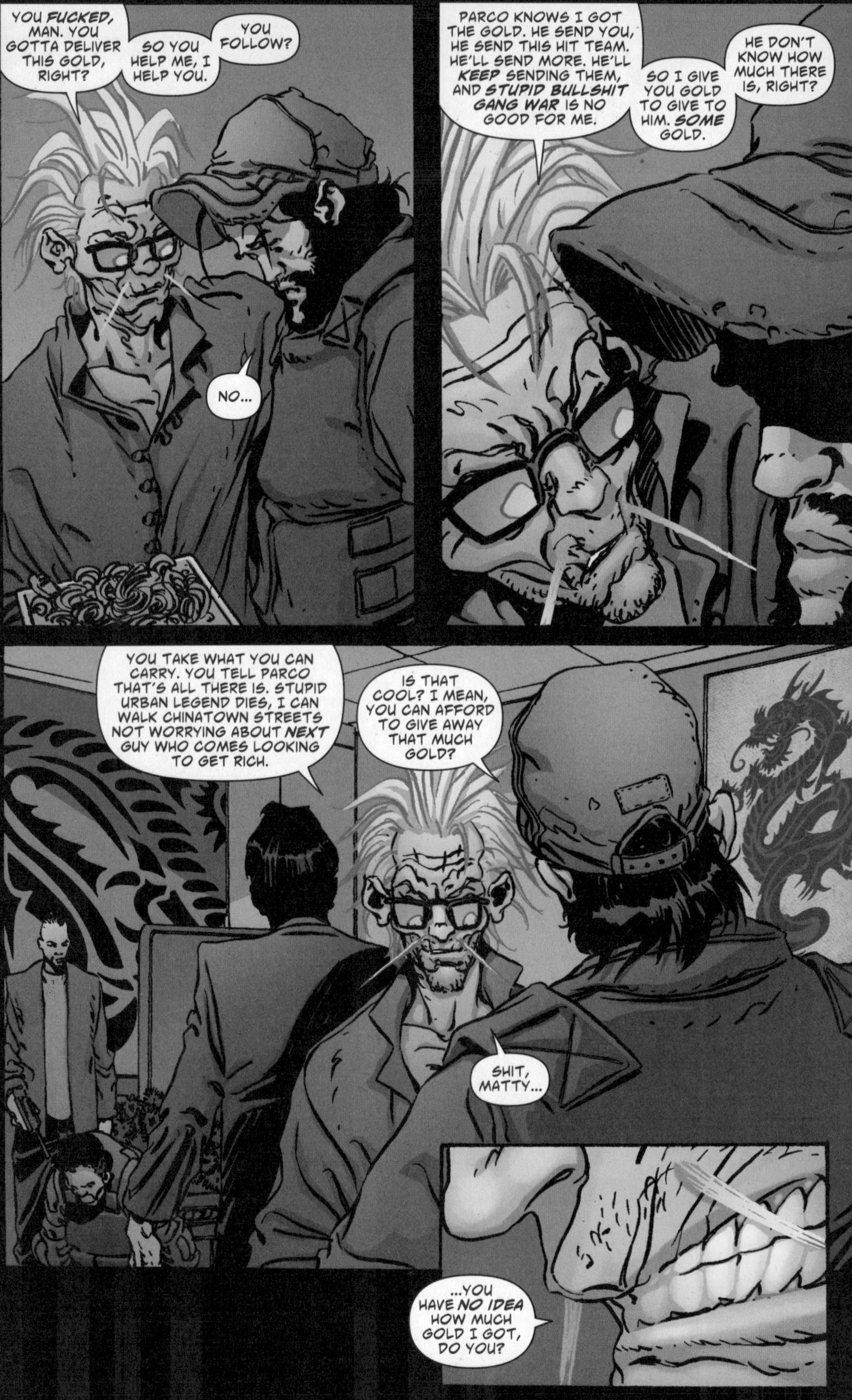

YOU *FUCKED*, MAN. YOU GOTTA DELIVER THIS GOLD, RIGHT?
SO YOU HELP ME, I HELP YOU.
YOU FOLLOW?
NO...
PARCO KNOWS I GOT THE GOLD. HE SEND YOU, HE SEND THIS HIT TEAM. HE'LL SEND MORE. HE'LL *KEEP* SENDING THEM, AND *STUPID BULLSHIT GANG WAR* IS NO GOOD FOR ME.
SO I GIVE YOU GOLD TO GIVE TO HIM. *SOME* GOLD.
HE DON'T KNOW HOW MUCH THERE IS, RIGHT?
YOU TAKE WHAT YOU CAN CARRY. YOU TELL PARCO THAT'S ALL THERE IS. STUPID URBAN LEGEND DIES, I CAN WALK CHINATOWN STREETS NOT WORRYING ABOUT *NEXT* GUY WHO COMES LOOKING TO GET RICH.
IS THAT COOL? I MEAN, YOU CAN AFFORD TO GIVE AWAY THAT MUCH GOLD?
SHIT, MATTY...
...YOU HAVE *NO IDEA* HOW MUCH GOLD I GOT, DO YOU?

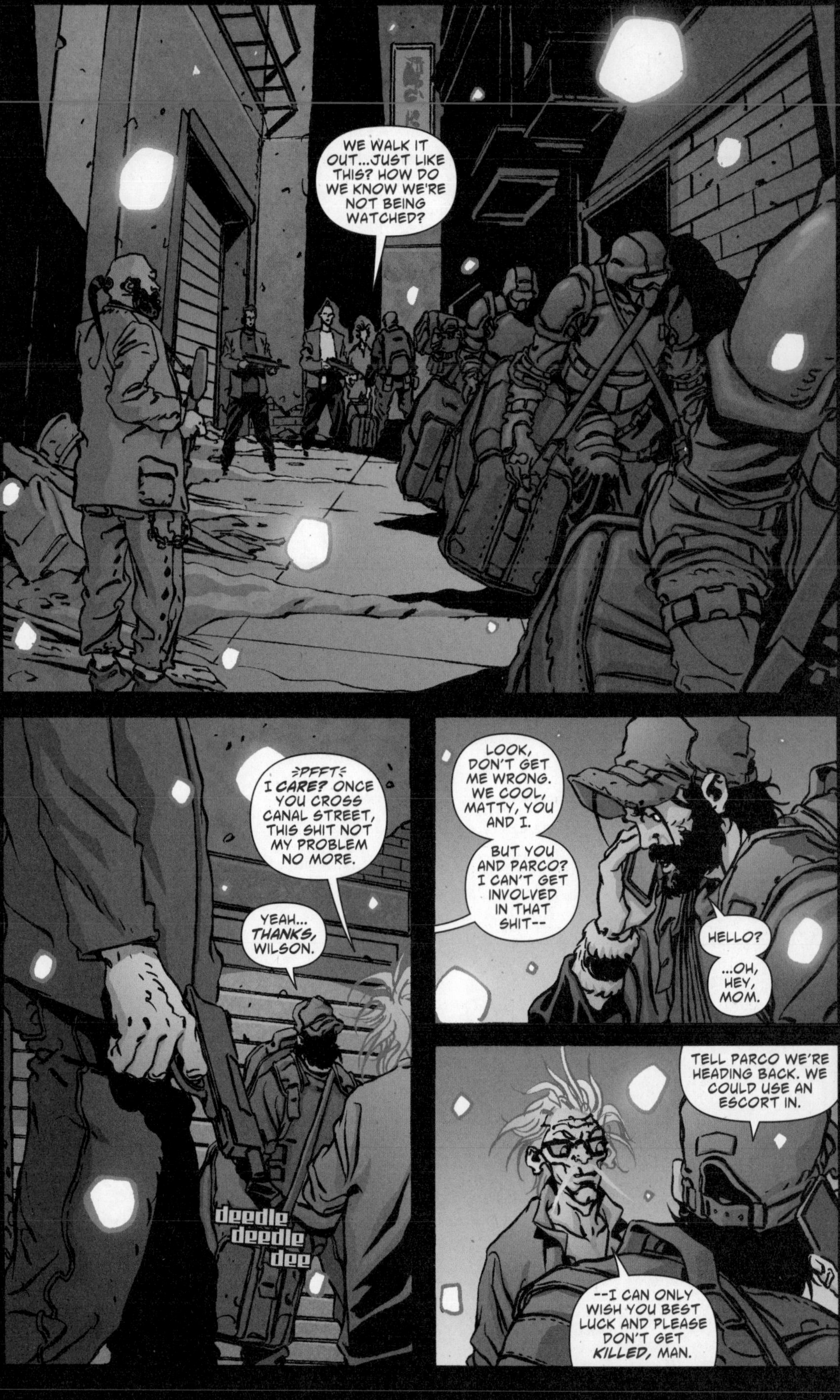
WE WALK IT OUT...JUST LIKE THIS? HOW DO WE KNOW WE'RE NOT BEING WATCHED?
PFFT I CARE? ONCE YOU CROSS CANAL STREET, THIS SHIT NOT MY PROBLEM NO MORE.
YEAH... THANKS, WILSON.
deedle deedle dee
LOOK, DON'T GET ME WRONG. WE COOL, MATTY, YOU AND I.
BUT YOU AND PARCO? I CAN'T GET INVOLVED IN THAT SHIT--
HELLO?
...OH, HEY, MOM.
TELL PARCO WE'RE HEADING BACK. WE COULD USE AN ESCORT IN.
--I CAN ONLY WISH YOU BEST LUCK AND PLEASE DON'T GET KILLED, MAN.

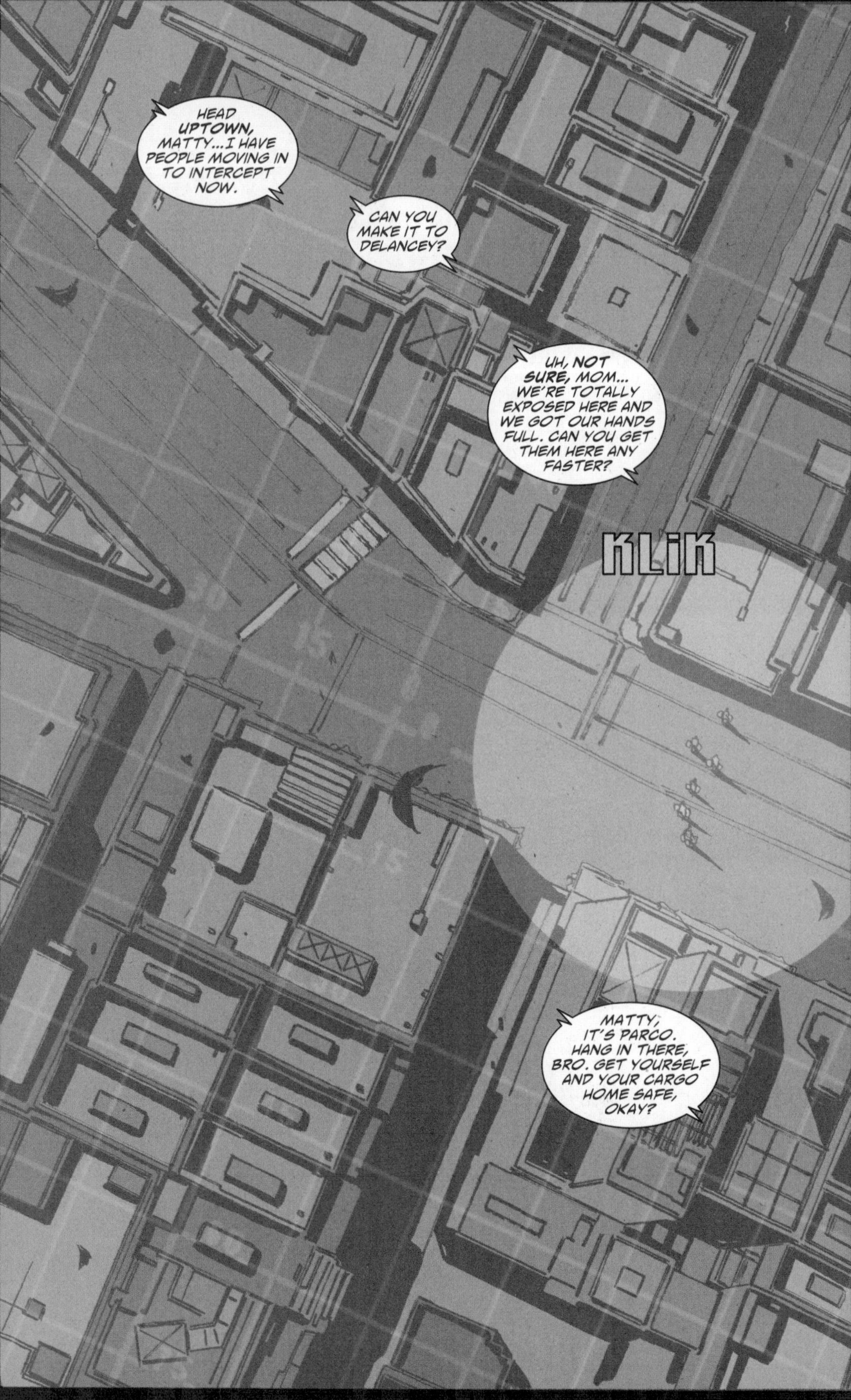
HEAD UPTOWN, MATTY...I HAVE PEOPLE MOVING IN TO INTERCEPT NOW.
CAN YOU MAKE IT TO DELANCEY?
UH, NOT SURE, MOM... WE'RE TOTALLY EXPOSED HERE AND WE GOT OUR HANDS FULL. CAN YOU GET THEM HERE ANY FASTER?
KLIK
MATTY, IT'S PARCO. HANG IN THERE, BRO. GET YOURSELF AND YOUR CARGO HOME SAFE, OKAY?

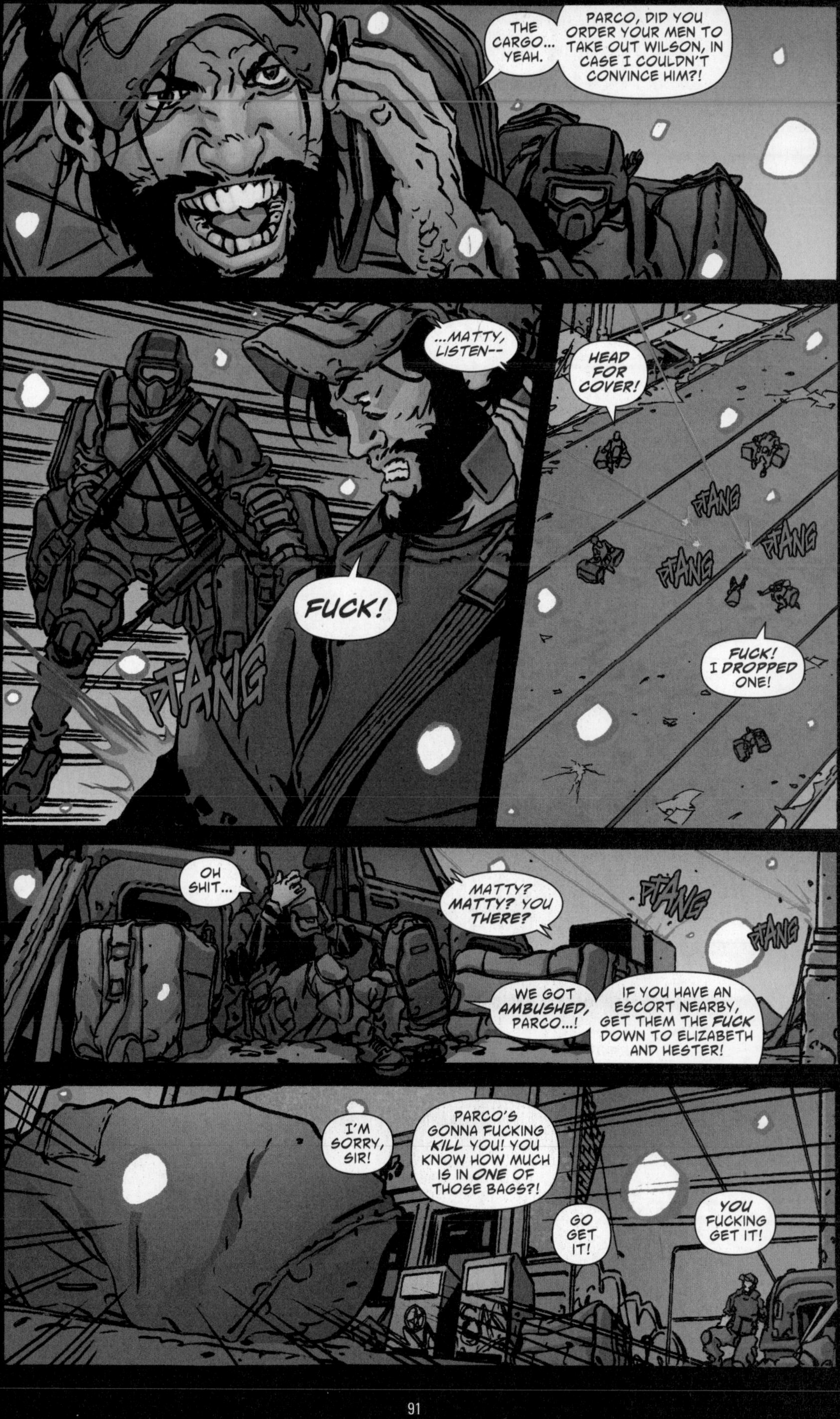
THE CARGO... YEAH.
PARCO, DID YOU ORDER YOUR MEN TO TAKE OUT WILSON, IN CASE I COULDN'T CONVINCE HIM?!
...MATTY, LISTEN--
FUCK!
PTANG
HEAD FOR COVER!
PTANG
PTANG
PTANG
FUCK! I DROPPED ONE!
OH SHIT...
MATTY? MATTY? YOU THERE?
PTANG
PTANG
WE GOT AMBUSHED, PARCO...!
IF YOU HAVE AN ESCORT NEARBY, GET THEM THE FUCK DOWN TO ELIZABETH AND HESTER!
I'M SORRY, SIR!
PARCO'S GONNA FUCKING KILL YOU! YOU KNOW HOW MUCH IS IN ONE OF THOSE BAGS?!
GO GET IT!
YOU FUCKING GET IT!

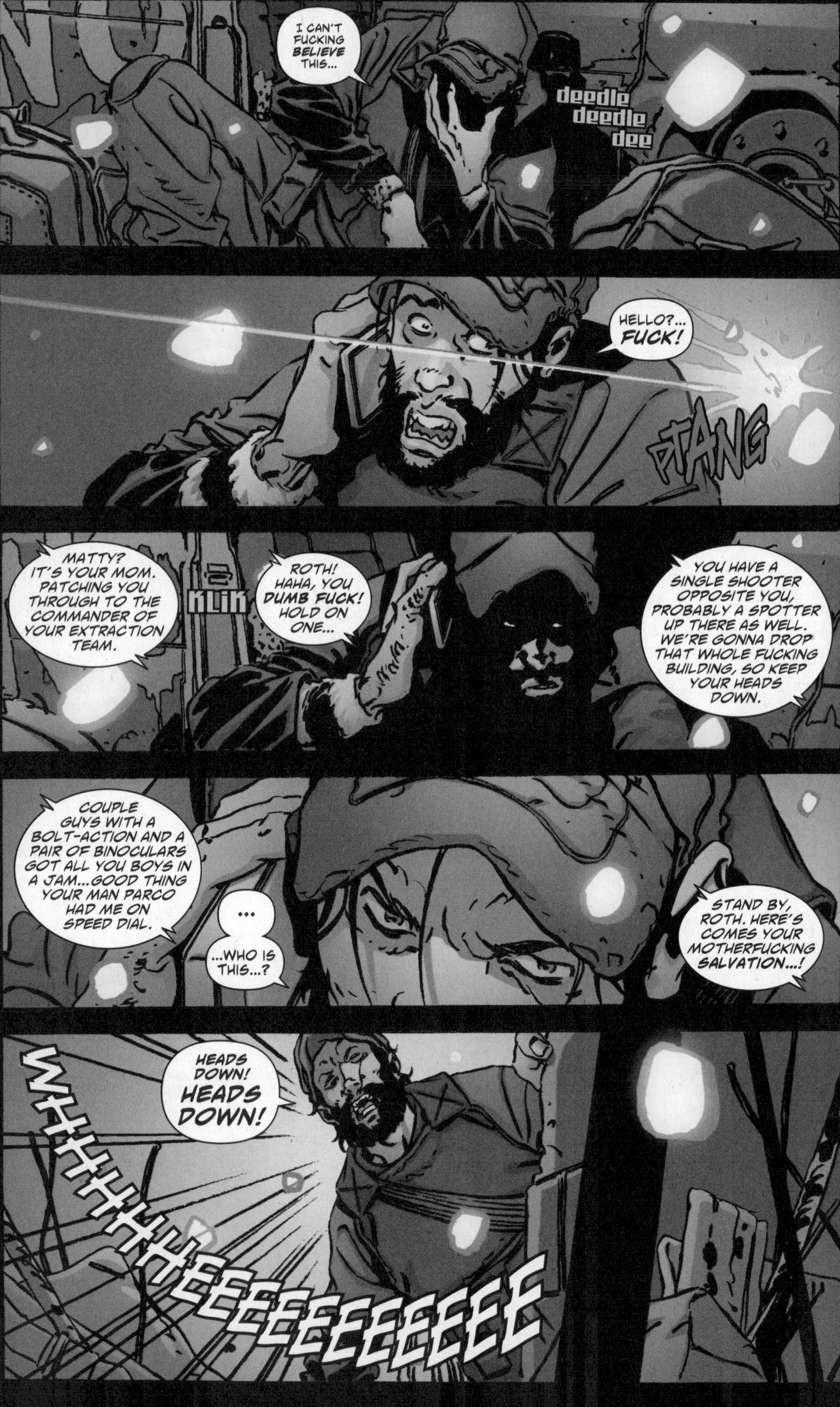
I CAN'T FUCKING BELIEVE THIS...
deedle deedle dee
HELLO?... FUCK!
PTANG
MATTY? IT'S YOUR MOM. PATCHING YOU THROUGH TO THE COMMANDER OF YOUR EXTRACTION TEAM.
KLIK
ROTH! HAHA, YOU DUMB FUCK! HOLD ON ONE...
YOU HAVE A SINGLE SHOOTER OPPOSITE YOU, PROBABLY A SPOTTER UP THERE AS WELL. WE'RE GONNA DROP THAT WHOLE FUCKING BUILDING, SO KEEP YOUR HEADS DOWN.
COUPLE GUYS WITH A BOLT-ACTION AND A PAIR OF BINOCULARS GOT ALL YOU BOYS IN A JAM...GOOD THING YOUR MAN PARCO HAD ME ON SPEED DIAL.
...
...WHO IS THIS...?
STAND BY, ROTH. HERE'S COMES YOUR MOTHERFUCKING SALVATION...!
HEADS DOWN! HEADS DOWN!
WHHHHHHEEEEEEEEEEEEEE

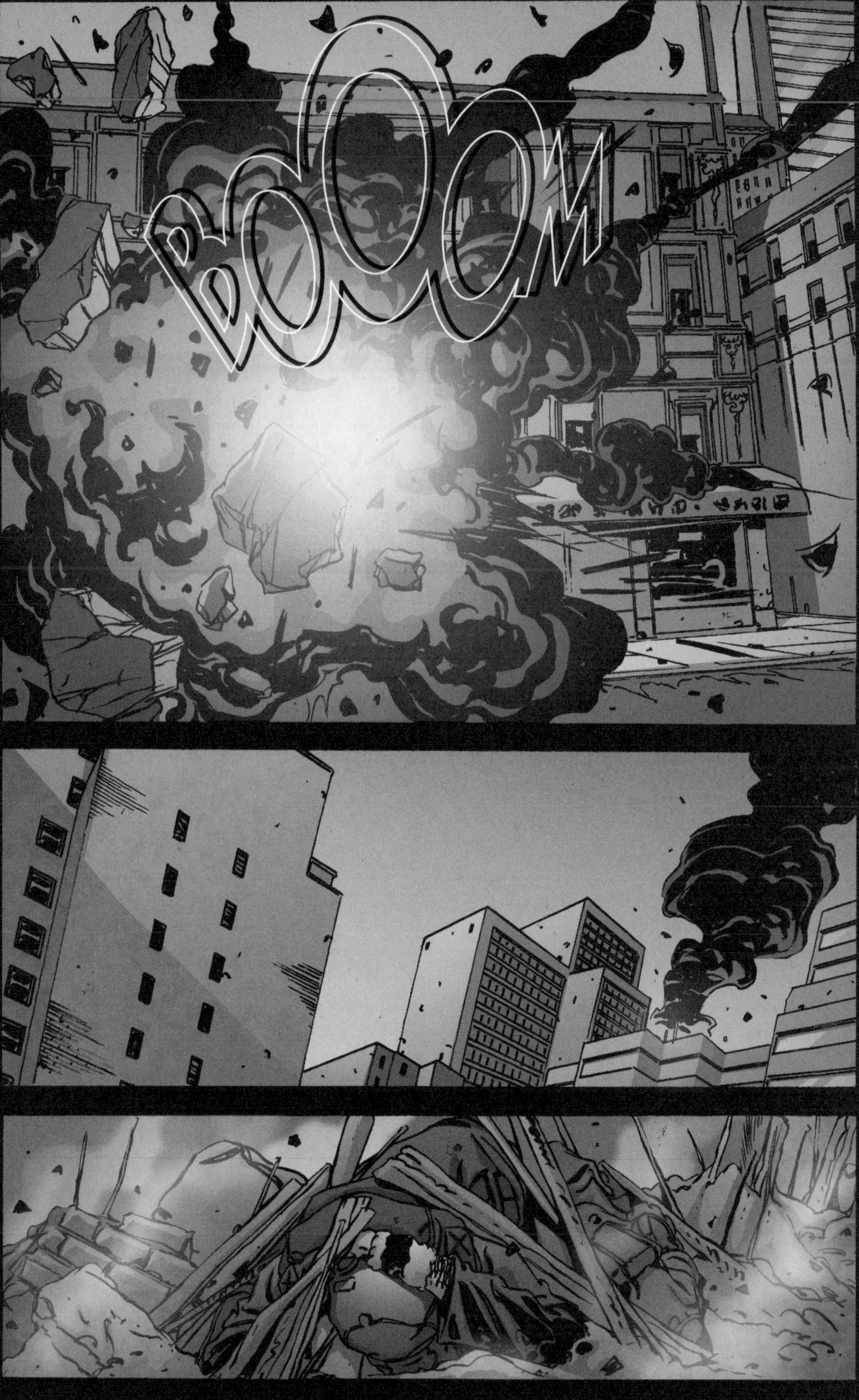
BOOOM

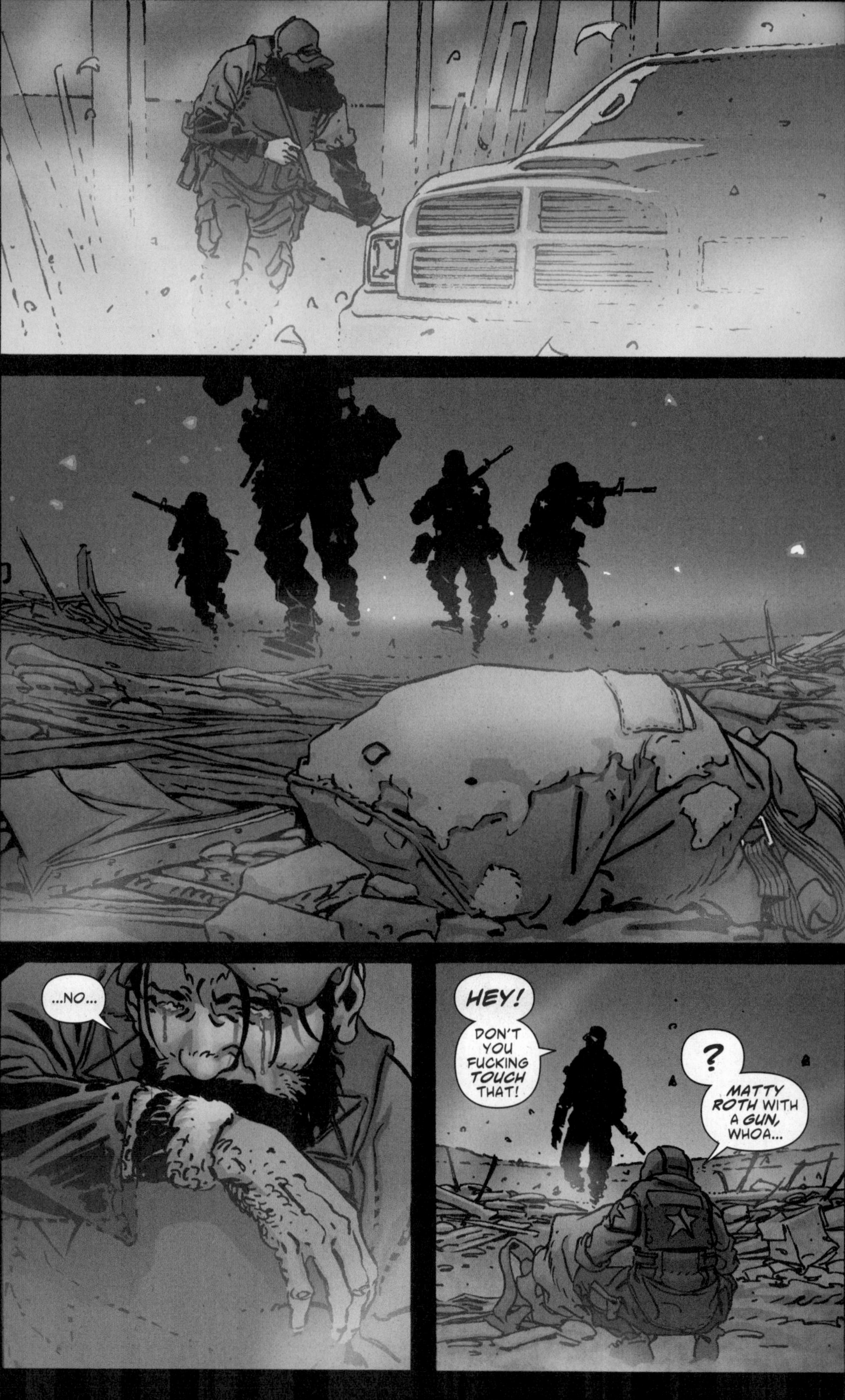
...NO...
HEY!
DON'T YOU FUCKING TOUCH THAT!
?
MATTY ROTH WITH A GUN, WHOA...

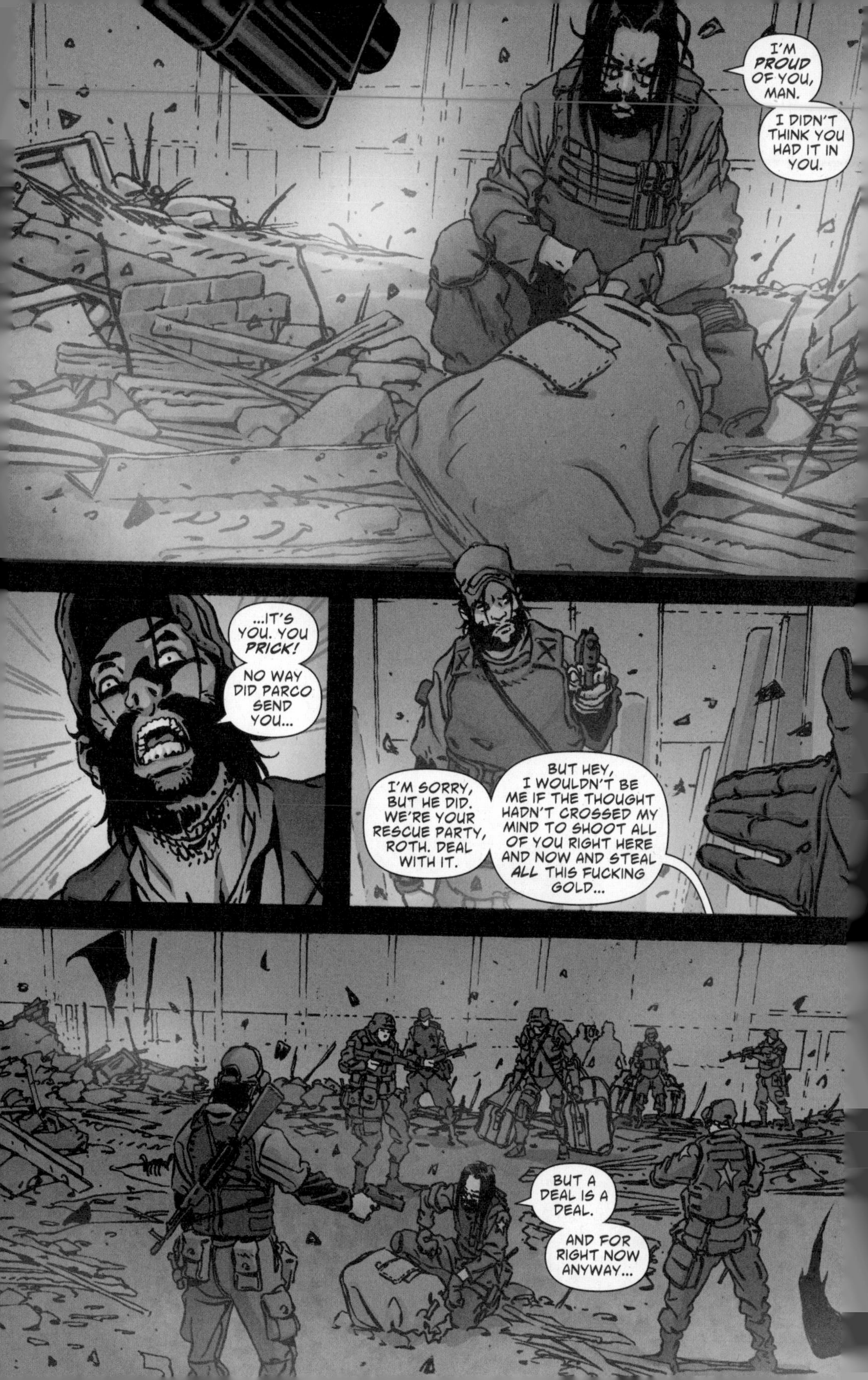
I'M PROUD OF YOU, MAN.
I DIDN'T THINK YOU HAD IT IN YOU.
...IT'S YOU. YOU PRICK!
NO WAY DID PARCO SEND YOU...
I'M SORRY, BUT HE DID. WE'RE YOUR RESCUE PARTY, ROTH. DEAL WITH IT.
BUT HEY, I WOULDN'T BE ME IF THE THOUGHT HADN'T CROSSED MY MIND TO SHOOT ALL OF YOU RIGHT HERE AND NOW AND STEAL ALL THIS FUCKING GOLD...
BUT A DEAL IS A DEAL.
AND FOR RIGHT NOW ANYWAY...

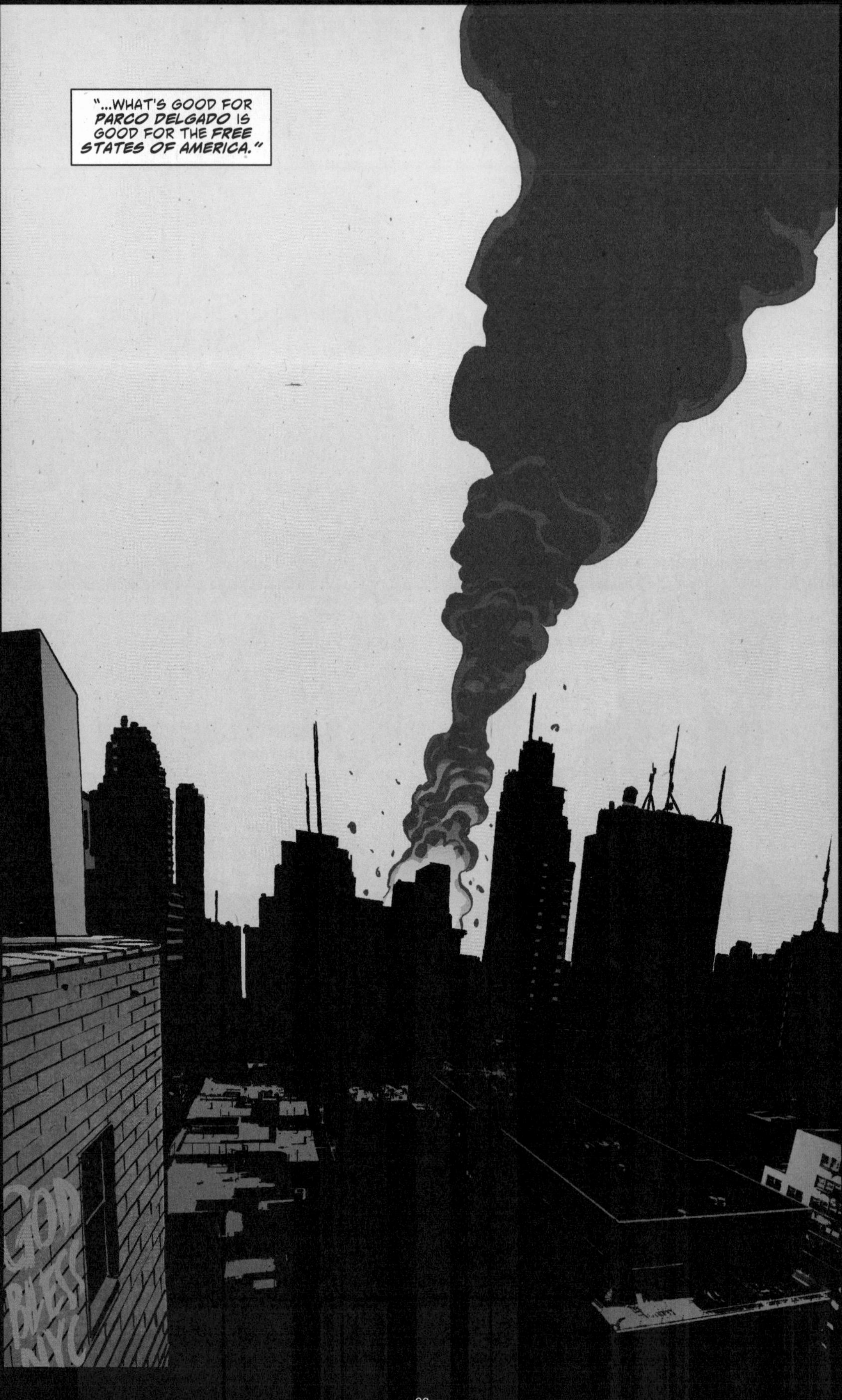
"...WHAT'S GOOD FOR PARCO DELGADO IS GOOD FOR THE FREE STATES OF AMERICA."
GOD BLESS NYC

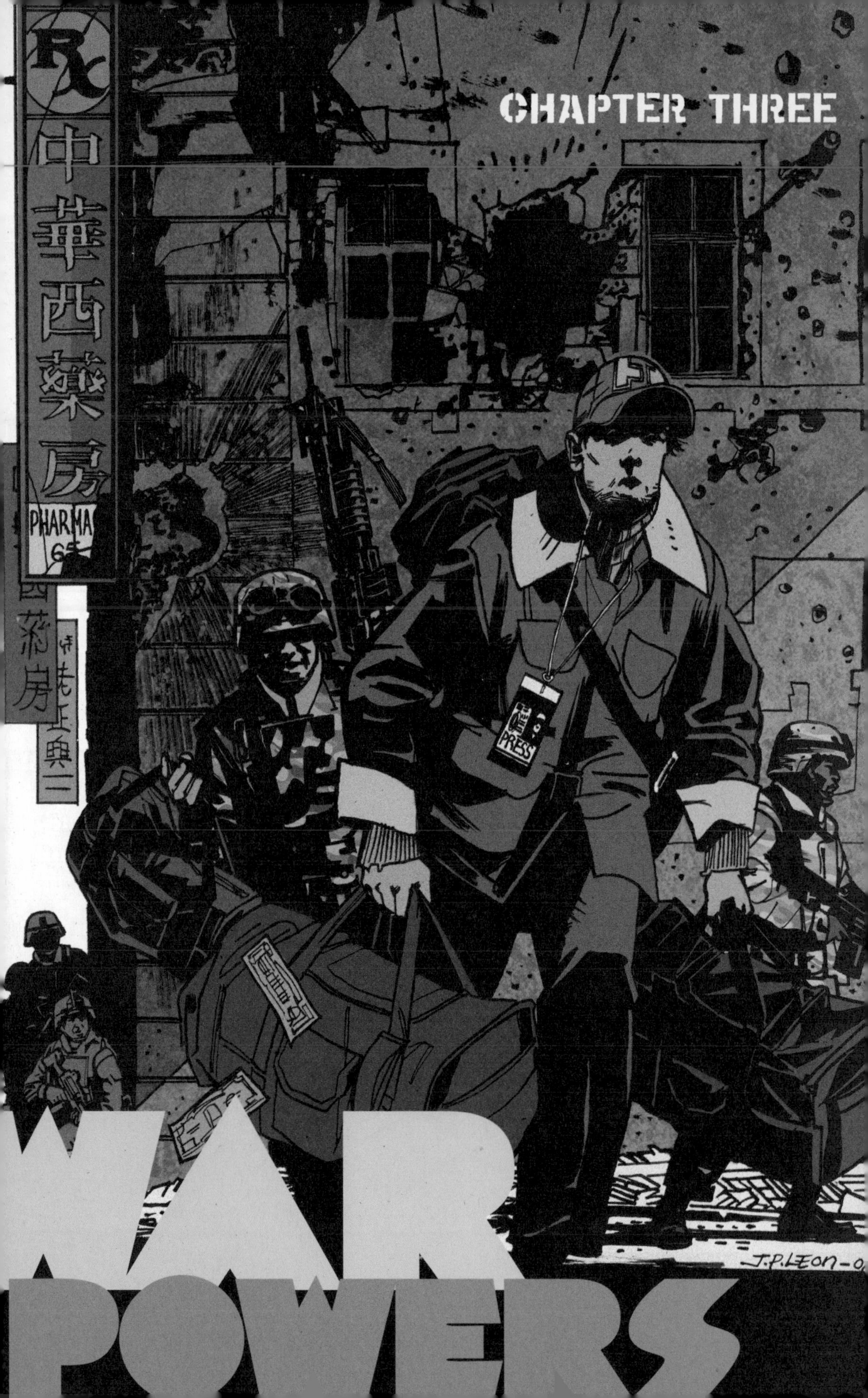
CHAPTER THREE
中華西藥房
PHARMA
PRESS
J.P.LEON
WAR
POWERS

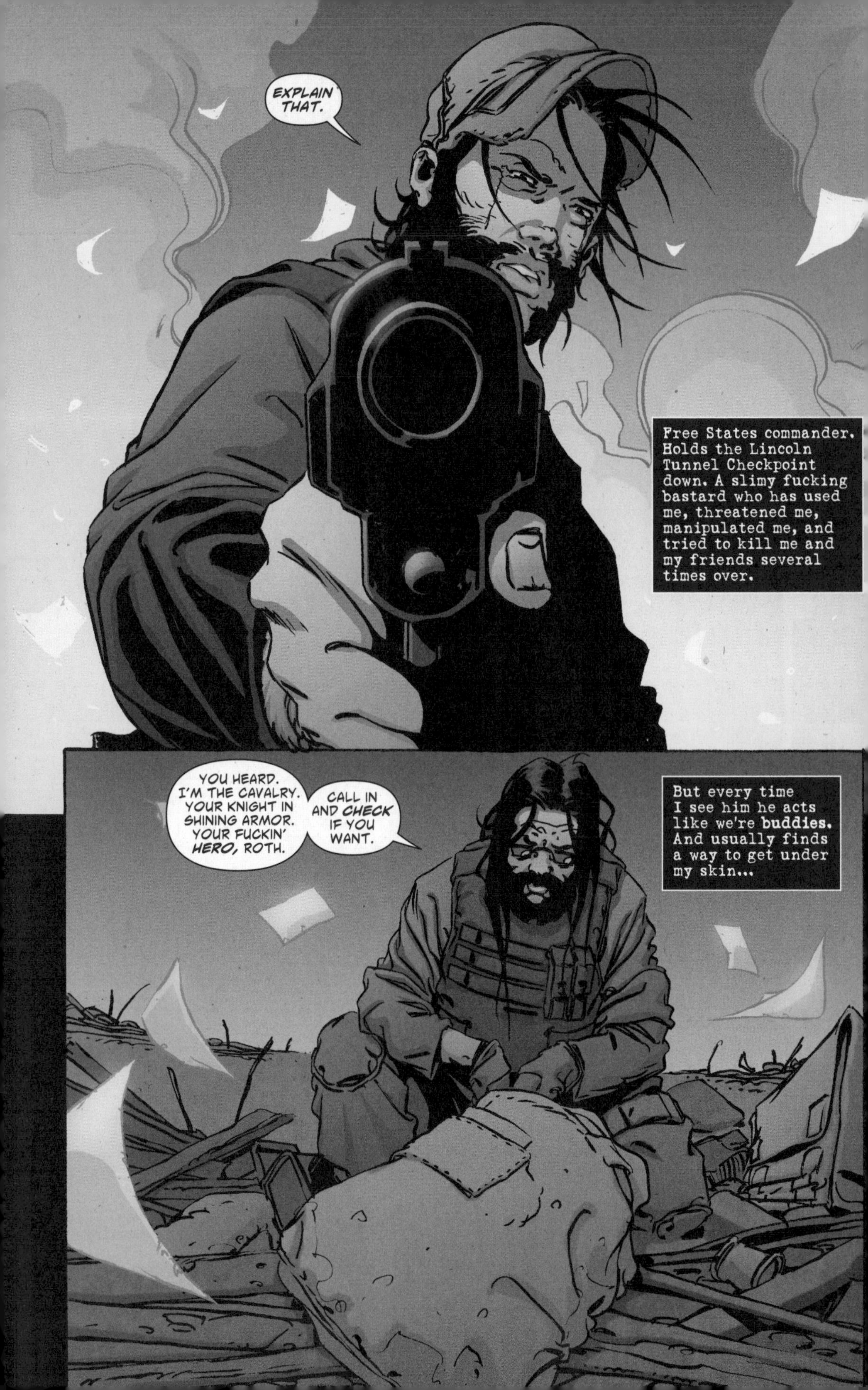
EXPLAIN THAT.
Free States commander. Holds the Lincoln Tunnel Checkpoint down. A slimy fucking bastard who has used me, threatened me, manipulated me, and tried to kill me and my friends several times over.
YOU HEARD. I'M THE CAVALRY. YOUR KNIGHT IN SHINING ARMOR. YOUR FUCKIN' HERO, ROTH.
CALL IN AND CHECK IF YOU WANT.
But every time I see him he acts like we're buddies. And usually finds a way to get under my skin...

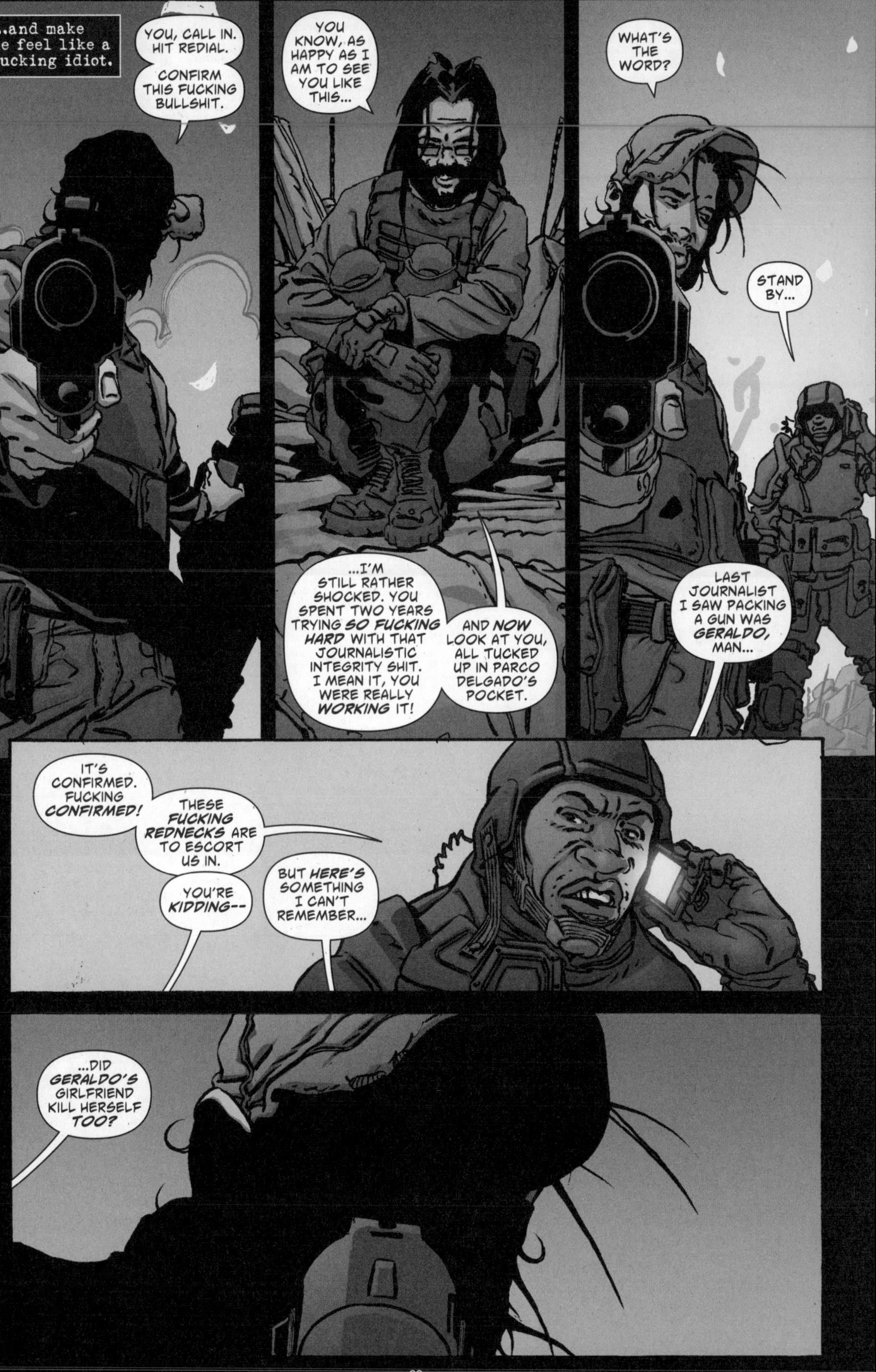

...and make me feel like a fucking idiot.
YOU, CALL IN. HIT REDIAL.
CONFIRM THIS FUCKING BULLSHIT.
YOU KNOW, AS HAPPY AS I AM TO SEE YOU LIKE THIS...
...I'M STILL RATHER SHOCKED. YOU SPENT TWO YEARS TRYING SO FUCKING HARD WITH THAT JOURNALISTIC INTEGRITY SHIT. I MEAN IT, YOU WERE REALLY WORKING IT!
AND NOW LOOK AT YOU, ALL TUCKED UP IN PARCO DELGADO'S POCKET.
WHAT'S THE WORD?
STAND BY...
LAST JOURNALIST I SAW PACKING A GUN WAS GERALDO, MAN...
IT'S CONFIRMED. FUCKING CONFIRMED!
THESE FUCKING REDNECKS ARE TO ESCORT US IN.
YOU'RE KIDDING--
BUT HERE'S SOMETHING I CAN'T REMEMBER...
...DID GERALDO'S GIRLFRIEND KILL HERSELF TOO?

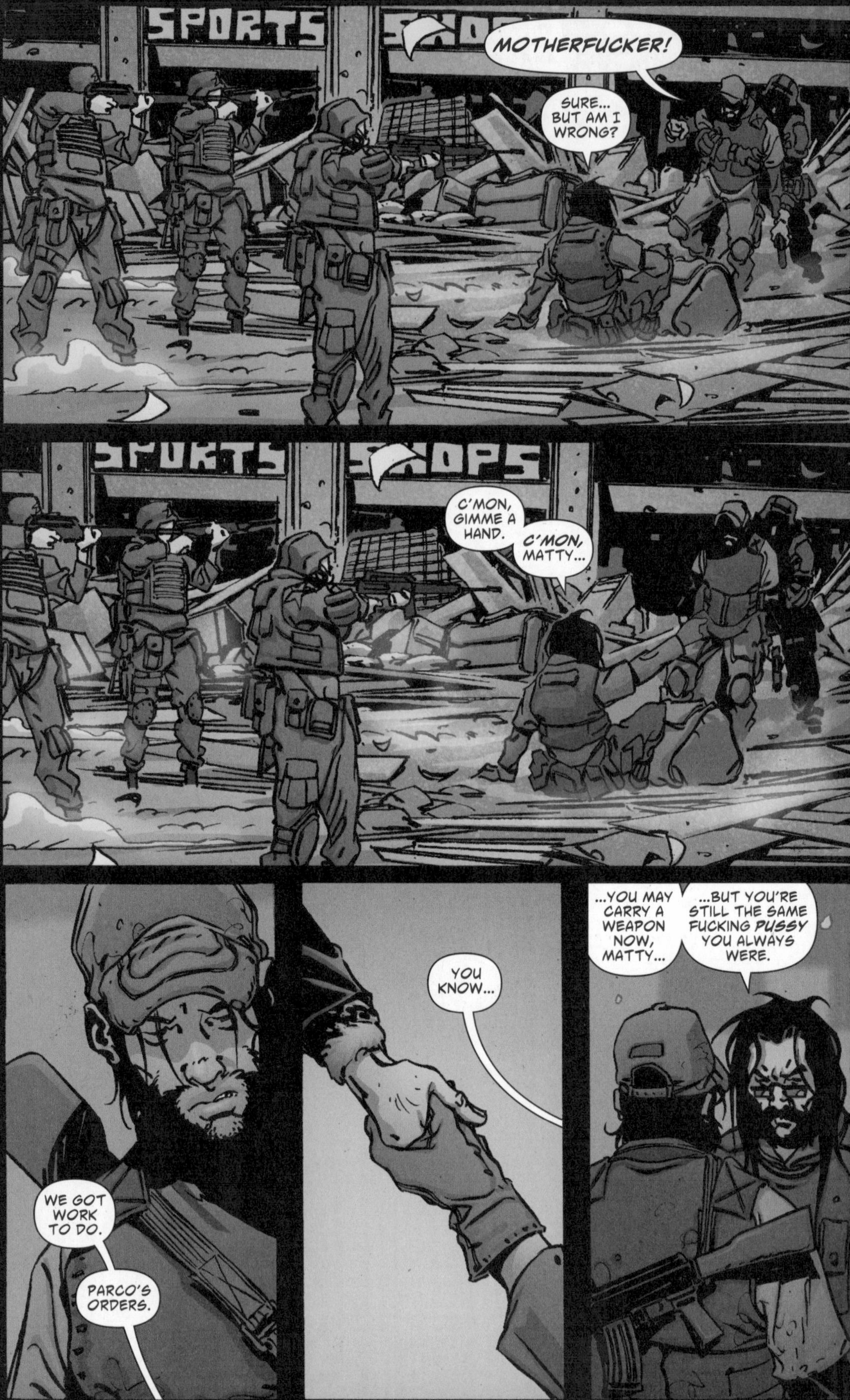
MOTHERFUCKER!
SURE... BUT AM I WRONG?
SPORTS
SPORTS SHOPS
C'MON, GIMME A HAND.
C'MON, MATTY...
WE GOT WORK TO DO.
PARCO'S ORDERS.
YOU KNOW...
...YOU MAY CARRY A WEAPON NOW, MATTY...
...BUT YOU'RE STILL THE SAME FUCKING PUSSY YOU ALWAYS WERE.

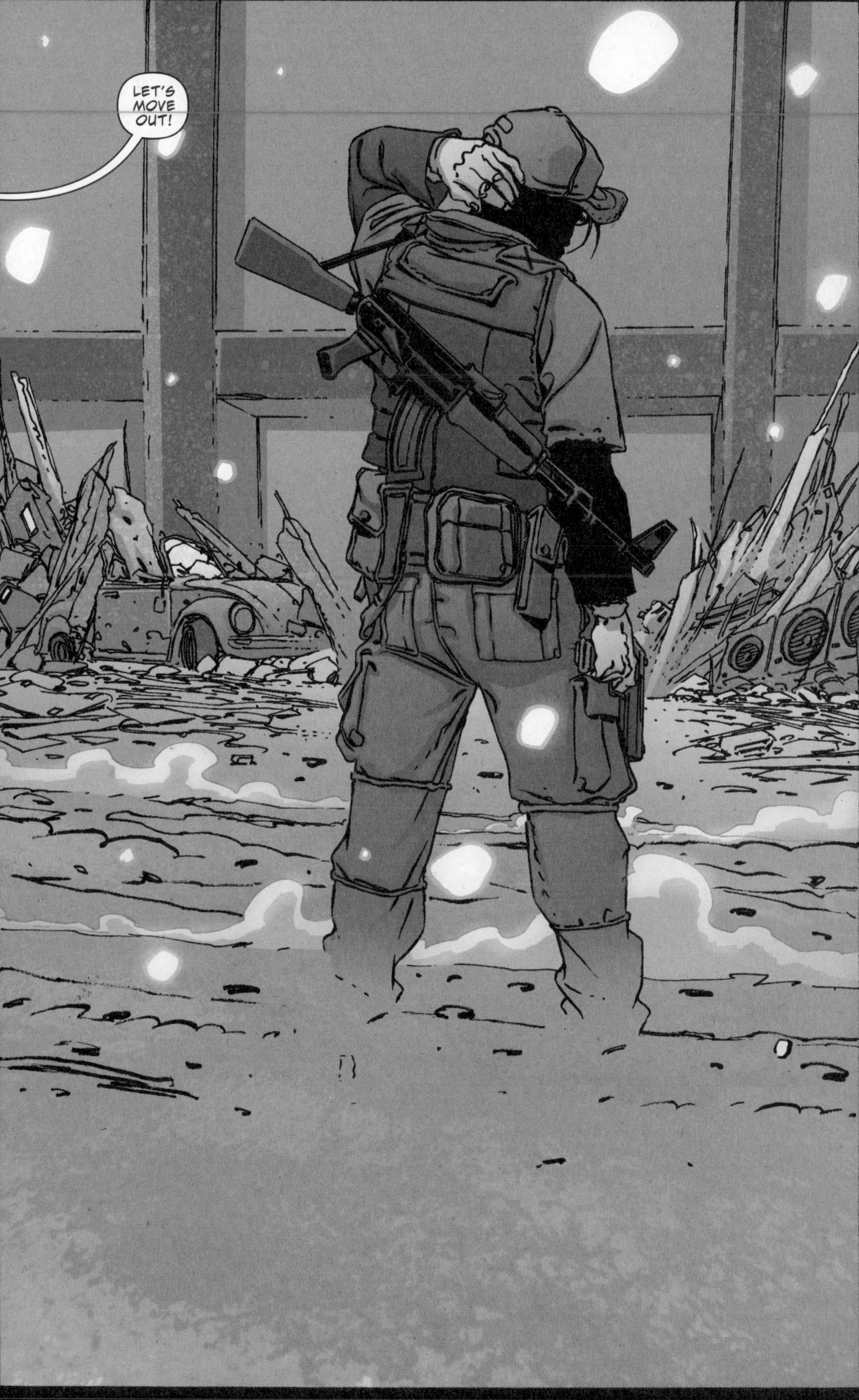
LET'S MOVE OUT!

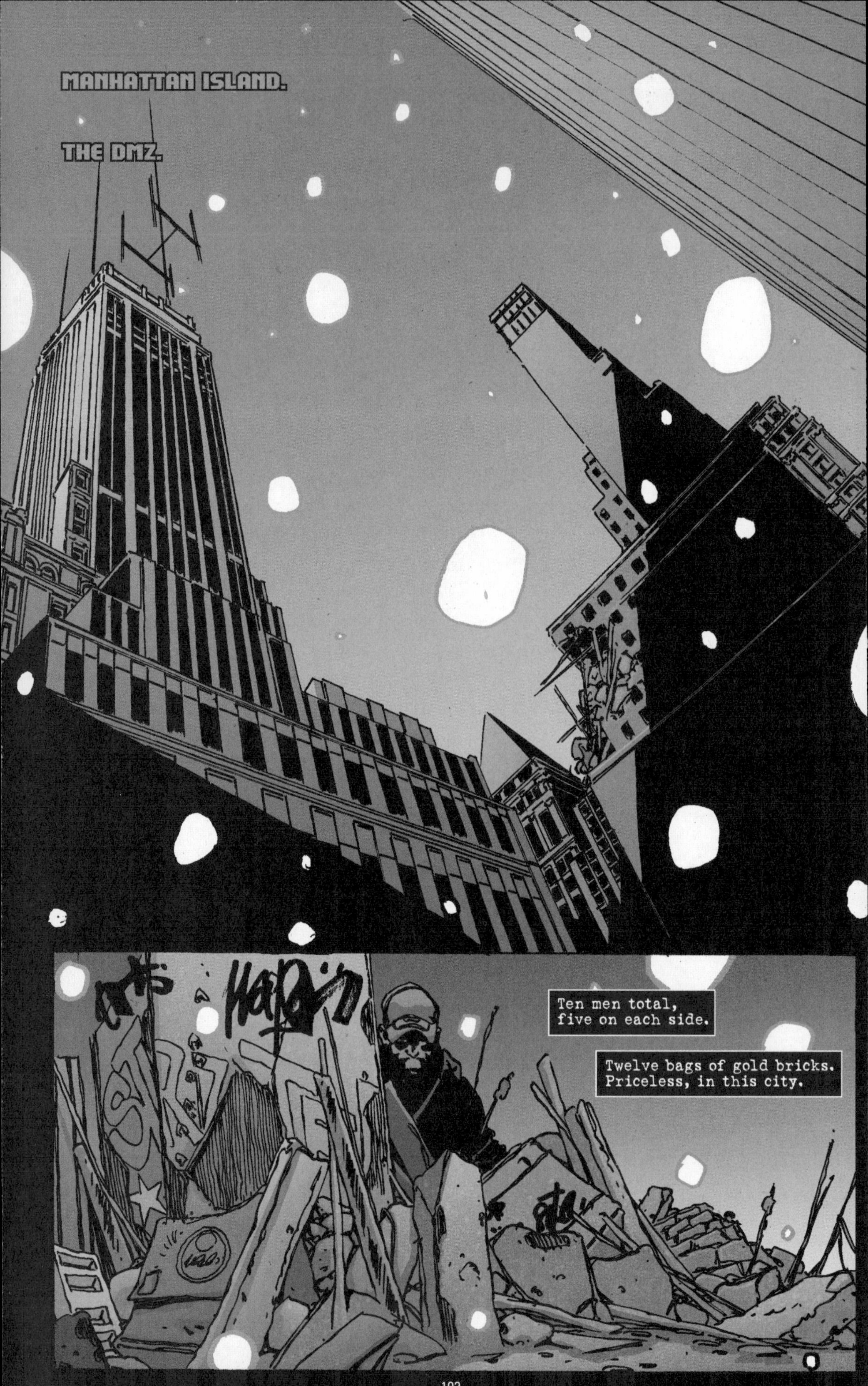
MANHATTAN ISLAND.
THE DMZ.
Ten men total, five on each side.
Twelve bags of gold bricks. Priceless, in this city.

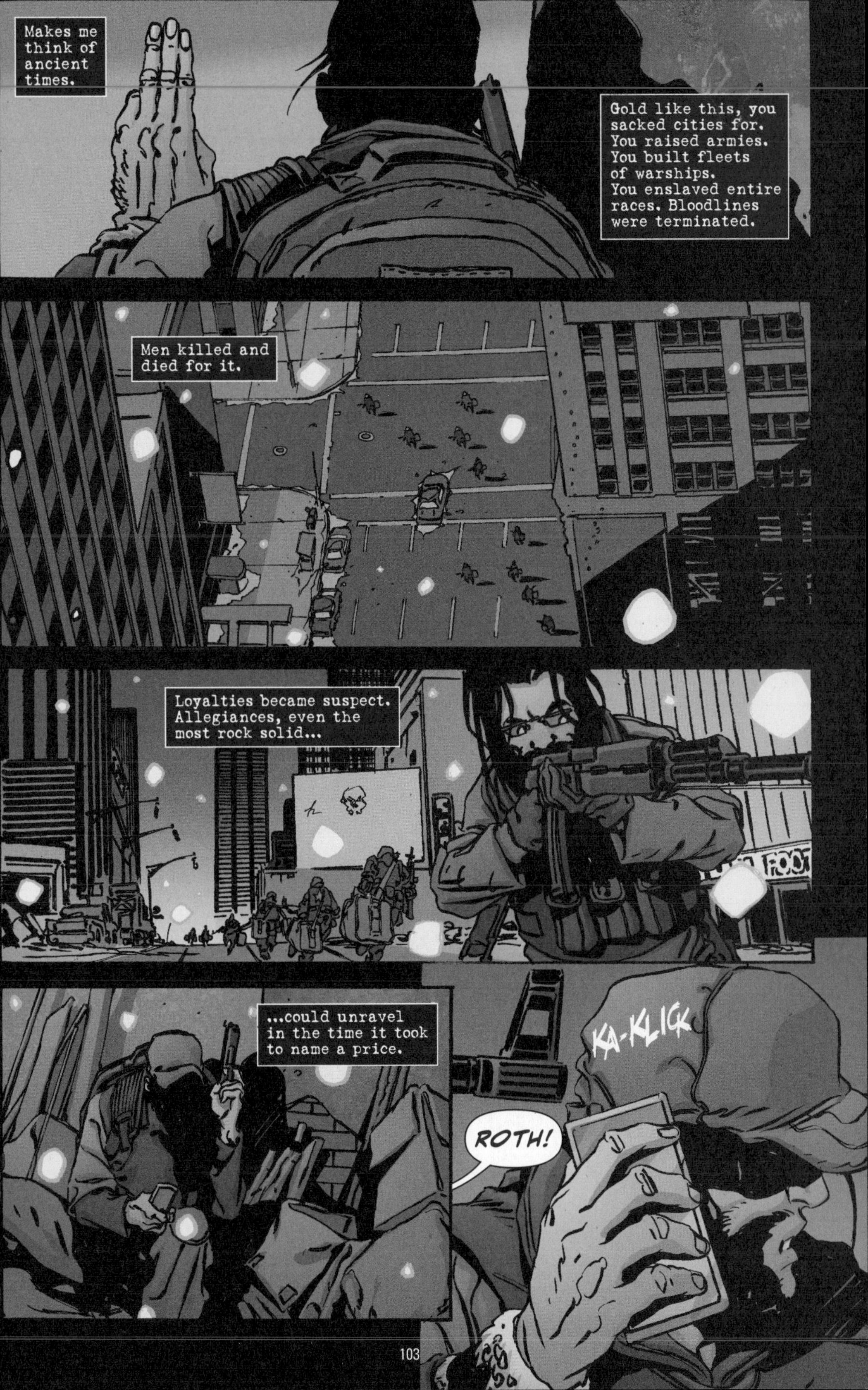
Makes me think of ancient times.
Gold like this, you sacked cities for. You raised armies. You built fleets of warships. You enslaved entire races. Bloodlines were terminated.
Men killed and died for it.
Loyalties became suspect. Allegiances, even the most rock solid...
...could unravel in the time it took to name a price.
KA-KLICK
ROTH!

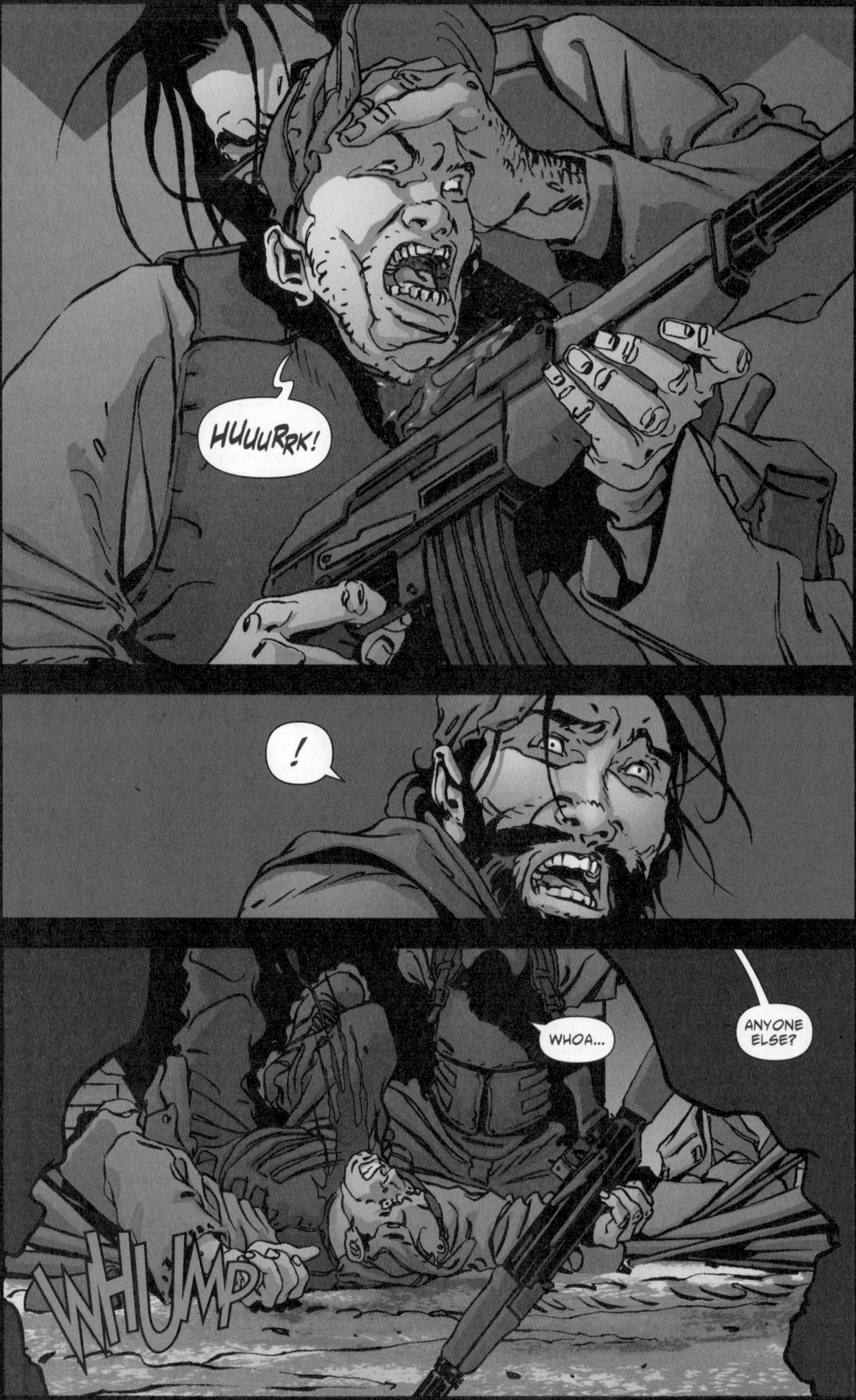
HUUURRK!
!
WHOA...
ANYONE ELSE?
WHUMP

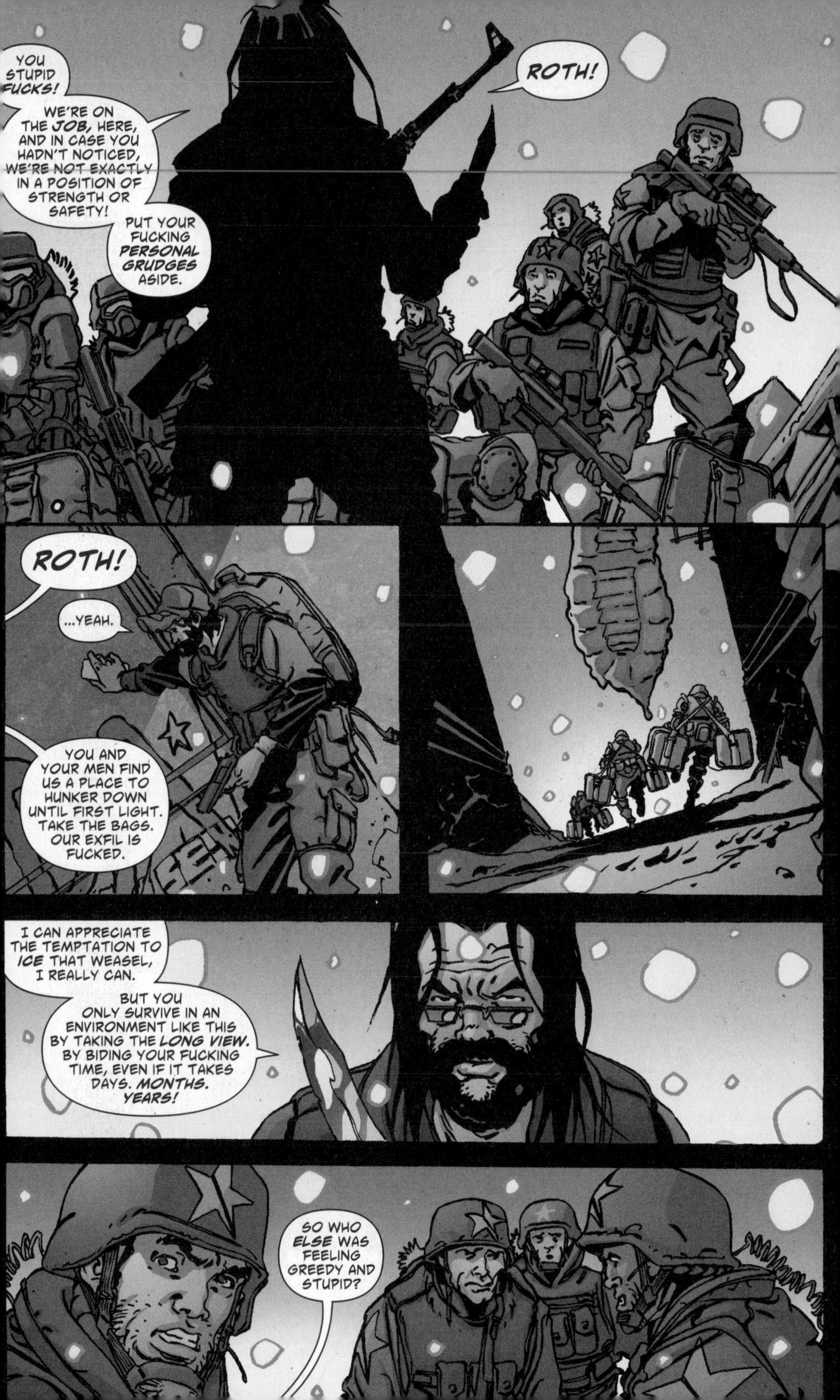
YOU STUPID FUCKS!
WE'RE ON THE JOB, HERE, AND IN CASE YOU HADN'T NOTICED, WE'RE NOT EXACTLY IN A POSITION OF STRENGTH OR SAFETY!
PUT YOUR FUCKING PERSONAL GRUDGES ASIDE.
ROTH!
ROTH!
...YEAH.
YOU AND YOUR MEN FIND US A PLACE TO HUNKER DOWN UNTIL FIRST LIGHT. TAKE THE BAGS. OUR EXFIL IS FUCKED.
I CAN APPRECIATE THE TEMPTATION TO ICE THAT WEASEL, I REALLY CAN.
BUT YOU ONLY SURVIVE IN AN ENVIRONMENT LIKE THIS BY TAKING THE LONG VIEW. BY BIDING YOUR FUCKING TIME, EVEN IF IT TAKES DAYS. MONTHS. YEARS!
SO WHO ELSE WAS FEELING GREEDY AND STUPID?

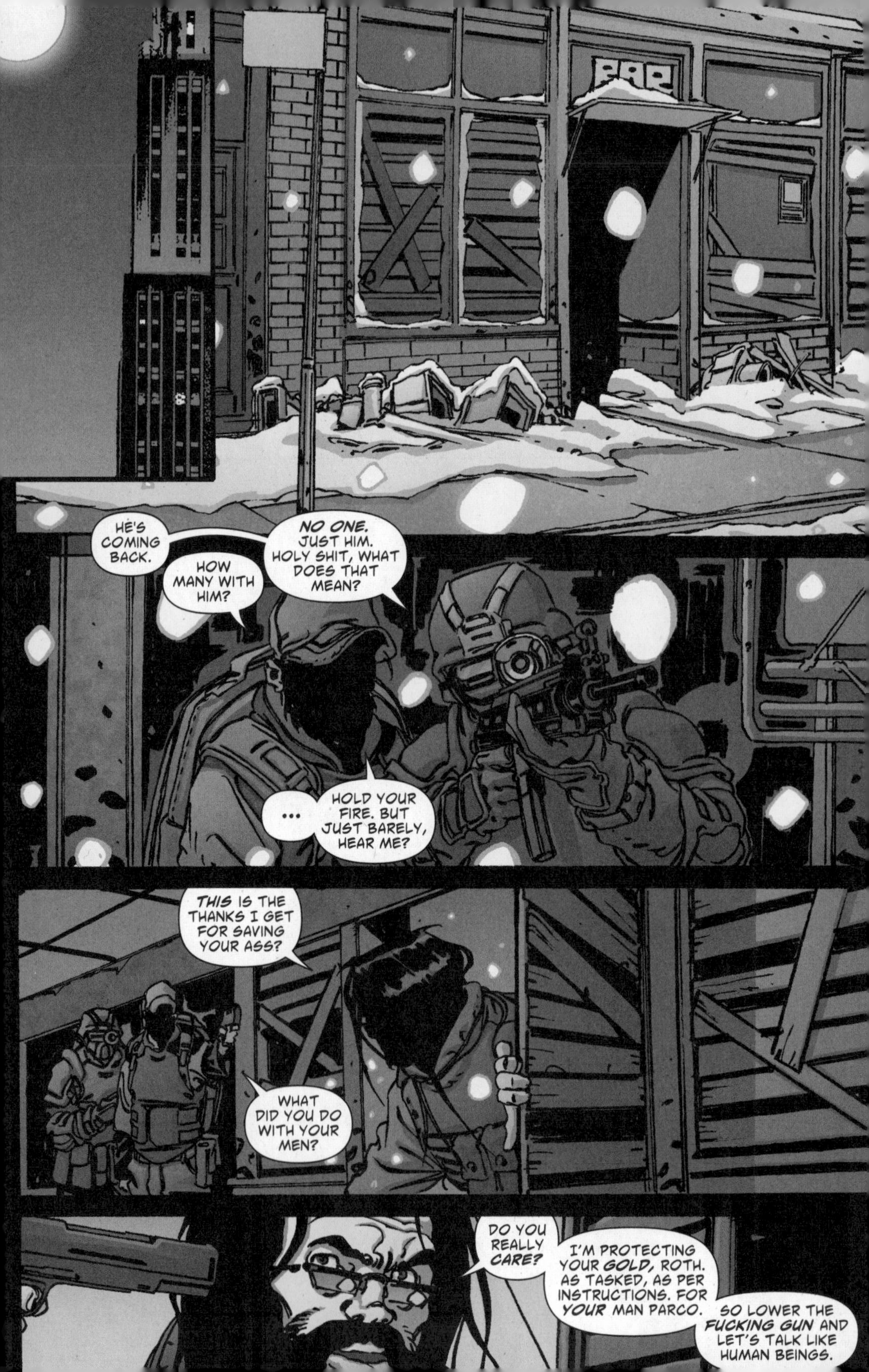
HE'S COMING BACK.
HOW MANY WITH HIM?
NO ONE. JUST HIM. HOLY SHIT, WHAT DOES THAT MEAN?
...
HOLD YOUR FIRE. BUT JUST BARELY, HEAR ME?
THIS IS THE THANKS I GET FOR SAVING YOUR ASS?
WHAT DID YOU DO WITH YOUR MEN?
DO YOU REALLY CARE?
I'M PROTECTING YOUR GOLD, ROTH. AS TASKED, AS PER INSTRUCTIONS. FOR YOUR MAN PARCO.
SO LOWER THE FUCKING GUN AND LET'S TALK LIKE HUMAN BEINGS.

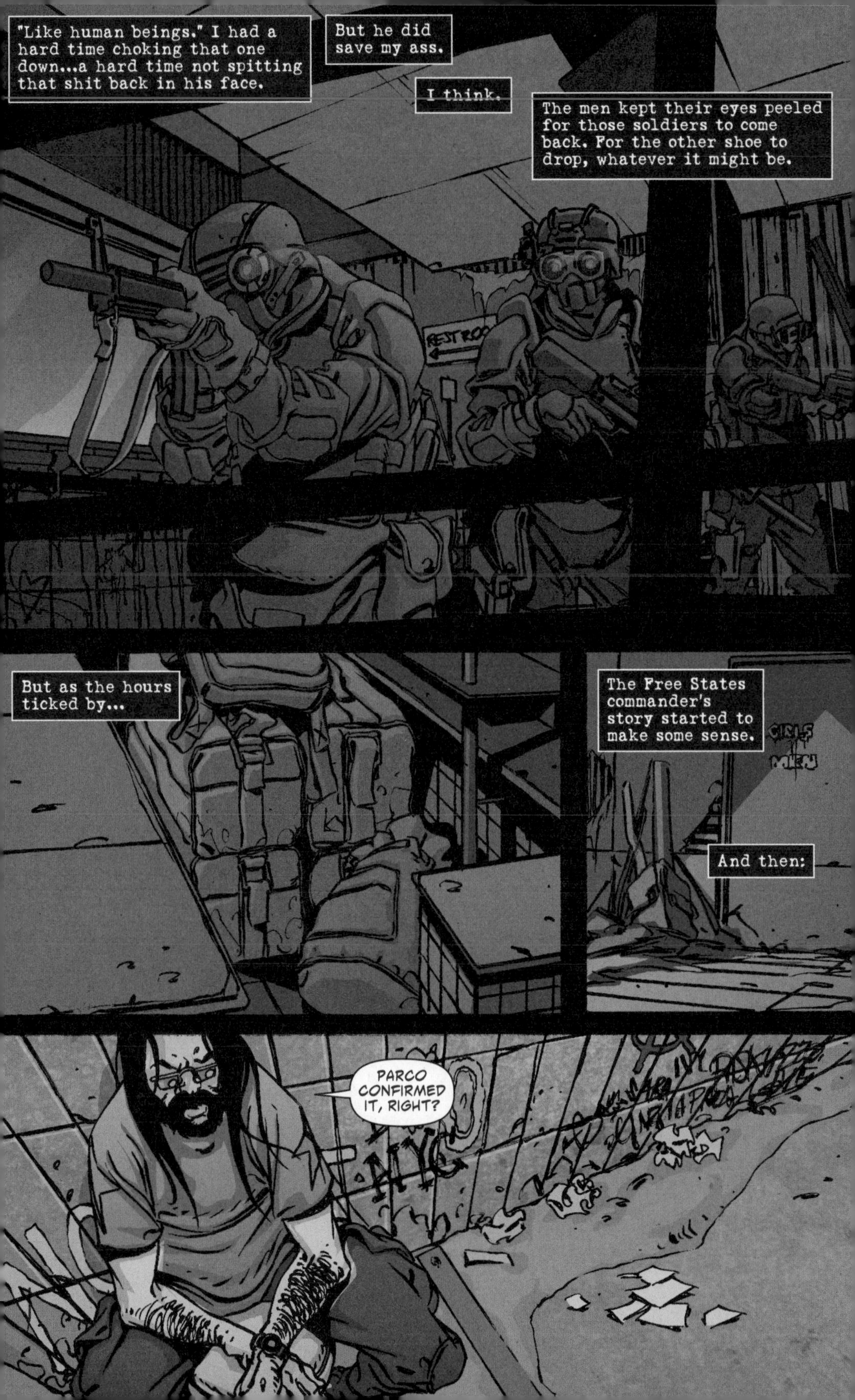
"Like human beings." I had a hard time choking that one down...a hard time not spitting that shit back in his face.
But he did save my ass.
I think.
The men kept their eyes peeled for those soldiers to come back. For the other shoe to drop, whatever it might be.
But as the hours ticked by...
The Free States commander's story started to make some sense.
And then:
PARCO CONFIRMED IT, RIGHT?

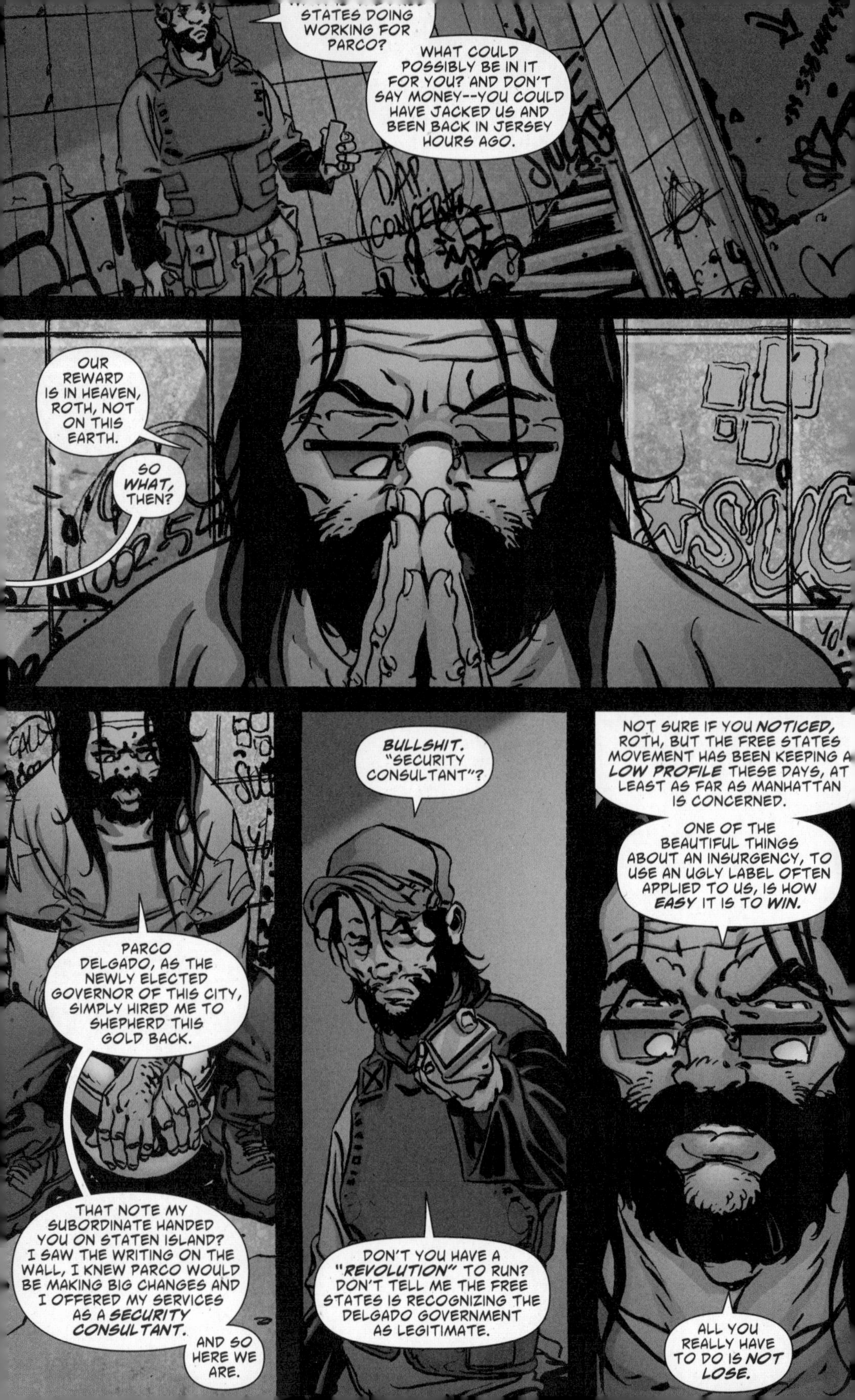
STATES DOING WORKING FOR PARCO?
WHAT COULD POSSIBLY BE IN IT FOR YOU? AND DON'T SAY MONEY--YOU COULD HAVE JACKED US AND BEEN BACK IN JERSEY HOURS AGO.
OUR REWARD IS IN HEAVEN, ROTH, NOT ON THIS EARTH.
SO *WHAT*, THEN?
PARCO DELGADO, AS THE NEWLY ELECTED GOVERNOR OF THIS CITY, SIMPLY HIRED ME TO SHEPHERD THIS GOLD BACK.
THAT NOTE MY SUBORDINATE HANDED YOU ON STATEN ISLAND? I SAW THE WRITING ON THE WALL, I KNEW PARCO WOULD BE MAKING BIG CHANGES AND I OFFERED MY SERVICES AS A *SECURITY CONSULTANT*.
AND SO HERE WE ARE.
BULLSHIT. "SECURITY CONSULTANT"?
DON'T YOU HAVE A *"REVOLUTION"* TO RUN? DON'T TELL ME THE FREE STATES IS RECOGNIZING THE DELGADO GOVERNMENT AS LEGITIMATE.
NOT SURE IF YOU *NOTICED*, ROTH, BUT THE FREE STATES MOVEMENT HAS BEEN KEEPING A *LOW PROFILE* THESE DAYS, AT LEAST AS FAR AS MANHATTAN IS CONCERNED.
ONE OF THE BEAUTIFUL THINGS ABOUT AN INSURGENCY, TO USE AN UGLY LABEL OFTEN APPLIED TO US, IS HOW *EASY* IT IS TO *WIN*.
ALL YOU REALLY HAVE TO DO IS *NOT LOSE*.

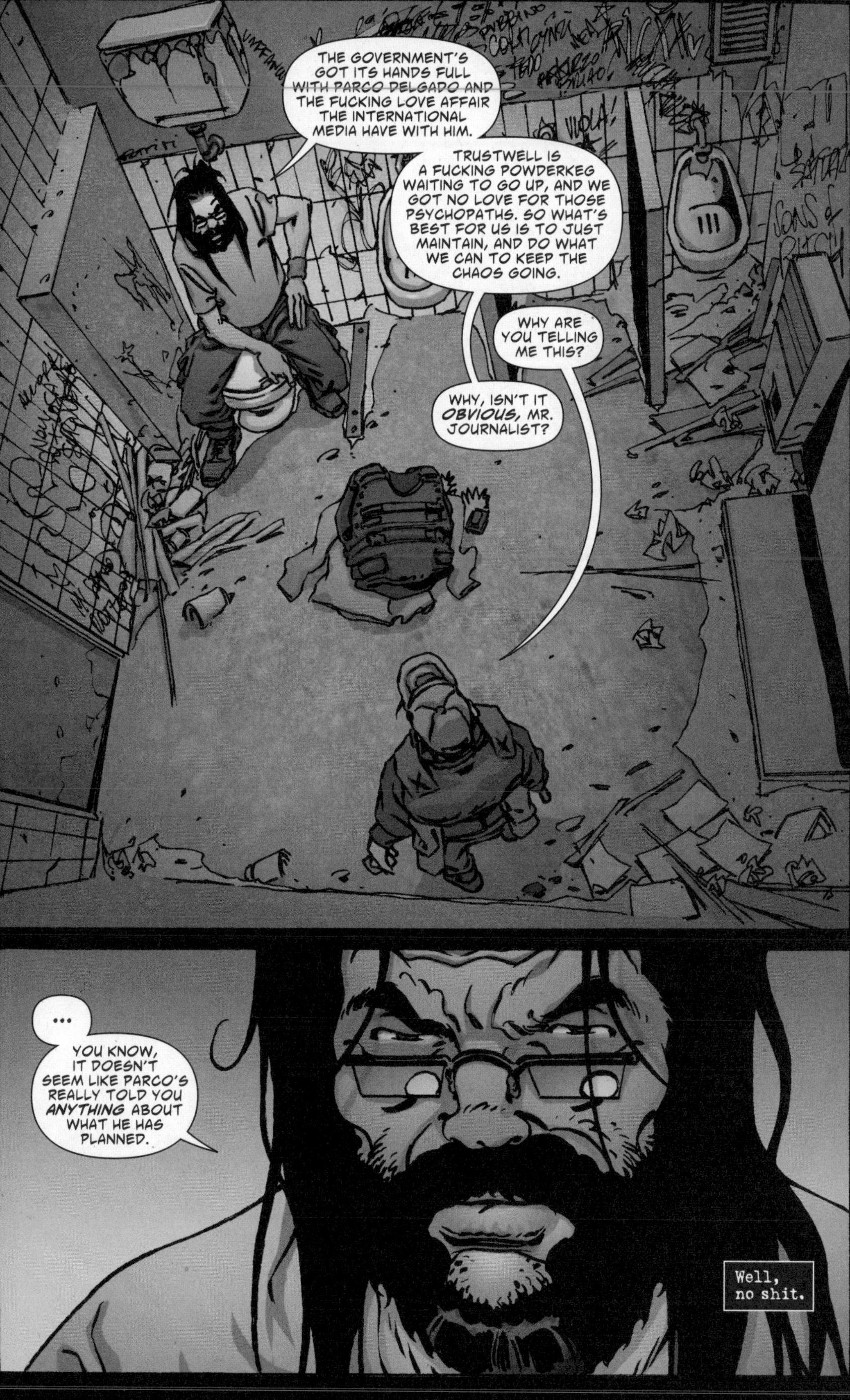
THE GOVERNMENT'S GOT ITS HANDS FULL WITH PARCO DELGADO AND THE FUCKING LOVE AFFAIR THE INTERNATIONAL MEDIA HAVE WITH HIM.
TRUSTWELL IS A FUCKING POWDERKEG WAITING TO GO UP, AND WE GOT NO LOVE FOR THOSE PSYCHOPATHS. SO WHAT'S BEST FOR US IS TO JUST MAINTAIN, AND DO WHAT WE CAN TO KEEP THE CHAOS GOING.
WHY ARE YOU TELLING ME THIS?
WHY, ISN'T IT *OBVIOUS*, MR. JOURNALIST?
...
YOU KNOW, IT DOESN'T SEEM LIKE PARCO'S REALLY TOLD YOU *ANYTHING* ABOUT WHAT HE HAS PLANNED.
Well, no shit.

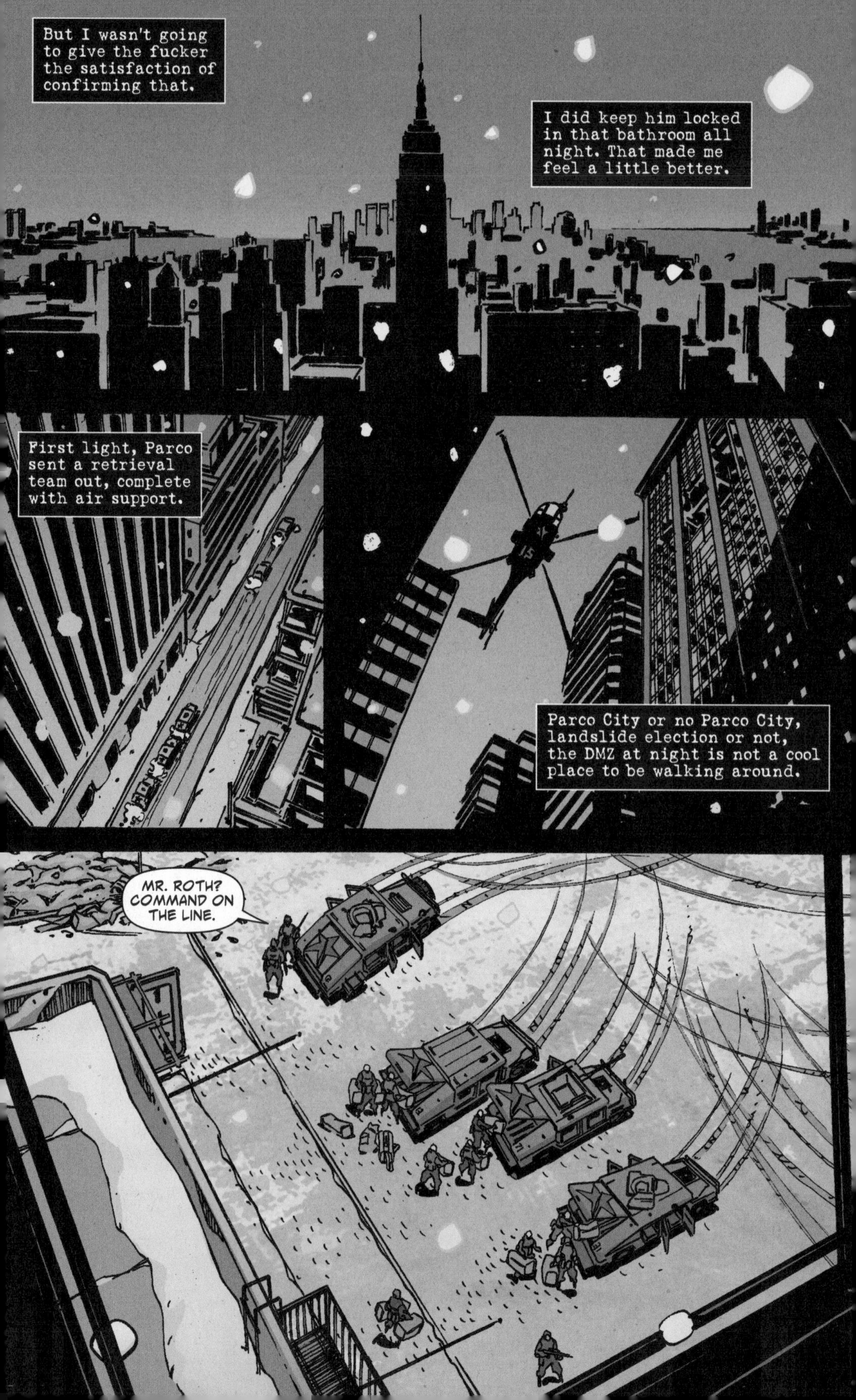
But I wasn't going to give the fucker the satisfaction of confirming that.
I did keep him locked in that bathroom all night. That made me feel a little better.
First light, Parco sent a retrieval team out, complete with air support.
Parco City or no Parco City, landslide election or not, the DMZ at night is not a cool place to be walking around.
MR. ROTH? COMMAND ON THE LINE.

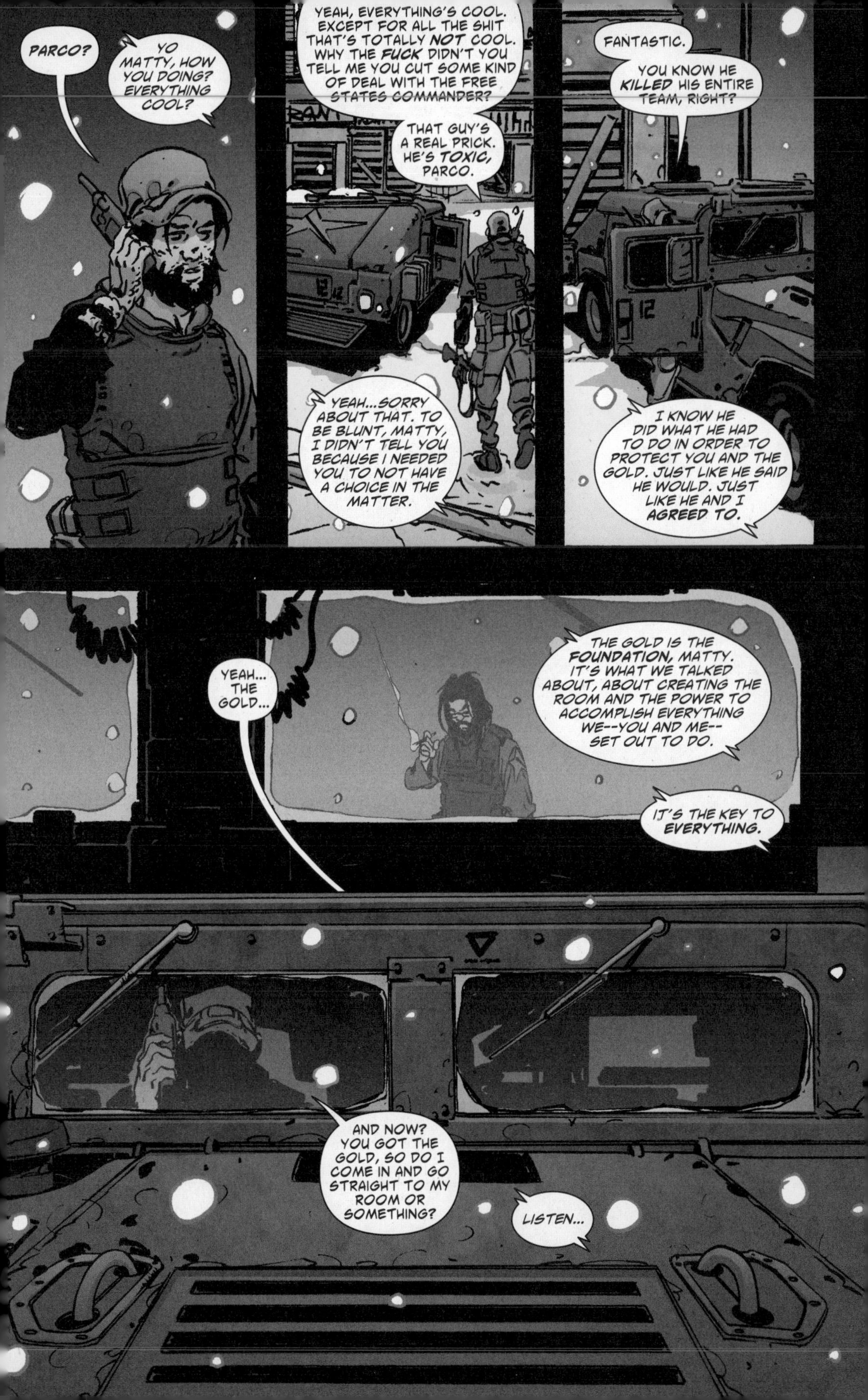
PARCO?
YO MATTY, HOW YOU DOING? EVERYTHING COOL?
YEAH, EVERYTHING'S COOL. EXCEPT FOR ALL THE SHIT THAT'S TOTALLY NOT COOL. WHY THE FUCK DIDN'T YOU TELL ME YOU CUT SOME KIND OF DEAL WITH THE FREE STATES COMMANDER?
THAT GUY'S A REAL PRICK. HE'S TOXIC, PARCO.
YEAH...SORRY ABOUT THAT. TO BE BLUNT, MATTY, I DIDN'T TELL YOU BECAUSE I NEEDED YOU TO NOT HAVE A CHOICE IN THE MATTER.
FANTASTIC.
YOU KNOW HE KILLED HIS ENTIRE TEAM, RIGHT?
I KNOW HE DID WHAT HE HAD TO DO IN ORDER TO PROTECT YOU AND THE GOLD. JUST LIKE HE SAID HE WOULD. JUST LIKE HE AND I AGREED TO.
YEAH... THE GOLD...
THE GOLD IS THE FOUNDATION, MATTY. IT'S WHAT WE TALKED ABOUT, ABOUT CREATING THE ROOM AND THE POWER TO ACCOMPLISH EVERYTHING WE--YOU AND ME--SET OUT TO DO.
IT'S THE KEY TO EVERYTHING.
AND NOW? YOU GOT THE GOLD, SO DO I COME IN AND GO STRAIGHT TO MY ROOM OR SOMETHING?
LISTEN...

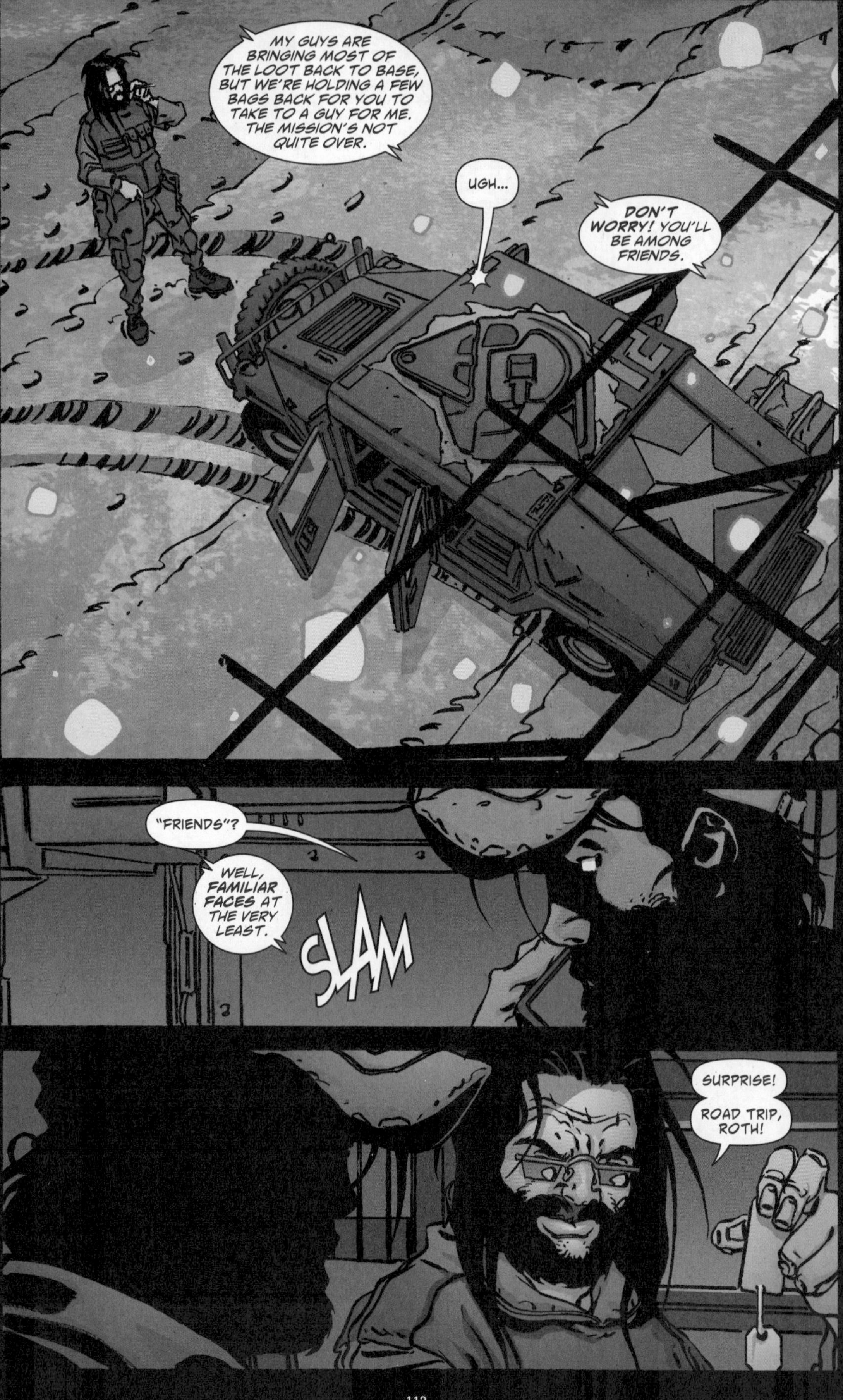
MY GUYS ARE BRINGING MOST OF THE LOOT BACK TO BASE, BUT WE'RE HOLDING A FEW BAGS BACK FOR YOU TO TAKE TO A GUY FOR ME. THE MISSION'S NOT QUITE OVER.
UGH...
DON'T WORRY! YOU'LL BE AMONG FRIENDS.
"FRIENDS"?
WELL, FAMILIAR FACES AT THE VERY LEAST.
SLAM
SURPRISE!
ROAD TRIP, ROTH!

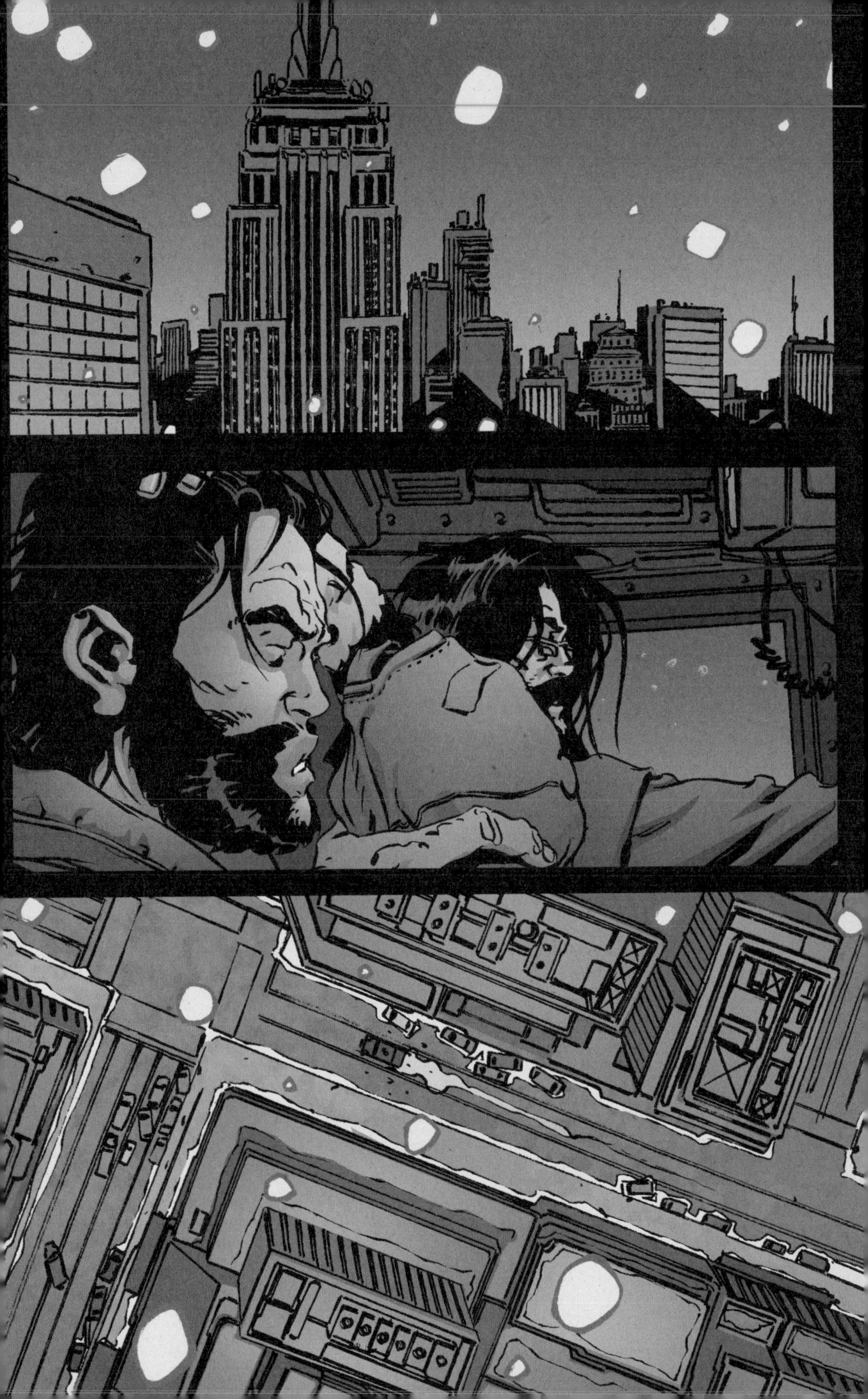

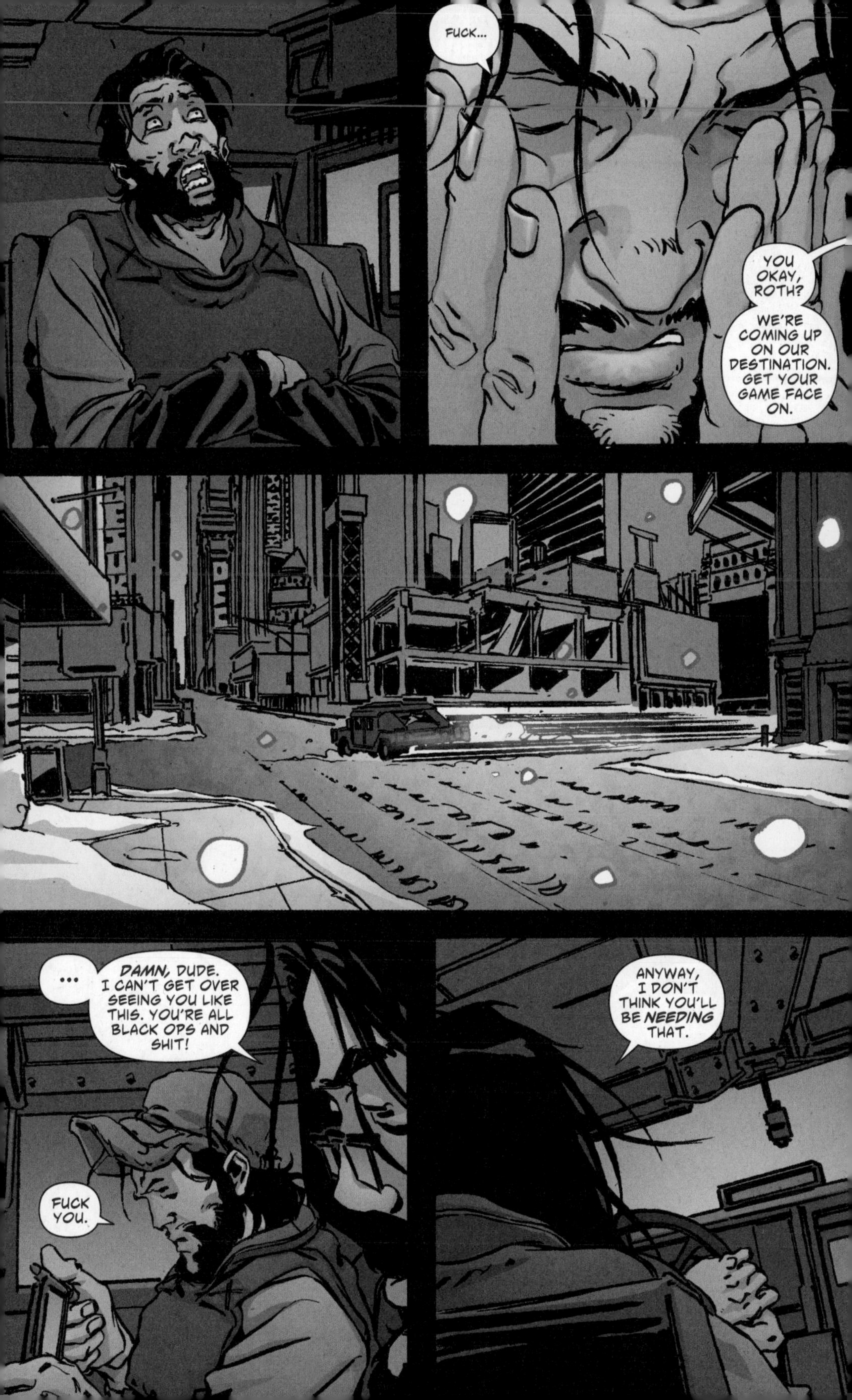
FUCK...
YOU OKAY, ROTH?
WE'RE COMING UP ON OUR DESTINATION. GET YOUR GAME FACE ON.
...
DAMN, DUDE. I CAN'T GET OVER SEEING YOU LIKE THIS. YOU'RE ALL BLACK OPS AND SHIT!
FUCK YOU.
ANYWAY, I DON'T THINK YOU'LL BE NEEDING THAT.

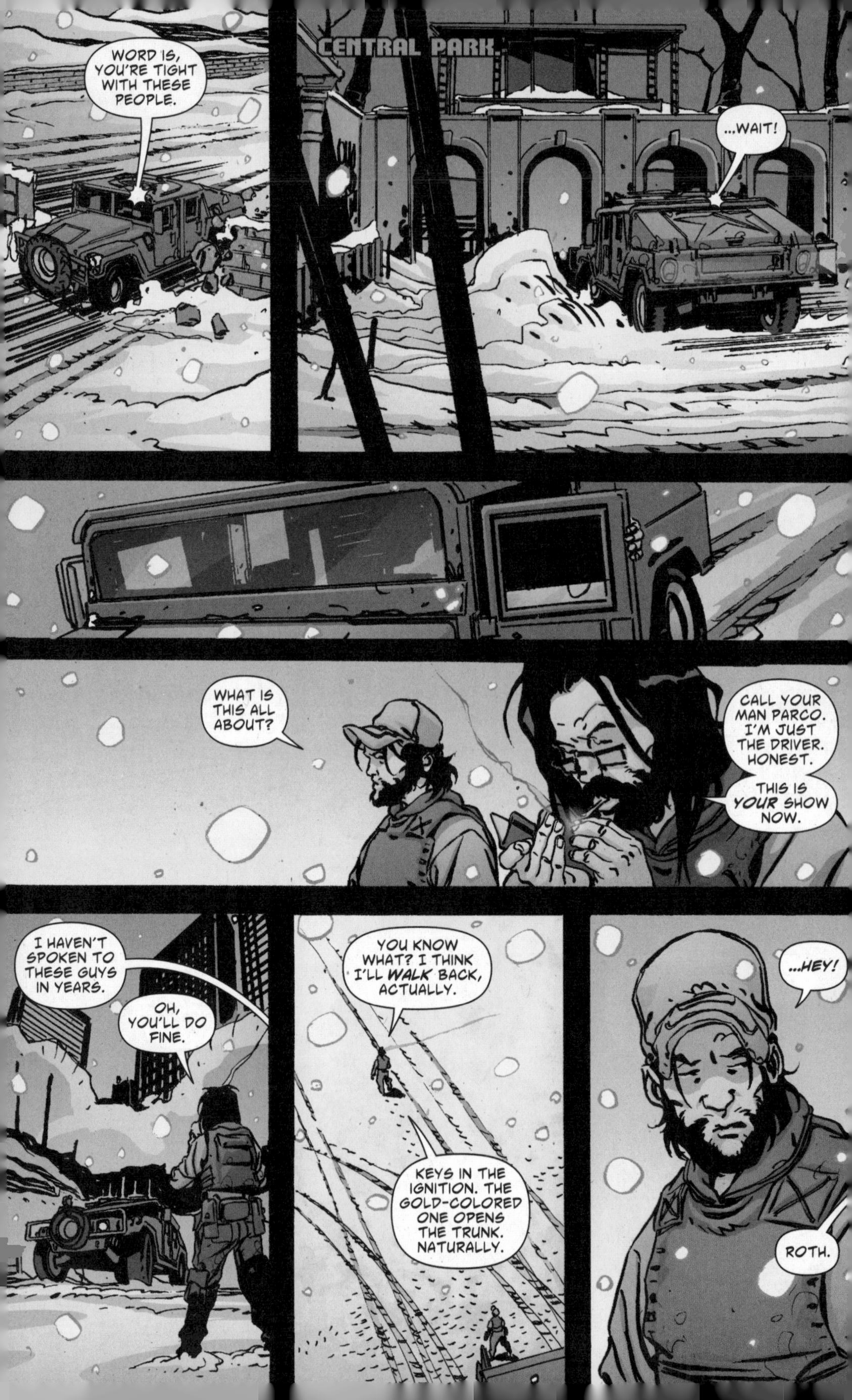
WORD IS, YOU'RE TIGHT WITH THESE PEOPLE.
CENTRAL PARK
...WAIT!
WHAT IS THIS ALL ABOUT?
CALL YOUR MAN PARCO. I'M JUST THE DRIVER. HONEST.
THIS IS *YOUR* SHOW NOW.
I HAVEN'T SPOKEN TO THESE GUYS IN YEARS.
OH, YOU'LL DO FINE.
YOU KNOW WHAT? I THINK I'LL *WALK* BACK, ACTUALLY.
KEYS IN THE IGNITION. THE GOLD-COLORED ONE OPENS THE TRUNK. NATURALLY.
...HEY!
ROTH.

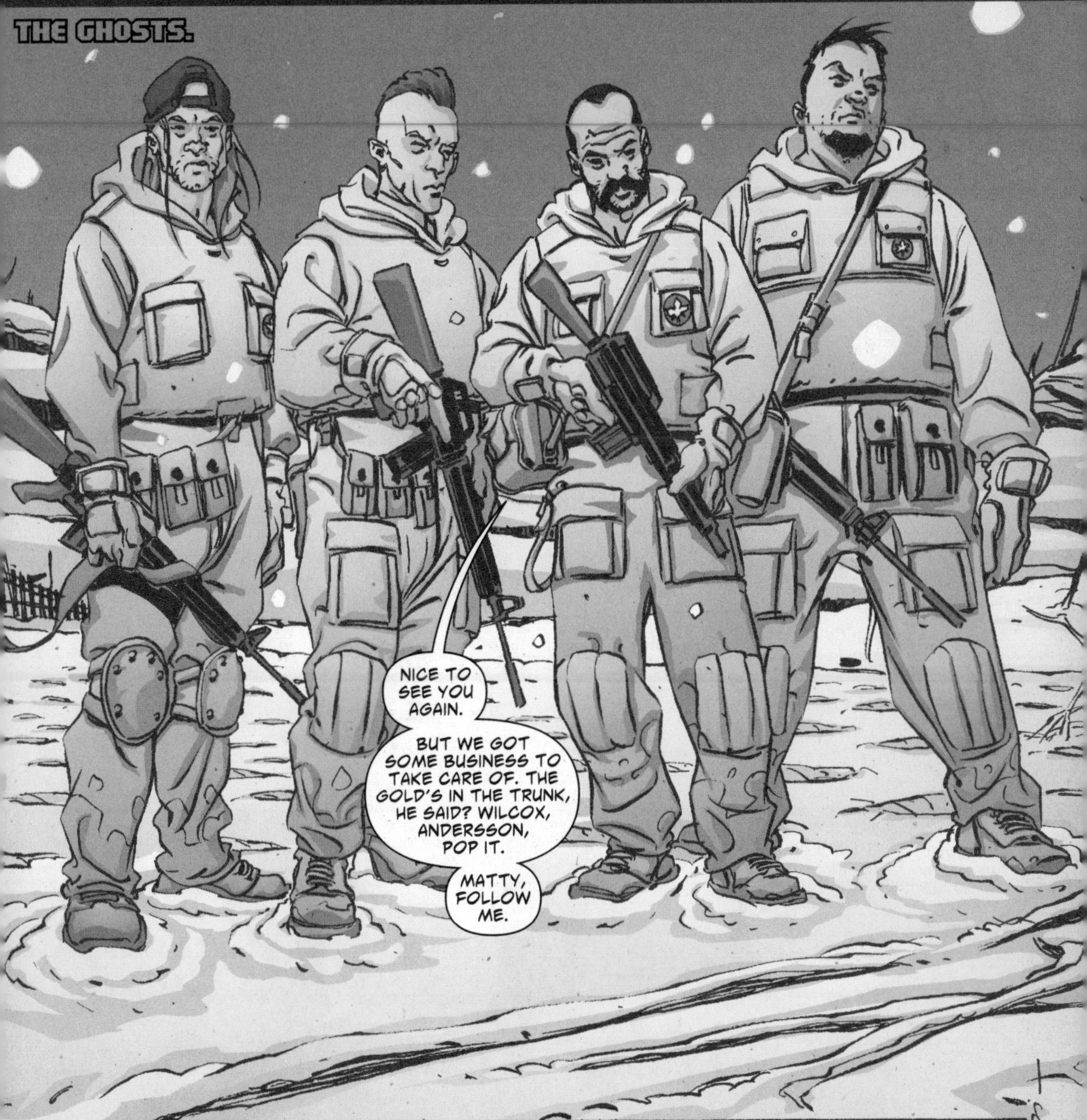
THE GHOSTS.
NICE TO SEE YOU AGAIN.
BUT WE GOT SOME BUSINESS TO TAKE CARE OF. THE GOLD'S IN THE TRUNK, HE SAID? WILCOX, ANDERSSON, POP IT.
MATTY, FOLLOW ME.

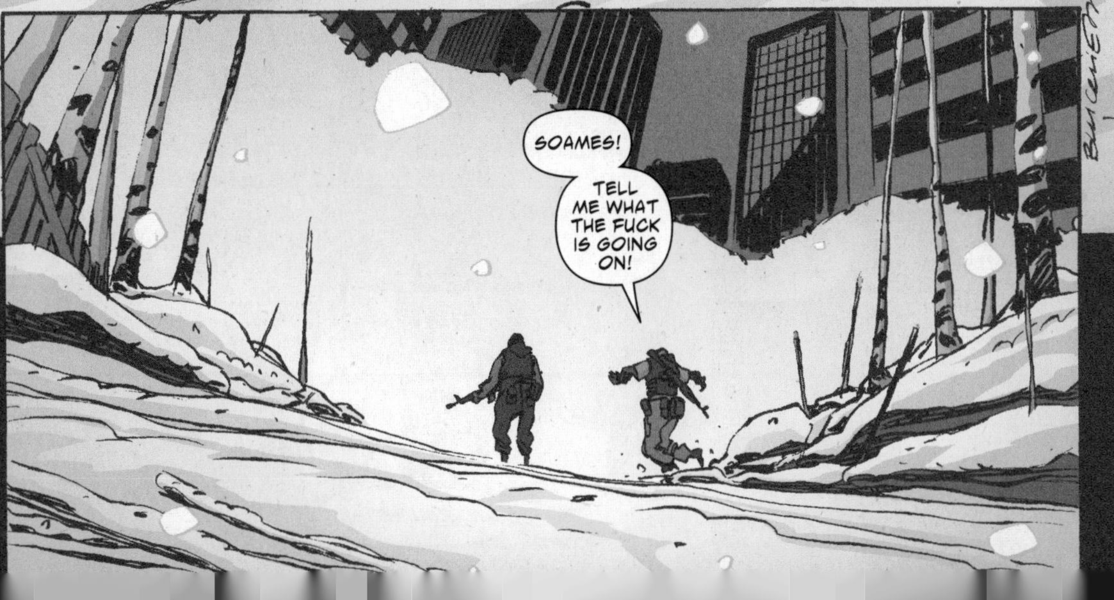
SOAMES!
TELL ME WHAT THE FUCK IS GOING ON!

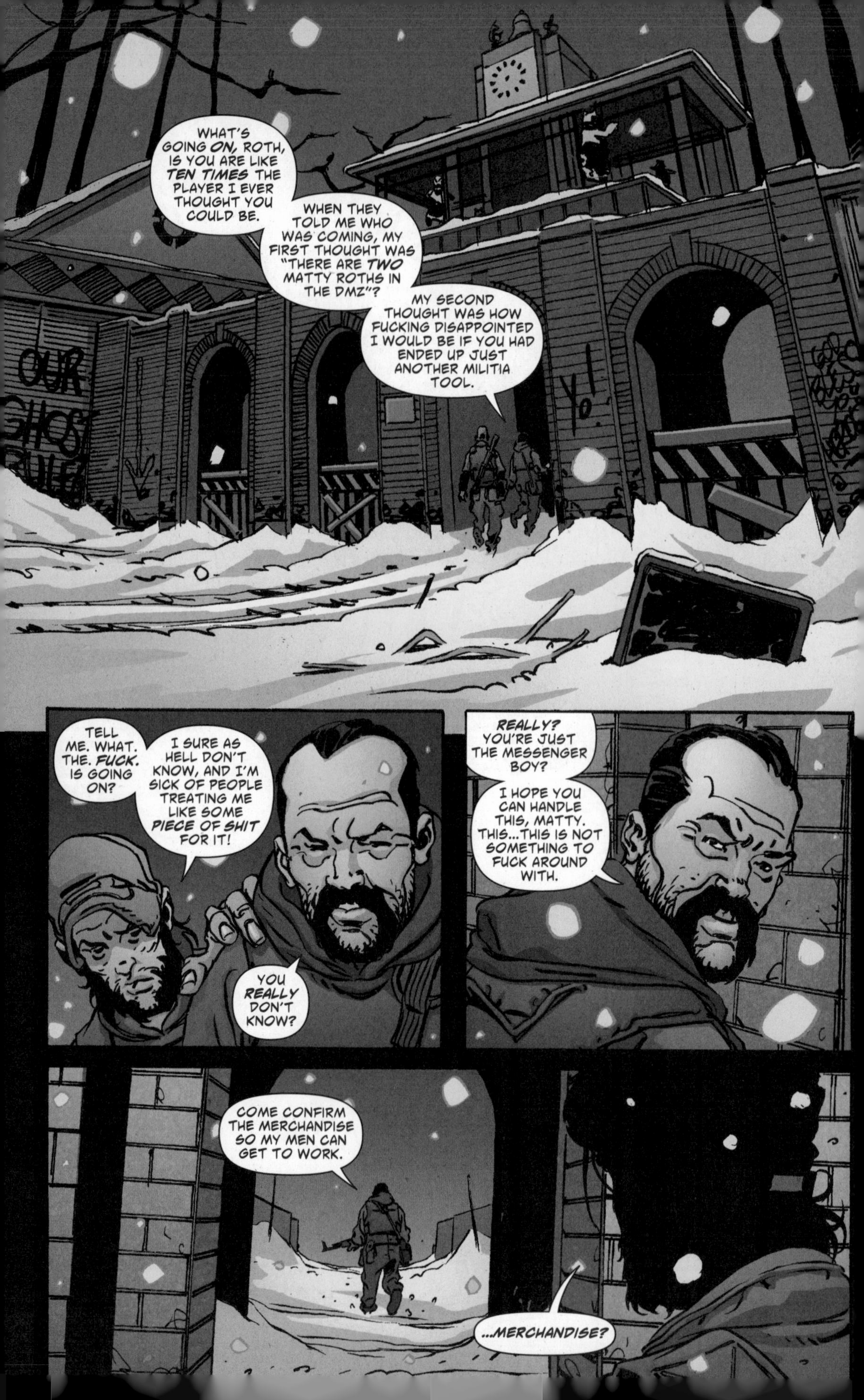
WHAT'S GOING ON, ROTH, IS YOU ARE LIKE TEN TIMES THE PLAYER I EVER THOUGHT YOU COULD BE.
WHEN THEY TOLD ME WHO WAS COMING, MY FIRST THOUGHT WAS "THERE ARE TWO MATTY ROTHS IN THE DMZ"?
MY SECOND THOUGHT WAS HOW FUCKING DISAPPOINTED I WOULD BE IF YOU HAD ENDED UP JUST ANOTHER MILITIA TOOL.
OUR GHOST RULE
YO!
TELL ME. WHAT. THE. FUCK. IS GOING ON?
I SURE AS HELL DON'T KNOW, AND I'M SICK OF PEOPLE TREATING ME LIKE SOME PIECE OF SHIT FOR IT!
YOU REALLY DON'T KNOW?
REALLY? YOU'RE JUST THE MESSENGER BOY?
I HOPE YOU CAN HANDLE THIS, MATTY. THIS...THIS IS NOT SOMETHING TO FUCK AROUND WITH.
COME CONFIRM THE MERCHANDISE SO MY MEN CAN GET TO WORK.
...MERCHANDISE?

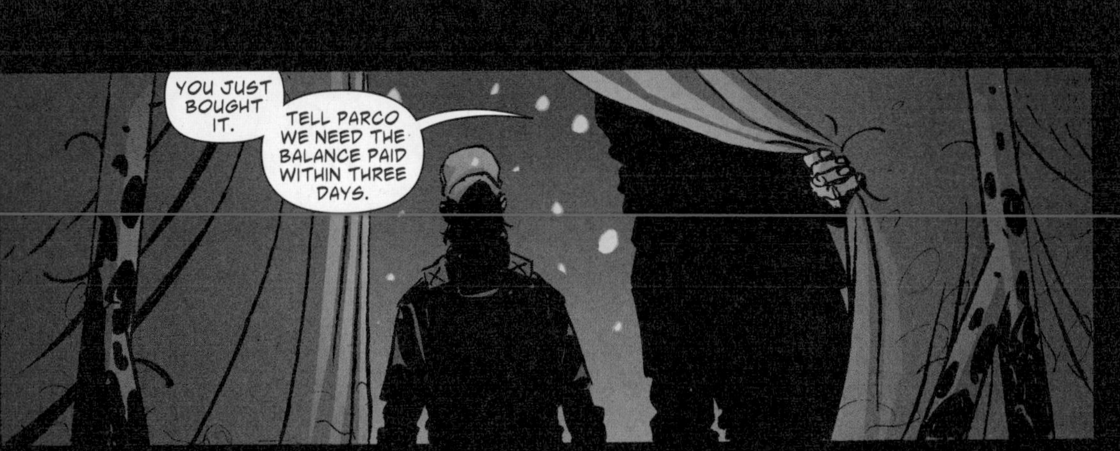
YOU JUST BOUGHT IT.
TELL PARCO WE NEED THE BALANCE PAID WITHIN THREE DAYS.

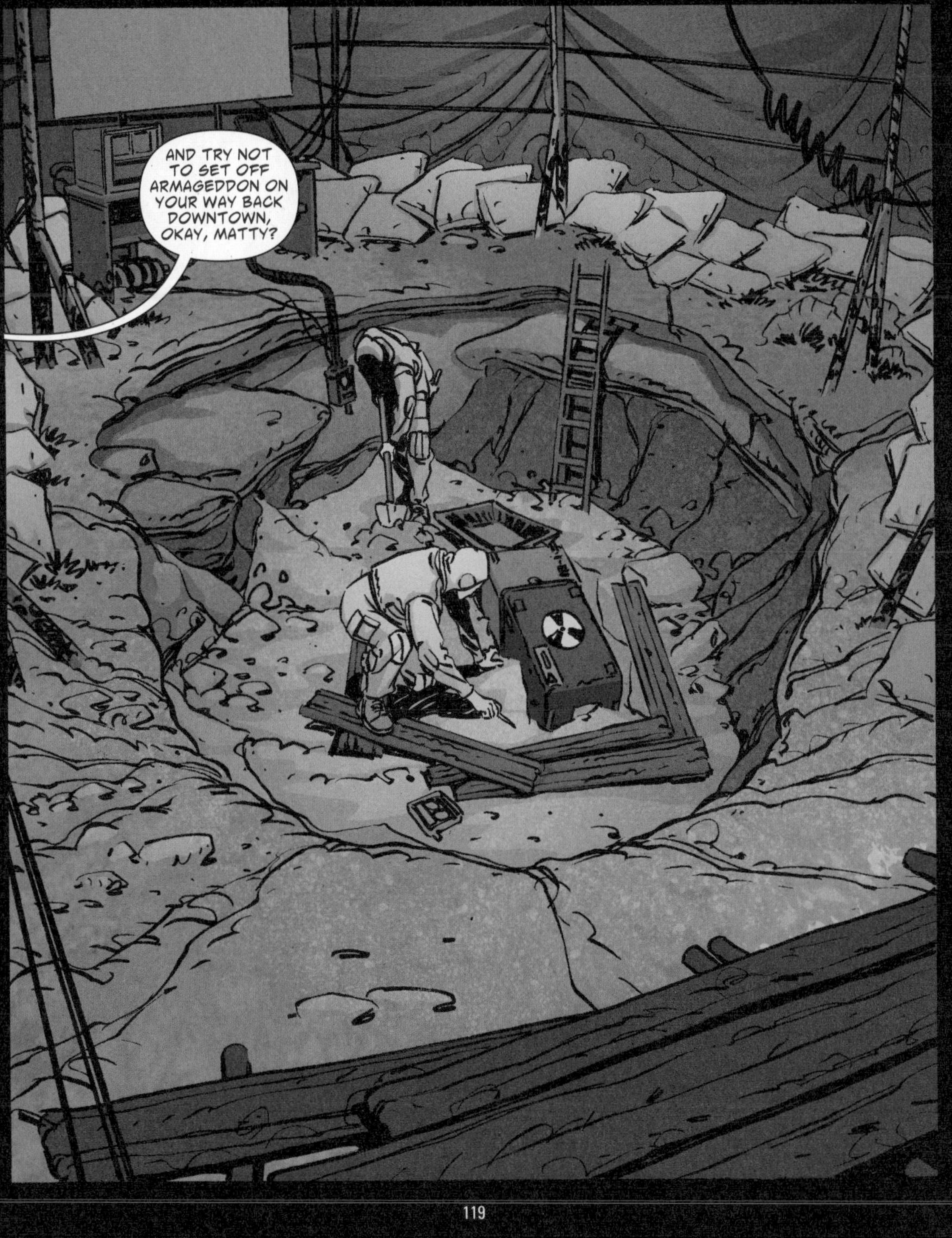
AND TRY NOT TO SET OFF ARMAGEDDON ON YOUR WAY BACK DOWNTOWN, OKAY, MATTY?

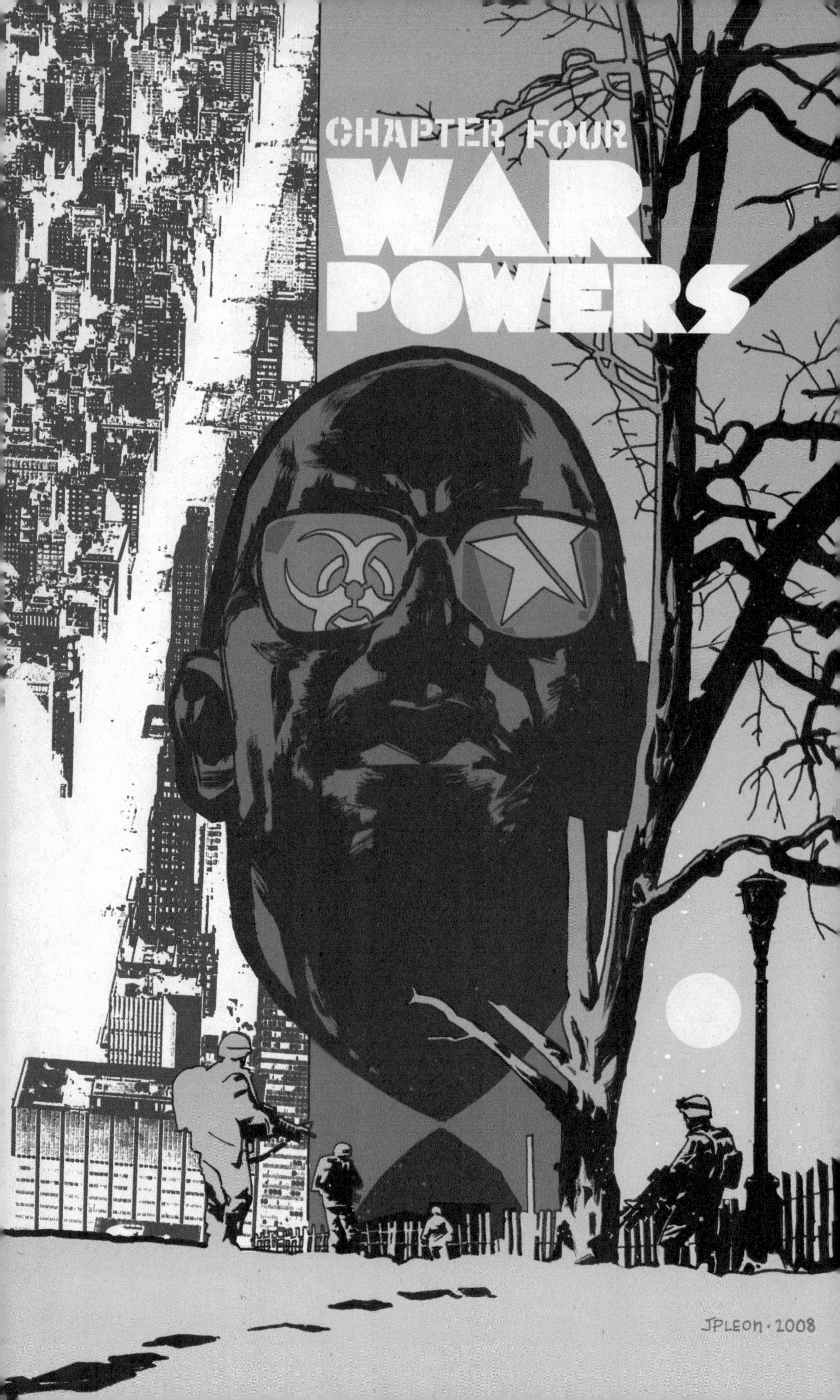

CHAPTER FOUR
WAR POWERS
JPLEON · 2008

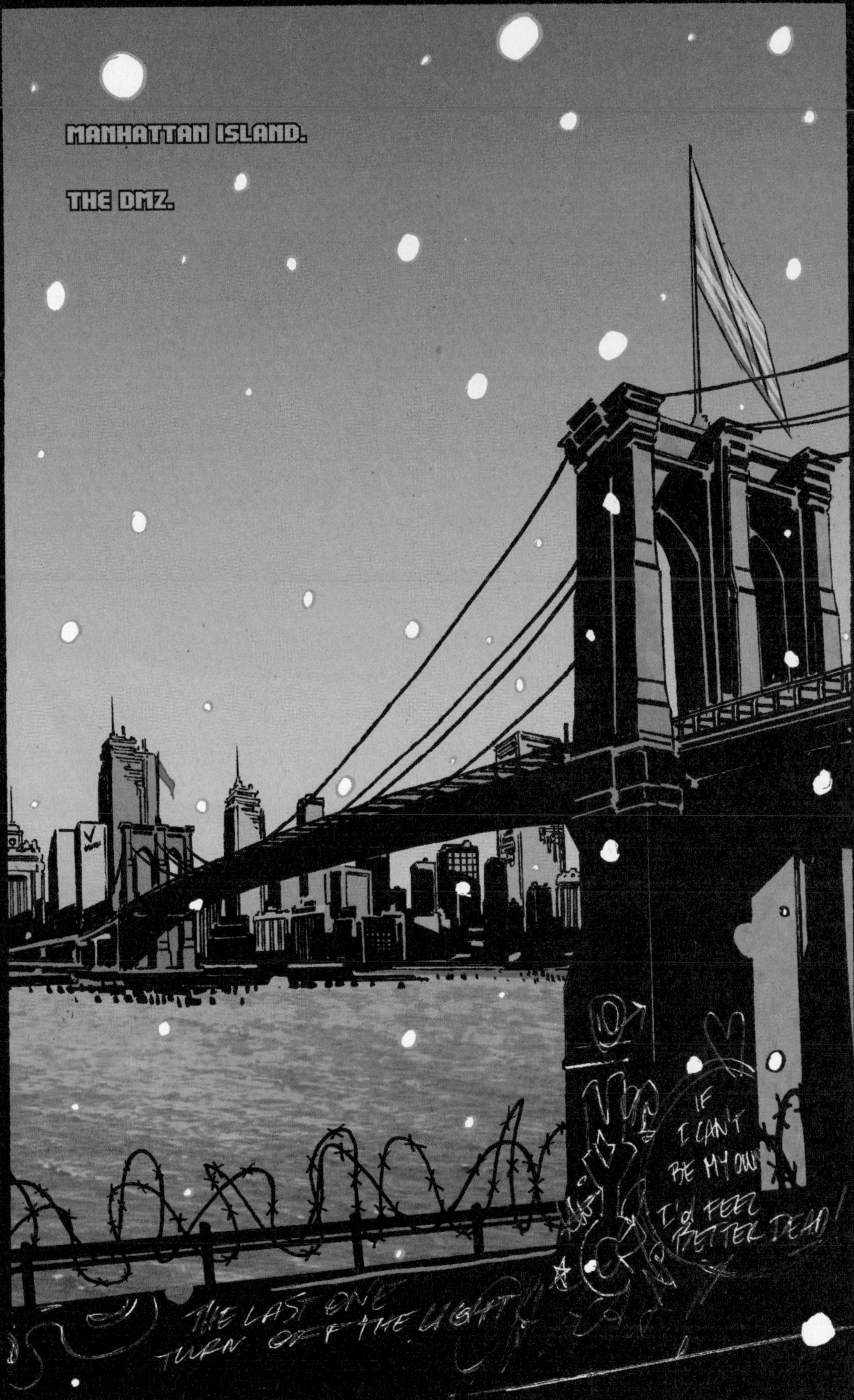
MANHATTAN ISLAND.
THE DMZ.
IF I CAN'T BE MY OWN I'd FEEL BETTER DEAD!
THE LAST ONE TURN OFF THE LIGHT!

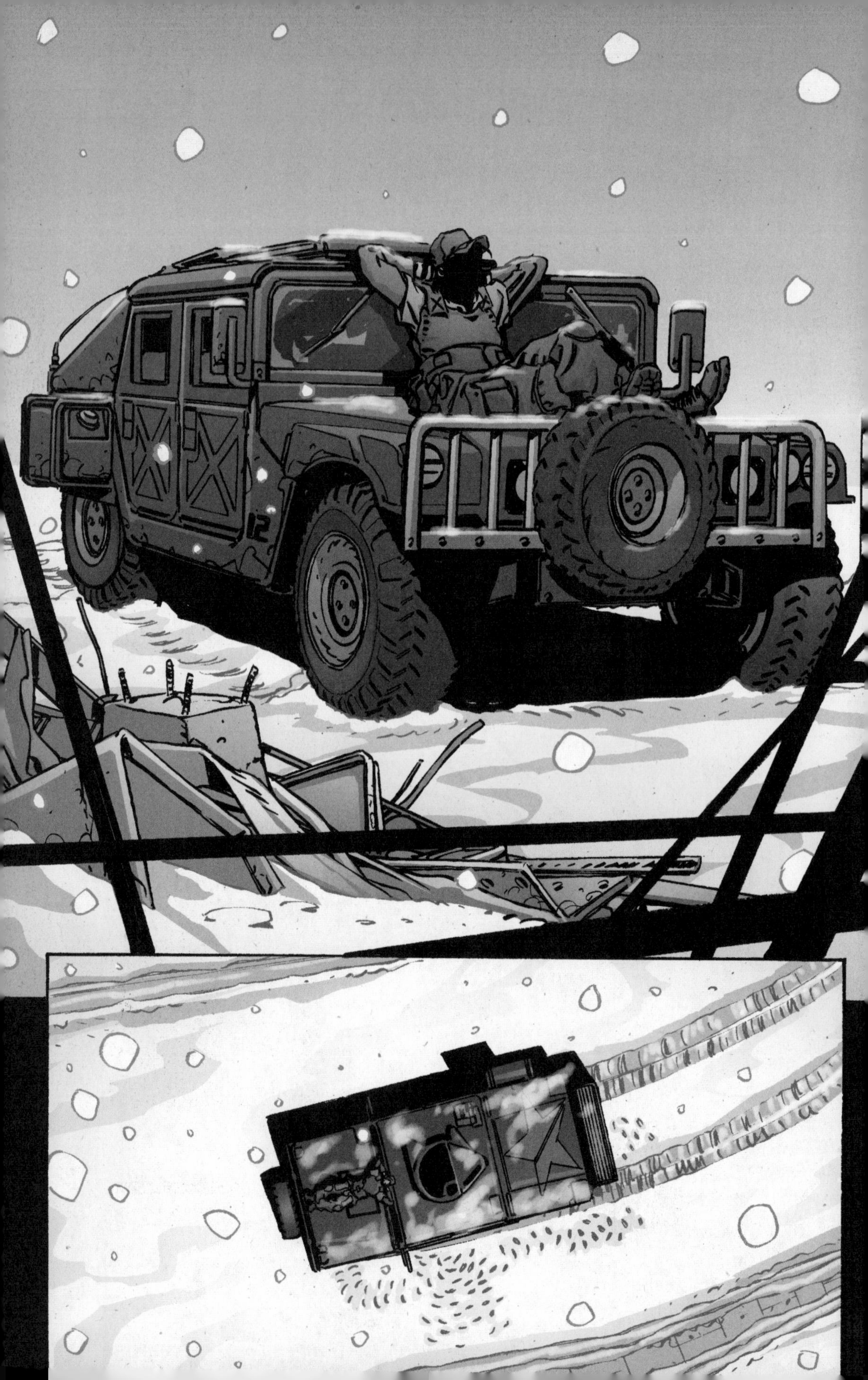

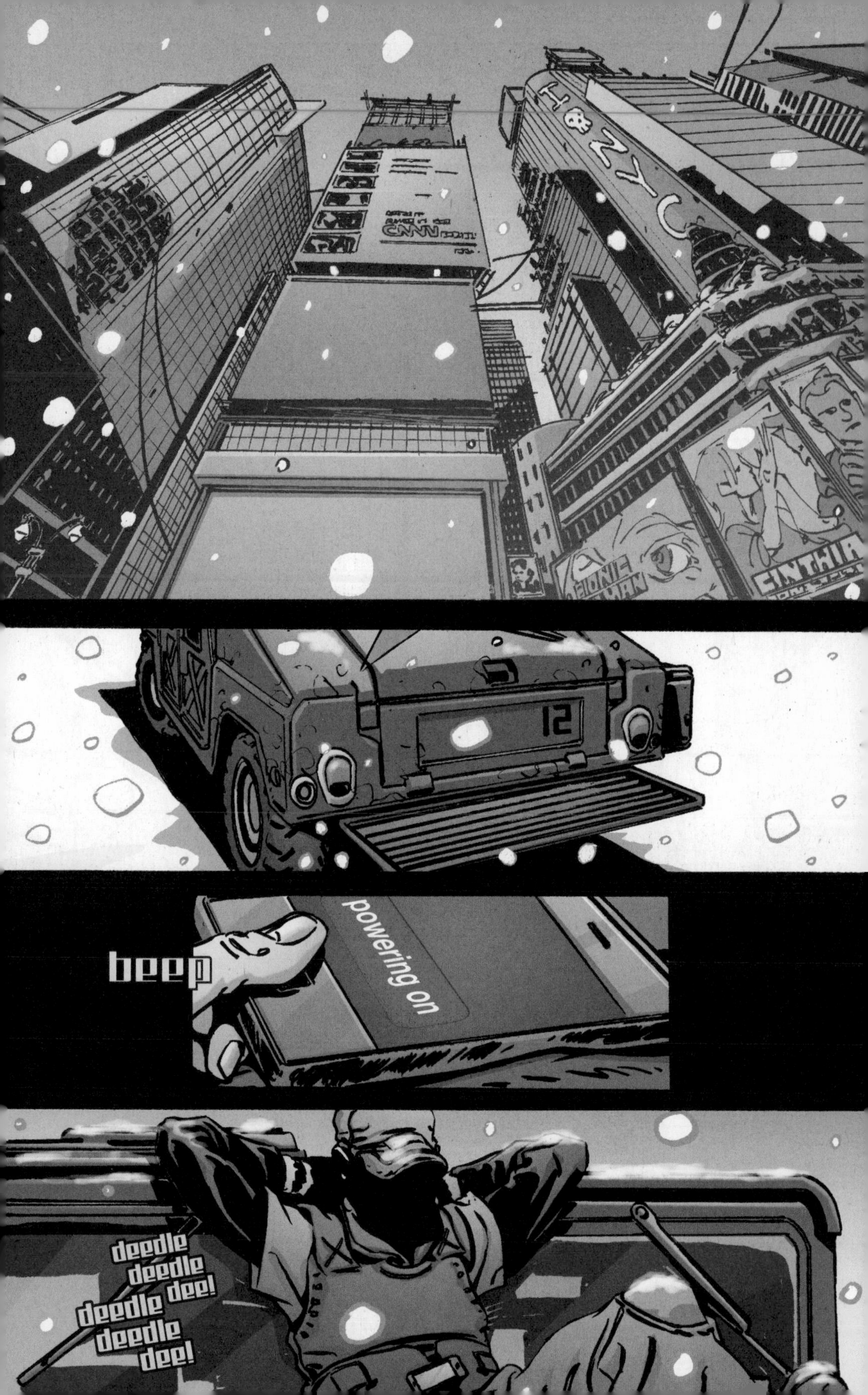
CNN
12
beep
powering on
deedle
deedle
dee!
deedle
deedle
dee!

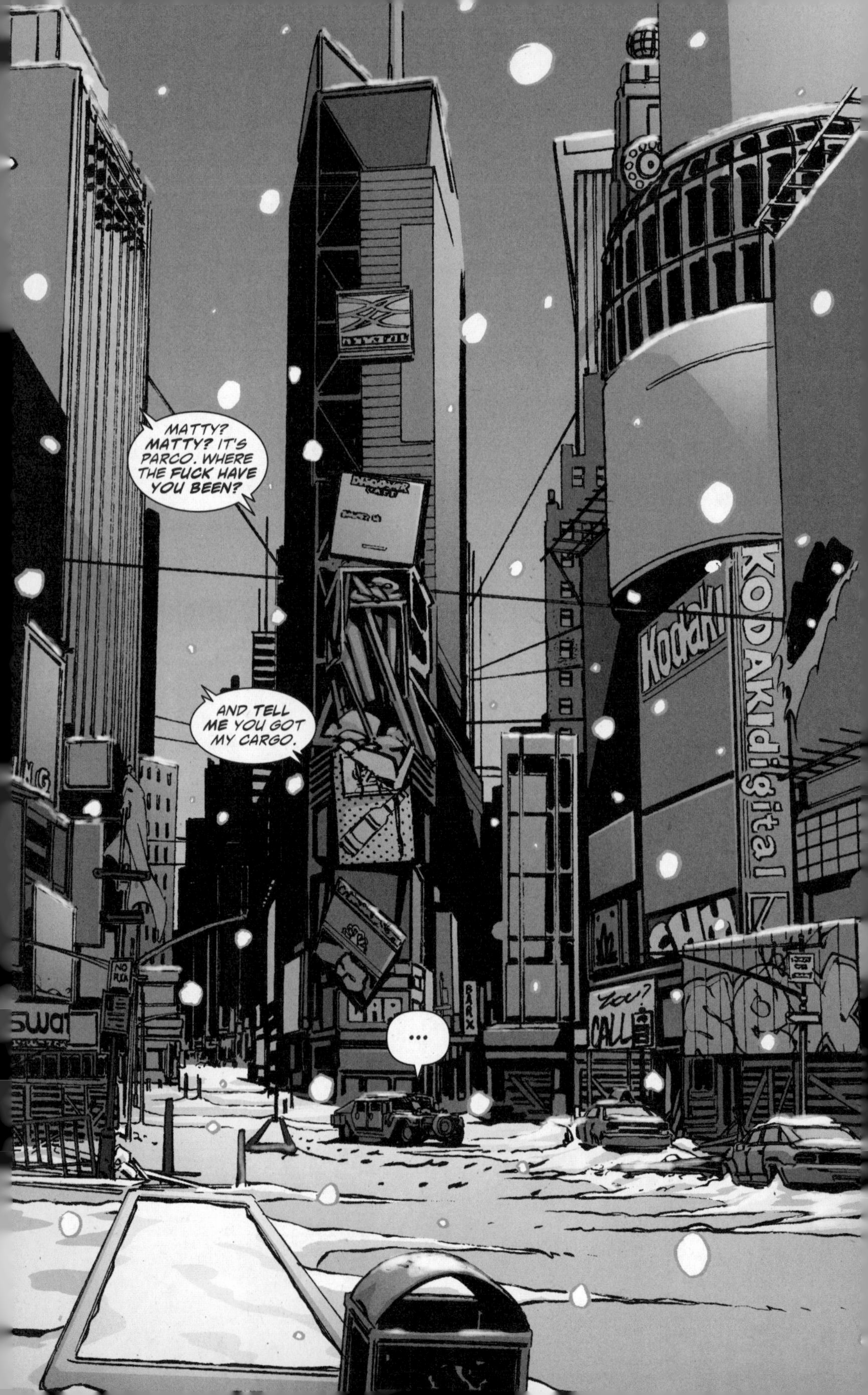
MATTY? MATTY? IT'S PARCO. WHERE THE FUCK HAVE YOU BEEN?
AND TELL ME YOU GOT MY CARGO.
...

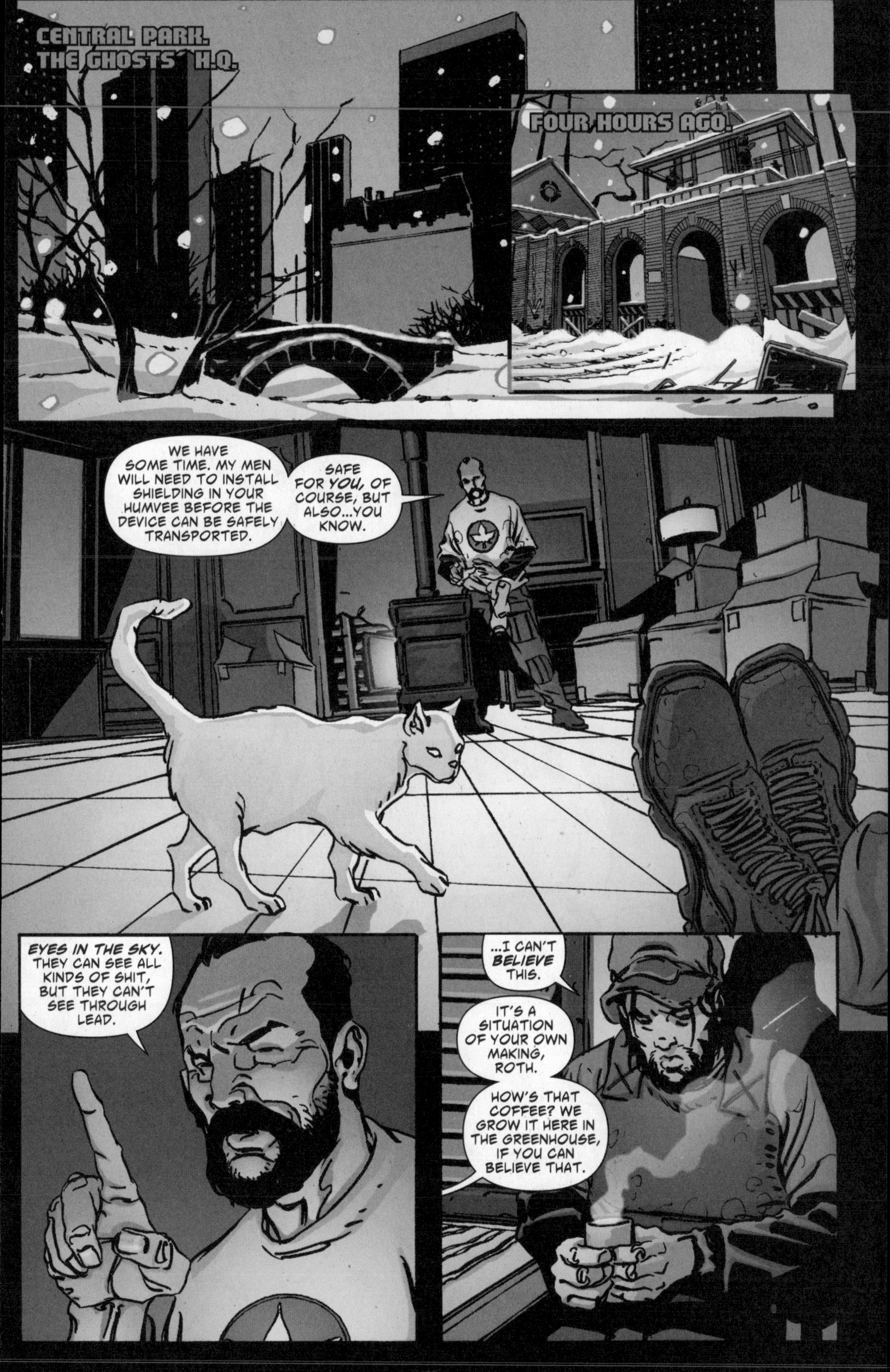
CENTRAL PARK. THE GHOSTS' H.Q.
FOUR HOURS AGO.
WE HAVE SOME TIME. MY MEN WILL NEED TO INSTALL SHIELDING IN YOUR HUMVEE BEFORE THE DEVICE CAN BE SAFELY TRANSPORTED.
SAFE FOR YOU, OF COURSE, BUT ALSO...YOU KNOW.
EYES IN THE SKY. THEY CAN SEE ALL KINDS OF SHIT, BUT THEY CAN'T SEE THROUGH LEAD.
...I CAN'T BELIEVE THIS.
IT'S A SITUATION OF YOUR OWN MAKING, ROTH.
HOW'S THAT COFFEE? WE GROW IT HERE IN THE GREENHOUSE, IF YOU CAN BELIEVE THAT.

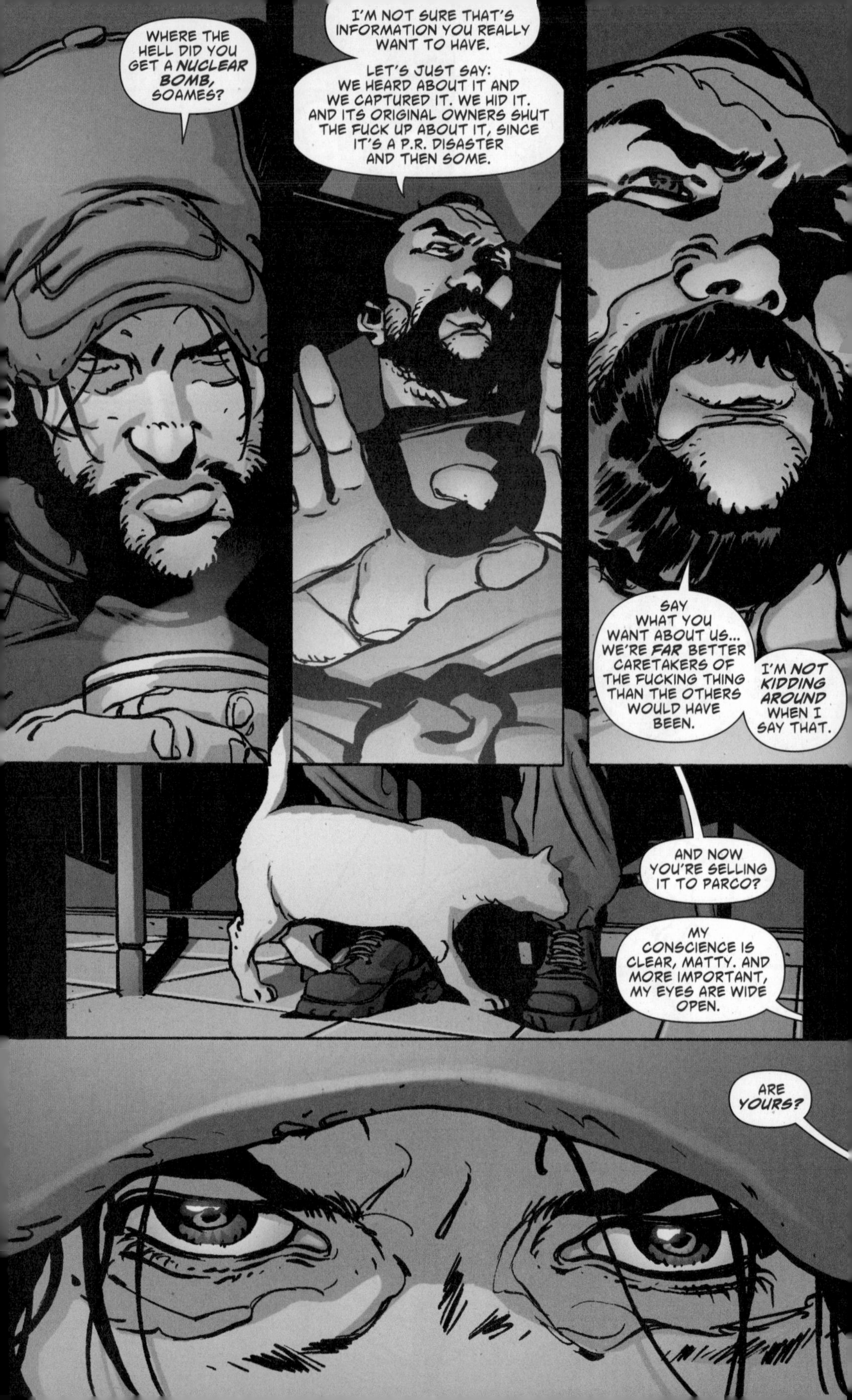
WHERE THE HELL DID YOU GET A *NUCLEAR BOMB,* SOAMES?
I'M NOT SURE THAT'S INFORMATION YOU REALLY WANT TO HAVE.
LET'S JUST SAY: WE HEARD ABOUT IT AND WE CAPTURED IT. WE HID IT. AND ITS ORIGINAL OWNERS SHUT THE FUCK UP ABOUT IT, SINCE IT'S A P.R. DISASTER AND THEN SOME.
SAY WHAT YOU WANT ABOUT US... WE'RE *FAR* BETTER CARETAKERS OF THE FUCKING THING THAN THE OTHERS WOULD HAVE BEEN.
I'M *NOT KIDDING AROUND* WHEN I SAY THAT.
AND NOW YOU'RE SELLING IT TO PARCO?
MY CONSCIENCE IS CLEAR, MATTY. AND MORE IMPORTANT, MY EYES ARE WIDE OPEN.
ARE *YOURS?*

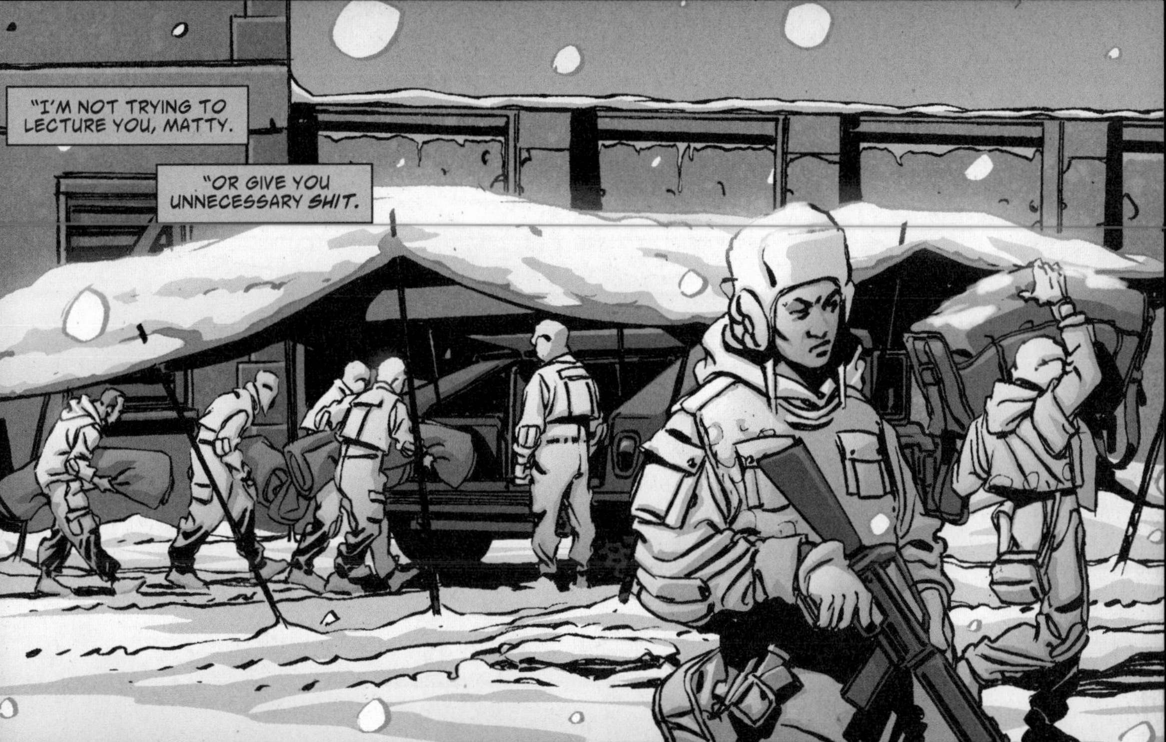
"I'M NOT TRYING TO LECTURE YOU, MATTY.
"OR GIVE YOU UNNECESSARY *SHIT*.

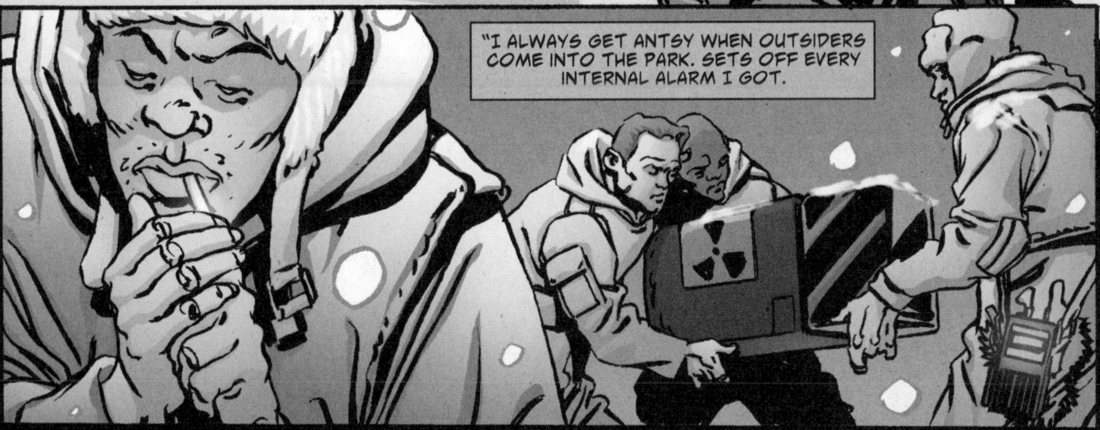
"I ALWAYS GET ANTSY WHEN OUTSIDERS COME INTO THE PARK. SETS OFF EVERY INTERNAL ALARM I GOT.

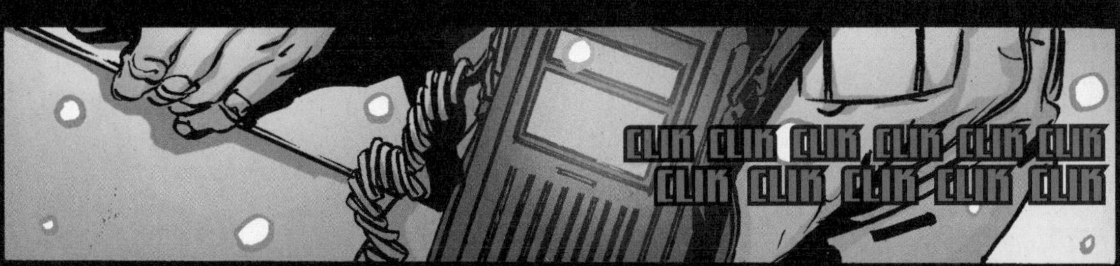
CLIK CLIK CLIK CLIK CLIK CLIK
CLIK CLIK CLIK CLIK CLIK

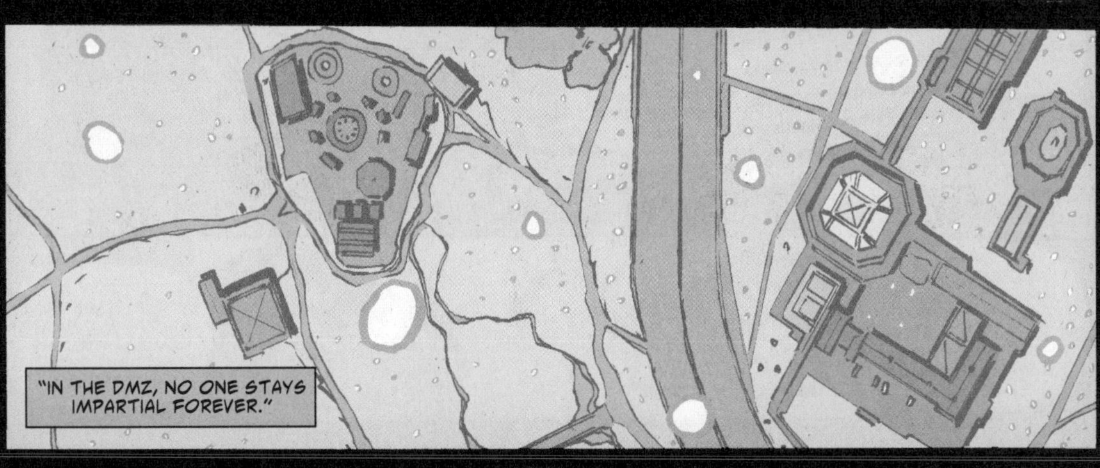
"IN THE DMZ, NO ONE STAYS IMPARTIAL FOREVER."

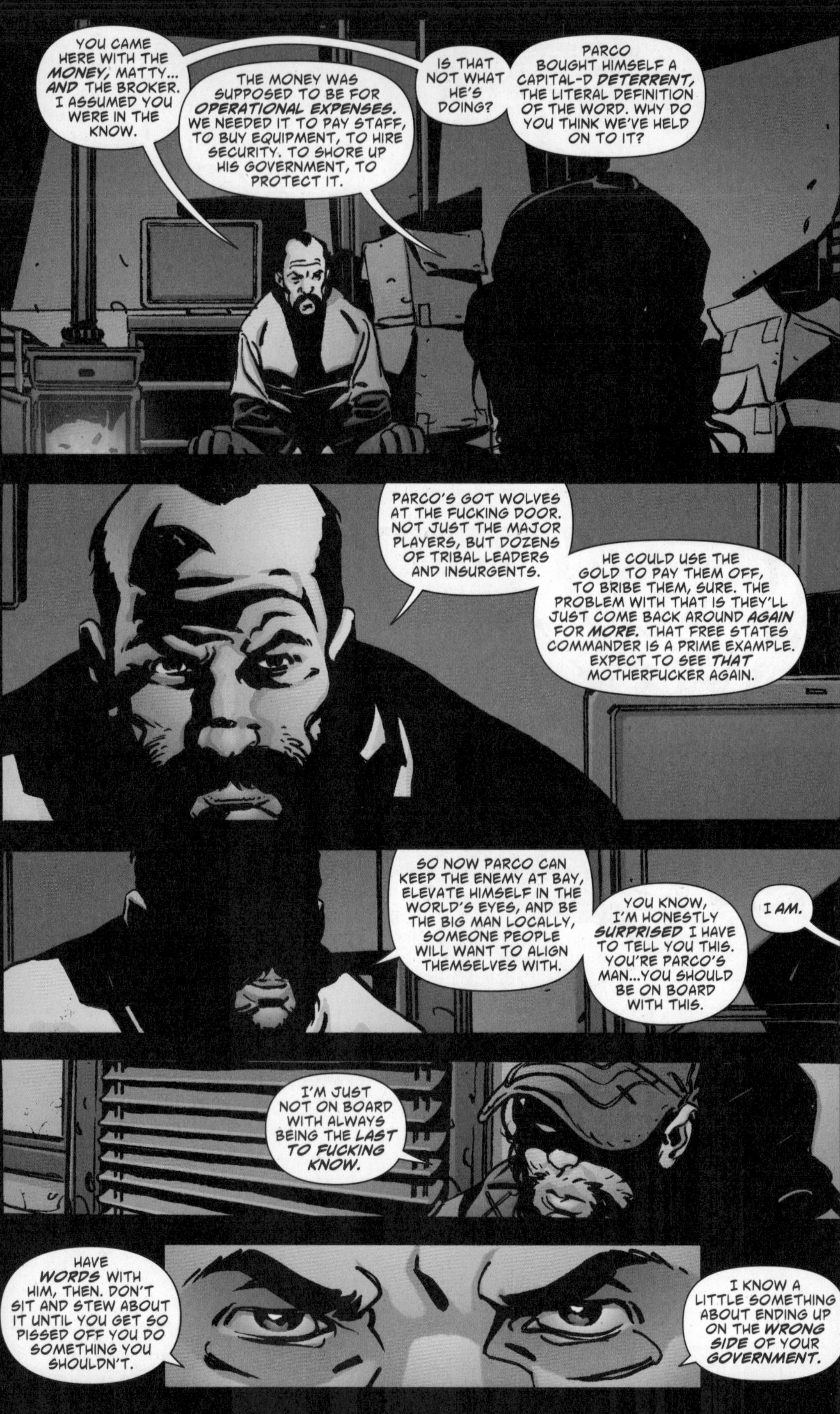
YOU CAME HERE WITH THE MONEY, MATTY... AND THE BROKER. I ASSUMED YOU WERE IN THE KNOW.
THE MONEY WAS SUPPOSED TO BE FOR OPERATIONAL EXPENSES. WE NEEDED IT TO PAY STAFF, TO BUY EQUIPMENT, TO HIRE SECURITY. TO SHORE UP HIS GOVERNMENT, TO PROTECT IT.
IS THAT NOT WHAT HE'S DOING?
PARCO BOUGHT HIMSELF A CAPITAL-D DETERRENT, THE LITERAL DEFINITION OF THE WORD. WHY DO YOU THINK WE'VE HELD ON TO IT?
PARCO'S GOT WOLVES AT THE FUCKING DOOR. NOT JUST THE MAJOR PLAYERS, BUT DOZENS OF TRIBAL LEADERS AND INSURGENTS.
HE COULD USE THE GOLD TO PAY THEM OFF, TO BRIBE THEM, SURE. THE PROBLEM WITH THAT IS THEY'LL JUST COME BACK AROUND AGAIN FOR MORE. THAT FREE STATES COMMANDER IS A PRIME EXAMPLE. EXPECT TO SEE THAT MOTHERFUCKER AGAIN.
SO NOW PARCO CAN KEEP THE ENEMY AT BAY, ELEVATE HIMSELF IN THE WORLD'S EYES, AND BE THE BIG MAN LOCALLY, SOMEONE PEOPLE WILL WANT TO ALIGN THEMSELVES WITH.
YOU KNOW, I'M HONESTLY SURPRISED I HAVE TO TELL YOU THIS. YOU'RE PARCO'S MAN...YOU SHOULD BE ON BOARD WITH THIS.
I AM.
I'M JUST NOT ON BOARD WITH ALWAYS BEING THE LAST TO FUCKING KNOW.
HAVE WORDS WITH HIM, THEN. DON'T SIT AND STEW ABOUT IT UNTIL YOU GET SO PISSED OFF YOU DO SOMETHING YOU SHOULDN'T.
I KNOW A LITTLE SOMETHING ABOUT ENDING UP ON THE WRONG SIDE OF YOUR GOVERNMENT.

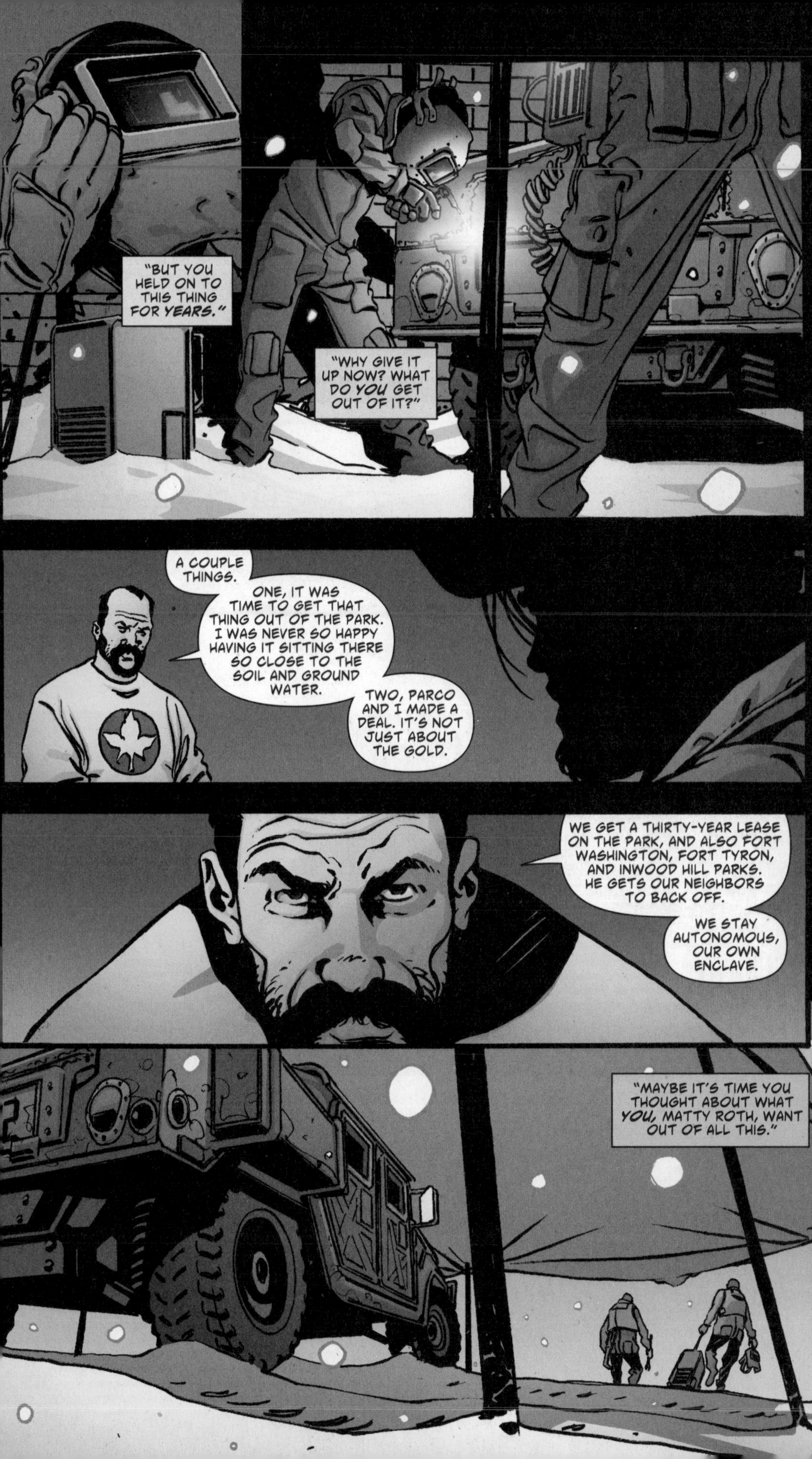
"BUT YOU HELD ON TO THIS THING FOR YEARS."
"WHY GIVE IT UP NOW? WHAT DO YOU GET OUT OF IT?"
A COUPLE THINGS.
ONE, IT WAS TIME TO GET THAT THING OUT OF THE PARK. I WAS NEVER SO HAPPY HAVING IT SITTING THERE SO CLOSE TO THE SOIL AND GROUND WATER.
TWO, PARCO AND I MADE A DEAL. IT'S NOT JUST ABOUT THE GOLD.
WE GET A THIRTY-YEAR LEASE ON THE PARK, AND ALSO FORT WASHINGTON, FORT TYRON, AND INWOOD HILL PARKS. HE GETS OUR NEIGHBORS TO BACK OFF.
WE STAY AUTONOMOUS, OUR OWN ENCLAVE.
"MAYBE IT'S TIME YOU THOUGHT ABOUT WHAT YOU, MATTY ROTH, WANT OUT OF ALL THIS."

"...recapping today's headlines, the delegation from the city of Manhattan, also known as "The DMZ," met today with representatives from the EU and Canada. The details of the meeting were not made public, but rumors of Parco Delgado's fledgling government being formally recognized were quickly squashed by analysts.

"'We are, of course, hopeful and eager for recognition,' Delgado press secretary Madelline Mastro said, 'but we also recognize that the DMZ is still an unstable and volatile region and we all have a lot of work to do.'

"Looking after the citizens of this city who so overwhelmingly voted us into office is our top priority.

"In related news, the U.S. Army Corps of engineers today completed work on the new Brooklyn Bridge security fence, specifically moving the barricades some twenty yards closer to the Brooklyn side.

"A newly declassified satellite survey conducted in the early days of the siege showed that the midway point was miscalculated, and the Delgado administration requested the error be corrected immediately."

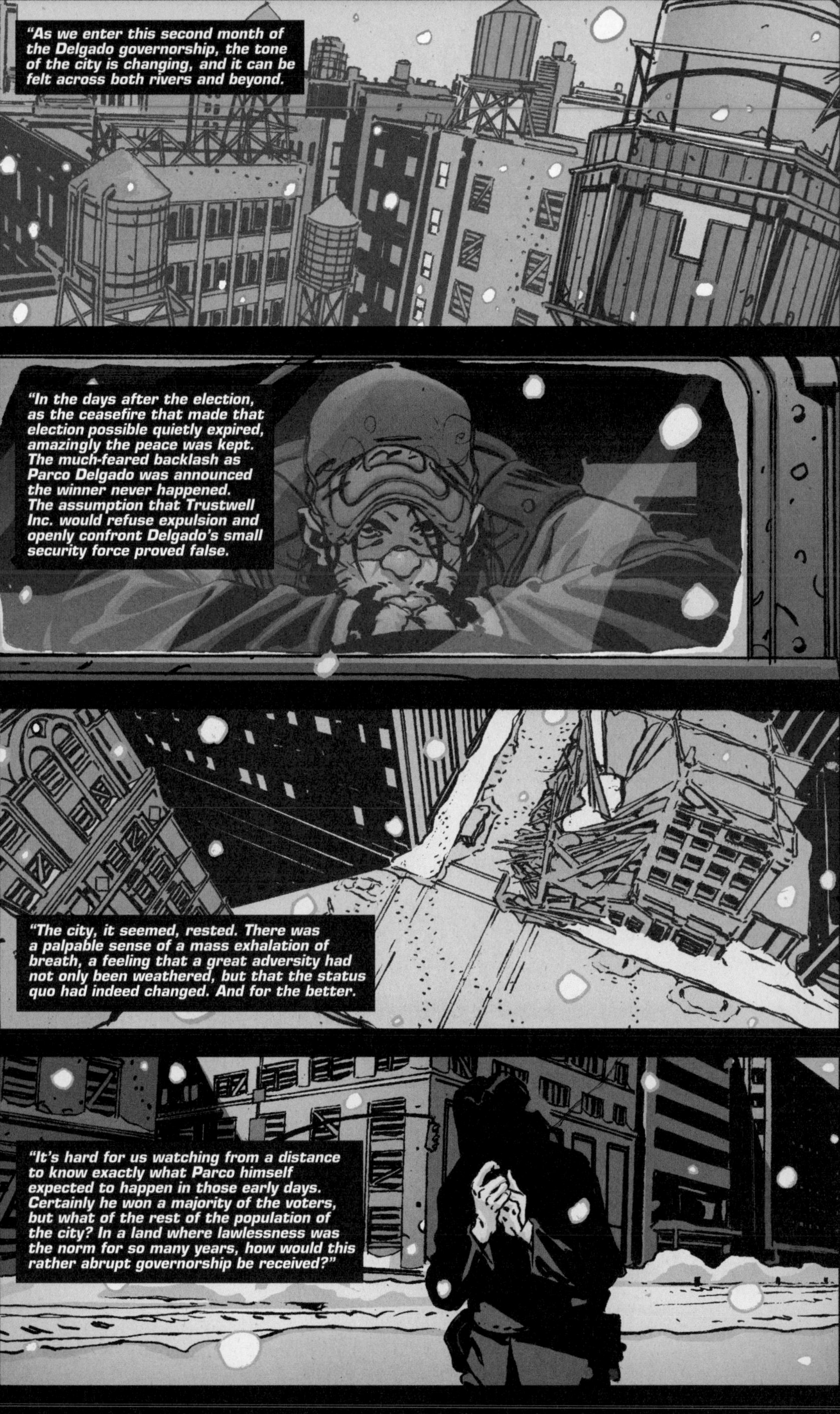
"As we enter this second month of the Delgado governorship, the tone of the city is changing, and it can be felt across both rivers and beyond.
"In the days after the election, as the ceasefire that made that election possible quietly expired, amazingly the peace was kept. The much-feared backlash as Parco Delgado was announced the winner never happened. The assumption that Trustwell Inc. would refuse expulsion and openly confront Delgado's small security force proved false.
"The city, it seemed, rested. There was a palpable sense of a mass exhalation of breath, a feeling that a great adversity had not only been weathered, but that the status quo had indeed changed. And for the better.
"It's hard for us watching from a distance to know exactly what Parco himself expected to happen in those early days. Certainly he won a majority of the voters, but what of the rest of the population of the city? In a land where lawlessness was the norm for so many years, how would this rather abrupt governorship be received?"

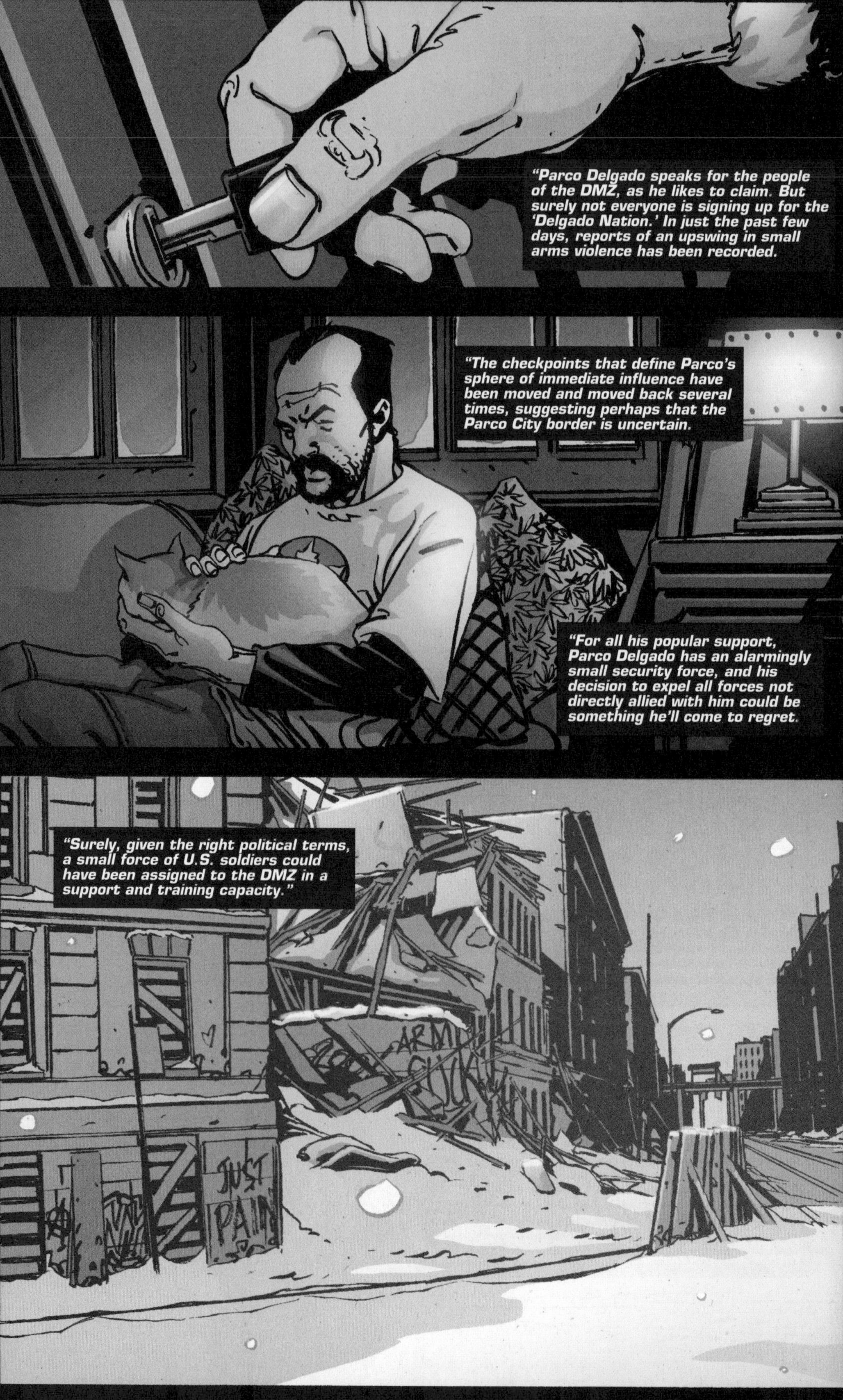
"Parco Delgado speaks for the people of the DMZ, as he likes to claim. But surely not everyone is signing up for the 'Delgado Nation.' In just the past few days, reports of an upswing in small arms violence has been recorded.
"The checkpoints that define Parco's sphere of immediate influence have been moved and moved back several times, suggesting perhaps that the Parco City border is uncertain.
"For all his popular support, Parco Delgado has an alarmingly small security force, and his decision to expel all forces not directly allied with him could be something he'll come to regret.
"Surely, given the right political terms, a small force of U.S. soldiers could have been assigned to the DMZ in a support and training capacity."
JUST

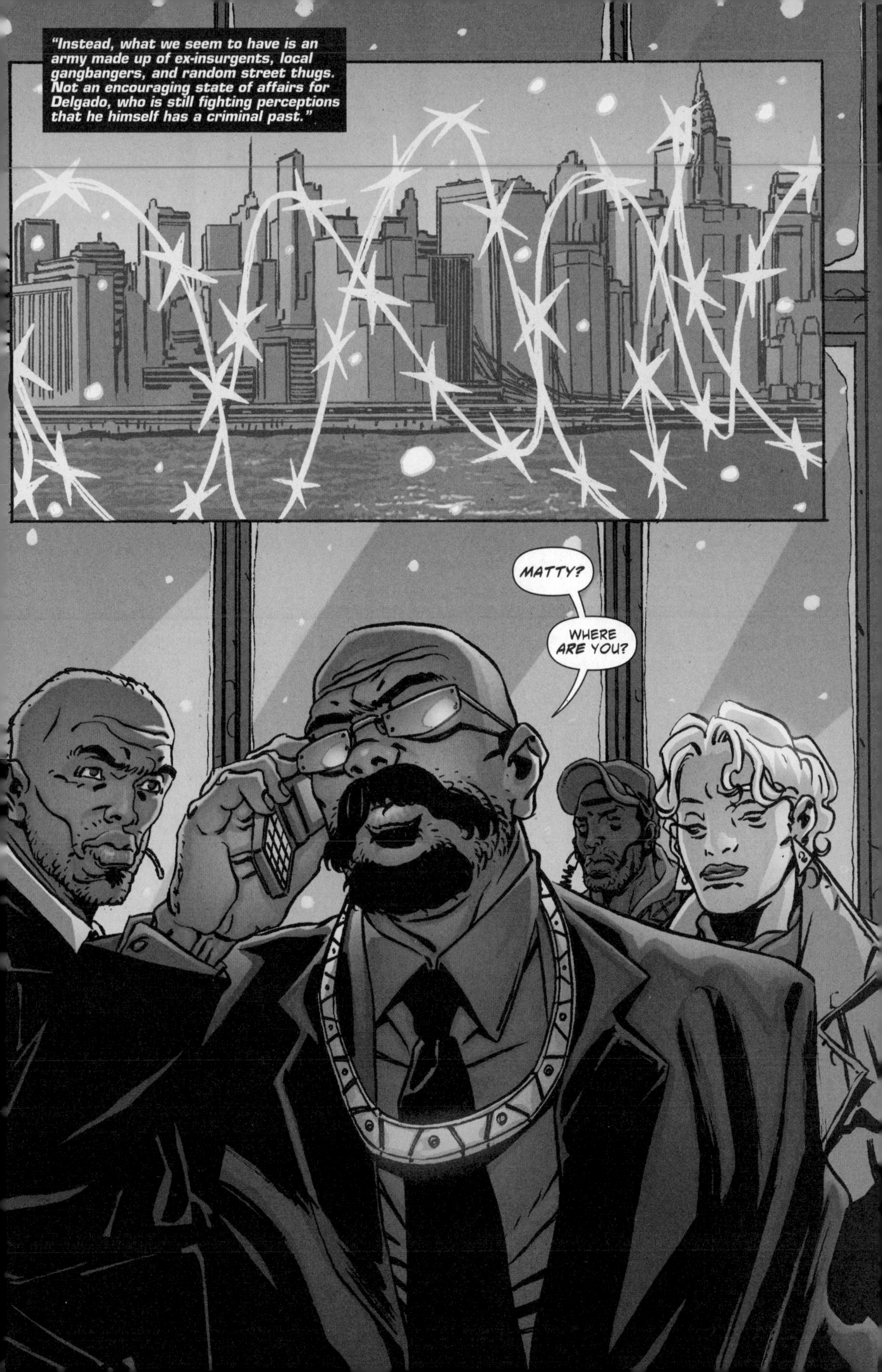
"Instead, what we seem to have is an army made up of ex-insurgents, local gangbangers, and random street thugs. Not an encouraging state of affairs for Delgado, who is still fighting perceptions that he himself has a criminal past."
MATTY?
WHERE ARE YOU?

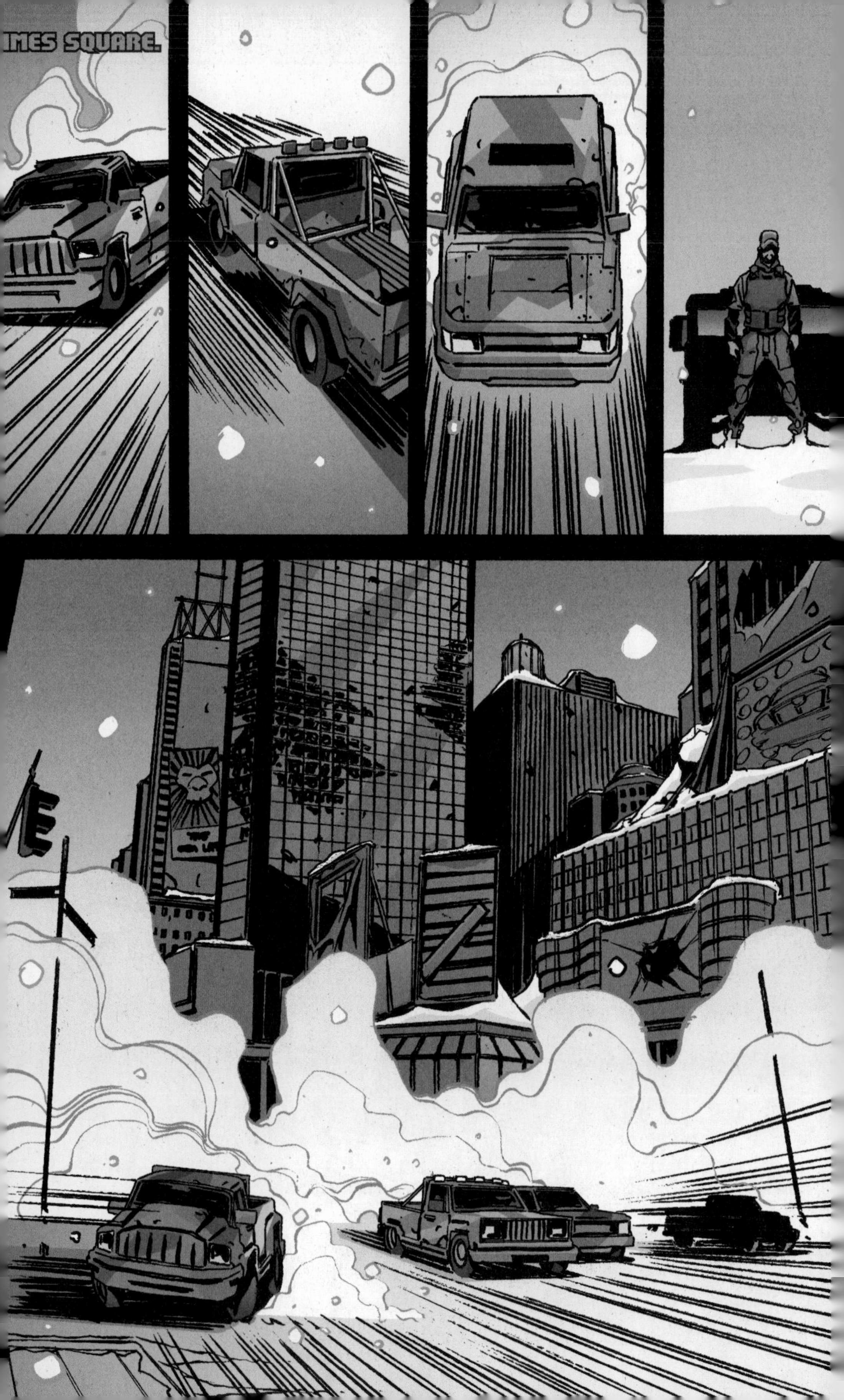

IMES SQUARE.

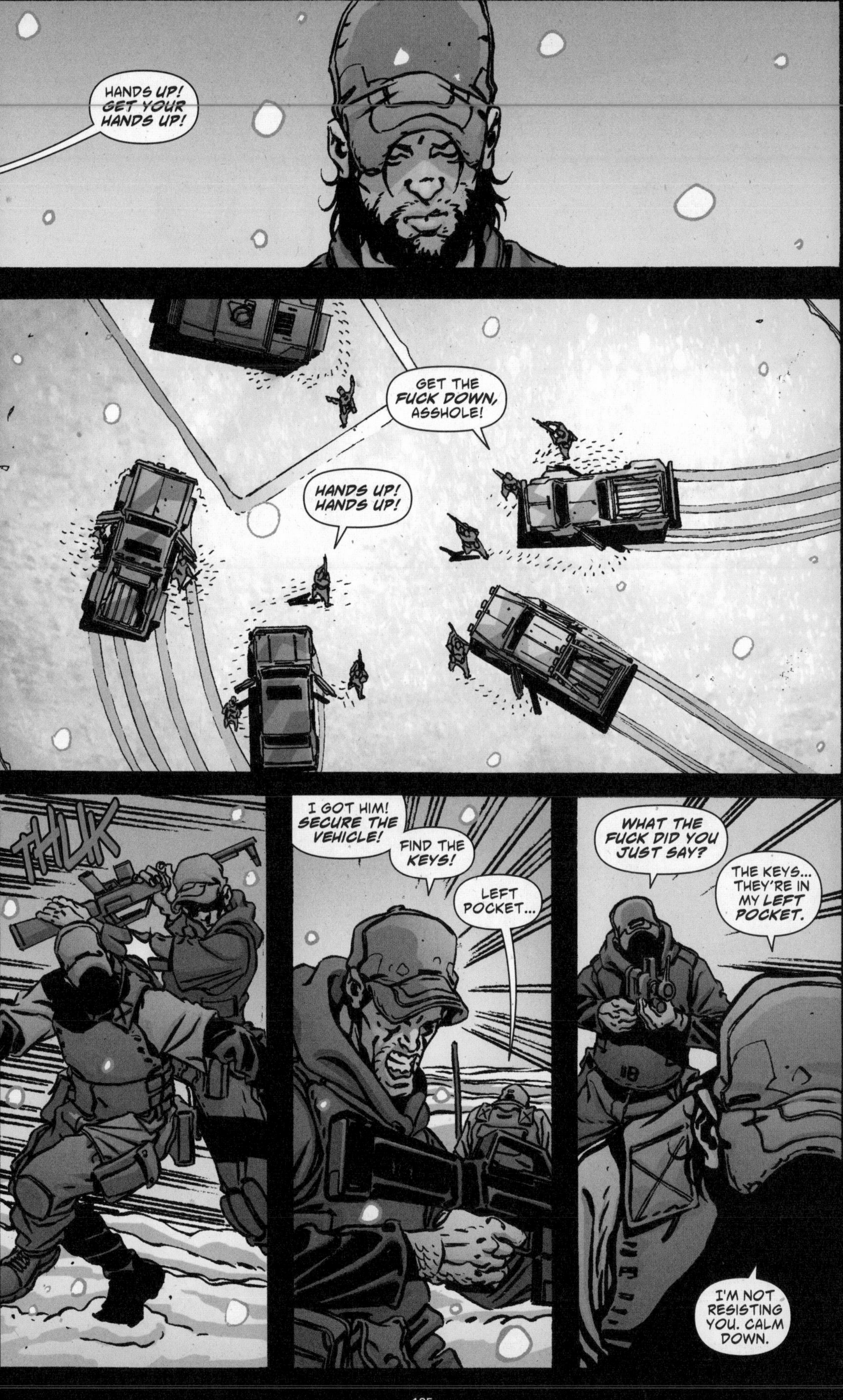
HANDS UP! GET YOUR HANDS UP!
GET THE FUCK DOWN, ASSHOLE!
HANDS UP! HANDS UP!
THUK
I GOT HIM! SECURE THE VEHICLE!
FIND THE KEYS!
LEFT POCKET...
WHAT THE FUCK DID YOU JUST SAY?
THE KEYS... THEY'RE IN MY LEFT POCKET.
I'M NOT RESISTING YOU. CALM DOWN.

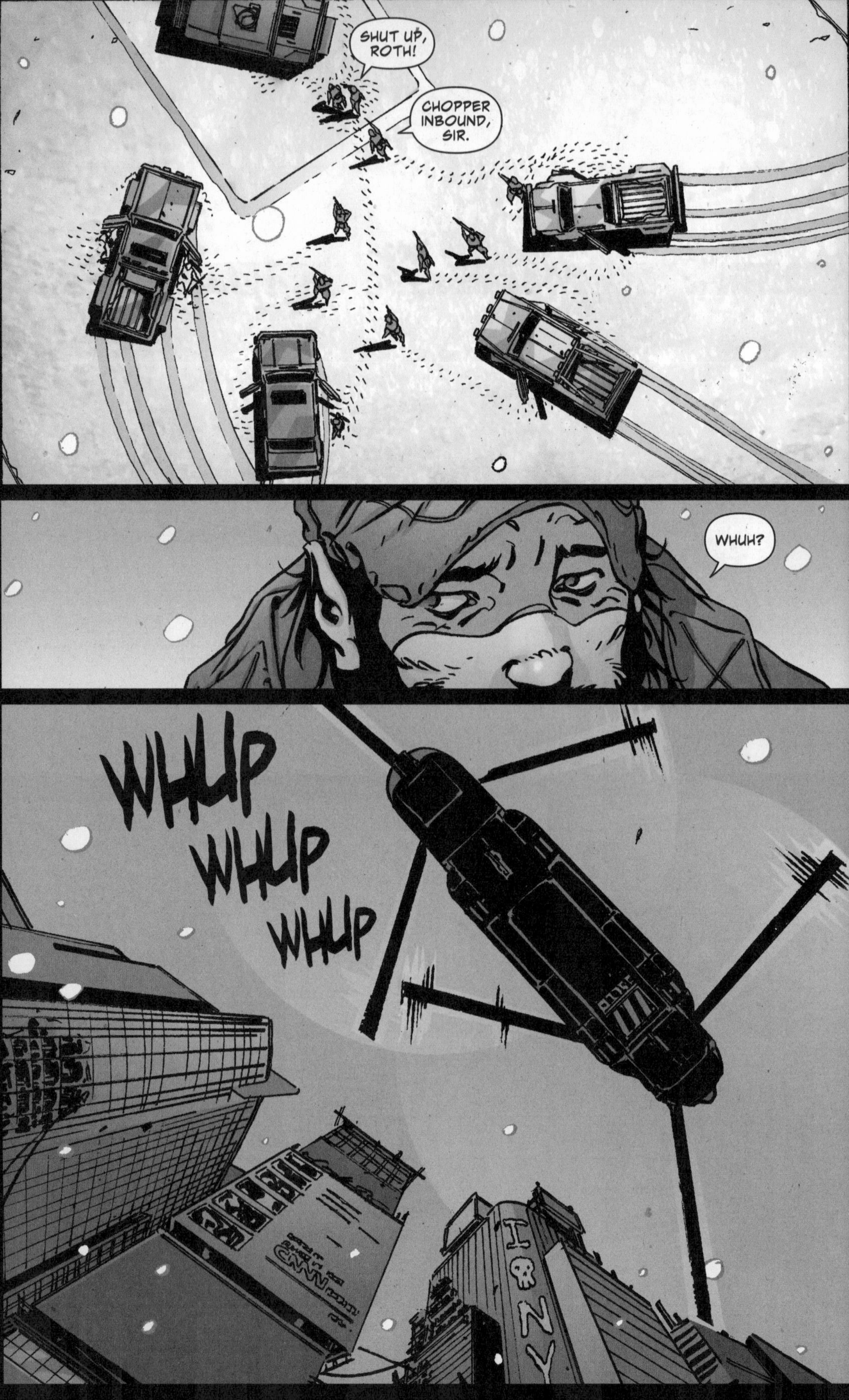
SHUT UP, ROTH!
CHOPPER INBOUND, SIR.
WHUH?
WHUP
WHUP
WHUP

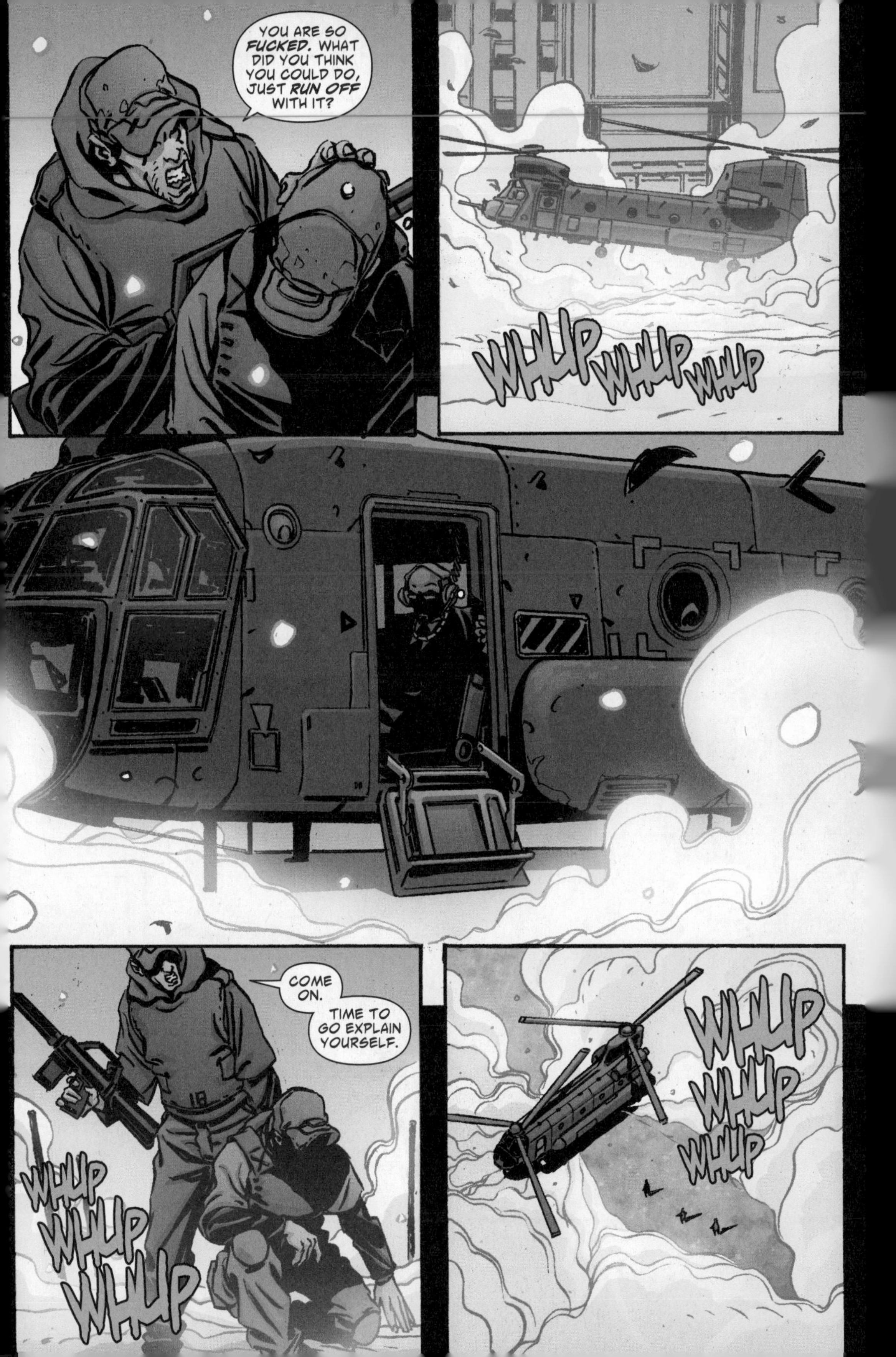
YOU ARE SO FUCKED. WHAT DID YOU THINK YOU COULD DO, JUST RUN OFF WITH IT?
WHUP WHUP WHUP
COME ON.
TIME TO GO EXPLAIN YOURSELF.
WHUP WHUP WHUP
WHUP WHUP WHUP

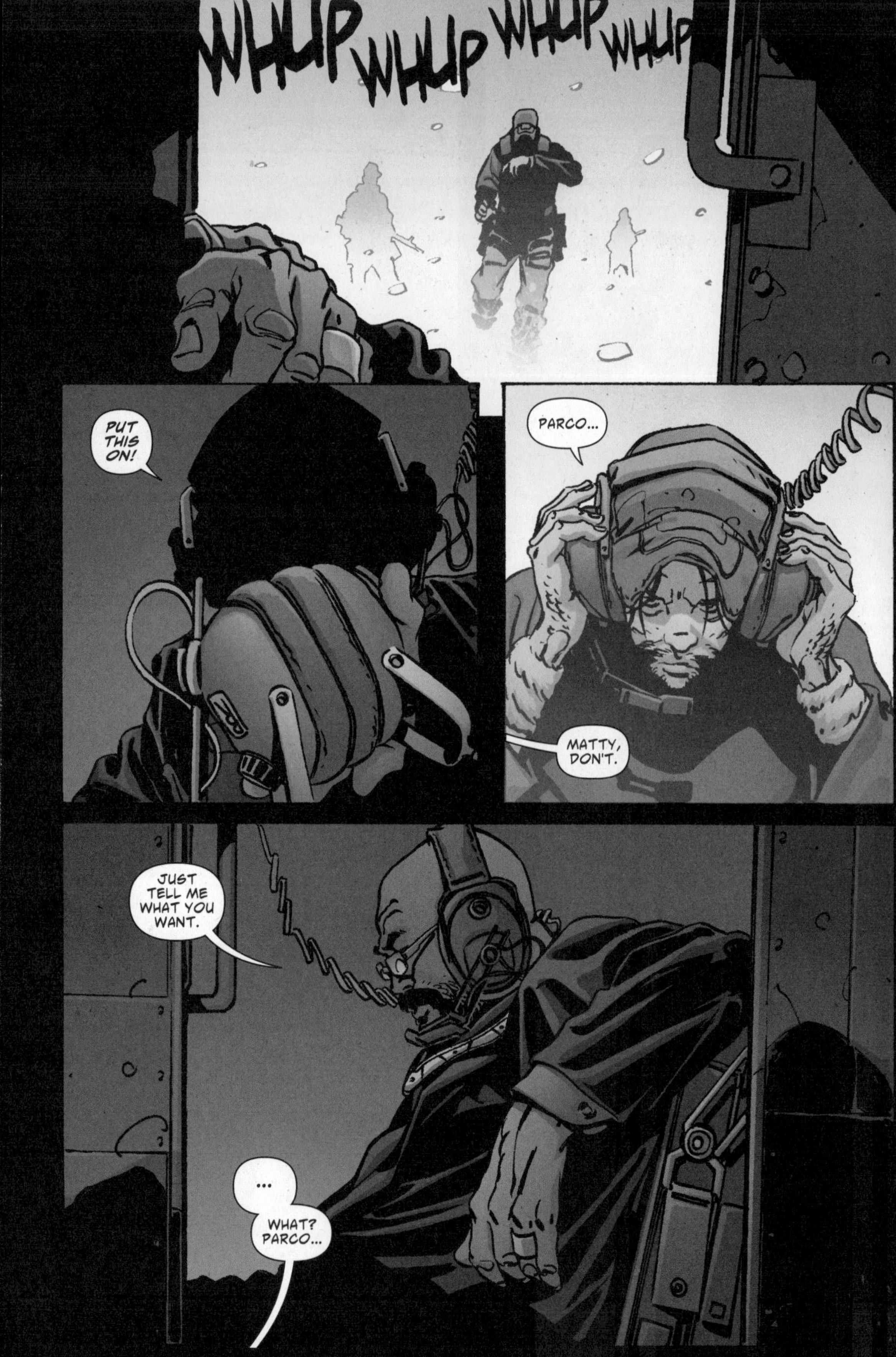

WHUP WHUP WHUP WHUP
PUT THIS ON!
PARCO...
MATTY, DON'T.
JUST TELL ME WHAT YOU WANT.
...
WHAT? PARCO...

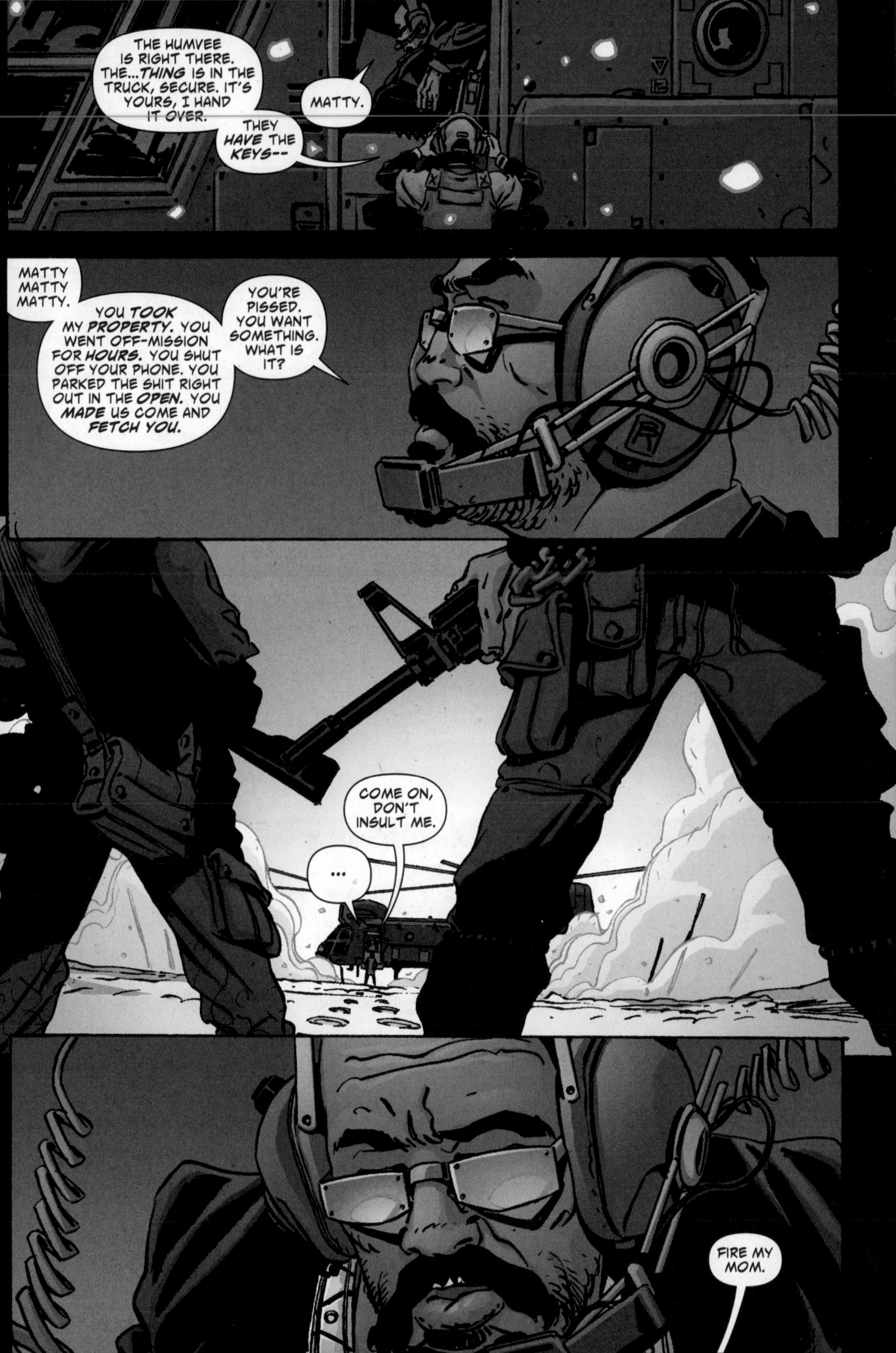
THE HUMVEE IS RIGHT THERE. THE...THING IS IN THE TRUCK, SECURE. IT'S YOURS, I HAND IT OVER.
MATTY.
THEY HAVE THE KEYS--
MATTY MATTY MATTY.
YOU TOOK MY PROPERTY. YOU WENT OFF-MISSION FOR HOURS. YOU SHUT OFF YOUR PHONE. YOU PARKED THE SHIT RIGHT OUT IN THE OPEN. YOU MADE US COME AND FETCH YOU.
YOU'RE PISSED. YOU WANT SOMETHING. WHAT IS IT?
COME ON, DON'T INSULT ME.
...
FIRE MY MOM.

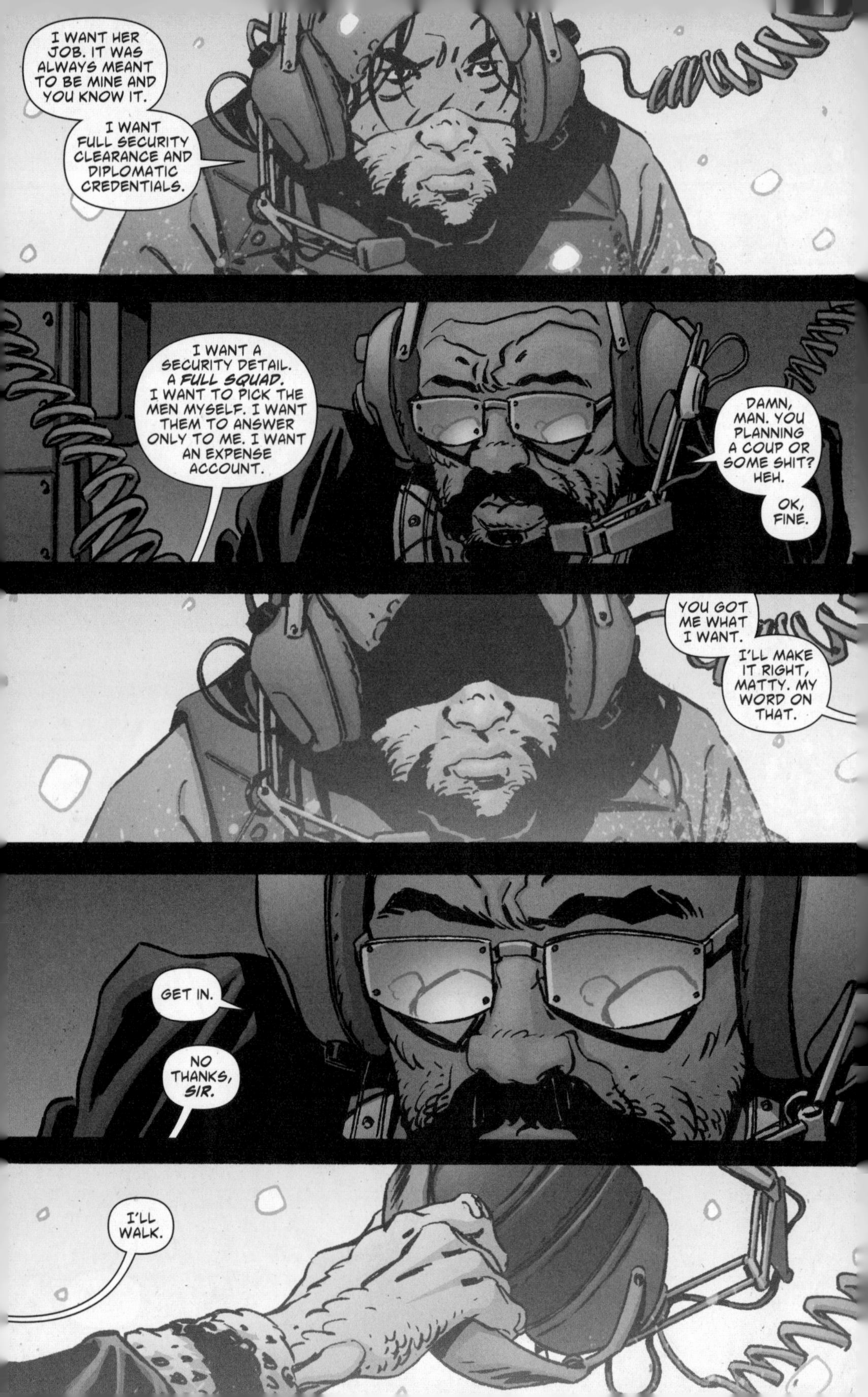
I WANT HER JOB. IT WAS ALWAYS MEANT TO BE MINE AND YOU KNOW IT.
I WANT FULL SECURITY CLEARANCE AND DIPLOMATIC CREDENTIALS.
I WANT A SECURITY DETAIL. A FULL SQUAD. I WANT TO PICK THE MEN MYSELF. I WANT THEM TO ANSWER ONLY TO ME. I WANT AN EXPENSE ACCOUNT.
DAMN, MAN. YOU PLANNING A COUP OR SOME SHIT? HEH.
OK, FINE.
YOU GOT ME WHAT I WANT.
I'LL MAKE IT RIGHT, MATTY. MY WORD ON THAT.
GET IN.
NO THANKS, SIR.
I'LL WALK.

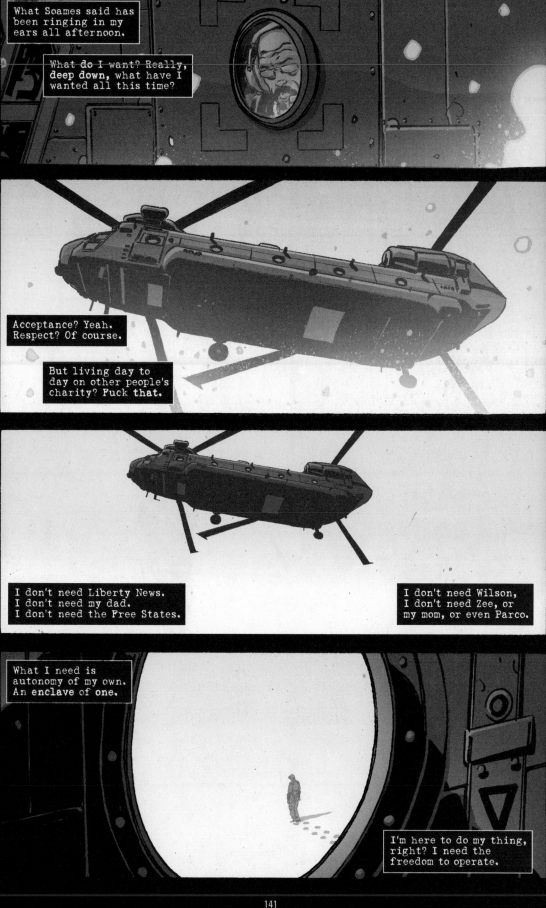

What Soames said has been ringing in my ears all afternoon.

What **do** I want? Really, **deep down**, what have I wanted all this time?

Acceptance? Yeah. Respect? Of course.

But living day to day on other people's charity? Fuck **that**.

I don't need Liberty News. I don't need my dad. I don't need the Free States.

I don't need Wilson, I don't need Zee, or my mom, or even Parco.

What I need is autonomy of my own. An **enclave** of one.

I'm here to do my thing, right? I need the freedom to operate.

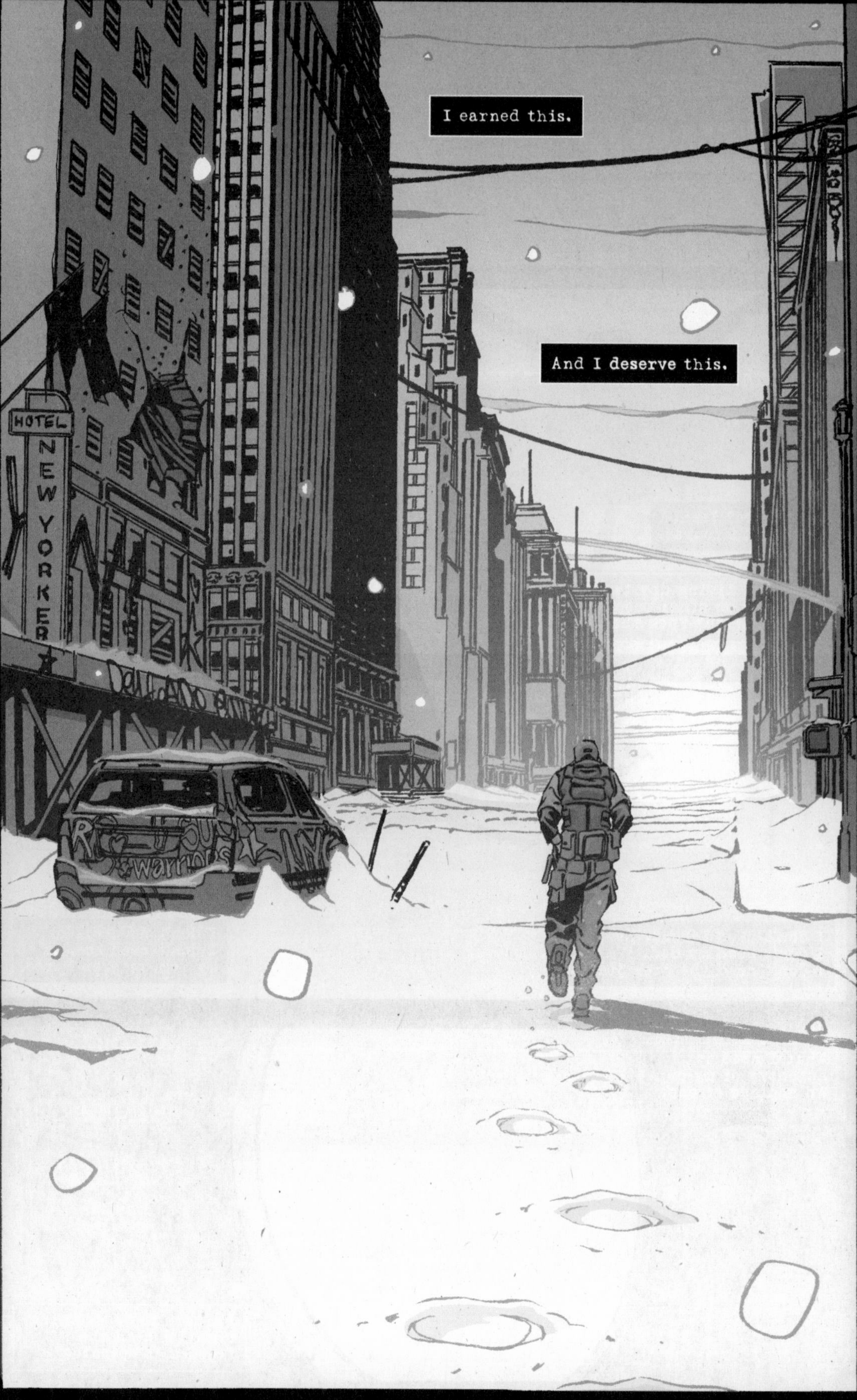
I earned this.
And I deserve this.
HOTEL
NEW YORKER

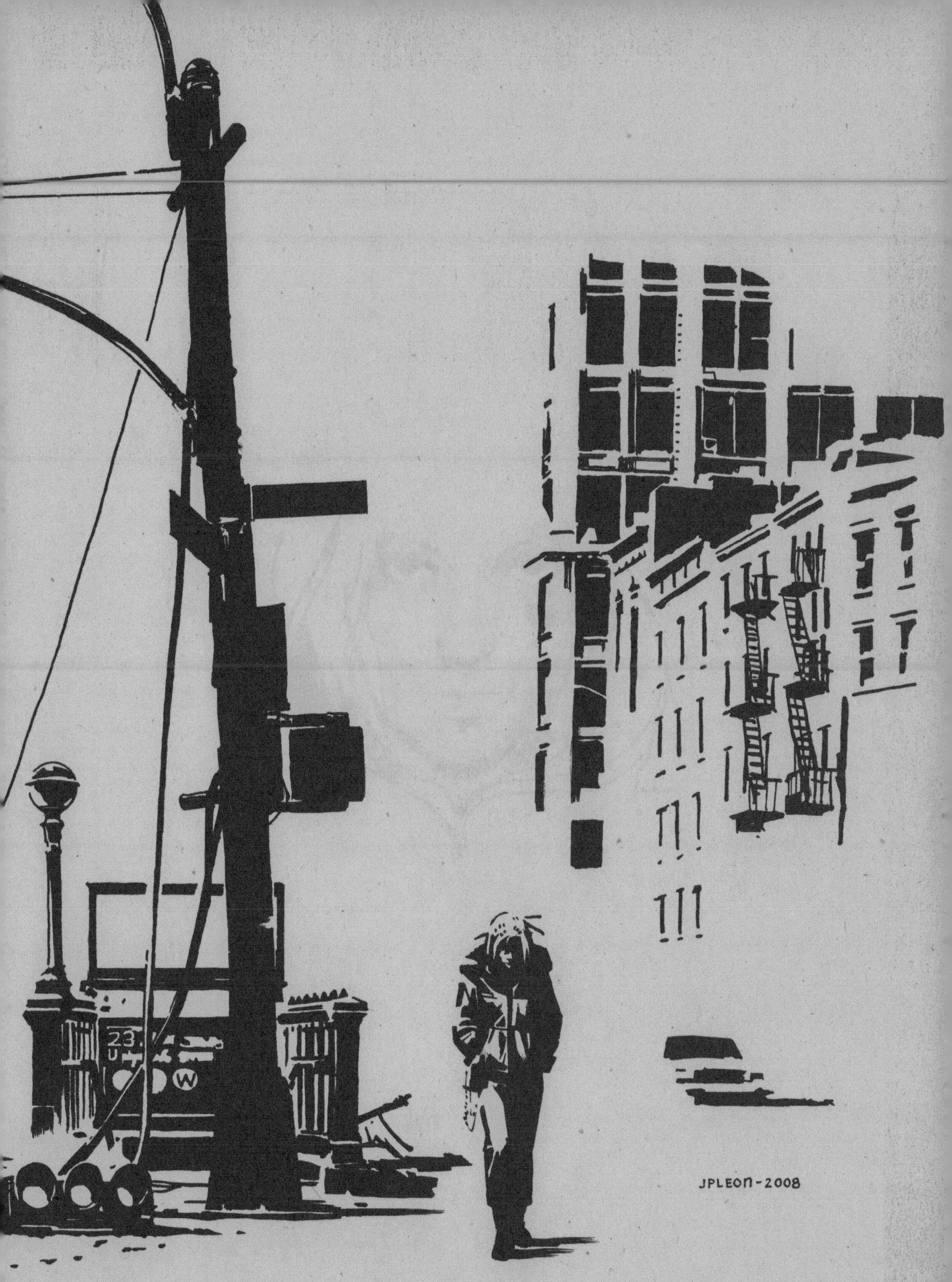
JPLEON-2008

ZEE, DMZ

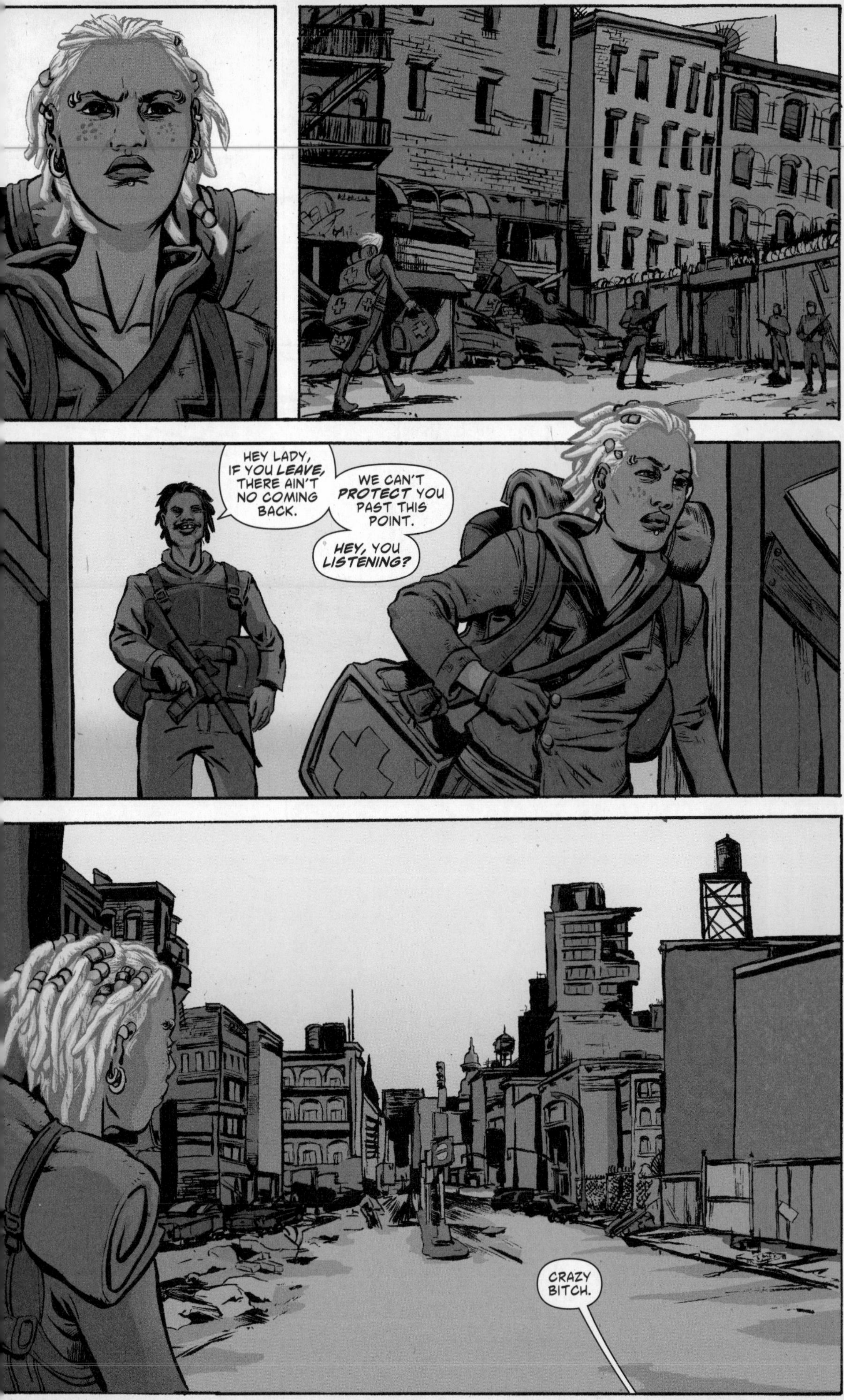
HEY LADY, IF YOU LEAVE, THERE AIN'T NO COMING BACK.
WE CAN'T PROTECT YOU PAST THIS POINT.
HEY, YOU LISTENING?
CRAZY BITCH.

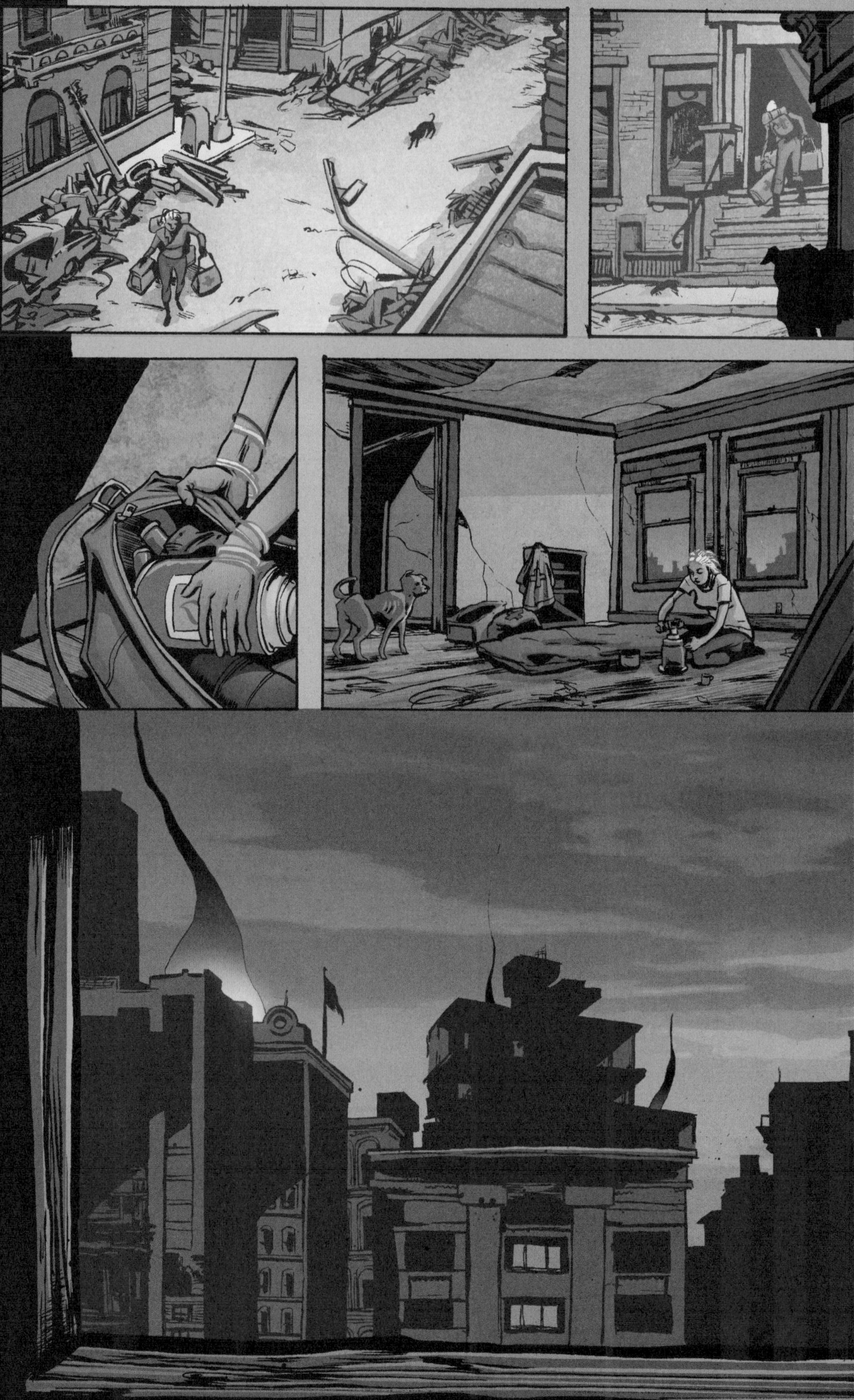

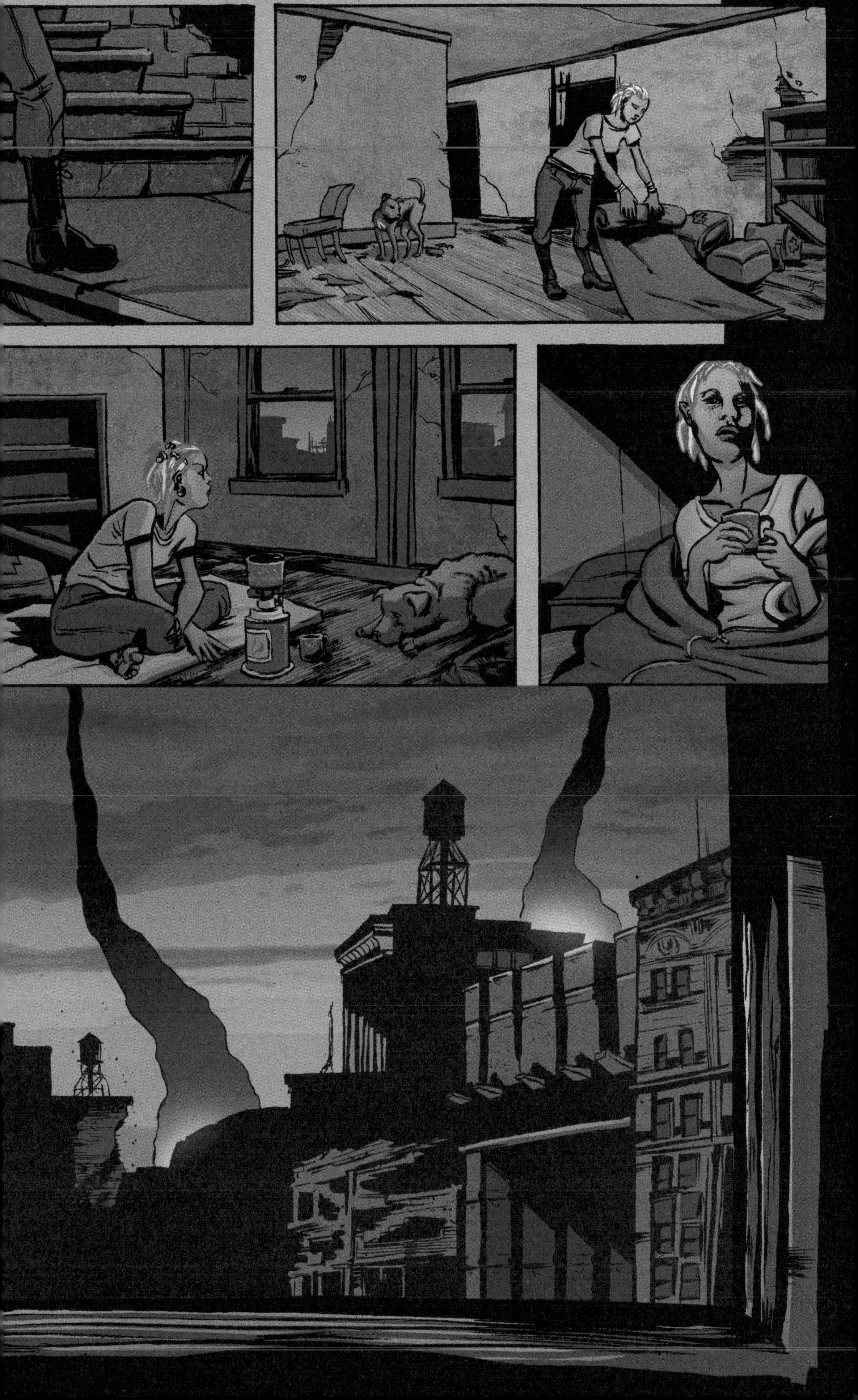

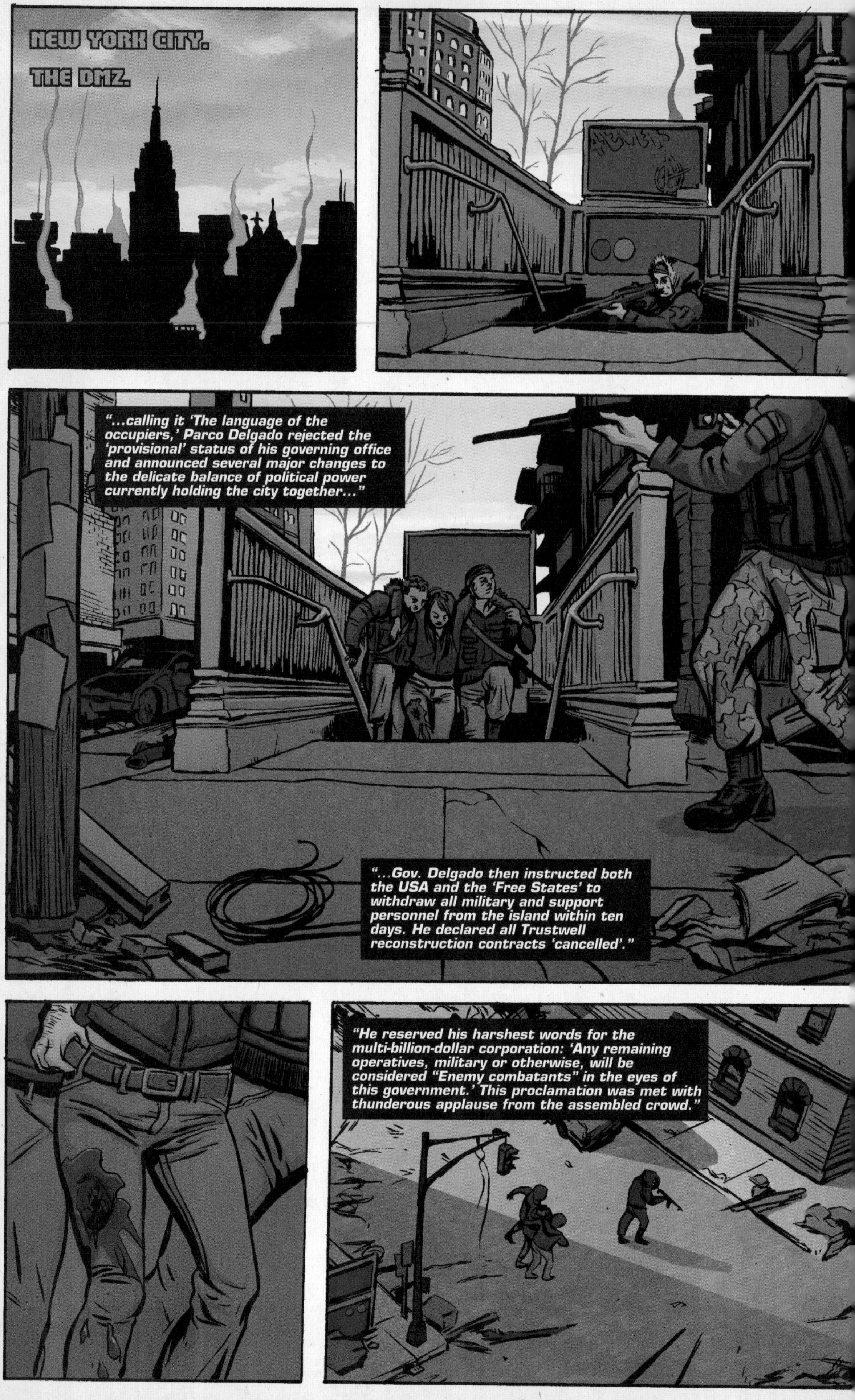
NEW YORK CITY.
THE DMZ.
"...calling it 'The language of the occupiers,' Parco Delgado rejected the 'provisional' status of his governing office and announced several major changes to the delicate balance of political power currently holding the city together..."
"...Gov. Delgado then instructed both the USA and the 'Free States' to withdraw all military and support personnel from the island within ten days. He declared all Trustwell reconstruction contracts 'cancelled'."
"He reserved his harshest words for the multi-billion-dollar corporation: 'Any remaining operatives, military or otherwise, will be considered "Enemy combatants" in the eyes of this government.' This proclamation was met with thunderous applause from the assembled crowd."

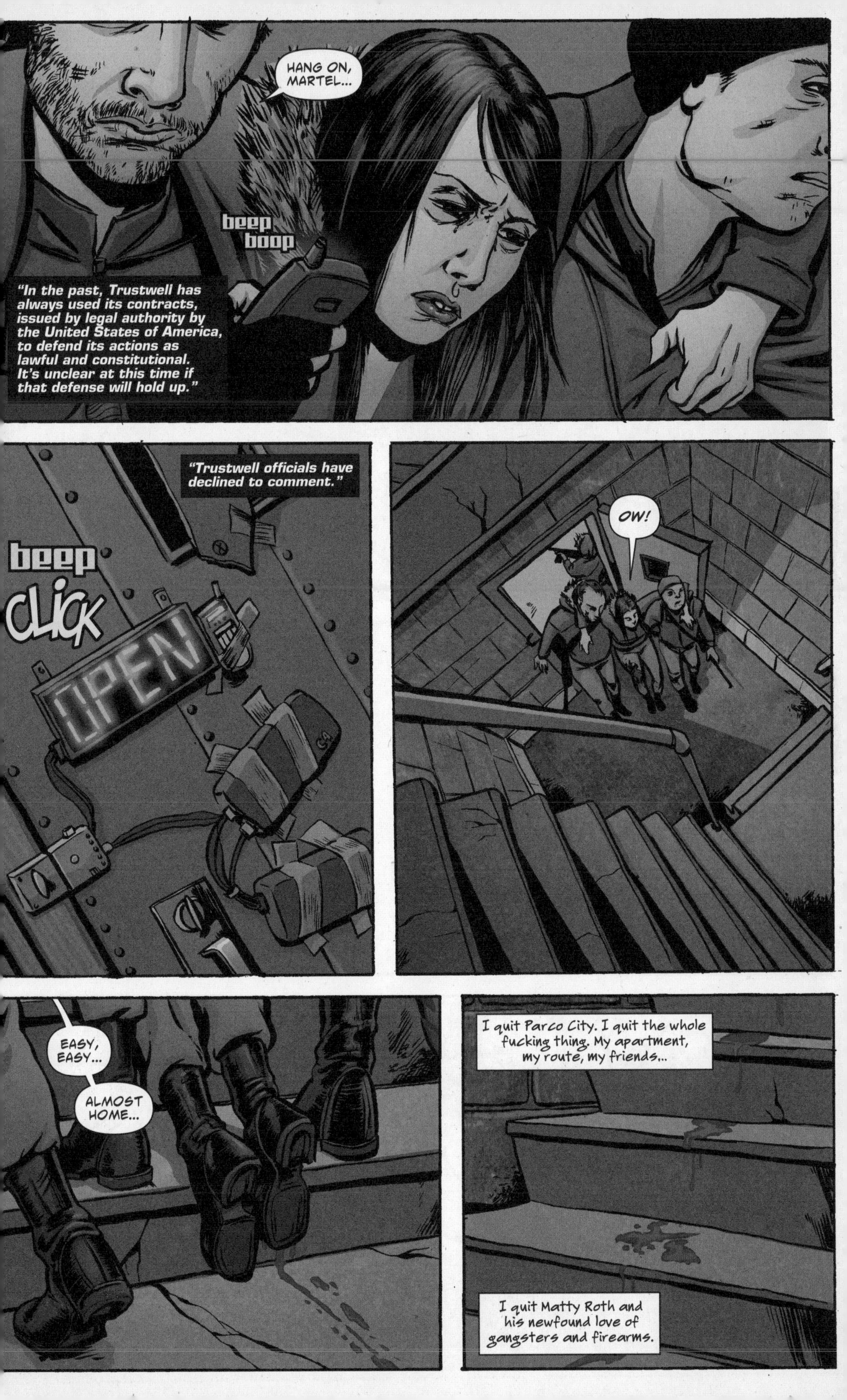
HANG ON, MARTEL...
beep boop
"In the past, Trustwell has always used its contracts, issued by legal authority by the United States of America, to defend its actions as lawful and constitutional. It's unclear at this time if that defense will hold up."
"Trustwell officials have declined to comment."
beep
CLICK
OPEN
OW!
EASY, EASY...
ALMOST HOME...
I quit Parco City. I quit the whole fucking thing. My apartment, my route, my friends...
I quit Matty Roth and his newfound love of gangsters and firearms.

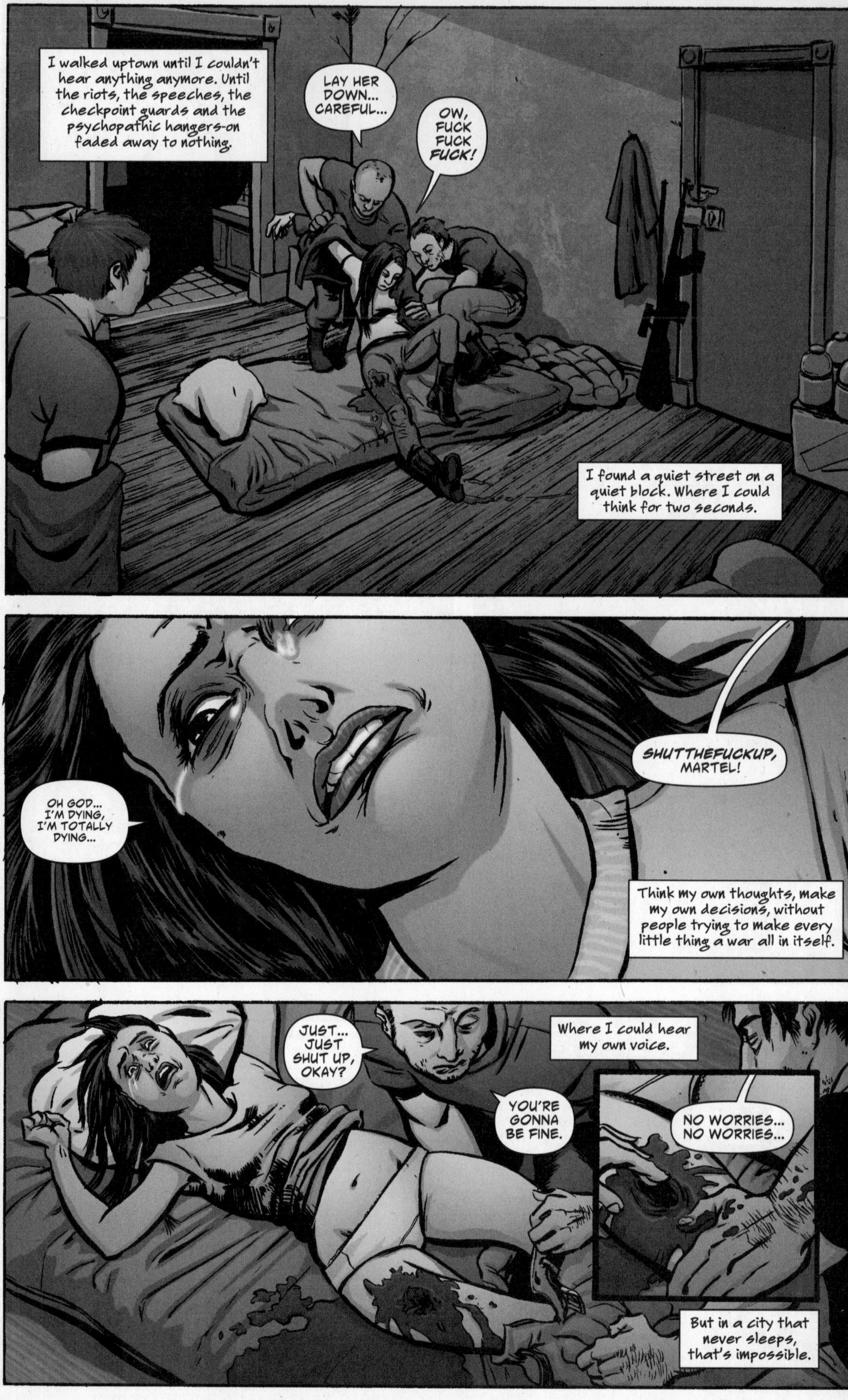
I walked uptown until I couldn't hear anything anymore. Until the riots, the speeches, the checkpoint guards and the psychopathic hangers-on faded away to nothing.
LAY HER DOWN... CAREFUL...
OW, FUCK FUCK FUCK!
I found a quiet street on a quiet block. Where I could think for two seconds.
OH GOD... I'M DYING, I'M TOTALLY DYING...
SHUTTHEFUCKUP, MARTEL!
Think my own thoughts, make my own decisions, without people trying to make every little thing a war all in itself.
JUST... JUST SHUT UP, OKAY?
Where I could hear my own voice.
YOU'RE GONNA BE FINE.
NO WORRIES... NO WORRIES...
But in a city that never sleeps, that's impossible.

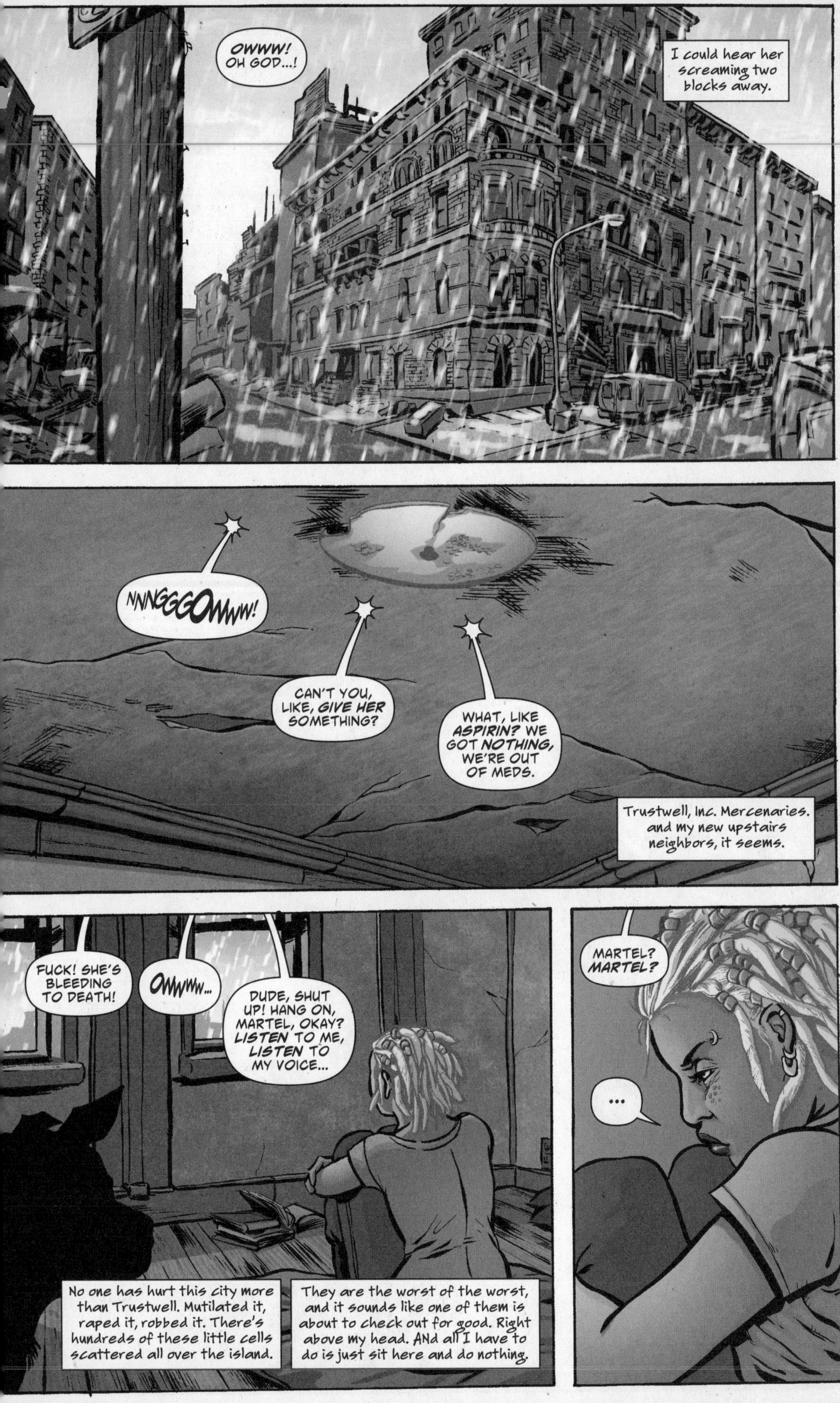

OWWW! OH GOD...!
I could hear her screaming two blocks away.
NNNGGGOWWW!
CAN'T YOU, LIKE, GIVE HER SOMETHING?
WHAT, LIKE ASPIRIN? WE GOT NOTHING, WE'RE OUT OF MEDS.
Trustwell, Inc. Mercenaries. and my new upstairs neighbors, it seems.
FUCK! SHE'S BLEEDING TO DEATH!
OWWW...
DUDE, SHUT UP! HANG ON, MARTEL, OKAY? LISTEN TO ME, LISTEN TO MY VOICE...
No one has hurt this city more than Trustwell. Mutilated it, raped it, robbed it. There's hundreds of these little cells scattered all over the island.
They are the worst of the worst, and it sounds like one of them is about to check out for good. Right above my head. And all I have to do is just sit here and do nothing.
MARTEL? MARTEL?
...

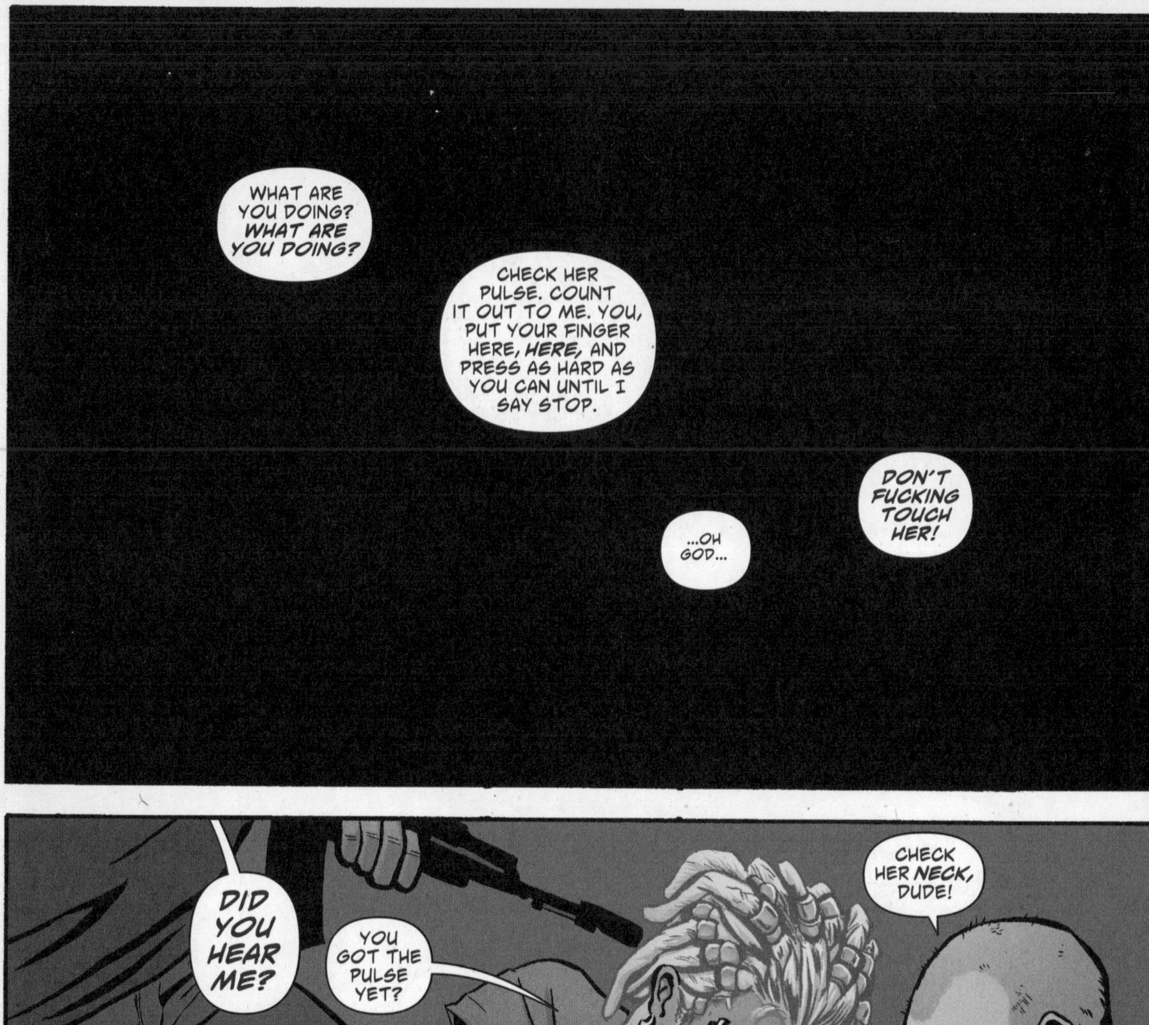

WHAT ARE YOU DOING? WHAT ARE YOU DOING?
CHECK HER PULSE. COUNT IT OUT TO ME. YOU, PUT YOUR FINGER HERE, HERE, AND PRESS AS HARD AS YOU CAN UNTIL I SAY STOP.
DON'T FUCKING TOUCH HER!
...OH GOD...
DID YOU HEAR ME?
YOU GOT THE PULSE YET?
I--I DON'T KNOW...
CHECK HER NECK, DUDE!
HANG ON, MARTEL...
I GOT YOU.

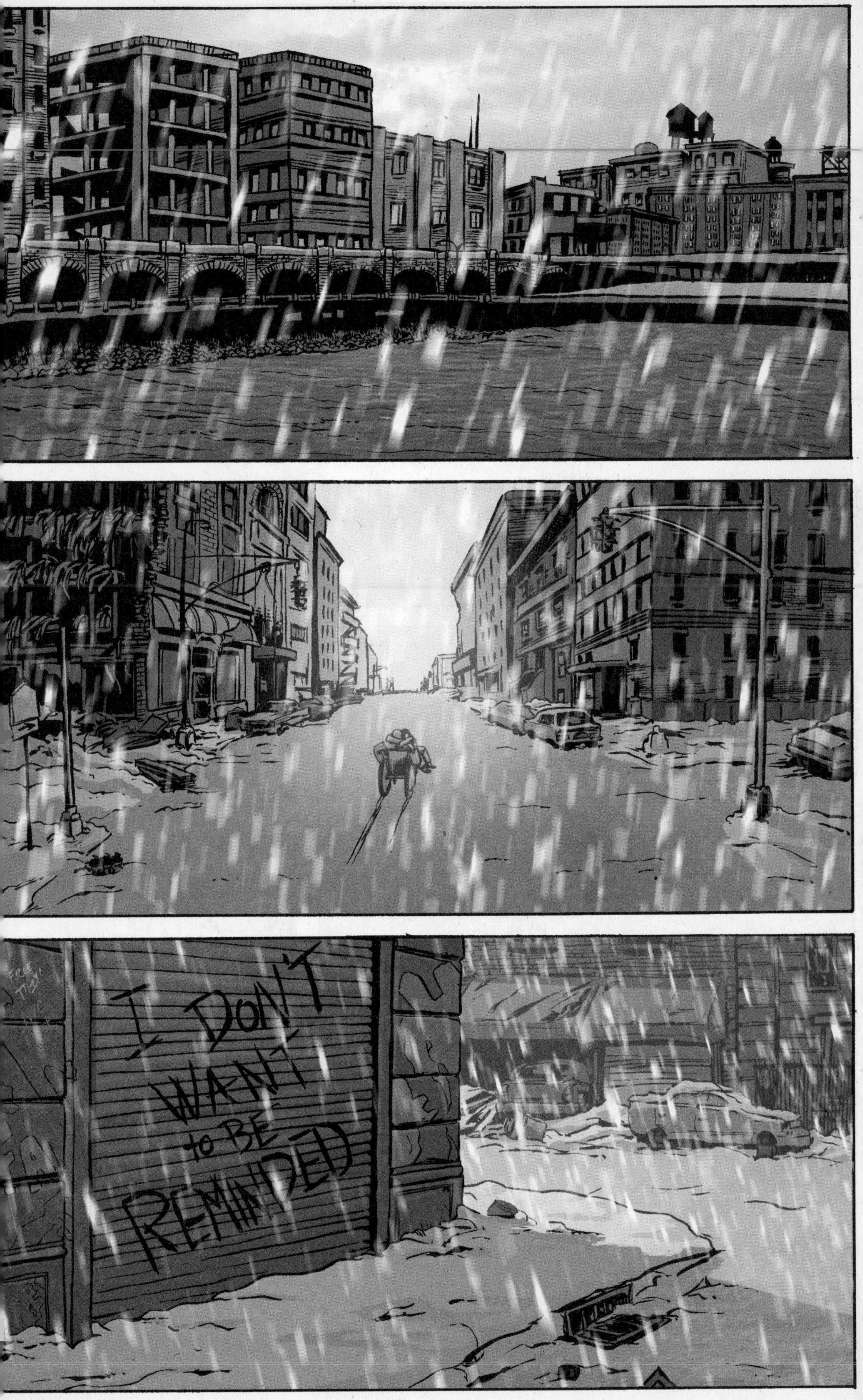
FREE TIBET!
I DON'T WANT to BE REMINDED

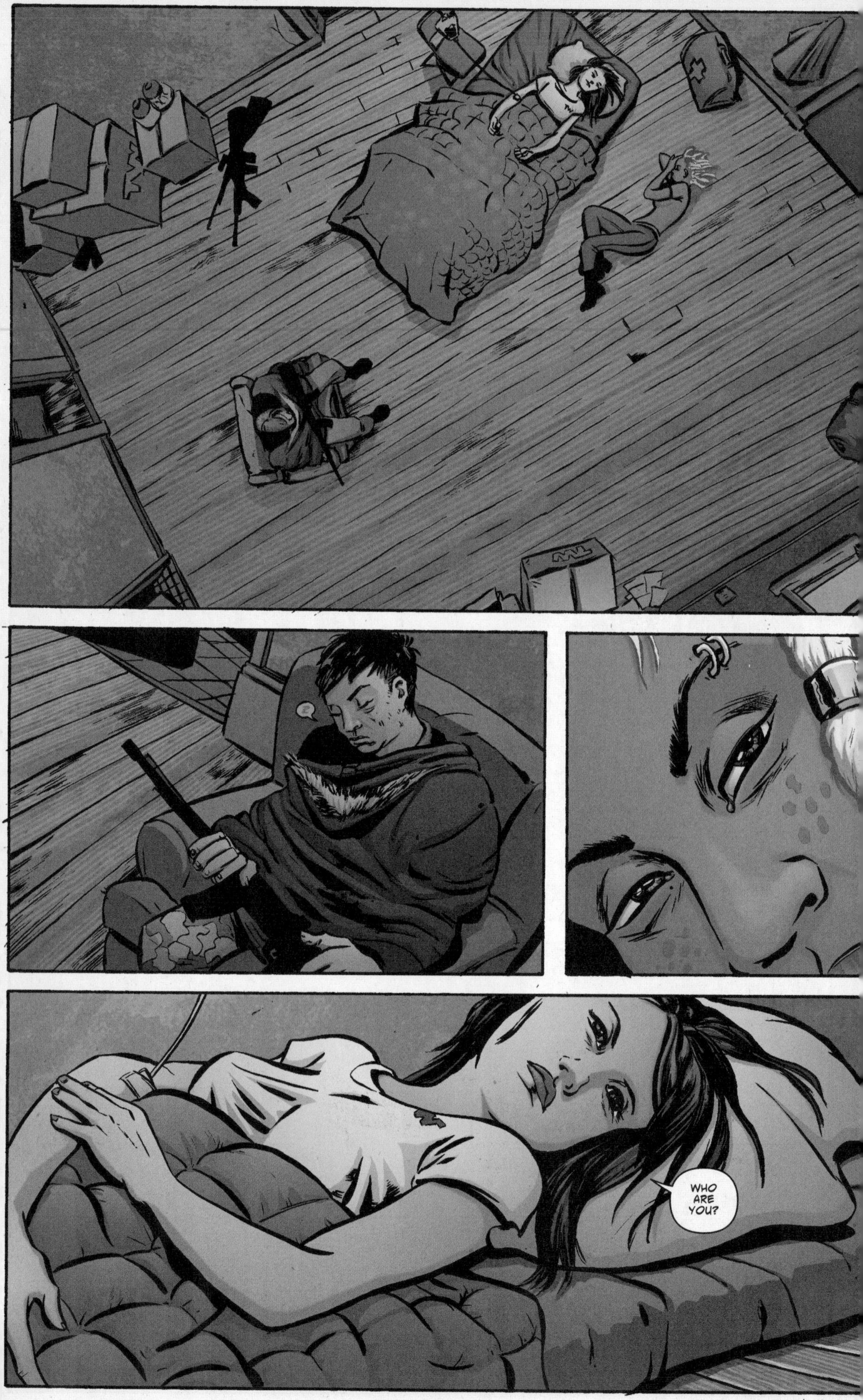
WHO ARE YOU?

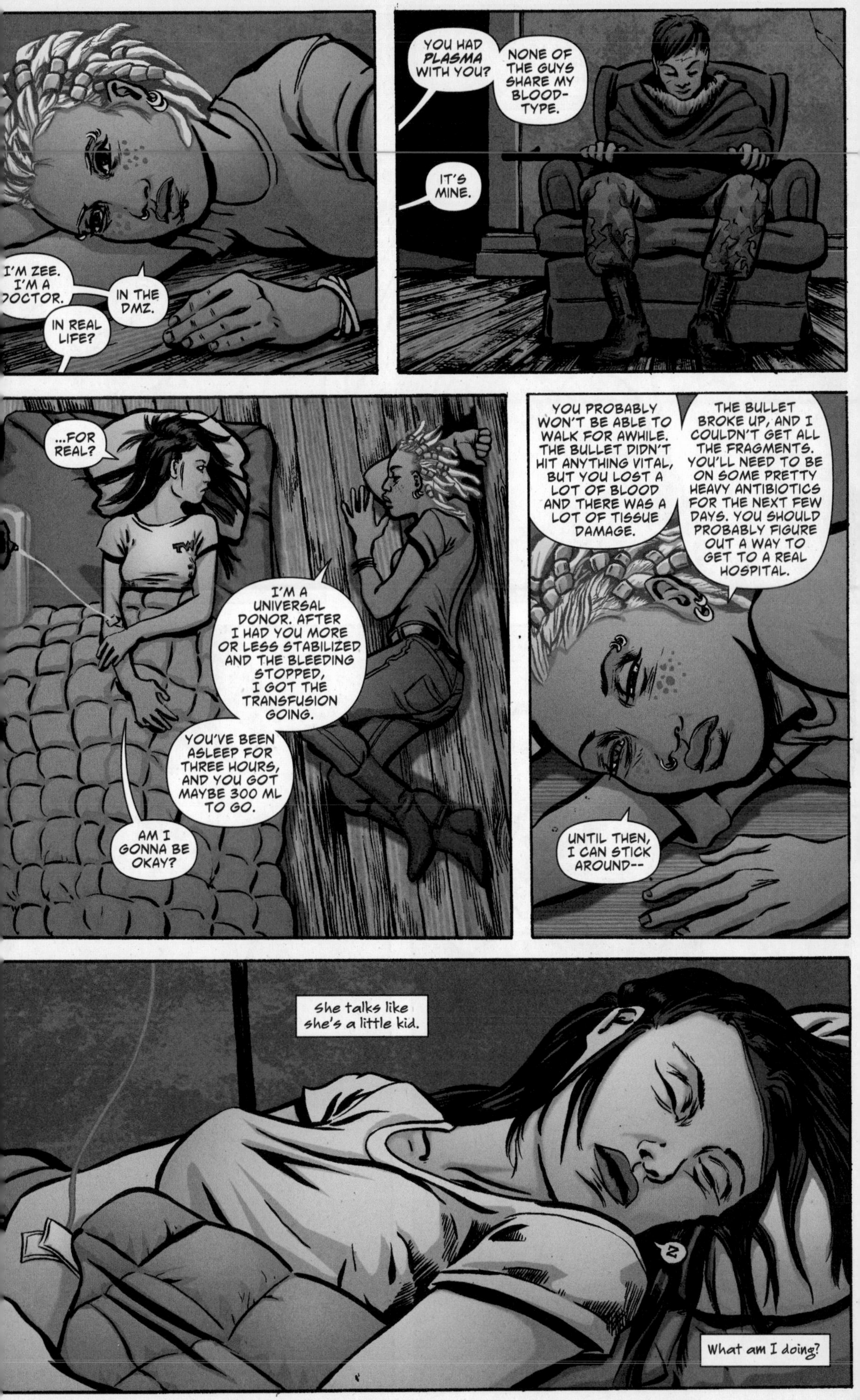
I'M ZEE. I'M A DOCTOR.
IN REAL LIFE?
IN THE DMZ.
YOU HAD PLASMA WITH YOU?
NONE OF THE GUYS SHARE MY BLOOD-TYPE.
IT'S MINE.
...FOR REAL?
I'M A UNIVERSAL DONOR. AFTER I HAD YOU MORE OR LESS STABILIZED AND THE BLEEDING STOPPED, I GOT THE TRANSFUSION GOING.
YOU'VE BEEN ASLEEP FOR THREE HOURS, AND YOU GOT MAYBE 300 ML TO GO.
AM I GONNA BE OKAY?
YOU PROBABLY WON'T BE ABLE TO WALK FOR AWHILE. THE BULLET DIDN'T HIT ANYTHING VITAL, BUT YOU LOST A LOT OF BLOOD AND THERE WAS A LOT OF TISSUE DAMAGE.
THE BULLET BROKE UP, AND I COULDN'T GET ALL THE FRAGMENTS. YOU'LL NEED TO BE ON SOME PRETTY HEAVY ANTIBIOTICS FOR THE NEXT FEW DAYS. YOU SHOULD PROBABLY FIGURE OUT A WAY TO GET TO A REAL HOSPITAL.
UNTIL THEN, I CAN STICK AROUND--
She talks like she's a little kid.
What am I doing?

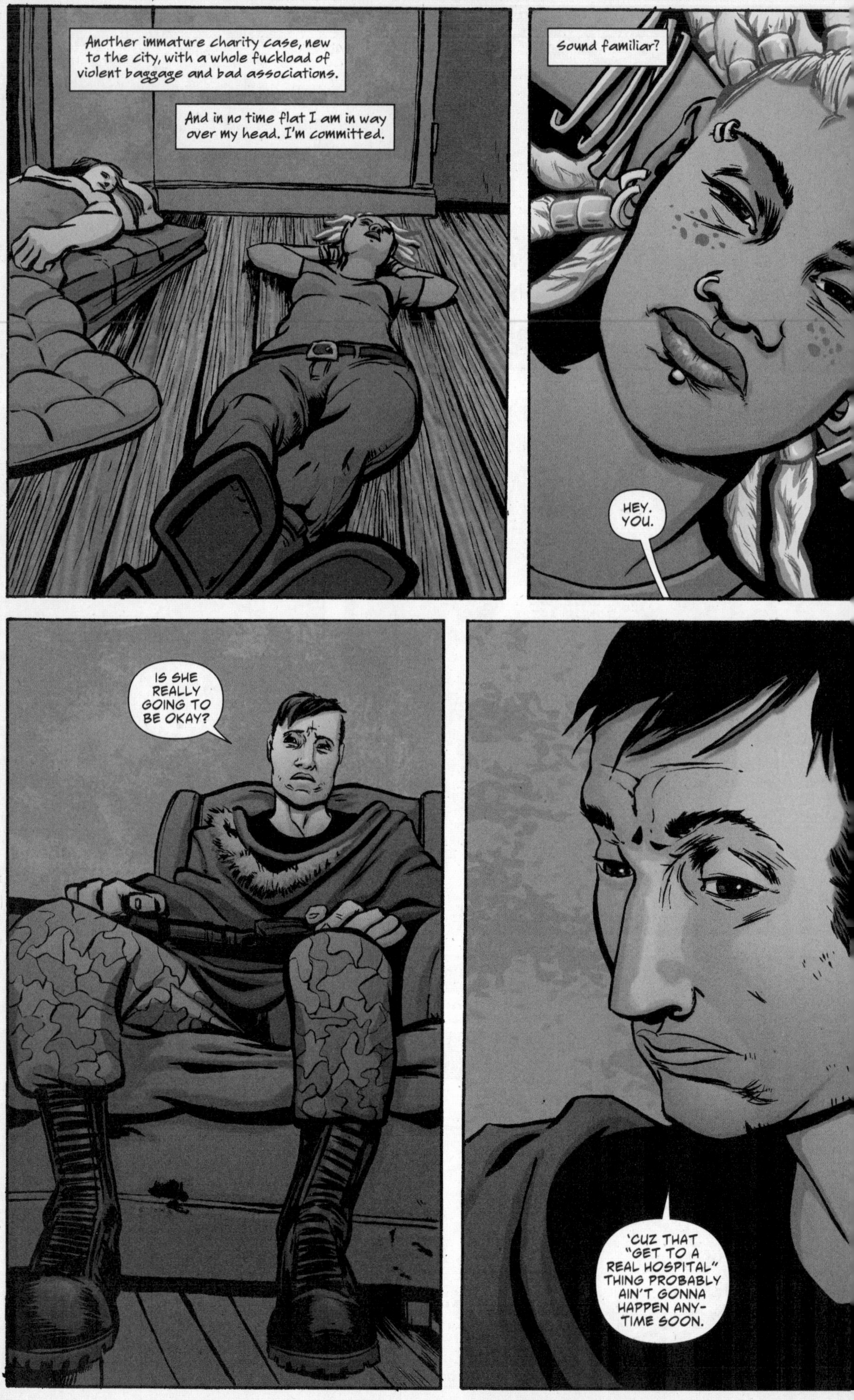
Another immature charity case, new to the city, with a whole fuckload of violent baggage and bad associations.
And in no time flat I am in way over my head. I'm committed.
Sound familiar?
HEY. YOU.
IS SHE REALLY GOING TO BE OKAY?
'CUZ THAT "GET TO A REAL HOSPITAL" THING PROBABLY AIN'T GONNA HAPPEN ANY-TIME SOON.

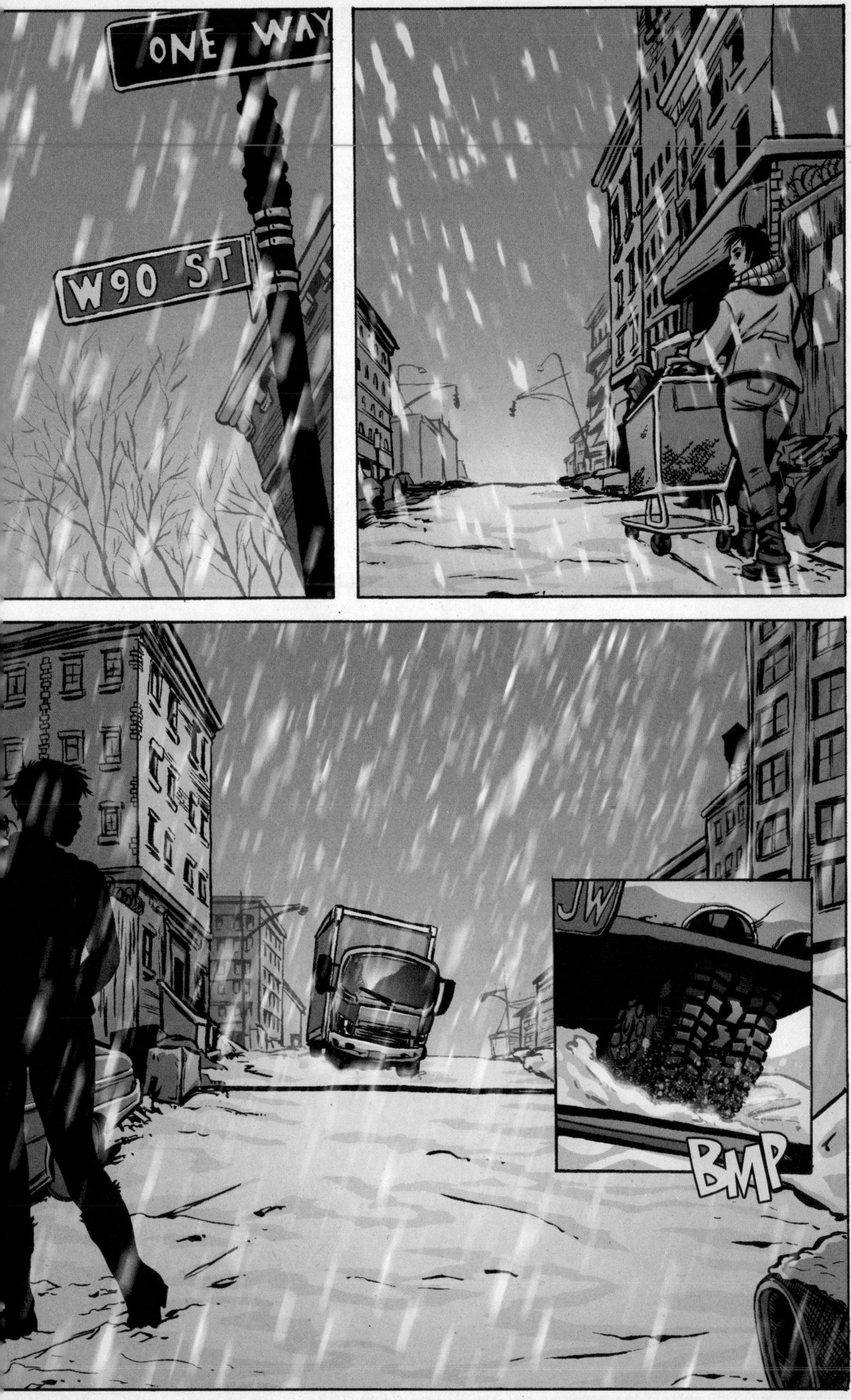

ONE WAY
W90 ST
JW
BMP

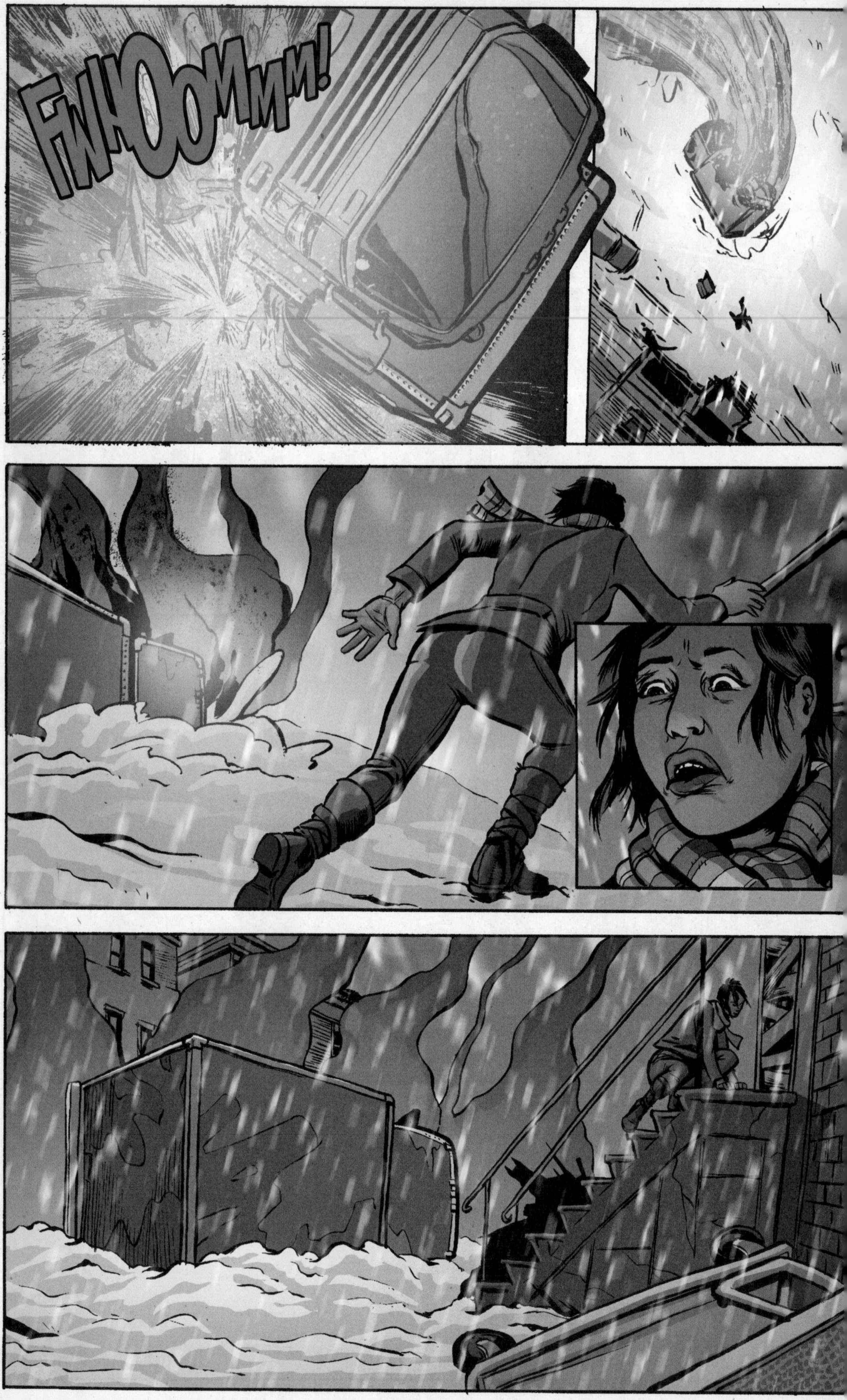
FWHOOMMMM!

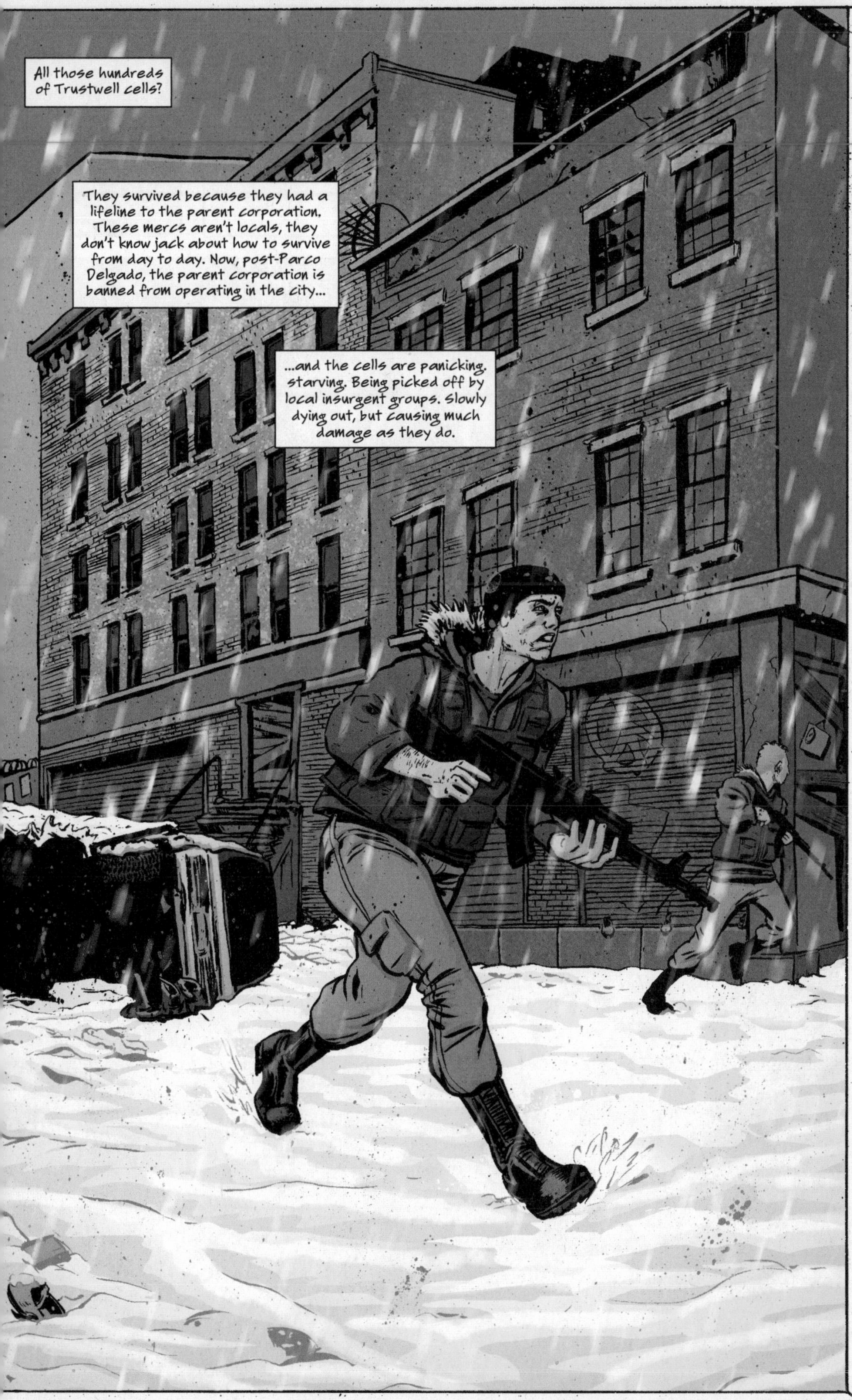
All those hundreds of Trustwell cells?
They survived because they had a lifeline to the parent corporation. These mercs aren't locals, they don't know jack about how to survive from day to day. Now, post-Parco Delgado, the parent corporation is banned from operating in the city...
...and the cells are panicking. starving. Being picked off by local insurgent groups. Slowly dying out, but causing much damage as they do.

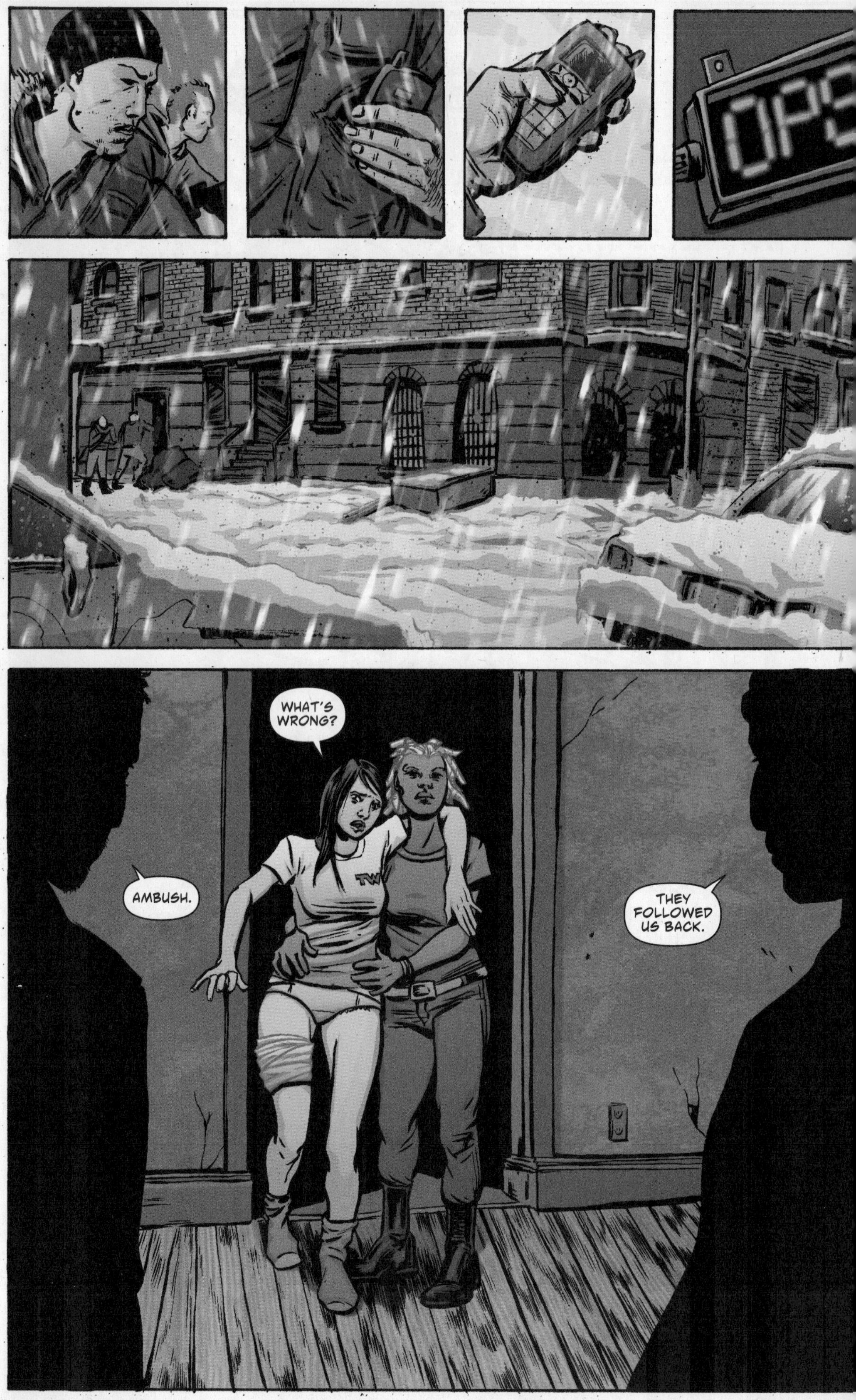
WHAT'S WRONG?
AMBUSH.
THEY FOLLOWED US BACK.

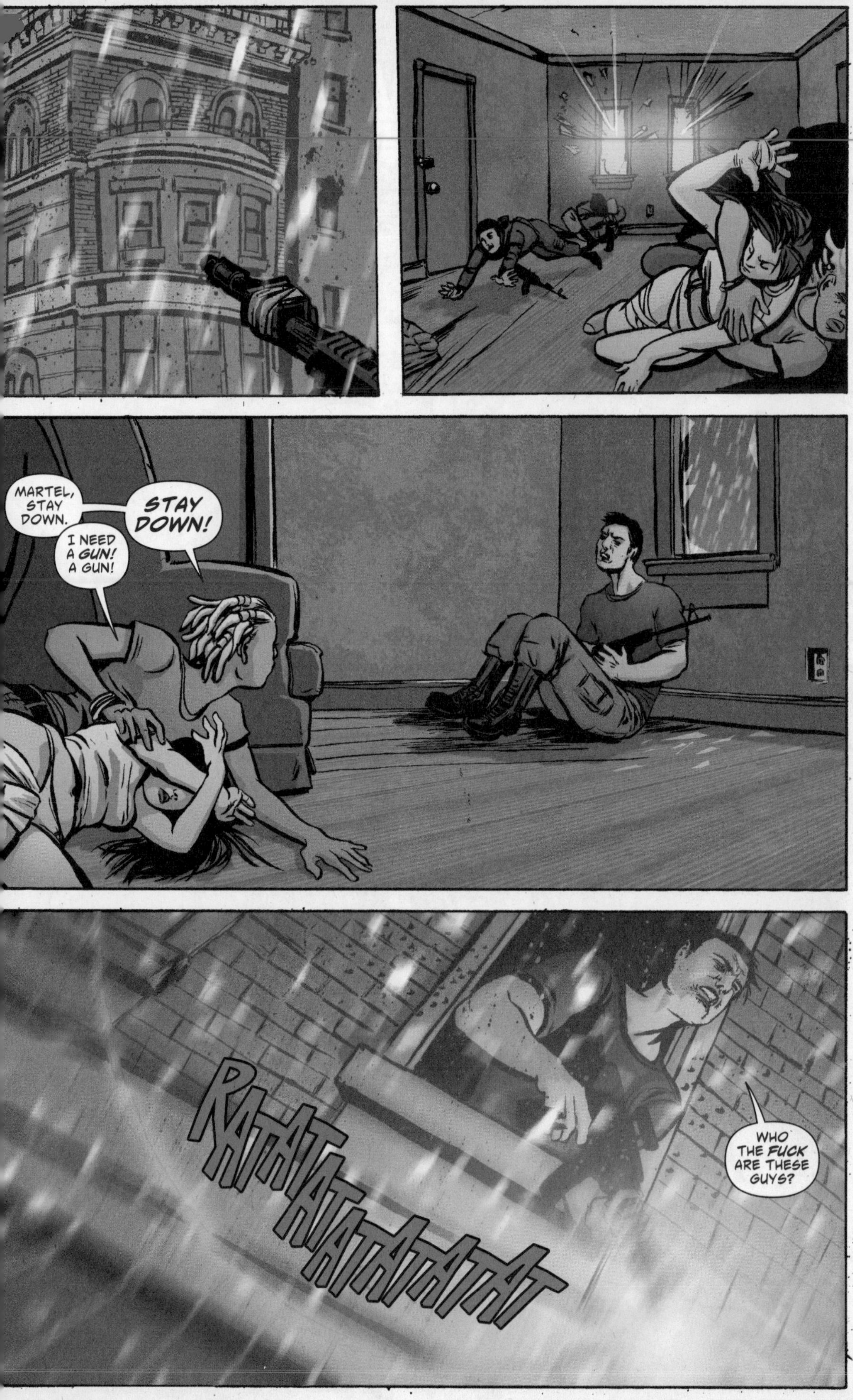
MARTEL, STAY DOWN.
STAY DOWN!
I NEED A GUN! A GUN!
RATATATATATATATAT
WHO THE FUCK ARE THESE GUYS?

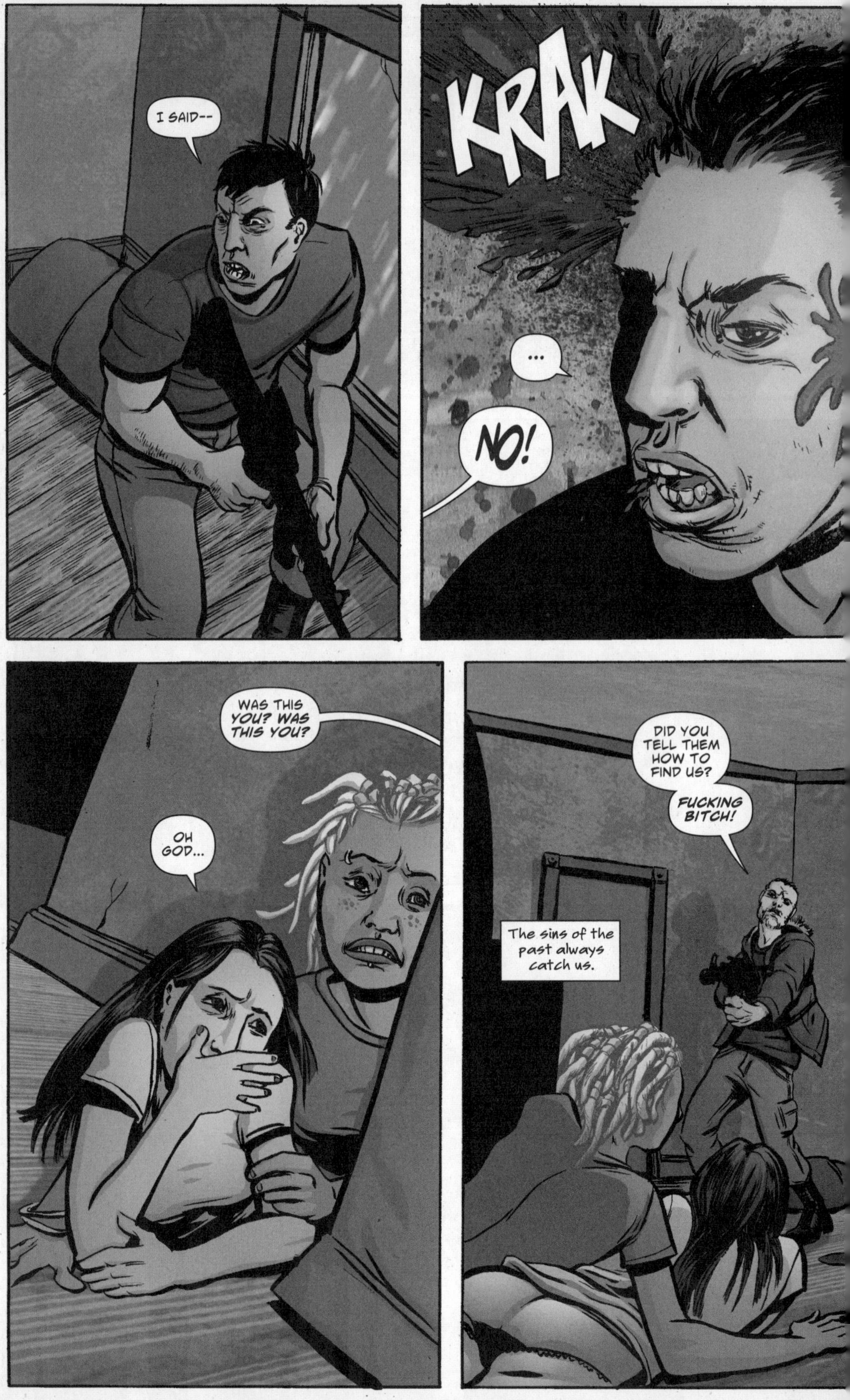
I SAID--
KRAK
...
NO!
WAS THIS YOU? WAS THIS YOU?
OH GOD...
DID YOU TELL THEM HOW TO FIND US?
FUCKING BITCH!
The sins of the past always catch us.

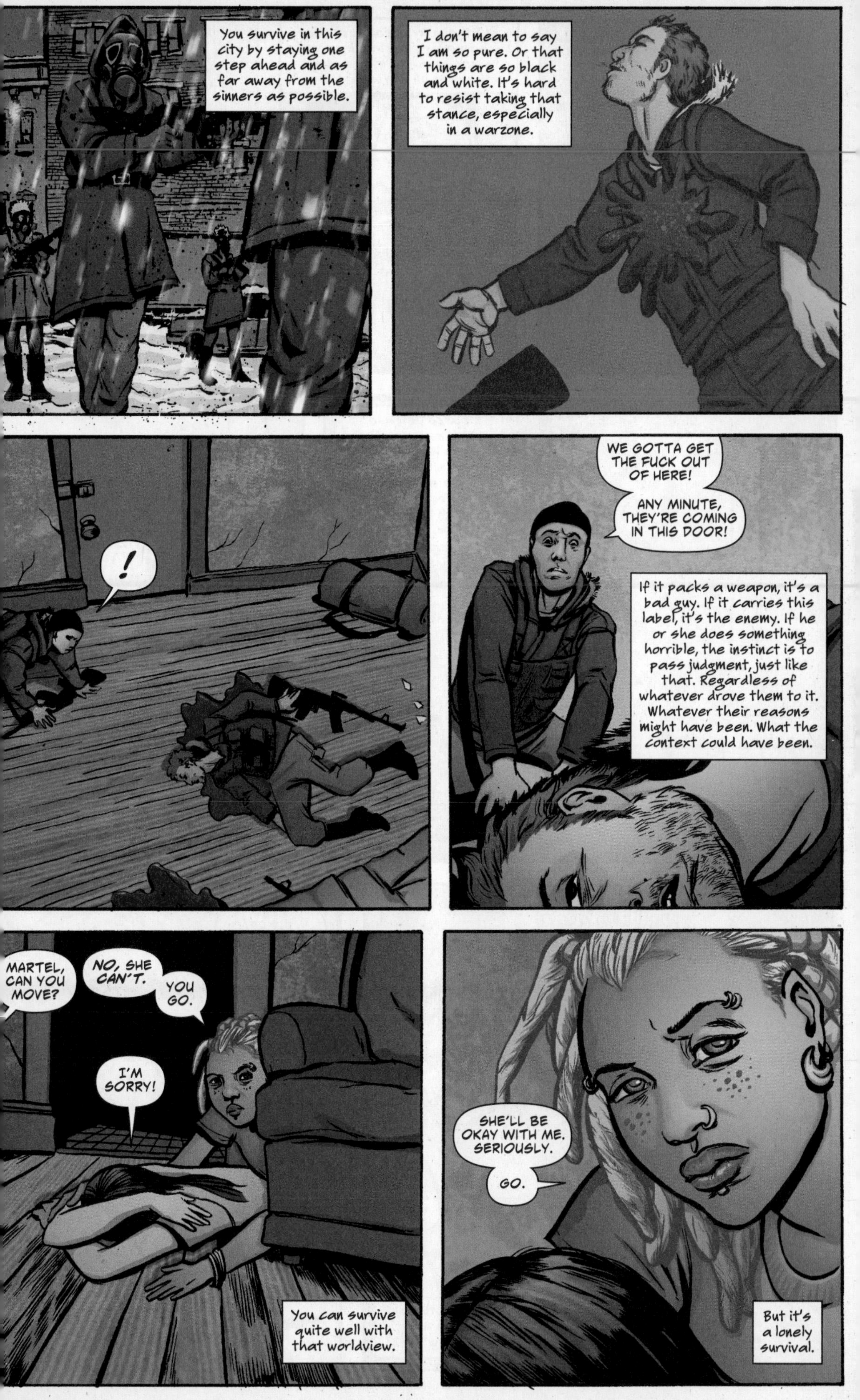
You survive in this city by staying one step ahead and as far away from the sinners as possible.
I don't mean to say I am so pure. Or that things are so black and white. It's hard to resist taking that stance, especially in a warzone.
!
WE GOTTA GET THE FUCK OUT OF HERE!
ANY MINUTE, THEY'RE COMING IN THIS DOOR!
If it packs a weapon, it's a bad guy. If it carries this label, it's the enemy. If he or she does something horrible, the instinct is to pass judgment, just like that. Regardless of whatever drove them to it. Whatever their reasons might have been. What the context could have been.
MARTEL, CAN YOU MOVE?
NO, SHE CAN'T.
YOU GO.
I'M SORRY!
You can survive quite well with that worldview.
SHE'LL BE OKAY WITH ME. SERIOUSLY.
GO.
But it's a lonely survival.

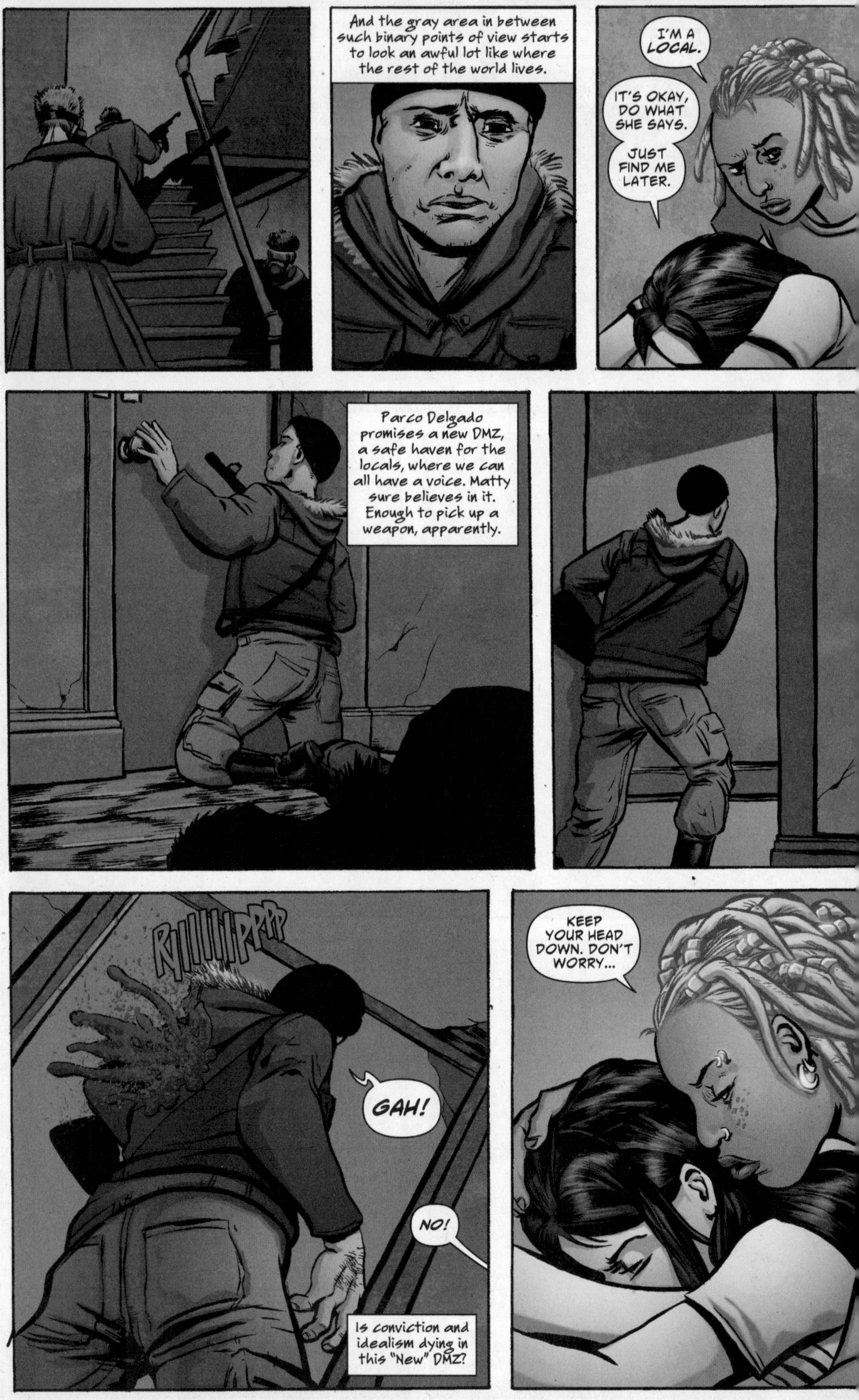

And the gray area in between such binary points of view starts to look an awful lot like where the rest of the world lives.
I'M A LOCAL.
IT'S OKAY, DO WHAT SHE SAYS.
JUST FIND ME LATER.
Parco Delgado promises a new DMZ, a safe haven for the locals, where we can all have a voice. Matty sure believes in it. Enough to pick up a weapon, apparently.
RJIIIIIPPP
GAH!
NO!
Is conviction and idealism dying in this "New" DMZ?
KEEP YOUR HEAD DOWN. DON'T WORRY...

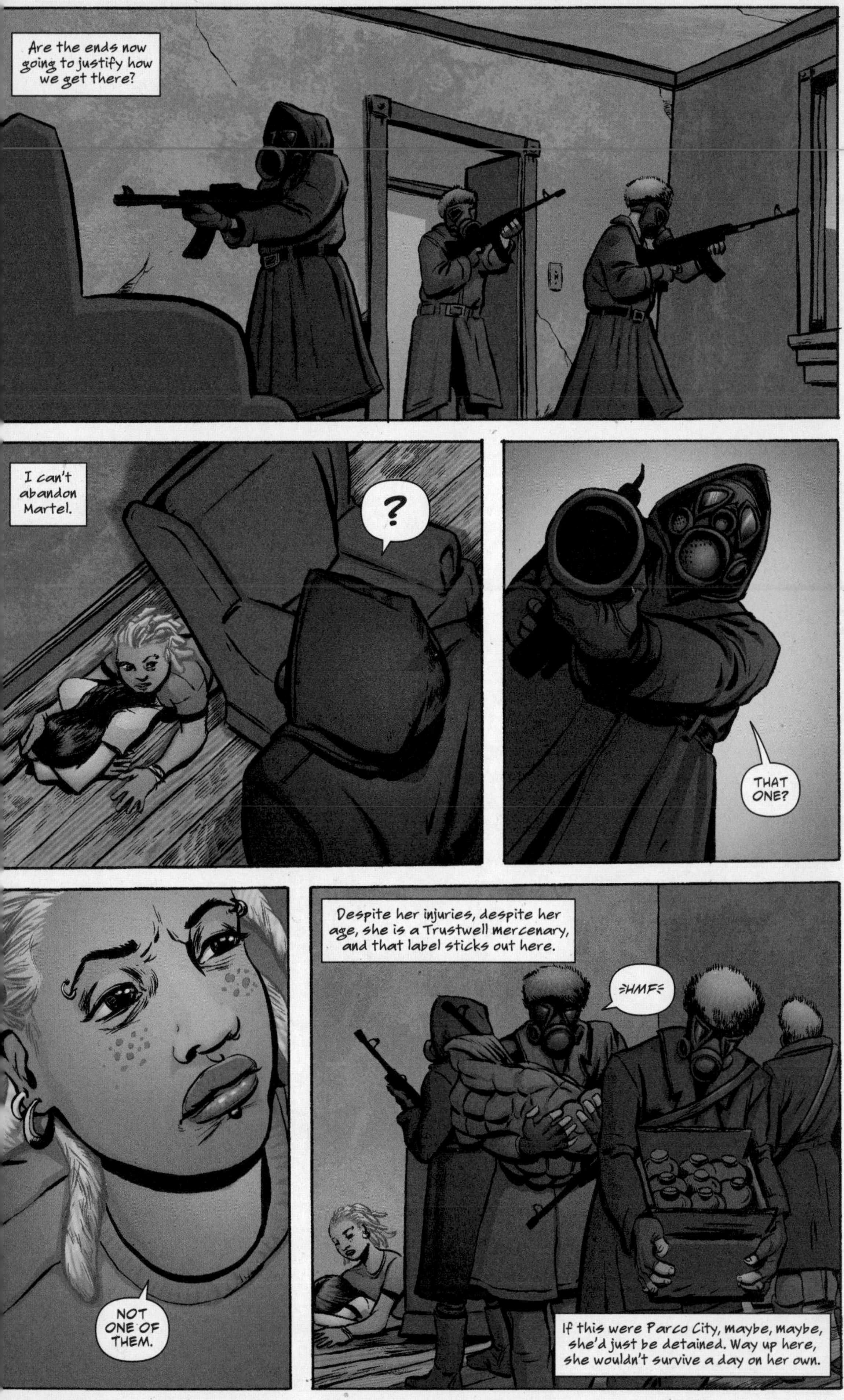
Are the ends now going to justify how we get there?
I can't abandon Martel.
?
THAT ONE?
NOT ONE OF THEM.
Despite her injuries, despite her age, she is a Trustwell mercenary, and that label sticks out here.
=HMF=
If this were Parco City, maybe, maybe, she'd just be detained. Way up here, she wouldn't survive a day on her own.

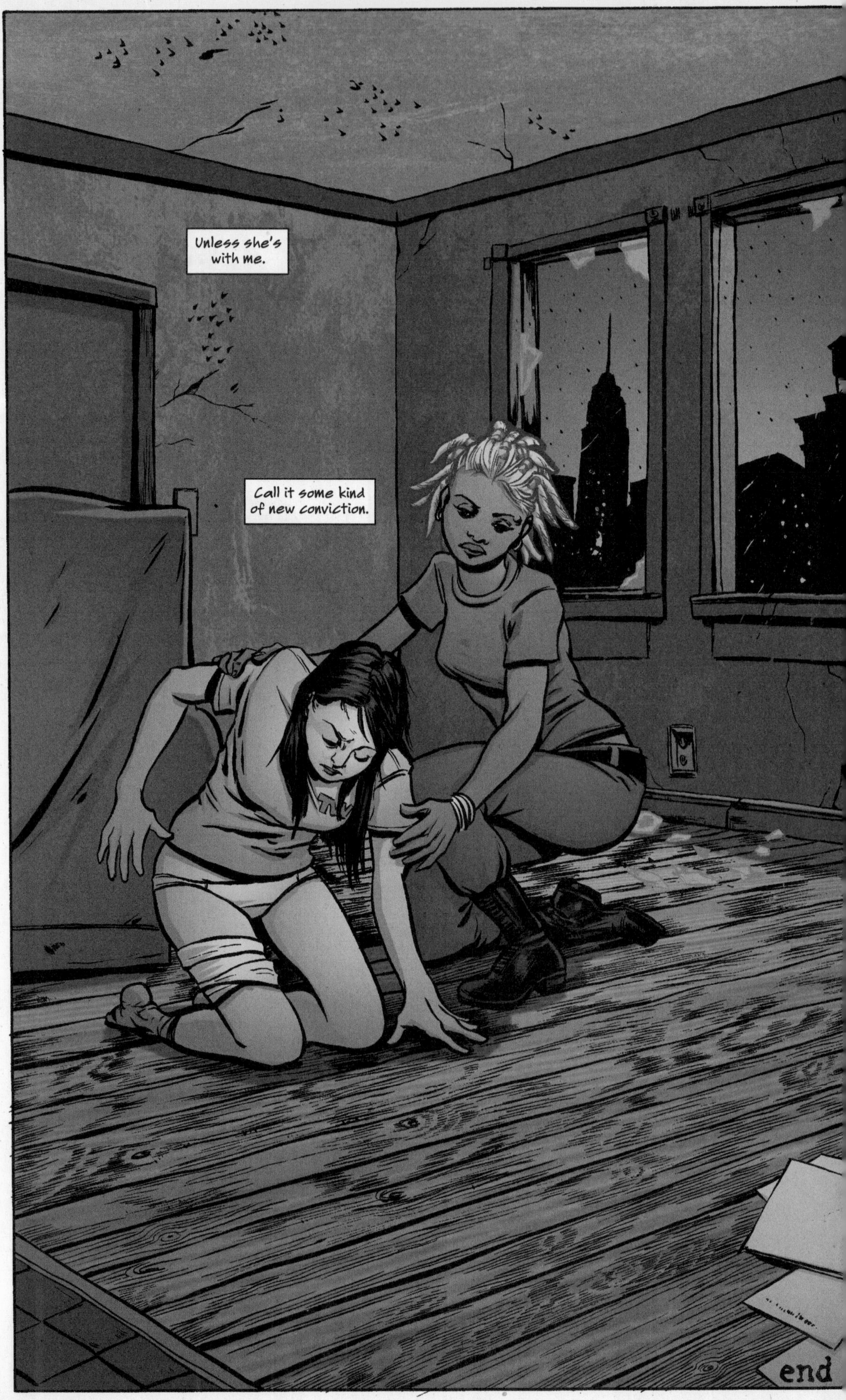
Unless she's with me.
Call it some kind of new conviction.
end

"Measures up to any summer blockbuster."
—TIME OUT NEW YORK

"One of the strongest ongoing series to come out of DC's Vertigo line in some time."
—THE ONION

FROM THE WRITER OF *NORTHLANDERS* & *DEMO*

BRIAN WOOD
with RICCARDO BURCHIELLI

DMZ VOL. 3:
PUBLIC WORKS

READ THE ENTIRE
SERIES!

DMZ VOL. 1:
ON THE GROUND

DMZ VOL. 2:
BODY OF A JOURNALIST

DMZ VOL. 3:
PUBLIC WORKS

DMZ VOL. 4:
FRIENDLY FIRE

DMZ VOL. 5:
THE HIDDEN WAR

DMZ VOL. 6:
BLOOD IN THE GAME

DMZ VOL. 7:
WAR POWERS

DMZ VOL. 8:
HEARTS AND MINDS

DMZ VOL. 9:
M.I.A.

DMZ VOL. 10:
COLLECTIVE
PUNISHMENT

DMZ VOL. 11:
FREE STATES RISING

DMZ VOL. 12:
THE FIVE NATIONS
OF NEW YORK

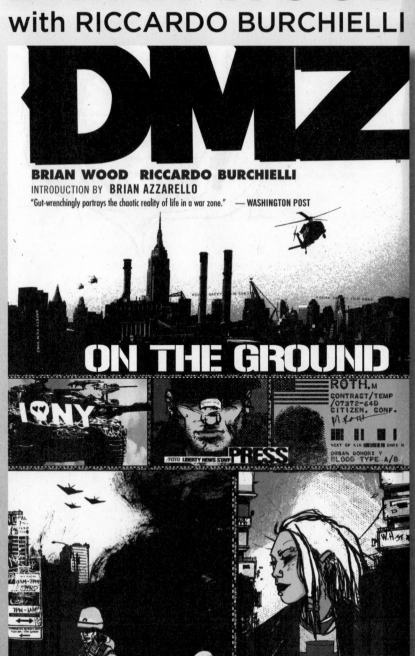